The Anatomy

of Swearing

ASHLEY MONTAGU

‹‹‹‹›››

*"Ha! this fellow is worse than me; what,
does he swear with pen and ink?"*
The Tatler, No. 13, 1709

PENN

University of Pennsylvania Press

Philadelphia

Originally published 1967 by The Macmillan Company
Copyright © 1967 Ashley Montagu
Paperback edition published 2001 by arrangement with
The Free Press, a Division of Simon & Schuster, Inc.
All rights reserved
Printed in the United States of America on acid free paper

10 9 8 7 6 5 4 3 2 1

Published by
University of Pennsylvania Press
Philadelphia, Pennsylvania 19104-4011

Library of Congress Cataloging-in-Publication Data
Montagu, Ashley, 1905–
    The anatomy of swearing / Ashley Montagu.
        p.   cm.
    Includes bibliographical references and index.
    ISBN 0-8122-1764-0 (alk. paper)
    1. Swearing.   I. Title.
GT3080 .M6 2001
394—dc21   00-067221

The Anatomy of Swearing

To

HARVEY AND JOYCE FLACK

Acknowledgments

To my wife, Marjorie, I owe many thanks for the many months of labor she spent together with me in the New York Public Library gracefully copying much of the material used in this book. To the librarians of the New York Public Library and the Princeton University Library I owe thanks for their many kind services.

ASHLEY MONTAGU

Contents

1   *Introduction: Why Swearing?*   1

2   *The Antiquity of Swearing*   5

3   *Cursing*   35

4   *The Origin of Swearing: The Curse and the Oath*   55

5   *Why Do Men Swear? The Physiology and*
    Psychology of Swearing   65

6   *Words Used in Swearing: Their Sources and the*
    Forms of Swearing   90

7   *The History of Swearing: Before the Reformation*   107

8   *Swearing in Shakespeare*   136

9   *Swearing in the Seventeenth Century*   154

10 *Swearing in the Seventeenth Century: As Observed*
    in the Urquhart and Motteux Translation of Rabelais   188

11 *Swearing in the Eighteenth Century*   200

12 *Swearing in the Nineteenth Century*   224

13 *Bloody: The Natural History of a Word*   239

14 *Damn!*   278

15 *The Four-Letter Words*   300

16 *Olla-Podrida*   321

NOTES   345

INDEX   359

[ix]

The Anatomy of Swearing

CHAPTER ONE

Introduction:
Why Swearing?

‹‹‹

Gentle, delicate, sublime critic; you, I doubt not,
are one of those consummate connoisseurs, who, in
their purifications, let humour evaporate, while they
endeavour to preserve decorum, and polish wit, until
the edge of it is quite worn off.

TOBIAS SMOLLETT, *The Adventures of Count Fathom,* 1753

SWEARING constitutes a species of human behavior so little understood, even by its most devoted practitioners, that an
examination of its meaning and significance is now long over-
due. The temper of the times in which we live having grown somewhat more complaisant, a consideration of this once tabooed topic
may not be considered out of joint. Swearing, because it is so little
understood, is still an equivocal form of conduct without social
sanction. Hence, it has long pursued a fugitive existence in all such
dark places as are not open to the light of social intercourse. That
is to say, among many people swearing is socially not tolerated in
any form. Nonetheless, such people may in private give expression
to their feelings in words somewhat stronger than they would
ordinarily use—for there are such phenomena as solitary swearers.
Swearing serves clearly definable social as well as personal purposes. A social purpose? But has not swearing always been socially
condemned and proscribed? It has. And that is precisely the point.
Because the early forms of swearing were often of a nature regarded as subversive of social and religious institutions, as when
the names of the gods were profanely invoked, their use in such
a manner was strictly forbidden. Subsequently, certain obscene
words were adopted as vehicles for the winged barbs of the swearer.

These, too, were words drawn from a strictly tabooed source, and outraged society once more instituted laws forbidding their employment for such profane purposes.

In England, and in every one of the United States, it is still a legal offense to swear. Every time someone forgets himself and through the mass media utters "a big D——" or "a big G——" there is an excited fluttering in the public dovecotes—or is it belfries? The silly season is, of course, always with us, and Mrs. Grundy is not yet altogether moribund. It is the general understanding that it is improper to swear, yet there continue to be a vast number of swearers. Because swearing is socially condemned, there are many who publicly join in its denunciation but privately take a somewhat different view of it. Whatever it is that causes some of us to swear, it is considered unseemly to yield to the temptation.

But what is in fact socially condemned? Is it the usurpation of the names of the gods in vain or the use of words considered obscene or suggestive? Or are these merely forms of swearing in their cradle period? Whether incunable or not, these are questions we shall be concerned with answering in the pages that follow. The many sophisticated forms of swearing we shall consider attest to the fact that since man first learned to speak imagination and inventiveness have been outstanding characteristics of his speech.

While the original purpose of the taboo on swearing has been forgotten, ill fame still surrounds swearing, so that today it is not held in much higher repute than it ever was. And so the swearer continues to utter his oaths *sotto voce*, as it were, like a smuggler cautiously making his way across a forbidden frontier. This is the pathos of profanity. As Holbrook Jackson once put it, "Faith, reverence, the virtues have hope—verily, they shall have their reward; but, despised and rejected of men, profanity walketh alone without hope or comfort in the future, staking all passionately in the present. Profanity, like virtue, is its own reward."[1] There are some who are ashamed of their swearing, yet swear and know not why they swear. It is a most unsatisfying, puling, primitive condition of irresolution to be in.

It is the purpose of this book to let the light of day into this forbidden, misunderstood, and furtively pursued form of human behavior, to present the curious inquirer with a conspectus of what the best minds and most accomplished practitioners of the art have said and done about swearing, and to endow the art, perchance, with a hope for the future.

It should, perhaps, be made clear that this book is not a manual in the art of swearing. It constitutes, rather, an inquiry into the history and nature of swearing, an analysis, an anatomy, of swearing. In its pages, quite possibly, oaths will be found suitable for almost every occasion. The discriminating reader will take to himself such hints and assistance as he thinks desirable. At most, the book may be regarded as an introduction to the theory and fine art of swearing. Our first task will be to examine swearing carefully in order to determine whether it deserves to be rehabilitated and treated seriously. When this has been done, the reader may decide whether or not he wishes to develop the art for himself. For it *is* an art, and it has suffered grievously at the hands of generations of unimaginative practitioners. However, the art has not wanted for distinguished performers. Their not inconsiderable accomplishments will be presented in the pages that follow as outstanding examples of what it is possible to achieve. The chronicle of the oaths of these stout and valiant swearers who have so boldly, and often imaginatively, enriched our language constitutes something more than an exhortation to the would-be swearer to go and do likewise. It constitutes also a contribution to social history.

The inventions and discoveries achieved by the virtuosos of swearing comprise a rich treasury, which is faithfully inventoried in these pages. The oaths that bloomed in the springtime and maturity of these swearers' powers displayed an originality, a virtuosity, a musicality, and an eloquence that not infrequently attained the summit of art. There shall be no censoring of their rhetoric, no disenvoweling or bowdlerizing of their words, no in-asterisking of them. Their oaths shall be left to stand exactly as they swore them, as the fit and proper monuments to both their inventiveness and their industry.

The definition of the forms of swearing will be provided in the body of the book. Until then it will be assumed that the reader understands what is meant by "swearing." Many precise and clear distinctions can, and in this book will, be drawn between various types of swearing, but before we achieve such a degree of proficiency, the reader will do no violence to his understanding if he thinks of swearing as cursing in profane, scurrilous, and vituperative language.

A word may be said here about the plan to be followed in this book.

We shall commence with an inquiry into the antiquity of swearing. We shall then proceed to discuss the history of swearing, from the earliest times to the present day, in a single land, England. The subject of swearing is such a vast one that any attempt to deal with the varieties of swearing throughout the world would be quite impossible. In any event, a universal history of swearing would not, I suspect, prove much more illuminating than one devoted to the study of the phenomenon among a single people. The forms of swearing appear to be basically similar among every people of whatever time, place, or state of cultural development. Wherever necessary, reference will be made to forms of swearing current among different peoples, but only where the comparison serves to illuminate a point.

Special attention will be devoted to such established swearwords as *bloody* and *damn,* as well as some others. Four-letter words will be freely and, I hope, inoffensively discussed. In earlier days the author would have been debarred from the innocent pleasure of sharing with the reader the particular examination of such tabooed words. Times have changed, and it is today possible to discuss the formerly undiscussable. So far, progress has been made. The reader uninterested in such demotic English may skip the chapter devoted to those astringent words.

To conclude, then, the present work may be regarded as a small and tentative contribution to a very large and inexhaustibly interesting form of human behavior, the offshoot of my desultory reading and intermittent research since 1927, when I read Robert Graves' delightful little book *Lars Porsena, or the Future of Swearing.* It occurred to me then that the subject would repay further investigation, that it would not be unamusing to take up the

> Phrases that Time has flung away,
> Uncouth Words in Disarray

and, pursuing their history, observe what light they might throw upon a much neglected form of behavior. The result is before the reader.

CHAPTER TWO

The Antiquity of Swearing

‹‹‹›››››››››››››››››››››››››››››››››››

However far some men have gone in the science of
impartiality, I am persuaded that there is not one
of them but would be surprised if he could be shown
how much farther he might go.

FULKE GREVILLE, *Maxims, Characters and Reflections*, 1757

How old is swearing? It is as old as man and coeval with language. How old is man? Very near two million or more years.[1] And speech? One may estimate that it began at about the same time. Interestingly enough many philologists have held that speech originated in utterances closely akin to swearing. According to this theory,

spoken language began . . . when a cry of pain, formerly wrung out by real suffering, and seen to be understood and sympathized with, was repeated in imitation, no longer as a mere instinctive utterance, but for the purpose of intimating to another, "I am (was, shall be) suffering"; when an angry growl, formerly the direct expression of passion, was reproduced to signify disapprobation and threatening, and the like. This was enough to serve as a foundation for all that should be built upon it.[2]

This view, here expressed by William Dwight Whitney, who, in the 1890s, was professor of Sanskrit and Comparative Philology at Yale, has found many distinguished proponents. The development of this theory runs something like this: Before men developed any articulate means of communication with each other, there were already in existence certain emotionally highly charged sounds or expletives. These sounds had arisen in response to the need of relieving angry feelings or giving expression to one's feelings upon a sudden shock or surprise. This need was fundamentally a physiological one and was only secondarily psychological. Such expletive sounds were not invented by man but were physiologically determined for him by the shape of his chest and the form of his nasal cavities, throat, and larynx. Such sounds would occur, as it were, in spite of himself and only upon the experience of some sudden shock, whether of pain, annoyance, or surprise. The elementary and undeveloped forms of such sounds are universally the same among all men of all lands and times. For example, the fundamental tone of the human voice is *ah*, or *a*, voiced as in "father." This sound, as an exclamation, is found among all known peoples, as are its variant forms *oh, oo, ow, ugh, oi, eh*, and so on. The elementary forms of these sounds are not acquired, nor are they inherited. They are physiologically determined; that is to say, physiologically determined in the sense that a volume of air suddenly expelled through the throat will cause certain specific sounds to be produced quite involuntarily. Since such sounds are initiated in the throat, they are vowel sounds, for that is where vowels are produced. For this reason the fundamental character of these expressions, no matter how obscured they may have become by the overlying cultural style, remains unchanged wherever men speak. It is evident that these words are of such a nature that they are capable of conveying their meaning to men who are unacquainted with each other's language, for it is the basic affective or emotional tone of the word that constitutes its meaning. Without their peculiar affective tones these physiological, or organic, words lose their meaning; for example, an expressionless *oh* or *ugh* means nothing, but given full organic value they assume significance. It is in this sense that Whitney wrote, at the beginning of the passage already quoted, "The tones significant of feeling, of which no one can deny the existence because they are still part of our expression, are fully capable of becoming the effective initiators of language."

While such a theory of language has its attractions, it can at best be regarded only as an explanation of the origin of some words and of certain parts and processes of language. Discussions of the origin of language are by no means unrewarding, not so much for what they tell us of the origin of language as for what they tell us of its elementary forms. As C. H. Grandgent has remarked, "How language originated nobody knows and everybody has told."[3] It is probable that most, if not all, theories of the origin of language have some substance, but alone or together they are at most capable only of suggesting how certain aspects of speech may have come into being.[4] The "bow-wow" theory holds that primitive words originated in the imitation of the sounds of animals, principally the barking of dogs. The "pooh-pooh" theory holds that language is derived from instinctive ejaculations called forth by pain or other intense feelings or sensations. The "ding-dong" theory claims that there is a peculiar harmony between sound and sense, that each thing has its peculiar ring, and that this was vocally imitated by primitive man. The "yo-he-ho" theory suggests that speech origi- nated in the breathing relief associated with intense muscular effort. More than one author has suggested that at least one of the most prominent uses of language is to dissipate superfluous and obstructive nerve force—in plain English, to reduce nervous tension. The "gestural" theory holds that speech came into being when men began to imitate with their tongues the gestures they made with their bodies. The theory that goes by the charming name of "tarara- boom-de-ay" has it that speech originated in the collective half- musical expressions of early man when his principal vocal exercise was a meaningless humming or singing. Suppose that a group of such early men have together succeeded in bringing down a great mammoth; they will at once spontaneously be filled with joy and will strike up a chant of triumph—say, something like "tarara- boom-de-ay." The sounds of the chant might easily come to mean "We have brought him down. We have conquered. Hooray! Let us give thanks." And so on from there. This theory has been sug- gested by Otto Jesperson, and it is remarkably true that what can- not be uttered can often be sung. Finally, there is the "tally-ho" theory, suggested by myself, that speech came into being as a result of the necessities of communication arising during the cooperative hunting of early man.[5]

What we learn from examining the various theories of speech is that most writers on the subject agree that it is highly probable that some of the earliest elements of speech were initiated by the desire to express oneself forcefully. Swearing, therefore, is prob- ably coeval with the birth of language; however, it cannot be regarded as the sole or even the principal stimulus to the origin of speech, but at most as a contributory or dynamic factor in its development. Something of the manner of the use of words among early men may be inferred from the studies that have been made on the languages of living nonliterate peoples. Such studies are important for the proper understanding of the role that words play in swearing.

❰ *The Use and Meaning of Words in the Languages of Nonliterate Peoples*

The study of the languages of nonliterate peoples has revealed the fact that words play the part essentially of *implements.* Words are regarded as capable of *doing* things, not however in themselves or when they are isolated, but when they are properly handled. In examining the structure of a "primitive" language we are at once impressed by the *operative* function that the words seem to possess. Malinowski writes of the language of the Trobriand Islanders:

A word *means* to a native the proper use of the thing for which it stands, exactly as an implement *means* something when it can be handled. Similarly a verb, a word for an action, receives its meaning through an active participation in this action. A word is used when it can produce an action and not describe one, still less to translate thoughts. The word therefore has a power of its own, it is a means of bringing things about, it is a handle to acts and objects and not a definition of them . . . Language in its primitive function is to be regarded as a *mode of action* rather than as a countersign of thought.[6]

Significantly enough, it is the *affective* value, the feeling tone, of the word that is bound up with its meaning; the *affective* value is also the sense of active participation in the action for which the word stands. This active participation (in the action for which the word stands) need not be overt, but may be, and indeed most usually is, only felt. The word "empathy," or feeling into, best expresses this participative character of the word complex. If we may anticipate a little here, it may be pointed out that in the process of swearing, the words employed are generally of notably high affective value and are preeminently used as implements wherewith to belabor their object. This was, for example, explicitly recognized in the behavior of certain Arabs who, when cursed, ducked their heads or fell flat on the ground in order to avoid a direct hit. I have also seen this very fully recognized in Union Square in New York by a young man who was for some reason being most proficiently sworn at by a slightly intoxicated Irishman. At every curse the young man pretended to wince, as if each oath was a stick upon his back, and to put a finishing touch to the performance, he raised an arm and ducked his head behind it, as if to ward off every verbal whack delivered by the irate derelict.

Among certain tribes of Australian aborigines when a man wishes to bespatter another he swears at him, but should he find that his words have been overheard by one who stands in a certain social relation to him, he will exclaim, "My mouth is foul." On such an occasion the individual will sometimes take a lighted firebrand and pass it backward and forward before his mouth in ritual purification.[7] The dynamic quality of such words is well illustrated here. The words are actually regarded as having befouled the user's mouth. Whether the words are in reality invested with a tangible power or not is of no consequence here, for the fact is that they are regarded as possessing befouling qualities, precisely as if they possessed them in some substantial physical form. Here the function of words in their affective aspect and as a mode of action is given proper emphasis. We must remember this "primitive" character of words and language.

([Swearing Among Nonliterate Peoples

The term "primitive" as applied to many nonliterate peoples is a misnomer, since the cultures of such peoples are in many ways no less complex than our own; hence, anthropologists prefer to use the term "nonliterate peoples," although that is not altogether satisfactory either. But it is the preferred term, and we shall continue to use it here when referring to those cultures and peoples that, at the time they were described, had not yet been seriously influenced by the more "advanced" cultures.

The information relating to swearing among nonliterate peoples is very limited. Ethnologists apparently have not considered the subject worthy their attention. Interestingly enough, the only reports on the swearing of nonliterate peoples that we possess come from two Australian ethnologists and refer to widely separated Australian aboriginal tribes. The white Australian, as we shall later have occasion to see, numbers among his fellows perhaps the most inveterate and unimaginative swearers that exist anywhere in the world today. May it not be that the interest of Drs. Herbert Basedow and Donald F. Thomson in the swearing of the aborigines owes something to this fact? However this may be, the culture of the Australian aborigines is generally held to be at a Stone Age level of technological development. It is, therefore, fortunate that such reports of the swearing of nonliterate peoples as we do have should relate largely to these aborigines.

Basedow writes, of Australian tribes in general, "A common disturbance of the peace is brought on by petty theft. One woman might, intentionally or otherwise, appropriate a small article belonging to another. When the article is missed by the owner, an argument ensues, which soon warms up to a strained pitch of excitement. Abusive epithets become prolific, which repeatedly embody references to excrement and other filth."[8]

We shall see from the next report, by Thomson, relating to the swearing of a number of tribes inhabiting the Cape York Peninsula, that references to excrement and other filth is also a common form of swearing among these relatively isolated peoples.

Thomson states that among the tribes investigated by him there was no general prohibition upon reference to the genitalia or the physiological functions of reproduction, defecation, and urination. Children grow up with no inhibitions in these matters except in the presence of certain relatives toward whom it is obligatory to exercise restraint. Children learn to swear at a very early age, as Thomson discovered when "In a camp of the Yintjingga tribe on the estuary of the Stewart River, a child about two years of age that was being suckled at its mother's breast, dropped the nipple to glower at me and exclaim in the Ompela language of its mother, 'Awu! kuna katta! kuna katta!' 'Devil! excrement foul! excrement foul!' "[9] Thomson tells us that nobody expressed concern or attempted to correct the child, whereas among other tribes he found that this would have been done at once.

As among ourselves, so among these tribes, "there are at least two, often a number, of words for each object, or for parts of the body. One of these words is generally considered to be the proper term to be used in ordinary polite conversation; the other is, in the words of my aboriginal informant, 'half swear.' "[10] In the use of these words, Thomson noted, a very definite etiquette is rigorously observed, and as he points out, the aborigines are here characterized "by a nice reserve and by a sense of 'good taste' that we are always apt to claim as our special prerogative."[11]

We begin to perceive that the swearing of the Australian aborigines assumes a most startling family likeness to our own. But before proceeding with its further examination, let us continue a little with our account of the forms of swearing among these Cape York tribes.

When our aboriginal . . . inadvertently strikes his toe against a stump or root he does not break out with an oath or obscene expression, but calls upon the name of a relative long deceased. Similarly, when a weapon upon which he is working, or a canoe lashing, breaks, he calls upon the name of a dead relation whose name has outlived the kintja (tabu) period following death. . . .

This practice of calling upon the name of a deceased relation, a mild and innocuous oath, is general among the native tribes of Cape York Peninsula, and is found in tribes in widely separated localities.[12]

Thomson writes that "in three years spent among these natives I never knew them to depart from their traditional behavior and to use foul or obscene expressions under stress of pain, fear, or surprise, although these are freely used under other circumstances."[13] He classifies the swearing employed by these tribes as consisting of two main types:

1. Unorganized swearing and obscenity, falling under no sanction and used by both sexes in quarrels, and as taunts to goad an enemy to fight. This type of swearing is known to the Wik Monkan people as kul ken-tanak, "anger make-for," i.e., "for the purpose of arousing anger," for which purpose it is deliberately employed. Under this category fall all the worst expressions in the language: deadly insults that it would be intolerable for any native to receive in public.

2. Organized or licensed swearing and swearing that is not only permissible, but obligatory, between those who stand in certain relationships under the classificatory system. It is carried out in public, and falls under a definite social sanction. This organized license is in direct contrast with the extreme tabu (kintja) of certain relationships, e.g., with the wife's mother, the wife's father, and the wife's brothers. It is supposed to induce a state of euphoria: in the words of my informants, to "make everybody happy." This falls again into two distinct types:

a. Obscenity pure and simple, consisting of more or less stereotyped references to the pudenda, and permitted between a very few relatives, frequently in the grandparent-grandchild generations, and almost always between persons of the same sex. Certain relatives are also permitted to snatch playfully at one another's genitalia, and even to handle the organs in public.

b. Bad language, consisting chiefly of references to the anus and to excrement, permissible or obligatory between a number of relatives, generally distant, with whom license of a restricted type is permitted. The use of obscenities, or any sexual behavior is prohibited.[14]

From Thomson's account it is evident that swearing frequently occurs among these tribes. Furthermore, there is also prevalent a special kind of swearing which is restricted to individuals who stand in a certain relationship to one another. The interesting thing about this custom is that it is not only socially sanctioned but obligatory on the part of the persons concerned. This type of behavior is known to ethnologists as the joking relationship, after the similar form of behavior first recorded for several Indian tribes of North America.

Without entering into a detailed discussion of the character of these joking relationships, it may briefly be said here that they are intimately associated with the kinship organization of the tribe and the relationship in which every individual is classified in relation to every other member of the tribe. For example, under the restraints of ordinary social life the strictest prohibitions govern the relations of oneself to one's wife's mother, the wife's father, and the wife's brothers. To balance these prohibitions the greatest freedom is permitted with a member of one's classificatory grandparental generation. Between the members of these generations organized obscenity and behavior of a playful sexual type, such as snatching at one another's genitalia—always in the presence of the other members of the tribe, whether of the prohibited degrees or not—is the normal form of behavior. As a rule restraint must be exercised with all one's blood relations, while the more distant in the classificatory system are the individuals, the greater is the freedom permitted in the joking relationship. But the greatest freedom is permitted between the grandparent and grandchild generations, or the *pola* (father's father) and his classificatory son's son, the *poladu*.

At the time when the sacred initiations take place at the sacred grounds and the men get together in a kind of temporary men's club, they exchange all sorts of obscenities and insults with each other, exchanges that in other circumstances would be intolerable. During all this the greatest good humor is maintained and much mirth is generated. When asked why they swear, the men actually reply, "Nothing, friend, make happy little but, no swear proper!"

If it is not already obvious, Thomson gives us the clue to the meaning of this kind of behavior. He writes: "There is no doubt that the exchanges under the joking relationship do provoke genuine mirth, as well as a ritual state of well-being, that counterbalances, relieves, and gives point to, the austerity and restraint that characterize much of the behavior under the kinship system."[15]

Will not the gentle reader pause awhile with me and reflect in admiration upon the remarkably humane and intelligent manner in which these so-called primitive peoples have handled a problem that the self-styled civilized peoples of the West have failed both to understand and to control, and have therefore condemned out of hand? Instead of condemning obscenity and swearing, the Australian aborigines have obviously made an endeavor to understand them. In this they have succeeded eminently well, and they have so utilized these forms of behavior as to make them serve extremely important and useful functions: as relief mechanisms for feelings that might otherwise be more dangerously expressed and as counterbalances, also of relief and well-being, to the rigors, austerity, and restraints of much of social life.

It is, indeed, not for nothing that all who have come to know the Australian aboriginal well have remarked upon the beauty of his character and the fact that he is a remarkably happy and well-integrated person.

Socialized, or organized, swearing is the Australian aborigine's method of providing for the socially sanctioned expression of those forms of conduct that are prohibited under other circumstances. It is the licitly provided escape valve that in a far cruder form finds expression in our own society at stag parties and in dirty jokes, obscene limericks,[16] and the like, where forbidden matters are discussed that, as Benvenuto Cellini would have put it, are to be mentioned only under the apothecary's counter.

This form of socialized swearing (which is also to be found among Eskimos) constitutes one of the most widely diffused and efficient devices for assisting to preserve the equilibrium of the individual and his society.

But let us continue.

In all the tribes investigated by Thomson, humorous and ribald remarks relating to various parts of the body are used in a jocular fashion, and most of these remarks are regarded as perfectly harmless unless they are addressed to a person who stands in a forbidden relationship. Here are some of the words that are so used among the Wik Monkan tribe of the Cape York Peninsula. Extending all the way from merely jocular references to the hands, face, and legs to obscene references to the pudenda, they constitute the grossest insults possible in the language:

meritti	big eye
yanantti	plenty hair
konn werra	wide ears
yank onk	long legs

ka onk	long nose
ma'a punta wakk	arm like grass
tump many'	little legs, thin legs, thin calves
kutjaketti	big head
kutajak onk	long head

These terms are obviously blood-brothers to our "rubber-neck," "baldy-locks," "flap-ears," "spindle-legs," "string-bean," "fat-head," and the like. While such terms are, on the whole, quite innocent, they may be converted for use in dead earnest, as when a woman may say to a man who is looking hard at her, "*Merriti!*" "Big eye," that is to say, "what are you staring at, you?"[17]

When a strong or offensive term is used playfully, the word *puk* ("child" or "baby") is sometimes prefixed. "When used to an adult it has the force of a diminutive, a term of affection that takes the sting from the word it accompanies. Thus, *waiya*, 'bad,' 'a bad one'; *puk waiya*, in its literal sense 'a bad child,' is much the same as 'you little devil.' "

Examples of more serious swearing in the Wik Monkan language are the following:

To a man:

po'o wantj wenta	vagina woman mad
kuntjitti	big penis
kuntj tantitti	fat penis
kuntj mankatti	big penis root
untitti	big scrotum
otjumti	plenty urine

To a woman:

pam wenta	man crazy
nok werram	wide inguinal fold ("You are exposing yourself")
po'o patj	no pubic hair, bald pubis
po'o ka onk	vagina nose, i.e., long clitoris
po'o kati	enlarged clitoris
po'o tantitti	fatty vagina
po'o konnitti[18]	big-eared vagina, i.e., enlarged labia minora

None of these terms, with the exception of one or two referring to the male pudenda that may be used in one of the joking relationships, is used jocularly; all are employed only in the serious quarreling that is the prelude to fighting and are spoken in a sharp tone of voice. They are expressions that are used when all restraint is cast aside.

Examining the forms of swearing employed among these Australian aborigines and the words utilized, we see that, with the exception of organized swearing, these are of the same nature as our own.

References to excrement and filth doubtless draw their sting for the purposes of swearing from the subjects' obnoxious qualities, which, as it were, may be hurled or spattered upon the objects of one's dislike. In order to be useful for the purposes of swearing, a word apparently must have reference to an object possessing, or thought to possess, force or power of some kind. Swearing is the process by means of which one seeks to use the power of something to chastise the object of one's swearing. The power of the thing is always intended to overcome the victim, is always to his disadvantage. The power may be a good, evil, or indifferent one. Thus, one may call upon the sun, commonly regarded as a powerful good, to burn up a neighbor's field—or his face. Or we may call our enemy a turd-face. Here the turd is evil, evil-smelling, and evil looking—powerfully so. Or we may liken his head to a block of wood, a rattle, or a bone—in themselves neither good nor evil things, but powerfully hard or shallowly noisy. The value of terms referring to excrement and filth for the purposes of swearing is fully recognized by the Australian aborigines, and were we in possession of the necessary information concerning other peoples elsewhere in the world we would doubtless find that this has been equally recognized by most or all of them. There is good reason to believe that the employment of such terms in swearing is very widely distributed if not universal.

Thomson's account of the native child of about two years who dropped his mother's breast to glower and swear at him, "Devil! excrement foul! excrement foul!" is interesting, as well as amusing. It is probable that the child was more than two years old, for white observers almost invariably underestimate the age of native children. It is quite a common thing for a three- or four-year-old native child to be suckled by his mother. But the important point is not the child's age or even that he swore, but the words he used and the reason for his swearing. The words give us the clue to the reason. The child's reaction, indeed, is a completely human and universal one. Observing a white man—a strange creature at best—the child could no longer in comfort proceed with its meal. Frustrated and perhaps a little frightened by this unusual creature—the white man —the child called him a name equivalent to our word "devil," referring, doubtless, to his presumed unearthly origin, and swore at him in order to beat him off.

The universality of this sort of response is well illustrated by the story told of a Devon yokel who on seeing a stranger walking down the road in his own direction remarked to his crony, "Aye, William, there be un stranger comen. Let's heave un brick at un."

What the little Stewart River aboriginal simply was doing was "heaving a brick" at the stranger, and he did this with the only implement at his command—swearing.

Among the Australian aborigines the name of a long-deceased relative is often uttered as an exclamation upon the experience of a sudden shock, such as stubbing one's toe against the root of a tree, or when something upon which one is working suddenly breaks. This may at first appear to have no counterpart among ourselves. But, as we shall see, this is not strictly so.

In order to understand why the Australian calls upon the name of some long-deceased relative to serve him as an exclamation, it is necessary to know something of the religious beliefs of these people.[19] We need not here concern ourselves with the details, since for our purposes it will be enough to know that the Australian aboriginal believes that when a person dies his soul either returns to the place from which it came or goes away to some distant region in which to dwell. The names of the dead are for a long period after their death considered sacred and must not be pronounced by any of their living relatives. Hence a great constellation of inhibited emotions is built up about the names of such deceased relatives. During the period in which these names are under a taboo, their owners are capable of working much mischief unless they are properly respected. Hence, the degree of awe in which their names are held is very high. It will then no longer be diffi-cult to understand why an Australian aboriginal invokes the name of a long-deceased ancestor when he seeks quick release for a sud-denly induced emotion. What is more natural than to exclaim by that very name whose use has for so long been prohibited? It is an innocent-enough exclamation now, but one that formerly would have brought dire consequences to the unsanctioned user.

To these natives such names serve precisely the same function as do the names of the gods, the saints, and the holy ones (from whom something of the taboos that had surrounded them have departed) for the civilized swearer of our own day. Had the Australians possessed saints and gods, they would have sworn by them, and had we been forbidden to mention the names of our departed relatives for a long time after their decease, we, too, would have sworn, or at least exclaimed, by them. Indeed, in civilized societies some people do swear by one or other or both of their departed parents.

Again, we may observe that there is here no essential difference between the form of swearing used by the Australian aborigines and that which characterizes civilized men under similar conditions. The only difference is that the Australian aborigines exhibit a marked restraint in the form of the exclamations that they use under conditions in which civilized men would employ foul and obscene expressions. Under the conditions of pain, fear, or surprise these natives indulge in none but the most innocent of exclamations. Such exclamations, however innocuous they may be, nonetheless constitute swearing, in much the same sense that it is swearing to utter the words "Holy Moses!" "Ye Gods!" or "Saint Patrick!"

It is of great interest to learn that under the conditions of a minor shock or surprise the aboriginal utters an exclamation that is the exact equivalent of the English "Oh, mother!" Here, as among ourselves, of course, the exclamation derives its power from the strong emotional attachment that exists between mother and child.

Swearing during quarrels, swearing as taunts to goad an enemy to fight, and swearing with obscene references to the pudenda are all familiar forms to us. During quarrels and in the taunts calculated to produce a fight, the most obscene and intolerable insults are used, such as "Go and have intercourse with your mother." This is an insult that no man will brook. Among these aborigines, as among Western peoples where the same oath occurs, incest is considered one of the worst crimes a man can commit. The great affective weight of such an oath is obvious. Similarly, oaths making reference to the pudenda or sexual organs draw their power and effectiveness from the great value placed upon these organs and the emotional investment that is made in them. Hence, any reference to another's organs as not being as they should be is both mortifying and shocking.

It is evident, then, that as far as the basic forms of swearing are concerned, the Australian aborigines, of Cape York at least, have developed all the forms that the so-called culturally more advanced peoples have. If we possessed a thoroughly complete account of their swearing practices, we should no doubt find that they indulged in still other forms of swearing akin to our own. In one respect they have developed far beyond any of the peoples of Western cultures: their sanctioning of swearing under the appropriate conditions. Here, with far greater insight and understanding of such matters than civilized societies have achieved, swearing has been recognized as a function of the human psyche of great power for good as well as evil. Australian aboriginal society has taken this power and utilized it for good, "to make everybody happy," as the natives themselves say. It is a sort of ritualized letting off of steam —the induction of a general feeling of well-being as a consequence of being permitted to enjoy to the full the freedom of what, under other conditions, is prohibited and would be considered the most heinous offense.

By contrast with our undiscriminating condemnation of swearing, these Australian aborigines have shown themselves far more intelligent than we of the Western world, who have neither recognized the nature and meaning of swearing, nor perceived how to utilize it for good.

Because in many ways the culture of the Australian aborigines is said to be the most primitive existing at the present time, it would hardly be justifiable to conclude that the forms of swearing that they now practice are akin to those practiced by the earliest men. But what we may say, with some degree of security, is that the swearing of the Australian aborigines suggests that the tendency to strong expression through speech testifies to the basic similarity of human nature among all peoples everywhere—whether they swear or not.

(Swearing Among the Ancient Egyptians

Among the Egyptians of antiquity swearing must have been a well-developed practice. I have, however, encountered only one record of an example of swearing, a case in which a workman was charged with swearing "By the Sovereign whose powers are mightier than death" during the twenty-ninth year of the reign of Ramses III. This oath was apparently considered one of great solemnity, for he who used it ran the risk of severe punishment.[20] Such an oath must indeed have possessed very great power, and it is self-evident why it should have been prohibited for all but the holiest of uses. We recall Carlyle's words "Men are praying—on the other side of a brick partition, men are cursing; and around them all is the vast, void Night."[21] Prayerfully to use the names of the holy ones is permissible; on the other side of the brick partition it is not. The appeals of those who pray and of those who swear are heard by the Great Powers, but while the first is socially allowed and even obligatory, the second is prohibited and condemned. In short, the sanctity of the Great Powers must be preserved by restricting their worship or celebration to specific times, places, and conditions and by prohibiting the taking of their names in vain at all other times. The names of the Great Powers must not be so commonly used as to become hackneyed words passed from mouth to mouth as so much free air. Nothing breeds contempt as much as familiarity, so no one must ever be allowed to be on familiar terms with the Great Powers. Hence, all reference to them is forbidden except upon the socially sanctioned occasions. And because the Great Powers have been rendered so inaccessible, so awful and powerful, men have, in the weakness of their anger, broken down and called upon these forbidden forces to bring disaster to the causes and the objects of their anger.

This double fault of swearing appears to have been long recognized not only by those who have condemned swearing, but by the swearers themselves. Swearing has always been censured as a weakness in the swearer, a lack of restraint and good taste, an illicit and irreverent coercion of the Great Powers, and, at the same time, a defiance of the Powers that Be. Thus, while weakly swearing, the swearer has found himself defying those very powers that, under normal conditions, he would not dream of abusing. It is in this fashion, as we shall later have many opportunities of judging, that weak men have often attempted to pass as strong ones by the frequency and boldness of their oaths. But this is to anticipate.

(Swearing Among the Jews

That the Jews of old were powerful swearers is very evident from the number and the character of the prohibitions that refer to the practice. The Third Commandment in the Decalogue is essentially an ordinance against profanity: "Thou shalt not take the name of the Lord thy God in vain, for the Lord will not hold him guiltless that taketh his name in vain." This also is laid down in Lev. 19:12: "Thou shall not profane the Name of thy God." Uttering the sacred name during an act of private or public worship or in any light, frivolous, or unauthorized manner was considered an offense so flagitious that it was punishable by death, as is fully exhibited in Lev. 24. Since our own attitudes toward swearing have been for the most part determined by the teaching of the Old Testament, we shall deal with its law and practice as it relates to swearing in some detail.

LEV. 24

10. And the son of an Israelitish woman, whose father was an Egyptian, went out among the children of Israel: and this son of the Israelitish woman and a man of Israel strove together in the camp;

11. And the Israelitish woman's son blasphemed the name of the LORD, and cursed. And they brought him unto Moses (and his mother's name was Shelomith, the daughter of Dibi, of the tribe of Dan:)

12. And they put him in ward, that the mind of the LORD might be shewed them.

13. And the LORD spake unto Moses, saying,

14. Bring forth him that hath cursed without the camp; and let all that heard him lay their hand upon his head, and let all the congregation stone him.

15. And thou shalt speak unto the children of Israel, saying, whosoever curseth his God shall bear his sin.

16. And he that blasphemeth the name of the LORD, he shall surely be put to death, and all the congregation shall certainly stone him: as well the stranger as he that is born in the land, when he blasphemeth the name of the LORD, shall be put to death.

This section of Leviticus forcefully illustrates what the God of the Jews himself ordained to be the punishment of those who blaspheme his name. And it makes very clear the heinousness of such an offense. The poor son of Shelomith had, in anger during a quarrel, misused the name of the Lord, and for this the Lord commanded that he be put to death. This, the Lord further commanded, was to be the punishment of all who committed a similar sin. The law thus made by God was to be often invoked for centuries afterward. Let it be observed that it was an obligation upon those who heard the swearer to bear witness against him, lest the guilt and the vengeance descend upon their own heads. Hence, it may be that something of the disapproval with which swearing has been viewed down the ages has been due to the fear of the consequences that might befall one who listened and tolerated without informing or at least demonstratively disapproving. This was, indeed, the basis of the appeal made in so many of the tracts that were published on the subject during the last five or more centuries.

For less noxious forms of swearing than the blaspheming of the name of the Lord the Old Testament prescribes lesser punishments. For the law regarding these we may again refer to Leviticus.

Lev. 5

1. And if a soul sin, and hear the voice of swearing, and is a witness, whether he hath seen or known of it; if he does not utter it, then he shall bear his iniquity.

4. Or if a soul swear, pronouncing with his lips to do evil, or to do good, whatsoever it be that a man shall pronounce with an oath, and it be had from him, when he knoweth of it, then he shall be guilty in one of these.

5. And it shall be, when he shall be guilty in one of these things, that he shall confess that he hath sinned in that thing.

6. And he shall bring his trespass offering unto the LORD for his sin which he hath sinned, a female from the flock, a lamb or a kid of the goats, for a sin offering; and the priest shall make an atonement for him concerning his sin.

7. And if he be not able to bring a lamb, then he shall bring for his trespass, which he hath committed, two turtle doves, or two young pigeons, unto the LORD; one for a sin offering, and the other for a burnt offering.

Here the sinfulness of swearing and of not informing against the swearer is explicitly stated. To cap all this, we have in Proverbs and Psalms the curse upon the curser.

Prov. 29

24. Whoso is partner with a thief hateth his own soul: he heareth cursing and bewrayeth it not.

Ps. 109

17. As he loved cursing, so let it come unto him: as he delighted not in blessing, so let it be far from him.

18. As he clothed himself with cursing, like as with his garment, so let it come into his bowels like water and like oil into his bones.

19. Let it be unto him as the garment which covereth him, and for a girdle wherewith he is girded continually.

This curse is, of course, a privileged one, but not all its threats nor all the terrors of punishment prescribed by the Lord against swearers have prevented men from blaspheming his name and lividly purpling the color of their speech. It would seem that if a law or proscription go against the nature of man, man's nature will rebel and go against the law and the proscription.

ECCLES. 9

2. All things come alike to all: there is one event to the righteous, and to the wicked; to the good and to the clean, and to the unclean; to him that sacrificeth not; as is the good, so is the sinner: and he that sweareth, as he that feareth an oath.

We may conclude the Old Testament teaching with regard to swearing with a saying of Solomon from Prov. 15:4: "A wholesome tongue is a tree of life; but perverseness therein is a breach in the Spirit."

From the great force and imperiousness of the Old Testament ordinances against swearing, it may be safely inferred that the Jews of antiquity were accomplished and frequent swearers. That the matter was serious is evident in Jer. 23:10: "because of swearing the land mourneth."

⟨ *The New Testament on Swearing*

The gentle spirit of Christ, in the Sermon on the Mount, speaks upon swearing so:

MATT. 5

33. Again, ye have heard that it hath been said by them of old time, Thou shalt not forswear thyself, but shalt perform unto the Lord thine oaths [cf. Num. 30:7: "If a man vow a vow unto the Lord or swear an oath to bind his soul with a bond, he shall not break his word; he shall do according to all that proceeded out of his mouth."]:

34. But I say unto you, Swear not at all; neither by Heaven: for it is God's throne:

35. Nor by earth: for it is his footstool: neither by Jerusalem; for it is the city of the great King.

36. Neither shalt thou swear by thy head, because thou canst not make one hair white or black.

37. But let your communication be, Yea, yea; Nay, nay: for whatsoever is more than these cometh of evil.

This passage is of great interest in many ways, but for us particularly because it affords some indications of what the oaths that tinctured the air in Christ's own day may have been like: *By Heaven! By the great Earth! By Jerusalem!* and *By my head!* These oaths, I am informed, occur to this day in Israel.

Christ's injunction against all swearing or vowing beyond "Yea, yea" and "Nay, nay" has been followed to the letter by only one Christian sect, the Quakers.

Another passage in the New Testament that may be taken, and has been taken, to include a reference to swearing occurs in Eph. 5.

26. Be ye angry and sin not: let not the sun go down upon your wrath:

27. Neither give place to the devil.

29. Let no corrupt communication proceed out of your mouth, but that which is good to the use of edifying, that it may minister grace unto the hearers.

And in JAMES 1, we have:

19. Wherefore, my beloved brethren, let every man be swift to hear, slow to speak, slow to wrath:

20. For the wrath of man worketh not the righteousness of God.

21. Wherefore lay apart all filthiness and superfluity of naughtiness, and receive with meekness the engrafted word, which is able to save your souls.

Such then are the judgments of the Old and New Testaments relating to swearing. They represent the authority upon which those who sought to guide and regulate the conduct of every individual who has been exposed to the Jewish and Christian tradition rested.

⟦ *Swearing in Ancient Greece*

That the heroes of Homer's *Iliad* swore we have no doubt, for they were mere troopers, and troopers have always sworn. But Homer, whose respect for the gods was a part of his poetic nature, did not exhibit this part of their heroism. The Greeks had a great pantheon of gods and mythological characters to draw upon for the adornment of their language, and no doubt they made good use of their resources. But at some early, unrecorded period, swearing appears to have been banned, and except for some rather mild oaths, the swearing of the Hellenes was refined and sophisticated.

Expletives were plentiful, and if a Greek suffered slight provocation, they would be employed to apostrophize the ruling divinities, as well as the shapes of field and flood, of earth and air. But the Hellenes do not appear to have forged their poetic oaths into weapons of malevolence and hurt—they possessed far more effective means of achieving such ends than mere verbal assaults. As soon as we have considered the actual forms of swearing in which the Greeks indulged, we shall pass on to an account of this other means.

Though the swearing of the Greeks was of a very light and innocuous kind, they were eminently a swearing people. Their reputation for swearing was so well known that Juvenal, in Satire VI, can only refer their immunity from swearing to the period when innocence was said to have prevailed upon Earth and before Jupiter had begun to let his beard grow.

It is all the more difficult to account for the mildness of Greek swearing, since it was an institution of considerable antiquity. Julian Sharman offered an ingenious explanation in 1888. He pointed out that the cities of Greece were full of strawshoes, men who made their calling known by placing a straw at their feet and who upon a suitable bid from a client were ready to give false evidence. In a nation too volatile and specious to be able to rely upon any system of reciprocal good faith, there was little place for confidence. It was from this circumstance that the Greeks earned for themselves the reputation of being the least trustworthy of all the untruthful nations of antiquity. In such a community, Sharman suggested, the fragile safeguard of an oath is, from sheer helplessness, the more rigorously demanded. In order, therefore, to protect the sanctity of the oath, the notion of an individual property or trademark in oaths came to be distinctively encouraged. "The specific appropriation of some distinctive oath raised the presumption that it implied an unequivocal pledge of sincerity."[22] In this way Zeno, the founder of the Stoic philosophy, swore continually *By the caper.* Pythagoras was accustomed, we are told, to swear by the number four, μα την τετρακτον. And Socrates swore *By the dog,* νὴ τὸν κύνα.

Hence, respectable oaths came to be institutionalized among the Greeks. There may be some truth in this theory, but it cannot possibly contain the whole explanation of the innocuousness of Greek swearing. For no people has ever abandoned its habits of swearing merely because the State considered it undesirable and forbade it. Of this we have abundant evidence in the example of modern Italy. Italy is a Catholic nation, and all Catholic nations are accomplished swearers, but with the exception of Hungary, none more so than modern Italy. In an attempt to induce Italians during Mussolini's regime to abandon their habit of swearing, the local authorities of many cities instituted a campaign against swearing. In trains and buses, for example, one often read signs admonishing passengers "Non bestemmiare per l'onore d'Italia" ("Do not swear for the honor of Italy"). No one ever observed that this ill-conceived campaign had the slightest effect. Indeed, this piece of political folly was treated as a huge joke in the most egregiously bad taste.

The whole history of swearing bears unequivocal testimony to the fact that legislation and punishments against swearing have only had the effect of driving it under the cloaca of those more noisome regions, where it has flourished and luxuriated with the ruddiness of the poppy's petals and the blackness of the poppy's heart. It has never been successfully repressed. Perhaps the bland swearing of the Greeks was due to the decree of the State, but if such decrees were ever issued, there exists no evidence of them. Or perhaps the tameness was achieved by the subtle device of granting the swearer property rights in individual oaths. But surely this could not have been so for all Greeks? There would hardly have been enough oaths to go around. As we shall see, the answer to this problem is probably to be found elsewhere. Meanwhile, let us consider some of the common oaths by which the Greeks swore.

The Hellenes swore by all the known gods and goddesses—Zeus, Jupiter, Mars, Apollo, Hercules, Dionysos, Poseidon, Demeter, Minerva, Juno, Venus, and others—and by the regions they inhabited. They swore also by the virtues, as Philocles does in Lucian's *The Lover of Lies* when he exclaims, "In the name of Hestia!"[23] That is, in the name of friendship. In the same work Lucian makes Tychiades swear the commonest of all Greek oaths, Μὰ Δι! (By Heaven!)[24] Variations of this oath were Μὰ Δια, νὴ Δια, νὴ τὸν Δια. The νη and τὸν could be placed before the name of any of the gods to lend greater affirmative force to one's oath, as in the common form Μὰ νὸν Ἀπόλλω! (Yea, by Apollo!). To swear by the godhead the Athenian had his Μὰ τὸν θεόη (Yea, by God), which in deference to ears polite he would soften to a simple Μὰ τὸν. Women swore by Juno, Hecate, Diana, Venus, Proserpine, and Ceres, and men by more masculine deities and by their genius or guardian spirit. Athenian women swore by Aglaurosus, Pandrosus, etc.

Aristophanes, in the first scene of his comedy *Ecclesiazusae* (*The Assemblywomen*), makes the most of the customary sexual distinction between masculine and feminine oaths. In the very first scene, in which the women are disguising themselves as men in order to pack and take over the Assembly, the following exchange occurs:

FIRST WOMAN: By the two Goddesses. . . .
PRAXAGORA: *By the two Goddesses?* Dunderhead, where did you leave your brain?
FIRST WOMAN: What's wrong? I didn't ask for a drink?
PRAXAGORA: No, but what man swears By the two Goddesses? The rest was beautifully stated. Right to the point.
FIRST WOMAN: Oh. By Apollo!

Thus was a near calamity averted.

Greek levity in swearing is supposed to be exemplified in Socrates' oath, *By the dog!* He is also reported to have sworn variously by the goose and by the plane tree. Those who believe in the piety of the philosopher agree that the habit of these oaths was assumed by Socrates as a foil to the irreverent mention of the gods that was then universal. Lucian attaches an intelligent meaning to these flippant expletives and represents Socrates as justifying their use. "Are you not aware," he is presumed to reason, "that the dog is the Anubis of Egypt, the Sirius of the skies; and in hell is the keeper of Cerberus?" Plutarch also comments on the oath, "Those that worship the dog have a certain sacred meaning that must not be revealed; in the more remote and ancient times the dog had the highest honours paid to him in Egypt."[25]

The annotators of Socrates' rhetoric may be correct in their explanation of the meaning of his canine oath, but it would be difficult to make out a like case for his swearing by the goose and by the plane tree. In passing, it may be mentioned that the Anubis of Egypt was not a dog but a dog-faced baboon—to this day known in learned circles as the Anubis (*Papio doguera*). It is probable that Socrates swore by the dog for the same reason he swore by the goose and the plane tree: because they were utterly idle and inoffensive expressions that nonetheless had some power, for the purpose of slightly opening a cock valve or perhaps intensifying an assertion. The Greeks swore by the garlic, the leek, and the onion, and indeed every other deity which grew and flourished in the market-gardens of Alexandria.

Such oaths were not euphemistic like the modern *Holy mackerel!* which is merely a euphemism for *Holy Moses!* but are more akin to the oath by which Baudelaire, the nineteenth-century French poet, swore: *Sacré-Saint-Ciboire! (Sacred Saint-Onion!)*[26]

A hilarious burlesque on Athenian swearing, and of Socrates' brand of it in particular, has come down to us in Aristophanes' comedy *The Clouds*. Socrates was actually present at the performance of this play, in which he saw himself portrayed as the central figure of the action.

Socrates is discovered swung up in a basket in his own thinking shop, giving utterance to innumerable heresies and follies. When Strepsiades is about to swear by the gods, he is at once interrupted by Socrates, who from the basket reminds him that the gods are a mere expression of vulgar superstition, not current coin in his system of philosophy. "By what then do you swear?" asks Strepsiades, "By the iron money, as they do at Byzantium?" But to this question Socrates made no answer.

The result, however, of the Socratic influence upon the young men of his time is intended to be shown by the circumstance of Strepsiades subsequently swearing *By the mist!* and by his reproaching his son for taking oaths in the name of a deity of the outside world. Presently, when Strepsiades is approached by a creditor who demands the return of twelve minae lent for the purchase of a dapple-gray horse, he is ready to swear any number of oaths *By the gods* that he is innocent of the debt. In the course of a few minutes his opinions have undergone a complete alteration. He now feels justified in being rid of his obligation to repay the debt by making use of declarations that Socrates has argued are no longer of any consequence.

"And will you be willing to deny it upon oath of the gods?" screams the creditor.

"What gods?" asks Strepsiades.

"Jupiter, Mercury, and Neptune."

"Yes, by Jupiter!" rejoins Strepsiades, "and would pay down, too, a three-obol piece besides to swear by them."[27]

Plato, who did not share Socrates' views on the gods, did not respect them in his accounts of Socrates' philosophy. Considering the gods superannuated, Socrates abjured swearing by them. Aristophanes made this eccentric view of Socrates the butt of his satire in *The Clouds*.

The fact that Socrates did not believe in the gods seems then to have been the reason why he, at least, did not swear by them. But if this was so with Socrates, it was not so with the majority of the Athenians, who continued to privateer on their own account with the gods as their allies, totally unmindful, and unminding, of the unorthodox Socrates' opinions.

An appropriate oath was considered an ornament of speech in ancient Greece. Demosthenes, the greatest of orators, made good use of such figures in his speeches. Longinus, in his treatise *On the Sublime*, a Greek work probably written at the end of first century (A.D.), has much of interest to say on the figures used by Demosthenes in one of his speeches.

The topic of figures now claims immediate attention, for these too, if rightly handled, may be, as I said, an important element in the sublime. However, since it would be a long and indeed an interminable task to treat them all in detail at this point, we will by way of strengthening our position merely run through a few of those which make for grandeur. To proceed then, Demosthenes is producing an argument in favour of his policy. The reference is to Demosthenes' defense against Aeschines of his aggressive policy, which had led to the disastrous defeat at Chaeroneia. He appeals to past history to prove that it was sound, however unsuccessful.[28] What was the natural way to treat it? "You were not wrong, men of Athens, in undertaking that struggle for the freedom of Greece, and you have proof of this near home, for the men at Marathon were not misguided nor those at Salamis nor those at Platea." But when in a sudden moment of inspiration, as if possessed by the divine afflatus, he utters his great oath about the champions of Greece, "It cannot be that you were wrong; no, by those who bore the brunt at Marathon." Then you feel that by employing the single figure of adjuration—which I here call apostrophe—he has deified his ancestors by suggesting that one should swear by men who met such a death, as if they were gods: he has filled his judges with the spirit of those who bore the brunt there: he has transferred his argument into a passage of transcendent sublimity and emotion, giving it the power of conviction that lies in so strange and startling an oath, and at the same time his words have administered to his hearers a remedy and an antidote, with the result that, relieved by his eulogy, they come to feel as proud of the war with Philip as of their victories at Marathon and Salamis. In all this by the use of the figure he is enabled to carry the audience away with him. True he is said to have found the germ of the oath in Eupolis:

> Nay, by the fight I fought at Marathon,
> No one of them shall scatheless vex my heart.[29]

But the mere swearing of an oath is not sublime: we must consider the place, the manner, the circumstances, the motive. In Eupolis there is nothing but an oath, and that addressed to Athens, when still in prosperity and needing no encouragement. Moreover, the poet's oath does not immortalize the men so as to beget in the audience a true opinion of their worth, but instead he wanders from those who bore the brunt to an inanimate object, namely "the fight." In Demosthenes the oath is carefully designed to suit the feelings of defeated men, so that the Athenians no longer regard Chaeroneia as a disaster; and it is, as I said, at the same time a proof that no mistake has been made, an example, a sworn confirmation, a eulogy, and a stimulus.[30]

Here we observe the distinction between the sublime and the common oath, and the creation—by Demosthenes—of an oath, as it were, in process: the deification of the men who fought at Marathon, to whom the Athenians owed so much and to whose memory they were so deeply emotionally attached. This is, in reality, an excellent example of the manner in which oaths come into being, both of the sublime and more often of the common kind. We can easily imagine that an oath such as Demosthenes created became a popular one, although there is no evidence in this case that this oath did become so. Perhaps the occasion upon which it was used was too serious, but under other circumstances we could well imagine it taking hold of the popular fancy. We shall have occasion to refer to some modern examples of this later.

One of the most famous oaths of Ionia was *By the cabbage!* Indeed, this was the favorite expletive of the Ionians, as it was among the favorite oaths of Socrates. It is very possible that the modern Italian expletive *Cavolo!* is the lineal descendant of the Ionian *By the cabbage!* (μὰ τηv κραμβηv).[31]

How did this odd oath originate? It would appear that the merchants of the Levant trading with the port of Rhodes had familiarized Athenian householders with a most excellent variety of cabbage, the *halmynis*. The plant, found in its highest perfection only upon the southern coasts of the Mediterranean, had a flavor so mellow that it surpassed all the indigenous varieties and was, moreover, highly prized by all Athenian topers as the most potent antidote to the effects of drink. No dinner table would have been complete without some preparation of this delicacy. It is more than doubtful whether the Rhodian cabbage had any other than a placebo effect upon the wine bibbers, but with this nostrum at hand they imagined they could defy the worst that the choicest

Chian or Lesbian vintages could do. So it came about that the very name of so inestimable a vegetable came to be held in such high esteem that it was customary to say that if one were permitted to blaspheme without offending the gods, it would be by mention of the Rhodian cabbage.

So wrote Lynceus, a citizen of Rhodes to Diagoras at Athens.[32] In a fragment of a lost poem by Arnaius[33] the lover solemnly invokes the cabbage as evidence of his attachment, and in the iambics of Hipponax (fl. 540 B.C.) there is found a suggestion of the vegetable even having entered into the realms of mythology:

> He falling down, worshipped the seven-leaved cabbage,
> To which, before she drank the poisoned draught,
> Pandora brought a cake at Thargelia to take the curse away.[34]

Another product of the earth by which the Ionians swore was the colewort.

In Crete Rhadamanthus is said to have made a law forbidding people to swear by the gods, though they were permitted to swear by the dog, the goose, and the plane tree.

In the book of his old age, *The Laws*, Plato, much admiring of Rhadamanthus, felt that every form of abuse in language should be forbidden. In a well-regulated state, he wrote:

Concerning abuse there shall be this one law to cover all cases:—No one shall abuse anyone. If one is disputing with another in argument, he shall either speak or listen, and he shall wholly refrain from abusing either the disputant or the bystanders. For from those light things, words, there spring in deed things most heavy to bear, even hatreds and feuds, when men begin by cursing one another and foully abusing one another in the manner of fish·wives; and the man who utters such words is gratifying a thing most ungracious and sating his passion with foul foods, and by thus brutalizing afresh that part of his soul that was once humanized by education, he makes a wild beast of himself through his rancorous life, and wins only gall for gratitude from his passion. In such disputes all men are commonly wont to proceed to indulge in ridicule of their opponent; but everyone who has ever yet indulged in this practice has either failed to achieve a virtuous disposition, or else has lost in great measure his former high-mindedness. No man, therefore, shall ever in any wise utter such words in any holy place or at any public sacrifice or public games, or in the market or the court of any public assembly; in every such case the magistrate concerned shall punish the offender; or, if he fail to do so, he shall be disqualified for any public distinction because of his neglect of the laws and his failure to execute the injunc-

tions of the lawgiver. And if in other places a man abstains not from
such language—whether he be the aggressor or acting in self-defence
—whosoever meets with him, if he be an older man, shall vindicate the
law by driving off with stripes the men who pamper passion, that evil
comrade; or, if he fail to do so, he shall be liable to the appointed
penalty.[35]

Plato, alas, had grown even more intolerant of the foibles of
humanity than he had been in the work of his maturity, *The
Republic*, exhibiting that hardening of the intellectual arteries that
sometimes befalls older men. But what is psychosclerosis in Plato
is still high intellect in other men, and it is of more than passing
interest to hear him utter the words that were so often repeated
in later centuries, and utterly without effect.

Greek cursing as it relates to Greek swearing will be considered
in the next chapter. Meanwhile, let us turn our attention to Rome.

(*Swearing in Ancient Rome*

Curiously enough, swearing was no more vigorously practiced
by the Romans than it was by the Greeks. It may be suspected
that the reason for this was the same as that which, as we shall
see in the next chapter, probably regulated the character of Greek
swearing.

Like the Greeks, the Romans swore chiefly by their gods—and
swore rather plentifully too. The form of the oath was often determined by the sex of the person using it. Thus, the inseparable twin
offspring of Jupiter and Leda, Castor and Pollux (whom Jupiter
later set among the stars to form the constellation Gemini), were
the gods by which the Romans most frequently swore. While
women, as a rule, avoided swearing by Pollux and swore instead
by Castor, men generally omitted swearing by Castor and swore
by Pollux. The feminine oath was *Mecastor!* or *Ecastor!*—the affixes
me and *e* being supplied to adapt the name to the purposes of
swearing. The oath *By Pollux* was sworn in the corrupted forms
Pol! and *Edepol!* While women occasionally swore by Pollux, they
left the masculine oath *By Hercules! (Mehercule!)* entirely to the
men and scrupulously avoided its use. The oath *By Hercules!* was
a very popular one, and through frequent use the vocative of
"Hercules" was reduced to the disyllabic form "Hercle." This was
often strengthened by the addition of "certe" and "certo." In pas-

sionate language this oath would even be used twice in the same sentence, as in the *Aulularia* of Plautus (*c.* 250–184 B.C.), the chief comic poet and comedy writer of Rome:

> Sic hercle tu ex istoc loco
> digitum transuorsum aut unguem latum excesseris
> aut si respexis, donicum ego te iussero,
> continuo hercle ego te dedam discipulam cruci.
>> Plautus, *Aulularia*, I, i, 56–60

In Plautus' comedy *Audria* we have a good example of the intensitive "certe" being added to the disyllabic "Hercle":

> Certe hercle nunc hic saipus fallit, haud ego.
>> Plautus, *Audria*, III, ii, 495

Similarly, the intensitive "certe" was added to "Edepol" in order to lend it more weight, as we again see from the *Aulularia*.

> Certe edepol equidem te civem sine mala omni malitia
> semper sum arbitratus, et nunc arbitror.[36]
>> Plautus, *Aulularia*, II, ii, 212–213

Even in the dignified prose of Cicero (106–43 B.C.) such expressions occasionally make their appearance: "Ab hercule maiores nostri longe aliter et de illo et de ceteris talibus existimabant" (*Pro Sex Roscio*, 18).

By Hercules! was such a favorite oath with the Romans that even the children were permitted to swear by it. However, Hercules himself, it was said, had sworn only on a single occasion: when, in a great crisis in his life, he clapped on the shirt of Nessus and in the most bitter imprecations inveighed against the credulity of Deianira, the cruelty of Eurysheus, and the jealousy of Juno, which resulted in the loss of the fair isle. This being the only occasion upon which he was believed to have sworn, the Romans, in recognition of such a singular example of forbearance, enjoined their children never to make light use of his sacred name. In the house one could swear *Di boni!* or *Per dios immortales!* but never by Hercules. The prohibition, however, extended only to the four walls of the house and its curtilage; out of doors the children were free to make what use of it they liked.

It is probable that the Romans may claim the original ownership of an oath that has spread throughout the Western world more effectively, perhaps, than any other. This is their *damnosa canicula*, which in France became *sacré chien* and in England, *damned*, or *cursèd, dog*.

The origin of the malediction *damnosa canicula* has been traced back to the Roman game of dice, in which two kinds of dice were used, the tali and tesserae. The tali had four even surfaces, the tesserae, six. On one side of the tali appeared the figure 1, and on the opposite side, number 6, the numbers 3 and 4 appearing respectively on the other surfaces. The tessera, or six-sided dice, bore on its additional faces the numbers 2 and 5. Both tali and tesserae were usually the knucklebones of an animal, frequently the gazelle. The uneven ends were planed smooth in the case of the tesserae, but the tali were left in their natural condition. In ancient Greece the game of knucklebones was played only by children, but in Rome the game speedily became the instrument of wagering and gambling. The game was played with four pieces, two tali and two tesserae. The best throw, called the Venus, occurred when each of the upturned faces presented different numbers. In the worst possible throw, each of the four pieces showed the same number: an ace. The name by which this worst of all possible throws was distinguished by the crapshooters of antiquity was the *canicula* or *canis*.

> Jure etenim id summum quid dexter senio ferret
> Scire erat in voto, damnosa canicula quantum
> Raderet.
> > Persius, *Satires*, III 48–49

It may well be imagined how some of our old Roman gamesters felt when after a particularly hopeful throw the four pieces turned up a *canicula: Damnosa canicula!* It was an obvious enough malediction, and it caught on. Such is the tenacity with which old sweeping habits cling to men that generations of them, to the present day, doggedly swear by this oath. They swear by it in the form in which it has been naturalized in their own language, without quite knowing its precise meaning and certainly not its origin. The account of the oath's origin should explain the seeming paradox that in a society like ours, in which the dog is an object of affection, it should be possible to use its name in so opprobrious a manner. The expression used refers not to the dog but to the name of the worst throw in the game of Roman dice.

Sporting men swore by Hippona, the Goddess and patroness of grooms, jockeys, and horses. Thus, Juvenal (A.D. 57?–138?) in his *Eighth Satire*, written about A.D. 116, writes of "Fat Lateranus,"

> He'll play the Groom, give Oats, and rub 'em down.
> If after NUMA's Ceremonial way
> He at JOVE's Altar wou'd a Victim slay,
> To no clean Goddess he directs his Pray'rs,
> But by Hippona most Devoutly Swears,
> Or some rank Deity whose filthy face
> We suitably o're stinking Stables place.[37]

The last two lines refer to the practice of placing paintings or statues of the Goddess in stables.

The Roman poet Ovid (43 B.C.–A.D. 17), who was ever ready to poke fun at popular faith and credulity, makes allusion to all the essential elements of the oath in certain of his amatory pleasantries:

> Believe that gods exist! She broke her vow;
> Her face, though beauteous then, is beauteous now.
>
> .   .   .   .
>
> By her own eyes my darling lately swore,
> And then by mine; and mine are aching sore.
>
> Were I a god I'd see no damage came
> To pretty maid for swearing by my name.
> Yes, I'd swear truth at any odds!
> You would not class *me* with the gloomy gods.
> But thou, fair damsel, use the great gods' prize
> More moderately; or spare at least, mine eyes.[38]

Swearing by one's own, or at another's, eyes was apparently a common Roman oath. Here is an example represented in an epigram by Nicarcus (translated by Walter Leaf):

> If you desire to paralyse
> Your enemy, don't "damn his eyes";
> From futile blasphemy desist:
> Send him to Blank the oculist.

It is significant that when Ovid, who thought so little of swearing, desired to accomplish what others achieved by swearing, he resorted to the curse. But this brings us to the next chapter.

CHAPTER THREE

Cursing

❮❮❯❯❯❯❯❯❯❯❯❯❯❯❯❯❯❯❯❯❯❯❯❯❯❯❯❯❯❯❯❯❯❯❯❯❯❯

You taught me language; and my profit on't
Is, I know how to curse.

WILLIAM SHAKESPEARE, *The Tempest* (I, ii), 1611

THE oath has been defined as a provisional curse, a definition that may serve to explain the popular tendency to regard swearing and cursing as identical. We have not yet reached the stage, in this book, that would permit us to draw our own conclusions concerning the forms and varieties of swearing. It may for the present suffice to say that cursing is a form of swearing and that swearing is a form of cursing. As we shall see later, however, it is strictly more accurate to consider swearing as the generic form and cursing as a species of it. The indications are that swearing preceded the development of cursing. That is, expletives, maledictions, exclamations, and imprecations of the immediately explosive or vituperative kind preceded the speechmaking and later rituals involved in the deliberate apportioning of the fate of an enemy. Swearing of the former variety is from the lips only, but the latter is from the heart. *Damn it!* is not the same as *Damn you!* Consider the phrase "Damn it, man, couldn't you think of that before?" Now try to substitute "you" for "it." It can be done, but it normally would not. The best one could do with that substitution would be "Damn you for a fool, why didn't you think of that before?" *Damn it!* is an immediate catharsis. *Damn you!* is the expression of unappeased and continuing anger or annoyance. But *Damn you!* is not a curse, although it partakes more of the nature of one —such as *May you be damned* or *May the Lord damn you*— than *Damn it* does.

One swears when the promise of relief and the achievement of effect are immediate. One curses when relief may be immediate but the effect of one's curse may be somewhat delayed. And so one's imprecations and expletives are generally couched in language suitable to the requirements of the present moment, whereas cursing is essentially couched in language that refers to the future. One swears at an enemy when he is within reach, one curses him when he may not be within immediate reach. While common swearing is not ordinarily allowed, cursing enjoys a certain social sanction in every community, and while cursing has been privateering on its own account for many centuries, it has always been considered a special prerogative of the priesthood. In order to understand the full significance of swearing, as well as of cursing, we shall have to consider its elementary forms here.

⟪ Cursing Among the Australian Aborigines

Verbal cursing among the Australian aborigines is unknown. The reason for this is that they have a vastly more effective means of disposing of an enemy, a means that is certain and whose effectiveness is known from experience to every member of the tribe. This is the magical means of "pointing" death at a person who may or may not be present or visible. The death-pointing instrument may be made of a small stick or a human forearm bone cut down to about three or four inches and sharpened at one or both ends. Usually, the death of some individual is to be avenged, and the bone is then taken from the deceased's body. After a specified ritual, the bone is pointed at the victim himself, at his habitation, or simply in the direction in which he lives. Then one of the witnesses of the ceremony conveys the facts to the unfortunate victim. "Overcome with consternation and terror, the fellow immediately begins to fret; and death will inevitably be the outcome, unless the counter-influence of a medicine-man or the tribal power can make itself felt beforehand."[1] Belief in the magical efficacy of such ceremonies is so profound that the "pointed" person invariably goes into a decline and dies unless, as Basedow states, some counterinfluence is brought to bear upon the situation.

Still another widespread method of procuring the prostration of an enemy practiced by the Australian aborigines falls into the class of sympathetic magic. This consists of taking some part of the victim's body or some object with which it has been in contact, such as hair, sputum, sweat, excrement, a footprint, or whatnot, and "singing" it during the performance of a special ceremony. These enchanting songs are calculated to entice the spirit-father of the doomed man to attend the ceremony.

A little later one of the principal performers marches forward, carrying a small ball of resin mixed with the burned excrement, together with a short stick representing the spirit-father. At a given moment, he begins to dance and, with his free hand, catches hold of his scrotum. When he arrives at the hole, in which the fire is burning, other men snatch the glowing embers and clear the ashes out of the way. The dancer throws the resin ball containing the excrement into the hole and covers it with hot sand. The moment it strikes the hot ground, the resin fizzles and crackles; and these sounds are taken to be the voice of the spirit calling the victim from the earth.[2]

Shortly after the ceremony these facts are conveyed to the individual who has been selected to die, with results that always terminate in his death from the power that he fears, unless he is by the proper means released from the spell.[3]

Any fully initiated man may practice such evil magic or employ a medicine man to perform it for him. When the grievance to be avenged concerns the whole tribe, the medicine man is officially employed to perform the necessary operations, much in the manner of modern churches that, in similar circumstances, have availed themselves of the commination service and the edicts of excommunication.

The Australian aborigines also make images of their enemies, which they destroy after the appropriate ritual, fully expecting that the same fate will overtake the original of the image. This is a very widespread practice not only among so-called primitive peoples, but also among many of the more superstitious members of civilized nations throughout the world.

These ritual death-procuring practices of the Australian aborigines represent their sanctioned form of cursing. It is a practical form of cursing, which yields practical results. Were such forms of cursing unavailable to the aborigines, they would undoubtedly have recourse to the far weaker verbal forms.

([Cursing Among the Maoris of New Zealand

Even to the present day the Maoris of New Zealand strongly believe in the power of the curse. Pregnant women especially must not swear or curse too much for this may endanger the baby's welfare. Ernest and Pearl Beaglehole give an example of what may happen if this taboo is broken, the case of an infant who was born with a deformed head, so that it looked like a dog's head. The people who saw the infant were frightened and said it must be a demon (*atua*). No one would touch it, and after three days it died. The old women averred that the cause of the deformity lay in the mother's cursing—not in the use of the white man's swearwords, but in the use of Maori curses that relate to a person's head.[4]

(Cursing Among the Jews of Antiquity

The Jews were probably the most accomplished cursers of antiquity. Their verbal forms of cursing have provided the pattern for the curses of the Western world for two millennia. But verbal cursing is a development that followed on practical cursing, and the ancient Jews were given to a very primitive form of practical cursing: sympathetic magic. This is exemplified by the nature and method of Jeremiah's curse upon Babylon (Jer. 51: 60–64):

So Jeremiah wrote in a book the evil that should come upon Babylon, even all these words that are written against Babylon. And Jeremiah said to Seriaiah, When thou comest to Babylon, and shalt see, and shalt read all these words; Then shalt thou say, O Lord, thou hast spoken against this place, to cut it off, that none shall remain in it, neither man nor beast, but that it shall be desolate for ever. And it shall be, when thou hast made an end of reading this book, that thou shalt bind a stone to it, and cast it into the midst of the Euphrates: and thou shalt say, Thus shall Babylon sink, and shall not rise from the evil that I will bring upon her.

The word "book" in this passage probably refers to a roll of papyrus and not to a clay tablet or one of stone, for Jeremiah's injunction is that a stone should be bound to this book so that when it is cast into the midst of the waters the "book" will surely sink. At a later period this problem was solved at one blow, by cutting the curse directly on a heavy material like clay brick, stone, or lead.

Jeremiah's curse against Babylon constitutes an excellent example of practical cursing. All the elements of the Australian aboriginal's sympathetic death magic are contained in it: the supplication formula, the incantation, the ritual casting, and the invocation that what has befallen the object should befall the original.

Throughout the region extending from Mesopotamia to the western shores of the Mediterranean the art of practical cursing appears to have flourished from early times and is far from extinct today.

Unauthorized cursing was a punishable offence, the severest penalties being inflicted upon the offenders, even to death. In Exodus 21:17 it is written, "And he that curseth his father, or his mother, shall surely be put to death."

◖ Cursing Among the Greeks

From the earliest known time, the Greeks were given to the practice of cursing by sympathetic magic, in much the same manner as that described for the Australian aborigines (except that "pointing" was unknown among the Greeks). It was common practice to take some castoff or nonessential portion of the earthly tabernacle of an individual, such as a nail paring, or a hair, and pronounce the proper formulary curse upon it, then either bury it or drop it into a deep well or a river, together with a tablet upon which the curse was incised. Many hundreds of such cursing tablets have been recovered by archaeologists from the earth and ruined wells of ancient Greece and the Ionian islands, and collections of the inscriptions on these tablets have been published.[5] Among the peasantry of modern Greece this primitive form of cursing was noted as recently as 1910.[6]

In Greece the cursing tablet took the form of a panel of lead or bronze or occasionally stone, which was called the αρα,* the ara,[7] literally translated as "the fastening down." Upon this tablet the curser incised or engraved his curse, usually following a definite formula. The curser lays his spell upon the person of his enemy, and frequently of his enemy's relatives too. Every portion of his body and every organ is named with meticulous care, fairly exhausting the anatomical nomenclature of the times. The list is generally brought to a close with a curse on the "psyche," the soul of the unfortunate victim, the whole being a perfect hymn of hate. His invocation testifies alike to the intensity of his animosity and the profundity of his faith.

---

* The name by which the Furies called themselves in their home beneath the earth is the name of Curses, 'Αραί.

When Plato speaks of imprecations, he uses the word *katadesis*, referring to the *tabulae defixionis* consigning the cursed persons to the gods of the nether world. Many of these tablets belong to the fourth century B.C. One, inscribed on the shard of a cup, reads, "I put quartan fever on Aristion to the death," and is of a date probably as early as the fifth century B.C. A large number of these cursing tablets have been found at Athens, and it is not altogether surprising to find the names of well-known persons on a number of them: Demophilus, the prosecutor of Aristotle and Phocion, as well as Demosthenes, Lycurgus, and other orators and politicians. As Nilsson has remarked, "The names mentioned show that belief in the magical power of these imprecations was not confined to artisans, hawkers, and such people, who also appear among those cursed. It must have been current even in the best of society."[8]

With a curse reinforced by the sympathetic magic of the burning brand Althea killed her son Meleager, and Theseus heavily cursed the Athenians when he departed from Sycros. Death came to the faithless Myrtilus from the curse laid upon him by his master Œnomaus, and with his dying breath he himself uttered a retaliatory curse upon the whole line of Pelops. Long before this Pelops had visited upon Laius of Thebes the curse of childlessness. The boiling to death of the wicked Pelias by his innocent daughters was the result of a curse uttered by Jason's mother, and Thyestes' curse was responsible for the end of his brother Atreus and his line, both sons of Pelops.

Oedipus' curses upon his children were granted by the gods, and so was Amyntor's when he cursed his son Phoenix, and Theseus' when he cursed his son Hippolytus. As Plato remarks in *The Laws*, "countless other parents cursed countless other sons, which curses of parents upon sons it is clearly proved that the gods grant; for a parent's curse laid upon his children is more potent than any other man's curse against any other, and most justly so."[9]

The Eurnolpid priests, according to both Diodorus and Plutarch, officially laid a curse upon Alcibiades for his rather obtrusive impiety. The Spartans objected to dealing with Pericles on the ground that his family, the Alcmaeonids, had been under a curse for three centuries.

So strongly was the curse entrenched in ancient Greece that it had become part of the official code, and the official curse was an accepted institution. Here are a few of some forty lines of such an official curse taken from two fifth-century B.C. pillars on the island of Teos:

Whosoever employs baneful drugs against the Teian state or against its citizens, may he and his family perish. Whosoever hinders the importation of grain into the land of Teos by any device or strategem, whether by sea or by land, or withholds grain from sale when it has been so imported, may he and his family perish. May any official who may fail to enforce this curse himself be subject to it. Whosoever shall fracture the pillars on which this curse is written or shall chisel out the letter or shall destroy the inscription, may that man and his family perish.[10]

Such official curses had the effect of a taboo. Anyone breaking the taboo had no one to blame but himself for the misfortunes that were bound to follow. It was a risk most Teians were probably unwilling to take.

At an early period in the history of Greece there was widespread belief in the destructive supernatural power of the curses of those who believed themselves wronged. Especially feared was the lethal potency of the poet's satire. Archilochus, a satirist of the seventh century B.C., wrote iambics that were literally believed to possess the power to kill. Indeed, "scorpion-tongued" Archilochus is said to have rimed several persons to death—a fact recalled by Ben Jonson at the end of his play *Poetaster*, in which he writes:

> I could doe worse,
> Arm'd with ARCHILOCHVS fury, write *Iambicks*,
> Should make the desperate lashers hang themselues.
> Rime 'hem to death, as they doe *Irish* rats
> In drumming tunes.

The meter in which Archilochus wrote his poems came to be known as "iambic" from "iamb," meaning "invective." G. L. Hendrickson says that "the popular fancy demanded and assumed, as a matter of course, destruction for the objects of the imprecations of the more famous iambists. That their ill-omened vows and invectives should be effective was a part of their preeminence, and that their victims should escape with less than death would have been a derogation of their fame."[11] Even in death the power of Archilochus' ill-omened invective could not be escaped, as a contemporary sepulchral epigram on Archilochus so ominously testifies: "Cerberus, whose bark strikes terror into the dead, there comes a terrible shade before whom even thou must tremble. Archilochus is dead. Beware the acrid iambic wrath engendered by his bitter mouth. Thou knowest the might of his words ever since one boat brought thee the two daughters of Lycambes."[12] The question of immediate interest, and of larger significance for the understanding of the development of magic and religion, is whether a person such as Archilochus was so effective because of his own extraordinary personal power or because he derived his power from the skill with which he wove his iambics—in short, his power over the word, which was itself believed to possess magical potency.[13]

As F. B. Jevons pointed out many years ago in a much neglected essay buried in one of those sterling books of essays that seem to be destined to remain unread from the day of their publication, extraordinary personal power is neither good nor bad,

but becomes the one or the other according as it is used for good ends or for bad, so it is in itself neither magical nor religious but comes to be regarded as religious if used in the service of the gods, and as magic if used otherwise. But it is not until gods are believed in that this power can be used in their service or regarded as their gift: only when belief in the gods has arisen can the person possessing power be regarded as having derived his power from them, or believe himself so to have derived it. It may well be that his power confirms his belief and strengthens it; it may perhaps even be that his power is the first thing to awaken him to belief in gods and to the possibility of communing with them in his heart. But the belief that there are superior beings is not the same thing as the extraordinary personal power which some men exert over others. Such belief and such power may indeed go together, but they do not by any means always go together; and accordingly the power cannot be regarded as the cause of the belief . . . magic does not come into existence until religion has come into existence.[14]

As a priest of Demeter, Archilochus was endowed with the power of manipulating the supernatural. It is, therefore, not surprising to find that he and his fellow iambists were so feared. The sixth-century satirist Hipponax was quite as much feared for his lethal verses as his predecessor Archilochus.

Customary in Greece was the ceremonial curse uttered on important public occasions. Demosthenes, in one of his orations demanded that "the curse" be recited: "This imprecation, men of Athens, is pronounced, as the law directs, by the marshal on your behalf at every meeting of the Assembly, and again before the Council at all their sessions."[15]

The priests of Zeus ritually pronounced the "curses of Bouzýges" at the third of the sacred plowings. Bouzýges was an old-time Athenian, the first ever to plow with a pair of oxen.[16] The "curses of Bouzýges" were uttered against those who failed to give succor to those in distress, who neglected to bury the dead with the proper rites, and who failed in similar obligations.

([Cursing Among the Romans

Practical cursing among the Romans was much the same as among the Greeks. Here is a typical inscription on a cursing tablet from the early Augustan period (50 B.C.) now in the Archaeological Museum at Johns Hopkins University:

Good and beautiful Proserpina (or Salvia, shouldst thou prefer), mayest thou wrest away the health, body, complexion, strength and faculties of Plotius and consign him to thy husband, Pluto. Grant that by his own devices he may not escape this penalty. Mayest thou consign him to the quartian, tertian and daily fevers to war and wrestle with him until they snatch away his very soul. Wherefore I hand over this victim to thee, Proserpina (or, shouldst thou prefer, Acherusia). Mayest thou summon for me the three-headed hound Cerberus to tear out the heart of Plotius, and mayest thou pledge thyself to give him three offerings—dates, figs, and a black swine—should he finish his task before the month of March. These offerings, Proserpina, I shall entrust to thee as soon as thou shalt have made good my vow. Proserpina Salvia, I give thee the head of Plotius, the slave of Avonia, his brow and eyebrows, eyelids and pupils, I give thee his ears, nose, nostrils, tongue, lips, and teeth, so he may not speak his pain; his neck, shoulders, arms, and fingers, so that he may not aid himself; his breast, liver, heart and lungs, so he may not sleep the sleep of health; his thighs, legs, knees, shanks, feet, ankles, heels, toes, and toe-nails, so he may not stand of his own strength. As Plotius has prepared a curse against me, in like manner do I consign him to thee to visit a curse on him ere the end of February. May he most miserably perish and depart this life. Mayest thou so irrevocably damn him that his eyes may never see the light of another month.[17]

This comprehensive curse follows the usual plan according to the then current formula. First the Queen of Hades is invoked, special care being taken to use her real and essential name, for this, as opposed to her nickname, inextricably bound the god, willy-nilly, to the curser's service. Under the inoffensive guise of prayer, the nether queen is now coerced to cast a series of veritable

Egyptian plagues upon the hapless victim. Their full tale is calculated to imbue with pain every significant feature of the man's anatomy from crown to toe. The next conspicuous item is the presence of precautionary clauses: Not till the goddess grants the wish will the fee be paid, and the petitioner, in a naïve retaliatory spirit, deals out his curse as the curse has been dealt out to him. The formula concludes with an impressive recapitulation, whose purpose is to leave no doubt that the victim is destroyed, body and soul, to all eternity. To make doubly sure, the document was folded, in order to enclose the victim's soul. The iron spike then driven through the tablet was certain to pierce the contained soul. It was this act of defixion that gave the form of the curse its name, *defixio*.

Sherwood Fox has propounded an attractive theory concerning the bioenergetics, as it were, of the cursing tablet's efficacy. He points out that the simplest form of the cursing tablet is a roughly rectangular sheet of lead about the area of half a dozen postage stamps. Upon this was incised the name of the victim, and the tablet was then thrown into a well, a stream or a river. In this easy and clandestine manner the curser buried or drowned his victim. The death stroke of the curse was calculated to destroy not only the body, but the soul too, to the end of time.

In the later period of the practice the spirits of those drowned at sea, or of the dead within the tombs into which the leaden tablets were cast, were brought in some mysterious way to communicate the wish of the curser to the gods of the lower regions, who were bound by the very nature of magic to put the curses into effect. In other words, the layer of lead was a letter, as it is actually called in one tablet; the grave or well was the letter-box in the nether postal service; the spirits of the departed, especially of those who had died violent or premature deaths, were the postmen; and the infernal gods were the receiving correspondents. To continue the figure, the proper incantation of a formula when the letter was dropped into the box was tantamount to a special stamp insuring prompt delivery and an equally prompt reply.[18]

Since practical cursing was for the most part indulged in by the uneducated classes, by the superstitious, it is not unlikely that something of this kind went on in the minds of such persons.

Reference may be made to several more examples of practical curses from Roman cursing tablets, together with the Greek forms of practical cursing, before we pass on to consider their significance for swearing. Here is an example of the shortest practical curse known. This lead tablet was brought to light at Salernum. The inscription reads

LOCVS. CAPILLO

RIBVS

EXPECT

AT. CAP

VT. SV

VM[19]

That is to say, *Locus capillo ribus! expectat caput suum* ("The stream is the place for the hair! it awaits its own head"). This we may read as meaning "Here lies the hair of John Doe deep in the stream, awaiting the head from which it came." This almost perfect iambic-trimeter curse is the most succinct and perhaps the most original that has come down to us.

A vindictive appeal of rejected affection, found on a cursing tablet at Latinium, reads as follows:

Just as the dead who here lies buried can neither speak nor converse, so may Rhodine, as far as Marcus Licinius Faustus is concerned, be dead and be unable to speak or to converse. Just as the dead is received neither among gods nor among men, so may Rhodine be unacceptable to M. Licinius and have as little influence with him as this dead man who here lies buried. O Father Pluto, I hand over Rhodine to thee that she may ever be an object of hatred to M. Licinius Faustus.

Sherwood Fox, who quotes this inscription, also gives an example of a similar curse that was published in a daily newspaper as late as 1910 in Nancy, France:

Great Saint Exterminus, I conjure thee to go and torment the soul and spirit of Madame Fernande X, . . . who now resides in Paris, through the avenues of her five natural senses. May she be tormented, besieged by the desire to leave her husband. So be it, Great Saint Exterminus, I conjure thee to go and torment the spirit of my own husband through his five senses. May he have only one idea—to give me money. Great Saint Exterminus, thou whose power is so vast, bring me once more to the man whom I love, I conjure thee. So be it.[20]

In a later part of this chapter we shall deal with several modern instances of practical cursing.

Perhaps the most remarkable example of a literary defixive curse is Ovid's *Ibis*, an amazing *tour de poéme*. In the epitome of his poem Ovid writes:

Heretofore my Muse has borne no weapons, and not a single stain of blood mars my pages. All the missiles I have hurled from my sling have missed their mark and bounded back only to the hurt of the one who hurled them. But now must the Muse don armour and her darts must strike the butt, for an insidious and skilful foe has done me a grievous injury. With his vicious lampoons he has exposed me to public ridicule and ignominy. But an eye for an eye, a tooth for a tooth, and a lampoon for a lampoon. Revenge is sweet. With the same curse with which Callimachus once sent the soul of Ibis to Tartarus thither do I now send thee and thine, O unnamed enemy.

Then follows the curse, a vituperative blast of 600 verses—a mandarin performance of considerable virtuosity following the well-worn path of the professional objurgator, the sorcerer, the maker of the tablets of defixion. First Ovid invokes the gods, the greater and the lesser, summoning them, as it were, within the magic circle to work his bidding. Next follows the curse, in which he prays down upon his victim all the dire afflictions to which human flesh is heir. Visit upon him, he entreats, pain, hunger, sleeplessness, impotency, care, mental anguish, and the consciousness of eternal disgrace. Let there be a pain in every member and in every organ of the body, in bone and muscle—pain beyond words to tell, pain so great that it will abide with the victim beyond the grave to the Styx and Acheron. Last of all, Ovid demands death—death by drowning, death by fire, death by torture, death by sword.

Fox thoroughly derails himself when he writes:

The whole piece is a burlesque—the incongruity between the consummate technique of a master of verse and the barbaric spirit of a plebian superstition is sufficient to give the *Ibis* of Ovid the place in the humorous literature of Rome which the curse in *Tristram Shandy* occupies in the literature of England. We are quite free to interpret the real intent of the poem as a *reductio ad absurdam* of a custom which because of its cruel intent had a disintegrating effect upon society.[21]

On the other hand, Ovid was never more serious, even though he may not for a moment have believed that he was possessed of Archilochus' power.

It is true, however, that the practice of defixive cursing was exercising a disintegrating effect upon society and was bringing the very gods into disrepute, for the gods were being demeaned by the practice and made ridiculous. A cursing tablet found on the site of an ancient Roman colony in Portugal shows us very clearly to what mean ends the gods were being invoked. The inscription runs: "O Proserpina, I ask, entreat, and implore thee to punish the person, whoever he be, who has borrowed, or stolen, or abstracted, from my wardrobe six shirts and two linen cloaks."

This was to make a jest of the sacrosanct, and so in the late Roman Republic and under the emperors the practice of defixive cursing was finally outlawed and heavy penalties were imposed upon those who were convicted of the offense. The effect of the new law was to drive the practice underground.

❴ Defixive Cursing and Its Relation to Swearing in Ancient Greece and Rome

We have seen that both the Greeks and the Romans were rather remarkably mild swearers. This is the more striking in view of the number and variety of their deities and fabled heroes and other figures. Why then did they swear with such little violence and even less crudity? The answer, perhaps, is to be sought in their actual swearing habits, habits that embraced the practice of defixive cursing. When one has available so effective a resource as defixive cursing, it is surely unnecessary to go to the trouble of belaboring one's enemy with mere words. The custom of defixive cursing had probably been inherited by the early Greeks from Babylonia and Assyria, and then bequeathed by them to the Romans. If, before this, Greeks and Romans ever swore, defixive cursing may well have had the effect of weakening the habit. Hence, under conditions provocative of serious anger or hostility the customary conventional means of responding to such a state would not have been an explosion of emotionally charged words but the formalized incision of the appropriate words in a defixive curse. The defixive curse actually assumed the place of vituperative swearing. With such a means as defixive cursing available to him, the individual could be certain of seeing his curses realized. Ordinary swearing being neither effectual, sanctioned, nor customary, it became somewhat attenuated. As Plato makes Adimantus say, if a man but will to injure an enemy the curse lay ready at hand as the weapon with which to effect it.[22]

It is because, we suggest, both the Greeks and the Romans had such an effective means of disposing of an enemy so readily at hand that common vituperative swearing never developed in either Greece or Rome. It is when a people can no longer curse with any assurance of success that swearing undergoes a luxuriant growth in which every element of cursing is incorporated into the common forms of swearing merely for the sake of the immediate relief it may grant the swearer. The decline in the cursing habits of a nation is a sure measure of the breakdown of its religious faith. As cursing declines, swearing increases in the richness of its variety, a variety borrowed from the outmoded forms of cursing. But while a people can curse with faith, they have little need of any other means of dealing with their enemies. A curse for Greek or Roman was not a mere oath, but a tangible thing. Hence, the expression "The curse laid upon him." The curse was something one could manipulate, direct, and place.[23] Both the Greeks and the Romans had the profoundest faith in cursing, and the Romans early reinforced the power of defixive cursing by incorporating into their earliest body of law, the Twelve Tables codified in 451–449 B.C., threats of punishment against those who should attempt by this form of cursing to injure the person, property, or family of a fellow citizen.

The reason, then, that the Greeks and the Romans swore so mildly was that they were free to curse so forcibly.

Let us now consider some examples of practical cursing that have survived in the modern world.

(Practical Cursing in the Modern World

In Catholic countries the example of the priest or monk who, from medieval days on, has with bell, book, and candle laid a curse upon some individual was not lost upon the masses. And so in Portugal, Spain, France, Italy, Greece, and Ireland, we find that the act of practical, and even defixive, cursing still survives. The art of defixive cursing is not, however, restricted to Catholic countries alone, although there can be little doubt that it is in such lands that the practice still flourishes to any appreciable extent. Forms of practical cursing are still to be found in every nation of which we have any knowledge. With examples of these we shall soon become acquainted.

It was Pope John XXII, who occupied the Holy See from 1316 to 1334, who gave the first definite stimulus to the witch hunting of the makers of defixive waxen images. Sharing all the superstitions of his time and conscious of his many political enemies, he regarded himself as a particularly vulnerable target for such perils. At the very outset of his reign he condemned Hugh Geraud, Bishop of Cahors, for a waxen-image cursing attempt on his life, and had him flayed alive and burned. At the end of the first year of his reign, in 1317, the barber-surgeon and some clerks of the Sacred Palace were executed on the accusation (among others) of making waxen cursing images. In France Enguerrand de Marigui, the minister of King Philip IV (1285–1314), was hanged because his wife and sister had made waxen images to bewitch Louis X. Another French king, Charles IV (1322–1328), was said to have been attacked through magic waxen images. And even Dante's name is mentioned by a witness in connection with a supposed attempt to destroy Pope John XXII.[24]

In certain parts of Tuscany it is, or was until very recently, a custom among the peasantry to wreak one's vengeance upon an enemy in the following way: The curser would obtain a stone, which he would then take to a running stream or river, into whose midst he would cast it as violently and as spitefully as he could, pronouncing at the same time the words:

> Non butto questa pietra,
> Ma butto il bene e la fortuna
> Della persona [name here] che il bene
> Gli vada nell' acqua corrente
> E cosi non abbia più bene!

> I cast not away this stone,
> But cast away the well-being and good fortune
> Of [name] so that his well-being
> Should flow away with the coursing water
> So that he may no longer enjoy any good!

This really is a defixive curse with the curse verbally expressed instead of being inscribed upon the stone. It is obviously the descendant of a curse that has seen better days. Indeed, the formula of this curse has its origin in many a Roman defixive curse, with its recurring *sic liqueat comodo aqua* ("so may his life flow away").

In Ireland, where every form of curse has enjoyed a long and notable career, there are naturally a large number of examples to choose from. A rather interesting form of practical cursing, which has persisted down to the present time, occurs in county Cavan. Near Black Lion, at the extreme north of county Cavan, use is made of a very original cursing stone, which consists of a large horizontal slab with twelve or thirteen *bullâns*, or basins, cut in it; in each *bullân*, save one, there is a large round stone. The curser takes up one of these stones and places it in the empty basin, and so on, one after another, till all have been gone over. During this performance he curses his enemy, and if he removes all the stones without letting any one of them slip (no easy operation, it is said, on account of their form), his curses will have effect. If he lets one slip, the curses will return on his own head.[25]

This form of ritual cursing at one time seems to have been widely practiced in Ireland, for similar cursing stones are known to have existed in many other parts of the land.

A truly defixive Irish form of cursing was the practice that was common in county Fermanagh until very recently. Tenants who had been given notice to quit their homes would, before doing so, collect a number of stones from every part of their farm. These they brought home and, having put a lighted coal in the fireplace, heaped the stones over it as if they had been sods of turf. They then knelt down on the hearthstone, and prayed that as long as the stones remained unburned every conceivable curse might descend upon their landlord, his children, and their children to the last generation. To prevent the stones from being burned by any chance, as soon as they had finished cursing, the stones were taken and scattered far and wide over the whole county. It is believed that many of the former families of the county died out as a result of being thus maligned.

An ancient and interesting parallel to this curse occurs in the Greek legendary story of Althaea's brand. The legend has it that the Fates told Althaea that her son Meleager would live just as long as a log of wood then on the fire remained unconsumed. Althaea contrived to preserve the log for many years, but when Meleager killed her two brothers, she threw it angrily into the fire, where it was quickly consumed, and Meleager expired at the same time.[26]

The Irish have long believed in the power of the rhymer. J. H. Hardiman tells us that the rural Irish of the 1820s feared nothing so much as "the satirical severity of their bards. Many a man, who would kindle into rage at the sight of an armed foe, will be found to tremble at the thought of offending a rhymer."[27]

An author in the brilliant Elizabethan satires published under the assumed name of Martin Marprelate utters his succinct curse after a style not uncommon in earlier days:

> I am a rimer of the Irish race,
> And have already rimde thee staring mad;
> But if thou cease not thy bold jests to spread
> I'll never leave thee till I have rimde thee dead.[28]

The nobility of England has always been distinguished by its partiality to the superstitious and the occult, as the unusually large number of names of English noblemen and noblewomen who are in the ranks of the followers of Mrs. Baker Eddy and Dr. Frank Buchman still bears witness. One of the most remarkable cases in the history of defixive cursing and the manipulation of the supernatural is that in which, at the beginning of the seventeenth century, the Countess of Essex was involved. The countess, like the lady of Nancy of our own time in a similar case, sought to win the Earl of Somerset for herself, but the earl's affection had already been bestowed upon another. Therefore the countess sent for Simon Formon, the astrologer and quack doctor, laying her desires before him. Thereupon wax images of the principals concerned were prepared and made to pass through the alembic of the magic ritual. All who stood in the way of the countess' desires were cursed, while the powers of darkness were invoked to cause Somerset's heart and eyes to look favorably upon her.[29]

To the horror of the court, in 1560, shortly after her ascent to the throne, a wax image of Queen Elizabeth with a pin jabbed through the heart was found in Lincoln's Inn Fields.

The witches of North Berwick tried to kill James VI of Scotland (afterward James I of England) with a wax image, but they were apprehended in the nick of time and executed.

James I, in his *Daemonologie* (1597), speaks of the practice of defixion in England and Scotland as being very common, and he attributes its efficacy to the devil. Baring-Gould, writing in 1866, tells us:

In Devonshire, witches and malevolent people still make clay images of those whom they intend to hurt, baptise the image with the name of the person whom it is meant to represent, and then stick it full of pins or burn it. In the former case that person is racked with rheumatism in all his limbs; in the second he is smitten with raging fever. Nider, in his "Hierarchy of Blessed Angels," speaks of a witch named Æniponte, who, by making an effigy of wax, pricking it with needles in diverse parts, and then burying it under the threshold of a neighbour's house whom she much hated, brought upon the neighbour insufferable torments and prickings in the flesh, till the image was found and destroyed, upon which those evils passed away.[30]

The practice of defixive cursing was widespread throughout Europe and the East.[31]

⟮ Common Cursing and Its Relation to Common Swearing

We have said that cursing is merely a special form of swearing, and we have thus far considered some special forms of cursing: the practical form of cursing as distinguished from the curse unadorned by anything more than the mood in which it is uttered. We have seen that the curse differs from ejaculatory or ordinary condemnatory swearing in being remote in action as compared with the immediacy of common swearing. But such a distinction holds true only for cursing that is either ritualized or in some other way formalized. In every other sense all cursing is indistinguishable in its character from any other form of swearing. There are, of course, fine differences, as a case in point will illustrate. When I exclaim, "Blast your eyes!" it is much the same as if I were to say, "May your eyes be blasted!" The mood of the one differs somewhat from that of the other. The first is explosive, the second a little more deliberate. The two forms exhibit a difference in the amount of bile involved. Cursing as compared with swearing would appear to be more malevolently intended, since it stems from conditions and a mood that have generally been of greater duration or intensity than those that give rise to swearing. The intention is also different. While the swearer swears for immediate relief, not caring a snap about anything else, the curser curses with the deliberate object of offending and discomfiting an enemy. When the hated one is beyond the reach of swearing, the tendency is to curse. This is clarified in "a man of the world's" definition of "anathemas" as "Imprecations which the ministers of religion hurl upon the heads of those who offend them, devoting them to eternal torments, when they have not the power to inflict upon them temporal ones."[32] The "temporal ones" for the ordinary man would be swearing, but if swearing would not suit the case he would curse. Coleridge recognized this distinction in the forms of swearing very clearly, without, however, distinguishing the one as cursing and the other as swearing. In the preface to his poem "Fire, Famine and Slaughter" he writes:

The images, I mean, that a vindictive man places before his imagination will most often be taken from the realities of life: there will be images of pain and suffering which he has himself seen inflicted on other men, and which he can fancy himself as inflicting on the object of his hatred. I will suppose that we heard at different times two common sailors, each speaking of some one who had wronged or offended him, that the first with apparent violence had devoted every part of his adversary's body and soul to all the horrid phantoms and fantastic places that even Quevedo dreamed of, and this in a rapid flow of those outrageous and wildly combined execrations which too often with our lower classes serve as escape-valves to carry off the excess of their passions, as so much superfluous steam that would endanger the vessel if it were retained. The other, on the contrary, with that sort of calmness of tone which is to the ear what the paleness of anger is to the eye, shall simply say "If I chance to be made boatswain, as I hope I soon shall, and can get that fellow under my hand (and I shall be on the watch for him), I'll tickle his pretty skin. I won't hurt him, oh, no! I'll only cut the —— to the liver." I dare appeal to all present which of the two they would regard as the least deceptive symptom of deliberate malignity—nay, whether it would surprise them to see the first fellow an hour or two afterwards cordially shaking hands with the very man the functional parts of whose body and soul he had been so charitably disposing of; or even perhaps risking his life for him.[33]

Robert Graves, who quotes this passage in his entertaining *Lars Porsena, or the Future of Swearing*, cannot agree with Coleridge, asserting, "No general distinction of motive can be made between swearers who adopt one or other of these methods."[34] This is somewhat an odd judgment from so sensitive an artist as Graves. "I do not think," he says, "that Coleridge's distinction between the violent swearer who does not really mean what he says and the quiet swearer who swears from real malignity is an essential one."[35] But isn't it surely obvious that there *is* a difference in the motives of the two kinds of swearers? The first, as Coleridge points out, merely indulges in his execrations as a kind of opening of his cock stops "to carry off the excess" of his passions. The motive here is immediately to belabor his adversary with the becudgeling words and thus to discharge himself of his animus. In the case of the second sailor the motive is somewhat different, as is the form of the swearing, which is plainly a curse. Here the second sailor, while venting some of his spite, is not expending all of it. He is retaining some to last him until he is in a position to strike more effectively. And the fact is, when he attains the proper position he generally does strike. The curser *is* generally more serious than the swearer. We may then, with Dr. Johnson, like a good swearer, but because the curser's mood is usually a malignant one, he cannot expect to win approval.

A general distinction may be made in the motive and intention of cursing as compared with swearing, but it can also be shown that many of the actual terms and phrases used in cursing, for the most part, have a somewhat different origin from those used in common swearing. In many cases such distinctions cannot be made, for the reason that a great part of the armament of swearing is drawn from cursing forms, while much of the power of cursing originates in swearing. Therefore, if any analysis of a curse or an imprecation were to be made with a view to ascertaining its cursory or other origins, each case would have to be examined on its own merits. This brings us to the question of the origins of the forms of swearing and the forms of cursing—a subject of great interest and importance, which we shall consider in the next chapter.

CHAPTER FOUR

The Origin of Swearing:
The Curse and the Oath

‹‹‹›››

Oaths are but words, and words but wind.
SAMUEL BUTLER, *Hudibras*, 1664

T HE investigation of the origin of any human institution or custom is a fascinating business, which is one reason why caution is necessary in such matters, lest the fascination of the subject overcome the critical sense and lead us into absurdity. Since no one now living was present at the birth of swearing, and since no one has left us an account of that momentous event, the best we can do is to attempt to put together such evidence as we have in order to reconstruct the probable conditions under which swearing developed. The most that can be done by such a method is to arrive at some plausible conjectures.

❐ *The Origin of Swearing and Cursing*

Swearing, interestingly enough, is not a universal phenomenon: American Indians do not swear, nor do the Japanese, nor do Malayans and most Polynesians. However, the occurrence of this form of behavior in so many human groups, including such long-isolated peoples as the aborigines of Australia, some examples of whose swearing were given earlier, has suggested to many writers on the subject that it constitutes a response to a fundamental urge deep-seated in the constitution of man. Is there such a thing, then, as an instinct of swearing? Does there exist such a thing as a psychophysical disposition that on the experience of a particular stimulus causes the organism to react by swearing? The existence of instincts in man is a discredited concept in modern psychology, and we prefer today to speak of "urges," "needs," or "drives" like hunger, thirst, sleep, rest, weeping, laughter, and sex. We may then repeat our original question: Is there, then, an instinct or innate drive to swear? In spite of claims that have in the past been made to the contrary, there exists not the slightest evidence that there is such a thing as an innately determined drive or urge to swear. The evidence indicates that swearing constitutes a learned form of behavior, a culturally conditioned response to the experience of certain conditions. Since the urge referred to, namely, the aggressive response to frustration, has often developed in the form of swearing, it may be concluded that swearing constitutes a form of behavior that developed early in the history of man. This seems a perfectly legitimate inference to make, and I believe we can treat it as one to which a high degree of probability attaches.

Given the culturally conditioned aggressive response plus the ability to speak, swearing behavior would seem to be inevitable, for the readiest form that spoken anger is capable of taking is either swearing or something closely akin to it. It is, of course, quite unnecessary to assume that the expression of his frustration was restricted by early man to speech. On occasion, he probably resorted to rather more violent forms of expression. It would, however, be a very great error to assume that early man was a violent creature, given to fighting and continuous bouts of agression. What we know of early man, from the condition of his skeletal remains and the cultural artifacts that have been recovered, strongly indicates that he was a peaceful creature who lived a highly cooperative life. That conflict between members of the same group and between different groups did occasionally occur is possible. Possibly also, an occasional life was lost in these conflicts. On the basis of the evidence available, however, we must assume that early man was not an aggressive creature. It is necessary to be clear upon these points, for they have a bearing on our argument.

If swearing is a form of human behavior of some antiquity, are there any means by which the earliest forms of swearing could be reconstructed? The answer to such a question can only be given in very general conjectural terms. There is every reason to believe that the earliest men practiced some form of religion— at any rate that they believed in supernatural powers and that they feared and probably worshiped these. Here, then, would be powers either to swear or to curse or to do both by. As we have seen, although the Australian aborigines possess a fully developed religion, they do not customarily swear by their powers, nor do they curse by them. There is no good reason, therefore, for assuming that early man behaved any differently, though he may very well have done so. There would almost certainly have been references to excrement—if we may assume, as I think we may, that such substances "stank in his nostrils"—filth, and any other objects that were strongly obnoxious. If such forms of expression did exist, and if the manipulation or invocation of the supernatural powers was at all practiced, then the conditions for the development of swearing and cursing were present. But as we have seen earlier, the belief in supernatural powers is not a *sine qua non* of cursing. What is necessary is a belief in *extraordinary* powers, and these can be personal. With the development of belief in the existence of supernatural beings, the ability to curse is, as it were, reenforced—powerful beings are now appealed to, to execute the judgment supplicated in the curse. The mere existence of supernatural powers is not in itself sufficient to generate the process of cursing. Only when the individual is forbidden to take judgment into his own hands is he likely to hit upon the idea of compelling the supernaturals to assist him in the execution of his judgment.

It is conceivable that in the early days of man's social development occasionally two individuals were sufficiently provoked to resort to physical blows, sometimes resulting in injury or death. It should, however, be obvious that a society that failed to put a prohibition upon such conduct would enjoy a life that was at best "poor, nasty, brutish, and short." The primitive human group is a small one, and each of its members occupies a vital position in its economy. The loss of a single adult male through injury or death is a serious matter. The individual, therefore, cannot be permitted to take the disposition of the life of his neighbors into his own hands. It is, therefore, forbidden, tabooed. The first taboos created by the earliest social group probably concerned the sanctity of life itself of the persons composing that group. It must have been realized that the summary injury or killing of one individual by another, in quarrel or for other reasons of no grave order, threatened the coherence of the group, so that it was, upon the recognition of this fact, forbidden for one person to injure or take the life of another without the sanction of the group. With the institution of such a taboo, early man found himself cut off from the possibility of taking direct action against an enemy for the purpose of disposing of him, and so he was forced to discover some indirect way of working his will upon him. The nature of the uncivilized mind is such that it tends to believe firmly that whatever things resemble each other are essentially the same and that whatever things have once been in contact with each other have established a bond, as it were, which ever after maintains the association. Following these principles, it is very likely that early man proceeded to make images of earth or other materials of his enemy and to vent his anger upon the image, which for him personified his enemy, by destroying or otherwise maltreating it, as he desired either to kill or merely to injure him. In so doing, his purposes were quite as fully realized, and the relief experienced was almost as great as if he had subjected the actual person of his enemy to such treatment as he had meted out to the image of the latter or to his property. It mattered not, for the time being at any rate, whether his enemy continued to live or uncomprehendingly to rot.

If death or injury could be brought about by this "indirect direct" attack, that is to say, an attack upon what was considered to be identical with the real object, the same effects could be produced by the proper appeal to the supernatural powers. Thus, by a more indirect method, early man could endeavor to secure the desired end through some other power. By this means one can secure what one wants without having to submit to the inconveniences entailed in securing the same object by means of the direct method. It is far easier to call in the aid of the supernatural powers, even though it be forbidden to do so, than to attempt to wreak vengeance upon an enemy with one's own hands.

But society soon recognized that activities such as these have no less a suicidal and disintegrating effect upon it than the effects of unprohibited violence itself, and a taboo upon the practice of such antisocial activities must, in time, have followed. The group reserved to itself the right to engage in such practices whenever necessary but forbade them to the individual. This, of course, would only have succeeded in causing the individual to practice in secret what he once practiced in the open, for in the privacy of his own time and place there was nothing to prevent him from performing the necessary ritual.

In reality, the simple processes of social development described above have been repeated again and again in every human society, from the most primitive to the most advanced. Cursing has been everywhere prohibited, except to the special class of medicine man or priest, and with its prohibition it has invariably taken on the new life that grows with the adaptation to the new environment of the secret and the occult.

Having thus far, and for the most part speculatively, traced the early origins of swearing and cursing, we can readily see that when, in the more recent period of man's development, belief in the powers of the supernatural was greatly weakened, much of the stock of the curser's fire and brimstone was taken over for the purposes of common, or garden, swearing. But this is to anticipate, for we have by no means completed our account of the origins of swearing and cursing.

As we have seen, throughout their history swearing and cursing have run a parallel course, for they really represent but slightly different aspects of the same phenomenon. Both draw their strength from external powers, both arise as a culturally conditioned response to a certain kind of angry urge, and both are calculated to produce a feeling of relief in their users. The only difference, ultimately, between the two forms of swearing appears to lie in the motive or intention, cursing tending to be more envenomed and malignant than swearing. We now trace something of the later origins of swearing and the curse.

◖ *The Oath, the Curse, and Swearing*

It is fairly evident that the character of much swearing greatly resembles the form of the judicial oath. The cockney's asseverative of surprise, *Gawd strike me pink! (Strike me dead!),* the sailor's *Shiver me timbers!* the common *The hell I will!* translated into the forms from which they originated are *May God strike me dead,* and *May I go to hell.* In other words, this is the legal procedure of calling down a curse upon oneself if one should deviate from what one has sworn to do or not to do. An enormous amount of our swearing takes this form, the form of the provisional curse, the oath. There can be not the slightest doubt that the pattern of much of our swearing has been determined by the judicial oath, or any form of oath that is administered by a socially elected body, whether priests, judges, or some other representatives of society.

The origin of the oath is hidden in the mists of antiquity, but the causes that brought it into being have been at all times and in all places the same: the desire of society to protect itself against the mendacity of the individual by causing him to call down upon himself the punishment of the Great Powers if he speak not the truth or keep not his bond. Apart from the power of the provisional curse, of the oath itself, there was also the power of society to punish any who might be discovered to have taken the oath falsely. In this way the oath came to draw its strength from the temporal as well as the spiritual domains. It hardly needs to be pointed out that every element of the primitive oath is preserved in our modern judicial oath: "I swear to speak the truth, the whole truth, and nothing but the truth, so help me God." In other words, "If I do not speak the whole truth, may God withdraw his help from me." This oath is of particular interest because it stands in the relation of direct paternity to one of the commonest asseverative forms of swearing of the cockney, *So 'elp me Gawd if it ain't true!* This is often contracted to the mere exclamatory *So 'elp me!* or *S'elp me!*

There would be no real point here to an account of the forms of the oath among primitive peoples[1] or among the peoples of antiquity,[2] for these all follow the same pattern of provisional cursing by appeal to the supernatural powers or to the elements. The later European forms of the judicial oath for our purposes sufficiently illustrate, and rather effectively, the manner in which the oath supplied the swearer with novel tropes and figures.[3] To illustrate this relationship we need only deal with the English forms.

❪ Recent Forms of Swearing Derived From Judicial Oaths

To call upon the gods and holy ones as witness to the truth or of the intention to fulfill an obligation constitutes one of the oldest forms of the oath. The majority of modern forms of swearing in which the gods and holy ones, their shrines, and even parts of their bodies are incorporated owe their being to the solemn oaths that were taken by them. After the introduction of Christianity into England, oaths were taken by the name of God and were administered on holy relics, sacred shrines, bishops' croziers, the cross, the robe, and the sacrament. Thus, such oaths as *By God, By the Eternal God, By Jesus, By Christ, By the cross, By the holy cross,*

By the holy sacrament, By the holy abbey, By Saint Dunstan, By the holy mother of God, By the Holy Ghost, By the Great Jehovah, By the Lord of Heaven, By the Great Father, By the Father of Light, By the saints above, By the holy saint Mary —all these and many more that will be dealt with later—were originally solemn Christian oaths taken only upon the most solemn of occasions. The reader may not recognize all these oaths as playing any role in modern swearing, but the fact is that at this very day all of them are still doing valiant service as part of the side arms and equipment of the modern swearer.

Apart altogether from the ethical values implicit in the pro-hibitions laid upon swearing by God himself and by the Holy Books, the Old and the New Testaments, we may begin to under-stand why the taking of an oath in a court of law or elsewhere has been so vehemently and consistently condemned by some Chris-tian sects, such as, for example, the Lollards in the fifteenth and sixteenth centuries, the Puritans in the seventeenth century, and the Quakers in the eighteenth century. These sects contended with more truth and justice than appeared evident to the minds of their persecutors and adversaries that the expletives of passion and irreligion have only been perpetuated by reason of the familiarity that has ensued as a consequence of the exaction of such oaths in the courts of law.

❬ *Recent Forms of Swearing Derived From Formal Cursing*

The subject of recent forms of swearing derived from formal cursing would fill the pages of a huge book, but we shall take only a few pages to deal with it. Throughout the history of the Christian church, cursing has formed a busy branch of its manifold activities. In this respect the Catholic Church has surpassed all others in the development of both virtuosity and variety in its curses. It is not surprising, therefore, that the example so promi-nently set by the Church should have proven worthy enough to have been paid the respect and flattery of imitation. Catholic swearers are, on the whole, far more accomplished in the art than the votaries of other Christian sects. This is not to say that more Catholics swear than other varieties of Christians do, but rather that when a Catholic does swear his range is both more extensive and intensive than the members of other faiths are able to accomplish. Whether this is so or not, the fact remains that almost all the Christian churches have at one time or another resorted to the curse as a punishment for certain offenses. Such curses have often been of the most horrendous kind. One of the most malignant, rendered famous by the quotation of half a dozen lines from it in *Tristram Shandy*, is that composed by Bishop Ernulphus. Ernulphus, or Arnulf (1040–1124), a French Benedictine appointed prior of Canterbury Cathedral by Anselm, subsequently became Abbot of Peterborough Cathedral and then Bishop of Rochester. It is to an extract from his *Textus Roffensis* that he owes the invidious distinction conferred upon him in *Tristram Shandy*. Sterne makes the bishop the supreme authority on cursing on the strength of his famous curse, which is here reproduced in full.

By the Authority of God Almighty the Father, Son, and Holy Ghost, and of the holy Canons, and of the undefiled Virgin *Mary*, the Mother and Patroness of our Savior, and of all the Celestial Virtues, Angels, Arch-Angels, Thrones, Dominions, Powers, Cherubins and Seraphins [sic] and of the holy Patriarch, Prophets, and of all the Apostles and Evangelists, and of the holy Innocents, who in the Sight of the Holy Lamb are found worthy to sing the new Song, and of the holy Martyrs and holy Confessors, and of the holy Virgins, and of all the Saints, and together with all the Holy and Elect of God: We excommunicate and anathematise him or them, Malefactor or Malefactors,—and from the Thresholds of the holy Church of God Almighty We sequester them, that he or they may be tormented, disposed and delivered over with *Dathan* and *Abiram*; and with those who say unto the Lord God, *Depart from us, we know not thy Ways*. And, as Fire is quenched with Water, so let the Light of him, or them, be put out for evermore, unless it shall repent him or them, and they make Satisfaction. *Amen*.

May the Father, who created Man, curse him or them. May the Son, who suffered for us, curse him or them. May the Holy Ghost, who was given to us in Baptism, curse him or them. May the holy Cross, which Christ for our Salvation triumphing over his Enemy ascended, curse him or them. May the holy and eternal Virgin *Mary*, Mother of God, curse him or them. May St. *Michael*, the Advocate of holy Souls, curse him or them. May all the Angels and Arch-Angels, Principalities and Powers, and all the heavenly Host, curse him or them. May the laudable Number of the Patriarchs and Prophets curse him or them. May St. *John*, the chief Fore-runner and Baptist of Christ, curse him or them. May St. *Peter* and St. *Paul*, and St. *Andrew*, and all other Christ's Apostles, together with the rest of his Disciples, and the four Evangelists, who by their Preaching converted the universal World, curse him or them. May the holy and wonderful Company of Martyrs and Confessors, who by their holy Works are found pleasing to God Almighty, curse him or them. May the holy Choir of the holy Virgins, who for the Honour of Christ have despised the Things of the World, curse him or them. May all the Saints, who from the Beginning of the World to everlasting Ages are found to be the Beloved of God, curse him or them. May the Heavens and Earth, and all the holy Things remaining therein, curse him or them. May he or they be cursed, wherever he or they be, whether in their House or in their Field, or in the Highway, or in the Path, or in the Wood, or in the Water, or in the Church. May he or they be cursed in Living, in Dying, in Eating, in Drinking, in being Hungry, in being Thirsty, in Fasting, in Sleeping, in Slumbering, in Waking, in Walking, in Standing, in Sitting, in Lying, in Working, in Resting, in Pissing, in Shitting, and in Blood-letting. May he or they be cursed in all the Faculties of their Body. May he or they be cursed inwardly and outwardly. May he or they be cursed in the Hair of his or their Head. May he or they be cursed in his or their Brain. May he or they be cursed in the Top of his or their Head, in their Temples, in their Forehead, in their Ears, in their Eye-brows, in their Cheeks, in their Jaw-bones, in their Nostrils, in their Fore-teeth or Grinders, in their Lips, in their Throat, in their Shoulders, in their Wrists, in their Arms, in their Hands, in their Fingers, in their Breast, in their Heart, and in all the interior Parts to the very Stomach: In their Reins, in the Groin, in the Thighs, in the Genitals, in the Hips, in the Knees, in the Legs, in the Feet, in the Joints, and in the Nails. May he or they be cursed in all their Joints, from the Top of the Head to the Sole of the Foot. May there not be any Soundness in him or them.

May the Son of the living God, with all the Glory of his Majesty, curse him or them; and may Heaven, with all the Powers which move therein, rise against him or them to damn him or them, unless it shall repent him or them, or that he or they shall make Satisfaction. *Amen, Amen, So be it.*

As Uncle Toby remarked in *Tristram Shandy*, "Our armies swore terribly in Flanders, but nothing to this. For my own part, I could not have a heart to curse a dog so."

It is no simple coincidence that every curse in Bishop Ernulphus' commination has appeared in the repertoire of the common swearer. It is not that these expletives were necessarily taken from this particular curse, but rather from the numerous similar models that have not been unhelpful to the swearer down the centuries.

Forms such as *God damn you, God rot your soul, Curse you, Damn your eyes, Blast you, Go to hell*, etc., it will readily be seen all have their origins in the curses of the Church, from which most secular ones are derived. However much the Church may have deplored swearing and cursing, its precepts have seldom been as effective as its example.

In thus briefly considering the cause and effect of promiscuous oath taking and cursing, we perceive that church and society in their endeavor to keep the faltering spirit of man staunch and straight have committed some grievous errors. The discipline that they sought to impose from without, it is now more than ever being realized, must emanate from within. Their seeking to support the temples of truth with the flying buttresses of the theological oath has weakened the central structure. Pelion was piled upon Ossa, oath upon oath, in inverse proportion, it would seem, to the regard in which truth was generally held. But as man's intellect has increased and his progress toward a greater, if not yet clearly defined, humanity has proceeded, the inducements to veracity have become more and more self-evident, as is summed up in the belief, which is daily seen realized, that truth is its own reward. In societies where such an attitude of mind and common practice prevails, however much and frequently some may fall by the way, there is no need of the doubtful security of the oath. Indeed, as many commentators have observed, the oath has outlived its usefulness and were better altogether discarded where it still survives in legal processes and proceedings.[4] As we shall later see, the oath has in all times been subject to criticism, and some of the finest passages in the writings of the critics have been devoted to its ridicule.

In societies in which the oath and curse have outlived whatever spirit was once imparted to them, sportive capital has been made of the residue. And as Julian Sharman put it, "An intervening age of irony probably sufficed to undermine the sanctity of the swearing obligation, until at last the oath of more sober times has come to be a common catchword, or the fustian ornament of somewhat spirited talk. In short, we shall always find that the sonorous expletive of recent days is nothing else than the once deliberative oath of Christian piety."[5]

CHAPTER FIVE

Why Do Men Swear? The Physiology and Psychology of Swearing

◄◄◄◄◄◄◄◄◄◄◄◄◄◄◄◄◄◄◄◄◄◄◄◄◄◄◄◄◄◄◄‹›››››››››››››››››››››››››››››››

When a gentleman is disposed to swear, it is not for any standers-by to curtail his oaths, ha?

WILLIAM SHAKESPEARE, *Cymbeline* (II, i), 1610

I N the foregoing pages we have seen that there is good reason to believe that swearing is a form of behavior of considerable antiquity. We have seen, too, that it occurs among most peoples, and we have concluded that swearing constitutes a culturally conditioned response likely to occur under certain conditions, principally of frustration. This fact seems to have been recognized by almost everyone who has ever devoted any thought to the matter; and with ready insight almost everyone appears to have recognized the function of swearing—namely, an effective means of permitting the escape of excess steam. Let us see what some of the authorities have had to say upon this matter.

François Rabelais (1494?–1553), the greatest, most proficient and most imaginative swearer the world has known, makes Panurge exclaim against that distinguished and inveterate cusser Friar John's swearing, and in so doing gives the first explanation of the "easement" function of swearing.

Oh, . . . you sin Friar John . . . it goes against my heart to tell it to you: for I believe this swearing doth your spleen a great deal of good; as it is a great ease to a wood cleaver to cry hem at every blow; and as one who plays at nine-pins is wonderfully helped if, when he hath not thrown his bowl right, and is likely to make a bad caste, some ingenious stander by leans and screws his body halfway about, on that side which the bowl should have took to hit the pin.[1]

Earlier in the same work, in that exquisite chapter in which Panurge consults the ephectic and Pyrrhonistic philosopher Trouillogan on the question of whether he shall marry or not, being much exasperated by the philosopher's evasive replies, Panurge exclaims, "By the death of a hog, and mother of a toad, O Lord, if I durst hazard upon a little fling at the swearing game, though privily and under the thumb, it would lighten the burden of my heart and ease my lights and reins exceedingly. A little patience, nevertheless, is requisite."[2] But Panurge's patience is sorely tried by the slipperiness of Trouillogan. Nonetheless, he finds that he must stay in the hope of extracting some advice from the philosopher, and so he calls upon a page to swear by deputy for him, "Page, my little pretty darling, take here my cap,—I give it to thee. Have a care you do not break the spectacles that are in it. Go down to the lower court. Swear there half an hour for me, and I shall in compensation of that favour swear hereafter for thee as much as thou wilt."[3]

The learned Dr. Rabelais has here stated the law of easements as well as it could be, and no book has given that law a more variegated exemplification than his.

Laurence Sterne in *Tristram Shandy* provides the following illuminating discussion:

"Small curses, Dr. Slop, upon great occasions," quoth my father, "are but so much waste of our strength and soul's health to no manner of purpose."

"I own it," replied Dr. Slop.

"They are like sparrow-shot," quoth my Uncle Toby (suspending his whistling), "fired against a bastion."

"They serve," continued my father, "to stir the humours, but carry off none of their acrimony; for my own part, I seldom swear or curse at all—I hold it bad, but if I fall into it by surprise I generally retain so much presence of mind ["Right," quoth my Uncle Toby.] as to make it answer my purpose, that is, I swear on till I find myself easy. A wise and just man, however, would always endeavour to proportion the vent given to these humours, not only to the degree of them stirring within himself, but to the size and ill-intent of the offense upon which they are to fall."

"Injuries come only from the heart," quoth my Uncle Toby."[4]

We have already had occasion to note that Coleridge considered the swearer's oaths as serving the function of "escape-valves to carry off the excess of their passions, as so much superfluous steam that would endanger the vessel if it were retained."[5]

To Julian Sharman the fact that the mildest of men are prone to swear under certain conditions

would seem to suggest some remarkable underlying motive as accounting for the wonderful omnipotence of swearing. It is possible that an occult virus congenial to its development is so insinuated into the composition of the human mind as to defy the power of ethics wholly to eradicate it. Can it be that the habit owes its existence and source of delight to some soothing and pleasureful qualities which like the solace of the tobacco-leaf or balm of the night shade, the world will not willingly forego?

We are disposed to think that the instinct of swearing is very deeply rooted in the mental constitution.[6]

Robert Graves, in his little volume on swearing, writes:

There is no doubt that swearing has a definite physiological function; for after childhood relief in tears and wailing is rightly discouraged, and groans are also considered a signal of extreme weakness. Silence under suffering is usually impossible. The nervous system demands some expression that does not affect towards cowardice and feebleness and, as a nervous stimulant in a crisis, swearing is unequalled.[7]

Graves considers the function of swearing to be nervous stimulation. This may well be, but as we shall soon discover, its principal action is that of a sedative rather than that of a stimulant.

The "disappointed man," W. N. P. Barbellion, reports the following conversation setting out his views on the function of swearing:

"Don't you ever swear?" I asked. "It's a good thing, you know, swearing is like pimples, better to come out, cleanses the moral system. The person who controls himself must have lots of terrible oaths circulating in his blood."

"Swearing is not the only remedy."

"I suppose you prefer the gilded pill of a curate's sermon; I prefer pimples to pills."[8]

In *Love's Labour's Lost* Shakespeare puts this view into three words when he has Biron say, ". . . abstinence engenders maladies" (V, i).

The view of the function of swearing expressed by the authorities quoted above—and it is one that has been proposed by many other thinkers, with some of whom we shall soon deal—may be said to assign to it the function of acting as a relief mechanism whereby excess energy is allowed to escape without doing anyone any serious injury, while doing the swearer some good. Those who have understood this function of swearing, even when they have thoroughly disapproved of swearing, have recognized its deep-seated nature and have wisely allowed that some forms of strong expression must be permitted in any properly organized society. This view may be illustrated from an article published in 1920, in the *Biblical World*. The writer, Henry Woodward Hulbert, says:

One of the notable theories of the origin of human speech, and a very plausible one, is that man began his invention of language by the use of interjections, cries of fear or pain or joy. At any rate the demand for expression along those lines may be accounted primitive and universal in man and not to be eradicated. We may be sure it will never cease to be a constituent part of the race. Utterance must be had for every phase of human life. Vigor of body, mind and heart will always call for definite strong, emotional expression. No study of our theme can stop with the negative side of it. It is imperative that, however imperfect human speech must always remain, it shall yet furnish man with words fitted to ease the mind under conditions of deep emotion and to convey one's feelings with force and effectiveness to others.

Music is a parallel instrument, rousing the soul of the performer to high states of feeling and conveying the same to others in a marked degree.[9]

The reference here to music is a very happy one and calls to mind the story told of Mark Twain, a redoubtable swearer, whose profanity on one occasion so much tried and exasperated his wife that she, in order to demonstrate to him what he sounded like to others, treated him to a somewhat unusual performance of really eloquent swearing. Mark listened until she had concluded and then dryly remarked, "The words are there, my dear, but the music is wanting."

The fact is that swearing is an instrument, which like any other can only be effectively played when it is sustained by a sufficient amount of feeling.

Hulbert's recognition of the "ineradicable nature of the tendency to strong utterances" and his acknowledgment of the desirability of furnishing "man with words fitted to ease the mind under conditions of deep emotion and to convey one's feelings with force and effectiveness to others" is really an event worthy of jubilant celebration, for it represents the first statement of its kind ever to have been published in a respected organ of the Christian church. In the year 1920 the sun was not observed to dance, the stars in their courses pursued the usual tenor of their way, the skies were not unduly lighted up, and no swearer, as far as I am aware, stopped in his tracks to cry out the news. Yet when it is considered to what extremes the misunderstanding of the swearer's nature has been carried by the church, all these events should have occurred, if only for a moment, to mark the glory of the sudden illumination that had transfigured one of its ministers. For this represents the first instance of such an act of understanding granted a representative of the church from its foundation to this very day. Hulbert's was, however, a lone voice within the church, and except for one or two others within it, very few understanding words have been uttered upon the subject by churchmen. Yet had the church shown such understanding of the nature of swearing as Hulbert has done, it is certain that the whole course and history of swearing would have been altered, and the church would by such means have achieved all that it has, by every means other than those based on the understanding of the facts, failed to achieve. It is one thing to know the facts; it is another to understand them.

The deep-seated nature and ineradicability of the tendency to strong expressions under the influence of certain conditions has been noted by many writers upon the subject and has been referred to by some already quoted. As one writer on swearing has put it:

Swearing is in the nature of things. Somewhere, deep down in the "onta," the noumenon, the "thing in itself," the immanent, the Seyen, in "Das Ich," or "Das Nicht-Ich," in substance, swearing must be. Now and then, in the collision and impact of matter, it emerges into phenomena, and emitting a spark or two, dives under again, into the rock-bottom of noumena.[10]

It is interesting that so many different writers agree that swearing is a fundamental form of human behavior and that its function is relief producing. But actually we still know very little about swearing. What is the character of the stimuli that induce swearing, and what are the physiological and psychological mechanisms through which it operates? These are really the most essential questions that one can ask about swearing, and their answers constitute the principal purpose and contribution of the present volume. All that has gone before has been but preparatory to this.

Let us then proceed.

◖ *The Cause of Swearing*

Is there any general law or principle that could be applied to the conditions that induce swearing? I think there is, and it is the purpose of this section to make that law or principle clear.

Let us begin with the behavior of children, and let us commence with the infant. An infant cries from the moment he is born; he begins to smile and to laugh a little some months later; he begins to speak at about twelve months and to walk at about fifteen months. The human infant exhibits the signs of frustration at a quite early age. These signs are usually observed following some deprivation such as the withdrawal of the nipple, the forcing from his hand of some object. Under such conditions all that the defenseless speechless infant can do is to respond to frustration by the only means at his disposal: by howling at the top of his voice, a performance that is usually brought to an end either by the return of the object whose loss caused the outburst or by sheer exhaustion. This represents the elementary form of the human swearing situation. With the acquisition of speech and experience the child learns to cry less frequently and to express himself in ways that are more effective and "naughty." When he grows to adolescence, crying and childish naughtiness are abandoned for the more manly forms of conduct; where one formerly wept, one now swears. This is well exemplified by an old *Punch* cartoon (April 2, 1913):

OLD LADY: Why are you crying, little boy?
LITTLE BOY: Because I bea'nt old enough to swear.

When a three-year-old accidentally knocks his head against the edge of the table, he either cries or runs complainingly away and is on bad terms for some time with the table, or else he gives it a thorough beating until, by either the first or the last means, he has relieved his feelings and has reestablished normal relations between himself and the table. The second mode of response, that of a whining retreat, offers no relief, no means of "letting off steam," and thus serves to preserve the feeling of anger toward the table. With age the child learns that a table is not an animate being, so that when he again knocks his head against the table it is highly significant that he now responds by *swearing* at it, however

mild his cussing may be: "Oh, shucks!" "Oh damn that table!"
As a "grown" individual, as a man, he knows that even though the
pain be sufficient and the occasion great enough to cause him to
weep, he cannot do so because he has learned to consider such
conduct unmanly. Relief by this means is closed to him, more
especially in the presence of others. To belabor the table physically,
as with a kick or a crash of the fist, is never entirely satisfactory.
Even in the privacy of his own room, where there is no one to
laugh at his childish lack of restraint and he is free to behave so,
there is no satisfactory relief in such conduct, and so he swears at,
he curses, the table. In this way most of us behave, not because
we privately believe in the animate nature of the table, but because
something in our nature causes us, on such occasions, to behave
as if the cause and the object of our angry feelings were something animate. Swearing may be used as an alternative method
for belaboring things that cannot, for some reason, be directly
chastised.

Such, in brief, has been the evolution of swearing. But the principal point to be emphasized here is that the capacity to respond
aggressively is already present in the infant, as is proven by his
responses to all forms of deprivation and frustration. His only means
of reacting to such deprivations and frustrations is by crying. He
uses the only instrument available; later, when the child acquires
the instrument of speech, he reacts to such situations through
such means as he has been taught, with the appropriate intensity.
Swearing is a learned form of behavior. It is not, as our aforemen-
tioned authorities have argued, a form of human conduct that
has its basis in the constitution of man. As we have seen, there
are many societies in which swearing does not occur at all. If
swearing were a constitutionally determined trait, it would be
universal. It is not. And even if it were, it is unsafe to argue that
the universal distribution of a trait means that it is therefore innate.
Like most other human traits, swearing is a learned form of human
behavior in cultures and under conditions in which it is encouraged.
Under such conditions one may learn to swear as a relief for angry
feelings of an aggressive quality that for one reason or another
cannot be expressed in any other way. The function of swearing
would appear to be to act as an effective substitute for the means
that it might be desired, but that it is impracticable, to apply in
order to "belabor" the object or secure a certain end. It thus serves

as a means of relief to the overwrought individual by affording adequate release to his aggressively angry feelings until a normal equilibrium is reestablished.

The infant's crying of frustration is a biologically determined response. The swearing to which he may learn to resort when he has learned to speak is an acquired, a learned, response. The one is designed to draw attention to his needs; the other serves quite another purpose.

Swearing, then, is an acquired way of responding, learned in accordance with the models that are culturally available, a response to frustration of some kind. The function of swearing is to provide an outlet for aggressive feelings thus induced, and in this manner to restore the normal psychophysical equilibrium of the individual.

Let us now in the light of this theory of the origin and nature of swearing consider the various situations, as we know them, that are customarily productive of swearing.

What are the conditions of everyday life that evoke swearing? On the basis of broad personal experience, we may answer that conditions that are thwarting or frustrating generally evoke swearing; that sudden shocks, surprises, disappointments, mortifications, and many similar conditions that produce angry feelings of great or little intensity are often provocative of swearing, and greatly relieved by it.

Frustration may be defined as the consciousness of the thwarting (or the deprivation) of an expected satisfaction. The response to frustration is always a feeling of aggressiveness. But not all aggressive responses to frustration take the form of swearing, though they are generally marked by hostile behavior of some sort. The relation of frustration to aggressiveness has been illuminatingly worked out by Dr. John Dollard and his colleagues at Yale University,[11] but these psychologists have failed to note the significance of this relationship for the phenomenon of swearing. The present writer first proposed this theory in connection with swearing in 1928 and in 1940 applied it to the analysis of the problem of race prejudice.[12] In 1901 G. T. W. Patrick of the University of Iowa, in an article, "The Psychology of Profanity," approached this explanation, but became disoriented in the quagmire of "instinct." In that article Patrick wrote:

Profanity is a primitive and instinctive form of reaction to a situation which threatens in some way the well-being of the individual, standing next to that of actual combat. Like all instinctive reactions, it does not generate emotion but allays it. The emotion arises when the reaction is delayed or inhibited. We are thus able to account for the "katharsis" phenomenon of profanity. It seems to serve as a vent for emotion and to relieve it. It really acts as a vent only in this sense that it brings to an end the intolerable period of inner conflict, of attempted inhibition, of repression and readjustment, and allows the habitual attitude to assert itself. The relief is only that of any completed activity.[13]

At this point let us examine the conditions that have been named above as normally leading to swearing and let us endeavor to ascertain whether frustration and angry aggressive feelings are the indispensable elements involved in the state of mind that gives rise to swearing.

Among the commonest everyday experiences that provoke swearing are sudden physical shocks, such as hitting one's knee or elbow or running into the edge of an open door. Eric Linklater, uncompromising artist that he is, has chronicled for all time the violence of the aggressive reaction that is likely to occur on such an occasion. In his novel *Magnus Merriman*, the following incident occurs.

He got up to look for a drink. The syphon was empty and he went to the pantry for another. The passage was dark and the door stood ajar. He hit his forehead hard against the edge of it, and flew into a rage.
"Good God damn and blast the bloody fool who made that door to everlasting hell, the lousy bastard!" he shouted, and kicked the dumb wood with all his strength.[14]

In this example, we find illustrated in high relief, as it were, every element and aspect of our theory of swearing. Here is an individual who wants a drink. He fully expects to have it without any thought of hindrance. He rises and walks toward the pantry with every assurance that he will soon be there and enjoying the anticipated drink—when, suddenly, he comes into violent and painful collision with the edge of the open door.

His feeling of well-being, of anticipated satisfaction, is suddenly rudely thwarted by this altogether unexpected and painful interposition of the door between himself and his objective. And here the sudden frustration elicits a verbal assault upon the maker of the door and a physical assault upon the door itself, as if both by their stupidity and malevolence had planned this piece of frustration from the beginning. The absent offender is cursed; the present offender is physically assaulted.

Let us take another example of a common experience.

You are walking contentedly along the street when suddenly you stub your toes against the curb and for a moment almost stumble. As likely as not you will—or feel inclined to—give utterance to some such expletive as *Damn!*

Here the anticipated uninterrupted walking is suddenly frustrated, a feeling of aggression immediately rises in us, and we give vent to it in an expletive.

If you are expecting to hit a nail on the head but instead hit your thumb, you may respond with *Ouch!* but the probability is that you will utter something more appropriate to the occasion, or at least feel like uttering it. Here, too, the anticipated activity is rudely frustrated by the painful deviation of the hammer from the nail to what it was not intended for, the thumb, and aggressive feelings well up and result in an expletive or a series of them.

In a classic case, a man already late for the annual dinner, unable to find his cuff links, frustrated beyond measure, is capable of language of the most violent kind. The aggressive response to this type of frustration by swearing is so common that its developing steps are obvious: the frustration, the aggressive feelings, and their expression in the learned behavior of swearing.

There is an inherent malice in inanimate objects, which some speak of as Resistentialism, the conspiracy among inanimate objects to resist the incursions and manipulations of the animate world—and most particularly of men. Hence, shoelaces have an uncanny way of breaking when their victim is in a particular hurry and there don't happen to be any to replace them. Studs decline to be coaxed into the places they normally freely go. Objects one held in one's hands a moment before suddenly vanish and remain unfindable for hours or days, until they as suddenly reappear in the very place one had last seen them. And so endlessly on do inanimate objects bedevil man. It is not to be wondered at, then, that the world of inanimate objects is so powerfully productive of swearing.

It is to be noted that whether the cause is an animate or an inanimate object, it seems almost always to be treated as if it were a conscious being, capable of receiving the full charge of our shotted words. We assault the door, the curb, the nail, or the cuff links as if they were capable of being affected by our verbal blasts, and when we are sufficiently enraged we are capable of kicking them, stamping upon them, and attempting to knock them out of shape. To provide a vehicle for working off one's accumulated frustration, there was put on the market, in the year of grace 1940, an assortment of pottery articles whose sole function was to break into a thousand pieces when hurled by those in search of an acceptable means of relieving themselves of accumulated tensions.

Any kind of frustration presents the conditions that make for swearing. The aggressiveness arising from the frustration, though it may not be consciously perceived as such, seeks to discharge itself upon the frustrating cause.

The relation of swearing to the chastisement of a living individual has been mentioned in the quotation from Patrick, in which he refers to that form of behavior as "standing next to actual combat." It is a form of conduct that has been recognized in popular speech in phrases such as "What a tongue lashing he gave him!" Shakespeare expresses this when he has Philip the Bastard exclaim:

> He speaks plain cannon fire, and smoke and bounce,
> He gives the bastinado with his tongue:
> Our ears are cudgell'd, not a word of his
> But buffets better than a fist of France.
> Zounds! I was never so bethumped with words
> Since I first call'd my brother's father dad.
> *King John*, II, i

We may also recall here the example, described earlier, of the youth in Union Square who pretended to receive every oath his Irish becusser hurled at him as if it were a physical blow. The verbal assault of swearing would appear to serve as a substitute for actual physical assault. Implicit recognition of this occurs in the old jingle:

> Sticks and stones may break my bones,
> But names will never hurt me.

By applying to him all the degrading epithets at one's command, the swearer reduces, in imagination at least, the object of his objurgations to that condition to which he would like to see him reduced in reality. The family resemblance should be obvious between such behavior and that of the native who maltreats the image of his enemy.

To a greater or lesser extent the element of physical assault is present in practically every form of swearing. Even the curse, with its delayed action, was "laid upon" the victim as the physical assault with cudgel or rack was. Swearing is a rather more civilized form of behavior that replaces physical violence. If physical combat between individuals and between nations could be replaced by the more sophisticated arrangement of a swearing contest, how much more satisfying that would be than our present barbaric method of settling disputes. Most profitably we could follow the example of the Eskimo contestants who assault one another with reproachful songs to a musical accompaniment and to the unfailing delight of the spectators. Great talents could in this manner find a useful outlet for their political skills.

The most cultivated form of swearing is invective, which may be defined as polite swearing. The shafts loosed in this form of verbal assault are often most skillfully wrought. Though the target may be discomfited, the wounds they inflict are seldom serious and upon healing frequently leave the victim all the better for having suffered them. The social function of ridicule, persiflage, and invective has not gone altogether unrecognized in its effect upon persons and upon institutions. Even nations may in this manner be taught their most enduring lessons, and precisely at those times when they are preening themselves on those great qualities before which goes the fall. Some day, when man has risen from the status of *Homo sap* to that of *Homo sapiens*, the worst kinds of individual conflicts and wars between nations will be fought not with the destructive power of armaments but with the constructive power of words, by the force of argument rather than by the argument of force. To a certain extent this has already been recognized by many societies. In every society those men are most admired who turn the tables upon their adversaries by the art and virtuosity of their words rather than by the resort to violence.

Perhaps one of the best and most famous examples of this is the exchange between the Earl of Sandwich and John Wilkes, the seventeenth-century demagogue. Enraged by a remark of Wilkes', the earl rose from his seat and, pointing a quavering finger at Wilkes, exclaimed, "That man will either die on the scaffold or of the pox." Wilkes in his turn rose and, bowing gracefully in the direction of the earl, replied, "My Lord, that all depends upon whether I embrace your principles or your mistress."

Wilkes benefited more from that verbal duel—and so, it should be added, have we—than from any number of physical duels he might have fought and won.

Speaking of duels, there is the story of the professor who, challenged to a duel by the man to whom he had said, "You stink!" declined to accept the challenge. "On what grounds?" demanded the offended challenger. "On the ground," replied the professor, "that since I would kill you, you would then stink worse than ever!" Exemplary thoughtfulness!

Physical combat is brutal and horrible in any shape or form. There can be neither biological nor social justification for it. Every society laying claim to being truly civilized would outlaw such forms of behavior forever.

The myth of the beast is still a myth, even though most people fervently believe in it. The truth is that other animals are not nearly as aggressive as so-called civilized peoples. Man's nearest relatives—the gorilla, the chimpanzee, and the orangutan—are the most unaggressive of creatures.[15] Nonliterate peoples are very little given to fighting, their individual and group combats being very mild affairs, indeed. Generally, as soon as the first blood is drawn the fight is at an end. We cannot, therefore, justly use our alleged ancestral past as the peg upon which to hang man's violence. Nor can we any longer justly speak of the survival of brutish or savage instincts within man that impel him to violent behavior. There is no such thing as an instinct or inborn urge to violent behavior of any kind. Men who are given to physical violence are not so by nature but by *nurture*. Soldiers will shoot to kill and maim others because they believe it is their duty to do so. Violent men learn their violence from the segment of the culture in which they have been conditioned, and those who resort to physical violence do so for every reason but an instinctive one. We no more fight with others by instinct or from instinct than we quarrel with others by instinct. Men will attack strikebreakers because they believe it is in their interest to do so and perhaps not uncongenial to them. Newspapers and men have engineered conflict and war and raised the battle cry against the "enemy" because there was profit in it. And men will fight to "defend their country" because they have been made to feel that their way of life, their lives, and the lives of their families are at stake. But in all this there is nothing remotely instinctive. It is not instinctive for men to fight. There is no general urge in man to combat or physical violence. The instinct theory of man's innate tendency to violence and warfare is a complete myth.[16]

The behavior of human beings has been molded by words and by conduct, and it is this organization of behavior, as it has been conditioned in human beings, that constitutes the basis of all human behavior—and not nonexistent innate "instincts." Man learns to be aggressive, just as he learns to be nonaggressive.

Man is naturally endowed with perfectly adequate means of restoring himself to his usual state of equilibrium without having to resort to any other means to do so. Time is an effective means, but there are innumerable built-in others. Physical violence is man's own invention. Weeping, laughter, and work are far more efficient.

Do any of the so-called lower animals exhibit behavior that may in any way be regarded as akin to swearing? The snarling of dogs and other animals may appear to resemble swearing, and there can be no mistaking the fact that the snarl of the dog is often a sign of annoyance. The function, however, of the snarl seems to be to serve as a warning, a caution to others, that it is dangerous to proceed further, rather than as a frustration-aggression relief mechanism. Angry barking is not of this nature, for it is clearly a direct expression of developed choler. In short, it is greatly to be doubted whether any animal other than man swears.

Among the order of mammals to which man belongs, the primates, behavior that looks suspiciously like the swearing of man has been frequently observed in monkeys, and especially in the chimpanzee. This assumes the form of violent shaking, repeated baring of the teeth, crashing and kicking with the feet, but rarely with any kind of vocal display.[17]

Swearing, then, constitutes a culturally conditioned form of behavior, serving the twofold purpose of permitting the excess energy of frustration to express itself in harmless verbal aggression and of restoring the organism to equilibrium. Swearing is the culturally conditioned verbal expression or venting of the aggressiveness that follows upon frustration. Hence, the desire to swear will be experienced only by those who have learned to swear under conditions that give rise to frustration.

Although the function of swearing has not yet been fully considered, the subject has been sufficiently rehearsed in the first part of this chapter to suggest something of the nature of that function. From our examination of the causes of swearing and from what we have thus far learned of its function, it seems that swearing may become so much a habit that it becomes "second nature," so that it appears to be almost constitutional. Indeed, in a man to whom swearing has become an ingrained habit it may become psychologically as well as physiologically very much more satisfying than either weeping or laughter.

([The Physiological and Psychological Basis of Swearing

Swearing, laughter, and weeping have in common the function of acting as relief valves for sudden surges of energy that require the appropriate form of expression. What these separate forms of behavior also have in common is the reestablishment of the psychophysical equilibrium of the organism.

The very simplest incongruity between events of any kind will produce laughter. The same events invested with a meaning of another kind will produce tears, and under still other circumstances, swearing. For example, when, just before the game is about to open, the star pitcher sends a message to the effect that owing to the development of hemorrhoids he will be unable to play, the announcement will be greeted by the crowd in different ways. Many supporters of the opposing team will, unsportingly, laugh with joy, with the pleasurable unexpectedness of this advantage to their side, and the incongruity between the cause and the effect will stimulate them to further laughter. To the fiancee of the player the announcement will come as a painful disappointment or shock, and she will shed tears of chagrin. To the supporters of our star pitcher, upon whom most of them had placed their hopes for the game, the announcement will act as a great blow, a tremendous frustration of their expectations, and they will often swear or feel like doing so in order to relieve their feelings.

This example illustrates the obvious fact that whether we will laugh, weep, or swear depends mainly upon the attitude we bear toward the things that elicit our responses. Our attitude toward certain groups of conditions may, at various times, undergo a series of changes, so that where we once laughed and then wept, we now swear or else are quite indifferent. Furthermore, upon occasion we may laugh when we might more adequately or more naturally weep, and vice versa, or we may swear when we might more appropriately laugh or weep, or we might altogether inhibit our desire to laugh, weep, or swear. It is even possible to telescope any two of these activities and give expression to them at one and the same time, as in hysterical weeping and laughter, or swearing and weeping, or swearing and laughter, although in the latter case the swearing is generally jocular.

While laughter and weeping may be regarded as inborn urges to react to specific stimuli in a specific manner, can the same be said of swearing? Babies, for example, are able to laugh and cry, but no case of a baby who could swear has ever been reported. To swear, one must have speech. The nearest thing to speech in the baby is crying, and so he expends such aggressiveness as he may feel by crying, the form his aggressiveness usually takes. When later he acquires speech, if he grows up in an environment in which it is permissible to do so he will learn to expend his aggressiveness through speech. Under such conditions the child will learn to use all the instruments available to him: physical assault, weeping, and name-calling such as "You *naughty* girl," "You *bad* boy!"—"naughty" and "bad" being the emotionally most heavily weighted words with which he is acquainted. On the other hand, some children, having from birth been exposed to the most horrendous swearing, will, like Tom Sawyer and Huckleberry Finn, not be at a loss for the proper words. The case of the two-year-old Australian aboriginal should be recalled. The actual swearing vocabulary is of course purely a matter of experience, and in many instances—particularly among youths who have been privately educated and shielded from all contaminating influences—a minimal swearing vocabulary may not be acquired, if at all, until much later. But it is the rare individual who can be so shielded that he does not overhear some expletive, however mild; and this he may eventually incorporate in his own vocabulary. Patrick quotes an amusing example of the way in which a "properly" brought up child may feel. The six-year-old son of a clergyman, a sturdy and combative child, but of good habits and careful training, having suffered some serious childish trouble with his playmates, came home and said, "Mama, I feel just like saying, 'God damn'; I would like to say 'Jesus Christ,' but I think that would be wrong."[18]

Don Talayesva, a Hopi Indian Sun Chief, tells how he was sent to school at Sherman, Arizona, and also introduced into the YMCA. He writes:

I learned to preach pretty well, and to cuss too. The Hopi language has no curse words in it. But at Sherman even the YMCA and the Catholic boys cussed like hell. At first so much of it made me tired; but when I got into the habit myself it was alright. When I wanted anything I would say, 'Give me that God-damn thing.' But I soon learned when and where it was appropriate to curse.[19]

Don Talayesva simply learned another language, and since swearing went with it, he learned that, too. But among his own people he never swore. "I made less and less use of the English language," he said, "except when I talked to Whites or wanted to cuss."

Frustration is a universal phenomenon, but whether or not aggressive feelings inevitably develop as a response to frustration, the desire to swear is not a universal phenomenon. The Quaker who abjures all swearing neither swears nor desires to. This does not mean that some people are able to control the expression of an innate urge. The urge simply is not there, and in the Quaker environment there is a prohibition upon learning to swear. American Indians early learn not to give way to emotion and are careful about both their weeping and their laughter—and these are entirely innate urges. May it not then be possible that control of the urge to swear may similarly be learned? It is certainly possible to learn to control the expression of innately determined urges, but as we have seen, there is no ground whatsoever for believing that swearing is such an innately determined urge.

The fact that the phenomena of weeping and laughter appear, as it were, more or less full-fledged in the human infant, while verbal swearing does not, could simply mean that the frustration-swearing urge must wait upon the development of speech just as the sexual urge must wait upon the physiological development of the reproductive organs before it can function properly. The sexual urge is a physiological one; swearing is not. Swearing is a purely artificial urge, culturally acquired, and is not in any sense part of the human constitution or the normal functioning of that constitution, as in weeping and laughter. Swearing is merely one form out of a large number of possible learned varieties of hostile or aggressive behavior. I believe that the evidence so far considered strongly suggests that swearing is a culturally acquired way of expressing anger. Anger is a complex emotion the expression of which may take the form of a hostile response

—it may be an oath, it may be a lampoon, it may be a laugh or a hundred and one other behaviors. In the case of swearing it is a special kind of anger that calls it forth. Although this kind of anger has gone unrecognized and unnamed, it exists and must be distinguished from the general blanket concept of anger that is generally recognized. All that can be said about it here is that it is a quick anger, an anger that rises suddenly as the result of a sudden stimulus, a stimulus of a frustrating kind, unlike the anger that is slow in its inception and calculated in its expression. Whatever the truth may be, it is clear that different conditions call forth different forms of anger and that with one of these forms of anger the desire to swear, as a learned form of response, occurs in some cultures or segments of a culture, but not in others.

Swearing, weeping, and laughter are all characterized by certain very definite physical accompaniments and physiological changes. Thus, laughter is characterized by distinctive muscular contractions of the diaphragm, the vocal cords, and the face, by an accelerated flow of the blood, by changes in respiration, and so on, resulting in a general heightening of the psychophysical tone of the body. Weeping is also characterized by muscular contractions of the diaphragm, the vocal cords, and muscles of the face, but instead of an acceleration, there is a deceleration in the flow of the blood and in the rate of respiration, accompanied by hypersecretion of tears from the lacrimal glands, resulting in a general lowering of the psychophysical tone of the body. In states of anger there is no necessary contraction of the diaphragm, but there is an increased tension of the muscular system in general, an increase in blood pressure and an acceleration of its flow, and an increased amount of sugar in the blood; respiration is increased and there is a general feeling of tension, which is gradually reduced as the swearing proceeds, and a state of relief ensues. But it would be a mistake to associate these changes with swearing, for what they are essentially associated with is the state of anger.

Thus, we observe that from the standpoint of psychophysiology, weeping and laughter appear to be closely related and have in common the function of serving to restore or preserve the normal mental equilibrium of the individual. Whatever the causes that evoke laughter may be,[20] its function seems to be to produce a temporary heightening of vital energy throughout the body, of such an intensity that the possibility of any noxious stimuli taking possession of the mind is completely precluded; the feeling of relief that ensues indicates that whatever tension there may have been is broken and signifies the return to a state of equilibrium.

Weeping, by lowering the general feeling tone of the body, breaks or reduces the shock of the stimulus and keeps the subject less intensely aware of it, meanwhile exerting a distinctively sooth- ing effect upon the mind until, by allowing the painfully induced and temporarily dominant energy of the shock to be worked off gradually, a return is made to the state of normal feeling tone. In the adult as well as in the child this not infrequently declares itself in a distinct sigh of relief.

In swearing, as a means of expressing anger, potentially noxious energy is converted into a form that renders it comparatively innocuous. By affording the means of working off the surplus energy of the emotion induced by frustration, the tension between the emotion and the object of it is decreased and the final disso- lution of the tension is expressed in a feeling of relief, which in its place is a sign of the return to a state of equilibrium.

A "good cry," a "good laugh," and "a good swear" have each in their way long been recognized as serving the useful function of bringing relief to the harassed mind.

It is clear, then, that in common with weeping and laughter, swearing serves a very useful function as a cathartic, that is, as an outlet for emotions that result, as it were, in a purgative effect, as well as a pacifying one. As Campbell has remarked in connec- tion with swearing, "the shouting and gesticulation which accom- pany an outburst of passion act physiologically by relieving nerve tension; and, indeed, as Hughlings Jackson has suggested, swear- ing may not be without its physiological justification. Passionate outbursts are generally succeeded by periods of good behaviour and, it may be, improved health."[21]

This relief-purifying-pacifying function of swearing has been recognized by many investigators, some of whose views have already been referred to in this chapter. B. G. Steinhoff has put the matter very succinctly. Swearing, he writes, "is a seton for harmlessly drawing off wrath and peccant humours." And then he goes off the rails by identifying the seton, which is a cultural artifact, with what is discharged through its means. "As it does not require to be taught, it may be safely inferred that it comes by instinct, or intuition, and thus it may finally be placed among the 'a priori' ideas."[22]

Shakespeare, who fully understood the significance, and every nuance and aspect of the function of swearing, clearly stated its relief function when he has Volumnia say:

> I would the gods had nothing else to do
> But to confirm my curses! Could I meet 'em
> But once a-day, it would unclog my heart
> Of what lies heavy to't.
>
> *Coriolanus*, IV, ii

To unclog the heart of all those troublesome and noisome vapors that oppress it is the service that swearing performs for man. What poisons circulate in the system of him who hoards his noxious humors! For him the complexion of life becomes the color of bile, a world full of unavenged personal wrongs and hated creatures for the announcement of whose death he hunts hopefully in the obituary columns of his daily paper. His biliousness robs him of laughter and the friendly token of a smile. His digestion becomes disordered, a clogging heaviness descends upon him and invades every part of his body, his thoughts and vital processes become bogged in a mire of thickening bile, which is continually being augmented by new upsurges of venom. As John Forthergill, that deipnosophical innkeeper, has put it, "All the steam, manufactured for use, is pent up, it can't escape through the natural channel but goes into the blood and bones and poisons."[23]

In order to prevent such a sorry state Saint Paul urged that though "ye be angry, sin not"; further, "let not the sun go down upon your wrath."[24] He does not say, "Be ye angry," as the King James version mistranslates, but "Ye be angry"—that is, "You are angry, don't be violent, don't swear, don't harbor malice, but make peace before the day ends." If this is what he meant, as it seems, then he just missed doing mankind a great service. How, being in anger, can one best be relieved of it without giving effective expression to one's anger? It is not enough to go out and climb a tree, or to chop one down, or to chop up one that has already been chopped down—at least these actions are not anywhere nearly as satisfactory as the real thing: a good swear. To forgive is admirable, but a good swear is more effective. It is unfortunate that this was not early recognized by the wise men of the East who laid down the canons of moral life for the West, for the apostle's advice to "let not the sun go down upon your wrath" would have been perfect if he had added, "by swearing your fill like the good men that ye are and bearing no malice."

The ill effects of not swearing are likely to be so great, while the evil effects of swearing are disposed to be so much less than the good effects, that mankind, having everywhere discovered this for itself, continues to swear and blast away despite all the interdictions and prohibitions of the reformers, secular or ecclesiastical.

Experimental studies abundantly confirm the universal experience. For example, D. M. F. Reiser and his co-workers, in a study of the physiological reactions to stress of enlisted soldiers, found that those who were free to "gripe" about army life with their interviewer were considerably less prone to exhibit an elevation in blood pressure than those who did not complain.[25] Similarly, S. H. King and A. F. Henry found that when the subjects studied by them under stress directed their rage against the experimenter they showed a less tense physiological reaction than those who controlled their anger.[26] Dr. D. W. MacKinnon found that in taking a test in which it was possible to cheat that those students who swore or cursed at the questions were likely to cheat without experiencing any feelings of guilt. This was in contrast with those students who kept quiet, blamed themselves for their own stupidity, and felt guilty and anxious during the test.[27]

These findings, as MacKinnon points out, tend to support the Freudian hypothesis that those who fail to gratify their aggressive impulses tend to become the object of them and to experience as a result a feeling of guilt.[28]

There are a great many other investigations of a similar sort that give support to the thesis that swearing constitutes a form of learned behavior calculated to reduce both physiological and psychological stress;[29] that it is a means of purging the organism, of eliminating what would otherwise accumulate as noxious humors. Its function is to provide an outlet for the spilling over of emotions under tension or pressure. Like laughter and weeping swearing represents a specific response to an acquired specific urge, and while producing a feeling of relief in the organism, it is itself perfectly harmless. Upon the psychophysiological turmoil and pressure of anger, swearing produces a tranquilizing, pacifying effect, a feeling of relief, of emotional satisfaction. Indeed, in a very real sense swearing may be regarded as an emotional orgasm, of greater or less intensity, as the case may be.

Any inhibition of swearing merely serves to accumulate the quanta of aggressiveness. Unless this aggressiveness can be expressed in some more acceptable manner, as in the business of the "attack" upon social problems of the Quaker, it is likely to prove disadvantageous to the general well-being of the individual.

Like laughter and weeping, the function of swearing is to produce a feeling of relief and to restore the organism to a normal state of psychophysical equilibrium.

Thus, we arrive at the important conclusion that as a functional form of human behavior, in those cultures in which it has been developed, swearing is a culturally learned form of behavior that serves functions similiar to those of laughter and weeping. But unlike them, it is not innately based.

❨ *The Sexual Factor in Swearing*

Beyond all else, we observe that the function of swearing, as it has been so many times eminently well described, is "to let off steam."

Now it may have occurred to the reader that something is still wanting in this explanation of the nature and function of swearing. If swearing may become so strong an urge, he may well ask, why is there such a difference in the expression of it between men and women? Are they differently endowed in this respect? To this we may profitably reply with another question: Why is it that men do not weep and women do? Are they differently endowed here too? I think that the probability is high that there is no difference in biological endowment in any of these respects and that such differences as we observe in the sexual expression of any of these functions are for the most part, if not entirely, determined by cultural factors.

In our society woman is indisputably the "gentler" sex, to whom violent activities and vehement expressions of any sort were until very recently forbidden. It wasn't done. Woman was too fragile and sensitive to be exposed to anything but the most refined expressions. She was too tender. As the Queen remarks when Posthumus swears *By Jove* and Iachimo swears *By Jupiter*,

> Beseech your majesty,
> Forbear sharp speeches to her: she's a lady
> So tender of rebukes that words are strokes
> And strokes death to her.
>
> *Cymbeline*, III, v

At best that was also the Victorian view. And so in the days of Victoria under conditions in which a male would swear, a female would burst into tears. This is still an outlet for her frustrated angry feelings that is always available to her and to which she may resort without incurring the contempt of her fellows, which accounts for the fact that until recently women rarely swore, for weeping rendered swearing unnecessary. It is of the most significant interest to note here that prostitutes, who have always been as notorious for their swearing as they have for their easy virtue, rarely weep, "but unpack their hearts with words, and fall a-cursing."[30] If women wept less they would swear more, a statement that derives some support from the fact that many modern women have grown to be ashamed of tears and quite belligerently proud of swearing.

Hence we perceive that until recently swearing in women was negatively sanctioned as unfeminine and bypassed by the resort to emotional expression through weeping. With the growing emancipation of woman from her former inferior status she has now altogether abandoned the privilege of swooning and has reduced the potential oceans of tears to mere rivulets. Today, instead of swooning or breaking into tears, she will often swear and then effectively do whatever is indicated. It is, in our view, a great advance upon the old style.

During World War II, when women were employed in large numbers in war industries, notices devised by women were occasionally seen, testifying to the thoughtfulness with which they used their new-found privilege. A typical notice, seen in an aircraft factory, read: "No swearing. There may be gentlemen about."[31]

⟮ Stress, Annoyance, and Social Swearing

The relationship between stress, annoyance, and swearing has been investigated by Dr. Helen E. Ross of the University of Hull during a university expedition to Arctic Norway. The group studied consisted of five men and three women between nineteen and twenty-four years of age, all of whom were zoologists, except Dr. Ross, who is a psychologist. As was to be expected among members of the middle class, the words used were blasphemous rather than obscene. It was observed that when the members of the expedition were relaxed and happy there was a noticeable increase in the amount of swearing. Swearing also increased under slight stress, but decreased with annoyance and fatigue.

When the group was relaxed and happy, the swearing was clearly of a social kind, a sign of being "one of the gang." This form of swearing, which was by far the most common, depended for its effect upon an audience, while annoyance swearing constituted a reaction to stress regardless of the audience.

Under conditions of very low stress, swearing was almost entirely of the social variety. With increasing stress social swearing diminished and annoyance swearing increased. "Under higher stress, social swearing almost entirely disappeared and annoyance swearing increased until it too reached a peak and began to drop. Under conditions of serious stress, there was silence."[32] This latter reaction suggests that swearing is a sign that a disagreeable situation is bearable—indeed, that the verbal expression of discomfort in the form of swearing helps to reduce stress.

Commenting on Dr. Ross' observations, the leader of the expedition, R. G. B. Brown, remarked that while it was certainly true that under conditions of extreme stress there was a decline in the swearing rate, this was also true of the speech rate in general. It was his own impression that under extreme stress fewer words are used, but that most of them are swear words.[33]

Among Dr. Ross' interesting findings was the fact that absence of an appreciative audience or the presence of nonswearers inhibited social swearing. The men who arrived in camp a week early felt obliged to watch their tongues when the women arrived. When half the group—including the only three nonswearers—left on a separate expedition, the swearing rate immediately doubled, and it remained consistently high. Dr. Ross suggests that this may have been due to an attempt to compensate for the lost members by this expression of increased solidarity.

When a medium swearer (female) spent two days with a heavy swearer (male), the swearing rates of both increased. But when the same female spent two weeks with a medium swearer (male), all swearing soon ceased, probably, suggests Dr. Ross, because the latter two needed the facilitative effect of a heavy swearer or a larger audience.

Dr. Ross' hypothesis that, in a given situation, those who swear are likely to suffer less from stress than those who do not swear is abundantly confirmed by common experience and by the results of experiment. And so are her observations that swearing is contagious and mutually reenforcing in certain situations, and also that a nonswearing environment of low intensity is capable of reducing swearing to the vanishing point. All of these observations testify to the fact that the presence or absence of swearing is a socially developed trait and strongly underscore the social nature of swearing.

CHAPTER SIX

Words Used in Swearing: Their Sources and the Forms of Swearing

<<<<<<<<<<<<<<<<<<<<<<<<<<<<<<<<<<<<<<<<<<>>>>>>>>>>>>>>>>>>>>>>>>>>>>>>>>>>

With some Poets, *Swearing is no ordinary Relief.*
It stands up in the room of Sense, gives Spirit
to a flat Expression, and makes a Period Musical
and Round.
JEREMY COLLIER, *A Short View,* 1698

To swear with propriety the oath should
be an echo to the sense.
RICHARD BRINSLEY SHERIDAN, *The Rivals,* 1775

ANY word carrying an emotional charge is capable of serving the swearer as ammunition for his purposes. The words of the swearer are shotted words, words charged with explosives, words invested with the powers of the gods, words bearing the forbidden potencies of the obscene: words violent, and words profanely contagious and polluting—scurrilous, rude, diminishing words, foul words, words polite and words otherwise, so long as they all carry an idea that is, or can be, effectively applied. All such words are grist to the swearer's mill.

Words possessing a high emotional charge are the most effective with which to swear, not because they normally force their way to the surface more readily than others, but because of their puissance they constitute the most pulverizing verbal projectiles at our disposal. Hence, the armament of words is drawn from the sacred; from the prohibited; from sex, the sexual organs and functions; from the obscene, from filth, the scatological, and all things offensive. These words carry with them the power invoked, borrowed—legitimately or illegitimately—from the gods, the holy ones, and the sacred, their spiritual and bodily powers and parts; these words refer to inanimate objects symbolizing ideas highly charged with emotional values.

The words used in swearing may actually be meaningless to the swearer in every other sense but that of his consciousness of their emotional or intensive value—both to the swearer and the sworn at. *Omne ignotum pro obsceno* is a fact that can be checked by the reader for himself if he will but try calling anyone unfamiliar with the "higher learning" a square of the hypotenuse, or a *corpus striatum,* or an existential, or anyone unfamiliar with the Hebrew alphabet an aleph, or a beth, or a gimel or especially a daleth. Robert Graves testifies to having witnessed a scene in which a man was thrown out of the Empire Lounge in London for having called a barmaid a *maisonette.* To which she, in high dudgeon, replied, "Indeed you're wrong, I'm an honest woman."[1]

In swearing an oath he who administers it need not believe in it himself, a fact that will not deter the swearer from taking the oath with every intention of keeping it, though in the full knowledge that the administrator does not believe in the powers by which the swearer swears. This is well illustrated in the exchange between Lucius and Aaron in Shakespeare's *Titus Andronicus*:

> LUCIUS: Who should I swear by? Thou believest no god:
> That granted, how canst thou believe an oath?
> AARON: What if I do not? as, indeed, I do not;
> Yet, for I know that thou art religious
> And hast a thing within thee called conscience,
> With twenty popish tricks and ceremonies,
> Which I have seen thee careful to observe,
> Therefore I urge thy oath; for that I know
> An idiot holds his bauble for his god.
> And keeps the oath which by that god he swears,
> To that I'll urge him; therefore thou shalt vow
> By that same god, what god soe'er he be,
> That thou adorest and hast in reverence
>
>   V, i

And Lucius vows. Such is the power of these miraculous words! Convincing alike to the convinced and the unconvinced.

So long as the words are sufficiently powerful, even if they are but a concatenation of meaningless sounds, they may serve as a conduit for the mounted passions. As Roderick Random put it, "It set all my passions into a ferment, I swore horrible oaths without meaning or application."[2]

Anything that is of emotional value to one social class or profession and not to another may form the instrument of swearing exclusively among that class or profession and to no other.

For example, many years ago in England the question of endowment and disestablishment was a subject of warm debate among ecclesiastics. *Punch*, in a skit on this dispute, represented two clergymen in the midst of a quarrel over a lady. "You be disestablished," says the one, "I shall give her flowers or whatever I like." "I'm disendowed if you shall; so there!" thunders the other.

Another example of the same thing may be found in Edward Thompson's excellent novel *A Farewell to India* (1931). Among the middle classes of England the O.B.E. (Order of the British Empire) was, after World War I, a much-sought-after decoration; however, it was so freely bestowed that it soon came to be generally held in contempt. In the novel, Alden, an Anglo-Indian missionary, exclaims, "I've told you that I don't care an O.B.E. what happens to the hostel."[3]

Here "O.B.E." does service, rather more imaginatively, for the "damn" that would not quite become an Anglo-Indian missionary's speech, and also, one may surmise, for "S.O.B.," reverberating from that locus of the clerical mind to which all such unmentionables are relegated. It is a pity, because had Alden been a really knowledgeable man, he could have damned away in an odor of undefiled sanctity, and as appropriately as could be. For according to some of our best authorities on the subject, the origin of the phrase "I don't care a damn" is purely Indian. In India the coin of least value is known as a *dām*. During the period when the Duke of Wellington, a powerful and imaginative swearer, was fighting and winning his battles in India, he is said to have invented the oath "I don't care a twopenny *dām!*"[4] Thus, instead of being a statement of the swearer's scorn or the theological threat contained in the prospect of damnation, the oath announces no more than the prosaic fact that the swearer does not care in the very least. On his return to England Wellington is said to have adapted the oath to the English scene by rendering it in a form that would be more easily understood, "I don't care a twopenny damn!"[5] Since this oath does occur in precisely this form prior to the advent of Wellington, and since an English coin of small value was added to the minute value of the Indian *dām*, it may well be that Wellington was responsible for popularizing this oath. Hence, it will be perceived that Alden, with propriety and a nice regard for the circumstances, could have used the term that, in ignorance of the true facts, he threw out in favor of a pretty nearly worthless decoration. (See pp. 296–298 for a full discussion of the expression.)

Constant and overabundant usage of certain common swearwords, which sparingly employed do good service, may deprive them of all value for the purposes for which they were originally intended. Such words become hackneyed and lose all the force and the value they once possessed. The strength has been drained out of them, and they become as colorless as any exhausted word can be.

Charles Marriott, in that admirable book *Modern Movements in Painting,* makes a very similar point. He writes, "In certain poems by Mr. John Masefield the word 'bloody' is by constant reiteration reduced to the ineffectiveness of the curate's 'Good gracious!' because the reader cannot but feel that it is only a euphemism for something stronger."[6]

A common misunderstanding of the character of swearwords is that they are in themselves obscene or in some way besmirched and besmirching. Nothing could be further from the truth, for this applies only to a very small proportion of the vocabulary of the worst of swearers, and not at all to that of most. Indeed, while many of the words that the so-called foul-mouthed swearer often uses may be of obscene origin, they are not necessarily used in an obscene sense. They are employed merely because they carry great emotional freightage and are prohibited by society—two electrical charges which endow them with the power to shock so necessary for the swearer's purposes. The foul-mouthed swearer does not swear in order to be obscene, but merely in order to deliver himself through the vehicle of appropriate shocking words of his passions. The obscene as such has no more appeal to most swearers than it has for nonswearers. In fact many a hearty swearer has been unutterably disgusted by the salacious inflection that the so-called nonswearer has so often given to the swearer's most innocent words. This is well illustrated by a passage in Bret Harte's *In the Carquinez Woods.*

"Ah, ha! Strong language, Mr. Daun," said Father Wynn, referring to the sheriff's adjuration, "but 'out of the fullness of the heart the mouth speaketh.' Job, sir, cursed, we are told, and even expressed himself in vigorous Hebrew regarding his birthday. Ha, ha! I'm not opposed to that. When I have often wrestled with the spirit I confess I have sometimes said, 'D——n you.' Yes, sir, 'D——n you.'"

There was something so unutterably vile in the reverent gentleman's utterance and emphasis of this oath that the two men, albeit both easy and facile blasphemers, felt shocked, as the purest of actresses is apt to overdo the rakishness of a gay Lothario, Father Wynn's immaculate conception of an imprecation was something terrible.[7]

The contaminating and defiling potencies of swearing are very real things. Margaret Cole, in her charming autobiography, *Growing Up Into Revolution*, relates:

Another relative, left widowed by a spouse whose choice of language had made her very unhappy at times, conceived the idea of having the house purified after him. This was done after some discussion, by the local priest; but shortly afterwards the house turned out to need structural repair; and when the workmen came in, it became sadly apparent that it was going to be polluted all over again. In despair, the owner appealed to the foreman, explained the delicate condition of the house, and begged him (since she realised that Men must swear) to ask them if they would be so kind as to go *outside* to do it.[8]

It is often the case that, as Samuel Butler put it, nice people are people with dirty minds, people who have spent the greater part of their lives in repressing and inhibiting the thoughts that the healthier-minded accommodate more easily or get out of their systems by free and uninhibited expression. Hence, when "nice people" swear they are as likely to use the mildest of words, in the consciousness that they are being very daring but that the occasion demands it. But the amount of obscene or vicious effect that they often inject into such words renders them extraordinarily unpleasant to hear, as in the case of an elderly priest attempting to play the roué.

Among "nice people" we find the exception to our rule that the words used in swearing are generally words heavily weighted with some emotional association. For among those respectable souls who abjure every form of unconventional swearing, it is quite possible to swear in the most thoroughly approved and sanctioned drawing-room language. But as long as the words used arise out of the frustrated and aggressive feelings and have as their aim the relief of those feelings by the removal or chastisement of their cause, it *is* swearing, whatever other name it may be called by.

The shapes that such conventionally permissible forms of swearing may take are numberless—all the way from the double entendre and the catty or cutting remark to the grossest of insults. It is possible to make jokes about an enemy and even offer him the vilest of insults, yet escape the consequences of such conduct by pretending that no harm was meant. "It was only a joke." This is one of the most blatant examples of the arrant cowardice of such forms of swearing, for in this form the most discrediting and humiliating things can be said about another with full impunity, because this kind of detracting swearer, for such he is, can always claim that he was only speaking in jest. If ever a truth was spoken in jest it has never been more seriously intended than in this kind of despicable jape.

Let it be known, then, to all men that this kind of jesting is the invariable work of a moral coward, a gutless creature who must always retreat into the mess of his own making and who derives his safeguards from that very mess, which no one else will approach. The catty remarks of which women are supposed to be so much more guilty than men partake of this character. A simple remark made by one woman to another, such as "Darling, is anything the matter? Are you sure you are quite well? You don't look *quite* your best," may contain an almost lethal dose of venom. This kind of swearing, developed to its most sophisticated form, is brilliantly exemplified in August Strindberg's autobiography, *The Confession of a Fool*, and in his play *The Father*, in both of which the story is told of the wife who, desiring to be released from her husband, almost succeeds in causing his death by a studied use, or rather misuse, of words.[9] The omnipotence of words was never more effectively illustrated.

Polite usage has its own vocabulary of swearwords and its own swearing devices. These enjoy the approval of society and their employment is thoroughly sanctioned and acceptable. It is in England that such usages reached their highest degree of development. To call a man an insufferable young puppy or an unmitigated cad or simply a cad were fighting words among the upper classes and their understudies, the middle classes. A gentleman, during the reign of Victoria, would call his adversary a cur or a cad, but never a bastard. The latter term, indeed, was sedulously avoided, for a sizable part of the nobility of England was of bastard origin, mainly as a consequence of the principal occupation of Charles II, who created more dukes and peers of the realm from the ranks of his bastard offspring than the Office of Intestate and Escheated Bastards could keep up with. One would have thought that after the lapse of a century or two the term would have lost its cutting edge. As the colonel remarked to the duchess who had been called "a bloody whore" by a London cabby, "I shouldn't worry, your Grace, I was in the army twenty years ago but they still call me colonel."

In Victorian England, words like "puppy," "cad," and "cur" had assumed so reprehensible a character that their application to any man signified an act of aggression capable of provoking the most heated of responses.

Today, anyone can call names. To call a person a drip, a square, a fink, an idiot, or cretin is but to follow the mode. Those more adept at words will think of vastly more refined ways of calling a man a bastard than by calling him a bastard. "Brown did you say? Oh, yes, I faintly recollect the creature. His dam I believe went in for uncertified motherhood. You were saying . . ." No form of swearing can be more devastating than that—unless it be the swearing of the contemptuous cold shower of silence, a coldness in inverse proportion to the heat it conceals. Which brings us to the subject of negative swearing.

Negative swearing, one of the least acknowledged of the fine arts, consists essentially in the use of inoffensive and gentle words in a situation so frustrating that their very triviality carries a force that could hardly be achieved by any other means. Robert Graves provides an excellent story illustrating this form of swearing.

A staff sergeant failing, after repeated swearing in the customary style of staff sergeants, to induce in a squad the supple gymnastic style he expected, gave the order to "Stand easy!" and called on the men to listen to a story. "When I was a little nipper," he began, "on my seventh birthday my dear old granny gave me a little box of wooden soldiers. Oh dear, you wouldn't imagine how pleased I was with them! I drilled them up and I drilled them down, and then one day I took them down to the seashore and lost them. Oh, you wouldn't believe how I cried! And when I came home to tea that night, late and blubbering, my dear old granny—her hair was white as snow and her soul whiter still— she says to me: 'Little Archie, cheer up!' she says. 'For God is good and one day you'll find your little wooden soldiers again.' And oh, good God, she was right, *I have*. You wooden stiffs with the paint sucked off your faces!"[10]

There is another story relating to a staff sergeant—Graves gives a version of this involving a general—which tells how on a certain day the bugler sounded the wrong call. The staff sergeant was about to let loose his figures of speech, when the forbidding eye of the colonel pulled him up quickly. With admirable presence of mind, passion choking him, his face crimson, he strode up to the bugler and, glaring upon the culprit, spoke the following words: "Oh, you naughty, naughty, naughty little trumpeter."[11]

Perhaps the most refined form of swearing is invective. This is a highly polished type of swearing, which among inferior performers takes the form of mere abuse. In the hands of a skilled artist invective combines all the qualities of irony, subtle humor, offensiveness most delicately but devastatingly put, and the complete annihilation of the subject for whom it is intended. In English parliamentary debates this form of swearing has often attained a high degree of artistry. In the House of Commons invective has taken both the long and the short forms. But it is in the shorter forms that it is best exhibited. Here is an example.

Many years ago when Sidney Webb (later Lord Passfield) had concluded a report, the member for Central Hull rose and said, "Mr. Speaker, I am not sure what I am to understand by the right honorable gentleman's report." Whereupon Sidney Webb rose and replied, "Mr. Speaker, the honorable member for Central Hell— I beg the House's pardon, Central Hull—is to understand exactly what he is capable of comprehending," and resumed his seat amid the peals of laughter that came from the benches and to the discomfiture of the unfortunate member for Central Hull.

On one occasion a rival politician remarked to John Horne Tooke (1736–1812), "I am told, Mr. Tooke, that you have all the blackguards in London with you." Tooke made instant reply, "I am happy to have it, sir, on such good authority."

To a Member of Parliament who asked John Philpot Curran (1750–1817) if he had heard his last speech, Curran replied, "I hope I have."

Of Dundas, a Member of Parliament, Richard Brinsley Sheridan (1751–1816) remarked, "He resorts to his memory for his jokes, and to his imagination for his facts."

Lord Palmerston remarked to Lord Beaconsfield in the House of Commons, "You owe the Whigs great gratitude, my lord, and therefore I think you will betray them. Your lordship is like a favorite footman on easy terms with his mistress. Your dexterity seems a happy compound of the smartness of an attorney's clerk and the intrigue of a Greek of the lower empire."

There is also Gladstone's judgment of Disraeli before he became Lord Beaconsfield, a judgment that with at least as much justice might have been applied to himself: "A sophistical rhetorician, inebriated with the exuberance of his own verbosity, and gifted with an egotistical imagination that can at all times command an interminable and inconsistent series of arguments to malign an opponent and glorify himself."

Of all the forms of swearing, invective alone lends itself to the printed page. Controversial issues often generate much heat, and only through the medium of invective can the principals concerned attack with all the wit and asperity at their disposal, for the words exchanged are in themselves of the politest. This form of swearing has both in wit and in literary craftsmanship often reached the greatest heights, both in prose and in poetry. While mere abuse may also be printed, and was frequently printed during the nineteenth century, the tendency today is to disallow it. At most, invective alone is permitted. It would today, for example, be impossible to obtain publication for such a letter as Swinburne addressed to Emerson in 1874. Actually, this letter was not published until 1918, long after the death of the two principals, when it was privately printed by T. J. Wise. I shall quote a passage from it here, merely in order to illustrate the difference between invective and abuse. Swinburne (1837–1909) had read in an American paper some abusive remarks about himself attributed to Emerson. He had written to Emerson stating that Emerson could not have been guilty of these remarks; but Emerson did not reply, whereupon Swinburne wrote the letter from which the following passage is taken.

A foul mouth is so ill-matched with a white beard that I would gladly believe the newspaper-scribes alone responsible for the bestial utterances which they declare to have dropped from a teacher whom such disciples as these exhibit to our disgust and compassion as performing on their obscene platform the last tricks of tongue now possible to a gap-toothed and hoary-headed ape, carried at first into notice on the shoulder of Carlyle, and who now in his dotage spits and chatters from a dirtier perch of his own finding and fouling; coryphaeus or choragus of his Bulgarian tribe of autocoprophagous baboons, who make the filth they feed on. . . .[12]

This is sheer abuse, and Swinburne, who was as touchy as a cat, could spit and scratch at those whom he had pretended to admire at the very slightest provocation. But when he himself was not involved, he could be as delicate and amusing in his invective as others, for example, as in his studies on Shakespeare.[13]

Compare the letter written by an American artist to an English critic with this excerpt from a letter written by an English poet to an American critic. James McNeill Whistler (1834–1903) wrote a letter to *The World*, published February 28, 1883, in which he apologized to Frederick Wedmore, who had complained that Whistler had defended himself against a criticism by misquoting "did not wish to understate Mr. Whistler's merit" as "did not wish to understand it."

... MR. FREDERICK WEDMORE—a critic—one of the wounded—complains that by dexterously substituting "understand" for "understate" I have dealt unfairly by him, and wrongly rendered his writing. Let me hasten to acknowledge the error, and apologize. My carelessness is culpable, and the misprint without excuse; for naturally I have all along known, and the typographer should have been duly warned, that with Mr. Wedmore, as with his brethren, it is always a matter of understating, and not at all one of understanding.

This is, of course, in every way a far superior performance to Swinburne's letter to Emerson. This is invective—a phrase neatly turned—and the other is mere scullion's abuse. This difference in reality signifies a very marked national disparity of taste in such matters. In England it is still considered no breach of taste to make the most personal remarks about an adversary in public debate. In America this is considered intolerable. Unfortunately, the art of invective has not flourished as well in America as it has on English soil. Yet nothing could be neater than Mark Twain's shaft aimed, characteristically, at the whole human race, "If you pick up a starving dog and make him prosperous, he will not bite you. This is the principal difference between a dog and a man."[14] Or take his comment on Chicagoans: "Satan (impatiently) to New Comer. 'The trouble with you Chicago people is that you think you are the best people down here; whereas you are merely the most numerous.' "[15]

Invective is at its best and is most immediately serving the function of swearing when it is the result of a personal and immediate frustration. When it is aimed at the representative or leader of some cause with which one is in violent disagreement, it is still invective, but there is generally a peculiar lack of passion about it, and the element of swearing is not so obvious in it.

We shall return to many more examples of invective later in this book. Meanwhile, we may draw to a conclusion our exemplifications of the kinds of words used in swearing, deduce some general law from them, and then proceed to their classification together with the forms of swearing.

We have seen, I think, that in every instance, including that of negative swearing, the words customarily used are always emotionally highly charged, while in negative swearing this charge is deliberately reversed. It happens that in polite swearing the words themselves may not be highly charged but the feeling that the swearer injects into them provides the charge suitable to the occasion. In every case there is an emotional association of some sort. This emotional association is generally an intrinsic part of the meaning of the word itself or else is extrinsically given to it either directly or by implication, as in negative swearing.

The condition that gives rise to swearing is an emotional one, and it is only through the vehicle of emotionally tinged words that it can, as a rule, express itself. Hence, *The Law of the Words Used in Swearing* is: All words possessing or capable of being given an emotional weight are the words that will generally be used for the purposes of swearing.

This means that practically all words may serve the swearer as makeweights; however, most swearers are not given to the abduction of words from their domesticated hearths, but are content to draw upon the large reserve of words that have performed time-honored service as swearwords. The swearer is not generally capricious in his choice of words, but follows along well-trodden paths. This we shall have occasion to judge for ourselves both from the examples of swearing that will be given in the pages that follow, and from the classification of the words and phrases that the swearer uses.

❴ *A Summary Classification of the Words and Phrases of the Swearer*

1. Names of supernatural or infernal powers, of gods, angels, and devils, such as God, Lord, Christ, Jesus, Jesus Christ, Jesus H. Christ, Great

Father, Merciful Father, Gracious God, Great Holy, By the Holy Spook, Great Jehovah, Gabriel, Lucifer, Beelzebub, Devil.

2. Names connected with the sacred matters of religion, such as the holy cross, the sacrament, the holy mass, God's wounds, God's blood.
3. Names or allusions to saints, priests, prophets, biblical characters, and persons conspicuous in church history, such as By the saints above, By all the saints, By the blood of the saints, Holy Mary, Holy Moses, Holy Peter, Patrick, Mark, Job, Thomas, Judas, Pope.
4. Names of sacred places, such as Jerusalem, Jericho, Goshen, the holy grave, By the Abbey.
5. Words relating to the future life, such as heavens, hell, bless, damn, and their numerous corrupted forms like, darn, dang, blast.

The above five classes of swearing sources will all be seen to have their origin in religion. Swearing, therefore, in any one of these classes constitutes *profanity*, which may be defined as the unsanctioned use of the names or attributes of the figures or objects of religious veneration. This is a general definition of profanity, and to adapt it to our purposes we need only add the words "in swearing" to the end of the last sentence. More generally, profanity is understood as the act of uttering or taking the name of God in vain, or of showing disrespect, irreverence, or contempt for sacred things.

Profanity is often confused with *blasphemy*, and this is readily understandable since it is often impossible to distinguish the one from the other. Blasphemy is defined as the act of vilifying or ridiculing the divine Being, the Bible, the Church, or the Christian religion.

It will at once be observed that an important difference between profane swearing and blasphemy lies in the fact that in the former there is generally not the slightest intention of either vilifying or ridiculing anything in any way connected with religion. On the other hand, the fact that the swearer borrows his words from religious sources may be taken as a token of his tacit respect for them. His misdemeanor lies in the fact that he has not shown the sufficient respect to refrain from their employment on unsanctioned occasions for unsanctioned purposes. In swearing by sacred things the swearer hardly ever dreams of showing disrespect, irreverence, or contempt for the things he swears by—when he does, he is a blasphemer. And that is the difference between profanity and blasphemy.

It will readily be seen, however, that it would be no difficult matter to show that profanity and swearing actually amount to one and the same thing. In reality they do not, as has been recognized by the courts of most countries in which profanity is generally treated as a common-law or statutory offense, while blasphemy is treated as a crime. In the ecclesiastical law of England and in the Puritan Commonwealths in Colonial America, profanity was punishable as blasphemy.

Profanity is also often confused with obscenity, but obscene swearing and profane swearing are very different things, for the one makes use of the sacred while the other employs the indecent. Concerning the origin of the indecent, as well as of the modesty that came into being to replace it, the following opinion of the courts of the United States deserves wider attention than it has thus far received. This opinion was handed down in 1877 in the case of *Ardery* v. *the State*.

Immediately after the fall of Adam there seems to have sprung up in the mind an idea that there was such a thing as decency, . . . and since that time, the idea of decency and indecency have [sic] been instinctive in and, indeed, a part of humanity. And it historically appears that the first most palpable piece of indecency in the human being was the first public exposure of his or her, as now commonly called privates; and the first exercise of mechanical ingenuity was the manufacture of fig-leaf aprons by Adam and Eve, in which to conceal from the public gaze of each other, their now but not then called privates. This example of covering their privates has been imitated by all mankind since that time, except perhaps by some of the lowest grades of savages. Modesty has existed as one of the most estimable and admirable of human virtues.[16]

This solemn and informative opinion should tell the reader more than whole volumes could why the obscene is indecent and the indecent is obscene. Possibly it is because of the character and opinion of such "nice people" as the judge who delivered himself of this masterpiece?

The term "profane," means, very briefly, the abuse of anything sacred. *Fanum* referred originally to a temple or consecrated place, and any act of desecration within or before it was termed "profane."

We may conclude, then, that the profane swearer is not, during his profanity at least, either a blasphemer or an obscene swearer. Indeed, strictly speaking, blasphemous swearing is quite impossible except to a casuist, for the swearer never really vilifies or ridicules the holy. Obscene swearing is, of course, a fact, but it has its origins in sources very different from those upon which profanity draws.

There is another source of swearing which derives its power from the peculiar geographic position at which the borderlands of the religious and the secular meet. This lies in

6. The names of ancestors and heroes, such as By the blood of my ancestors, By all those who came before me, By the blood of my father, By the ashes of George Washington, By my father's ghost, By George (Saint George, the patron saint and hero of England), By the ghost of my grandmother, By the ghost of Priam, By my father's sword, By my dead father. (These oaths can, of course, be rendered as expletives.)

There are also the forms of swearing by

7. The names of a ruler, sovereign, or symbol of authority, or the attributes of any of these, such as By Augustus Caesar, By the King's head, By the Royal Robe, By the power of the King, In the name of the King, By the Kingly Crown, By the purple robe, Peter the Great, By the great United States, Christopher Columbus, Amerigo Vespucci, Daniel Webster.

All the forms of swearing referred to in the three preceding classes derive their force from the power of animate beings or the objects that they have invested with power. There is, however, a class of swearing that draws its power from the realm of the natural inanimate. This is

8. Oaths by natural objects, forces, and phenomena, such as the sun, moon, stars, the man in the moon, the holy blue, thunder and lightning, blood and thunder, the hurricane, Harry cane, great clouds, the boiling sea. (The common German oath *Donnerwetter* is an example of this class.)

Still another class of swearwords are derived from the power that attaches to the prurient, to parts and functions of the body that are not ordinarily mentioned in polite society and to which reference in vulgar words is regarded as obscene. This is the class of

9. Vulgar or obscene words, such as shit, fuck, cunt, arsehole, piss, tit, tail, whore, ponce, pimp.

A further class of swearwords must be created for the reception of a single word and its various forms. A word that is forbidden —no one knows why—eminently a swearword and a remarkable proof of the fact that that which is forbidden assumes an importance simply because it is forbidden is the word "bloody." This is a vulgar word, but it is not vulgar in the same sense as the words which fall into class 8; it is in a class by itself, so much so that we shall devote a chapter to its discussion. We have then

10. The word "bloody" and its various forms, such as bleeding, blooming, blankety, blinking, bleeder.
11. Expletives, including words or phrases having unusual force for various reasons, such as Stap my vitals, Blow me down, Shiver my timbers, Confound it, Hang it, Gracious, Goodness.

Classes 7–11 are sources from which the modern swearer still derives his materials. A good proportion of the many hundreds of words and phrases that form these materials, as well as their euphemistic forms, will be considered in the pages that follow. But since this book is a history as well as an anatomy of swearing, it will be necessary to consider here the additional classes of swearing that have more or less become obsolete as sources for the modern swearer but that served swearers in former days truly and well.

12. Oaths in the names of classical divinities, such as, By Jupiter, Jove, Zeus, Mars, Pluto, Ammon, All the Furies, Furiation.
13. Oaths by animals, plants, and their products, such as By beans, turnips, gum, tar, by the duck, goose, hen, the plane tree, the cabbage, the bulls of Bashan, the golden calf, mustard, the dog, cat, mackerel, codfish.
14. Oaths in the name of valued personal attributes or inanimate symbols of honor, such as By my truly, By my sincerity, By my maidenhead, By my honor, By my halidome, By my sword, Honest Injun.

The cursing or denunciatory oath makes use of all these sources, so that there is no distinction upon this ground between swearing and cursing.

Having now considered the sources of swearing, let us proceed to the definition and classification of the forms of swearing.

⟨ *The Classification of the Forms of Swearing*

In order to clarify the sense in which the terms descriptive of the various forms of swearing will be used in the following pages, and to reduce the confusion that at present exists as to the forms and character of swearing, it will be necessary here to define them with some precision. A good deal of the ground we have already traversed will therefore be summarily retraversed here.

Swearing is the act of verbally expressing the feeling of aggressiveness that follows upon frustration in words possessing strong emotional associations.

Cursing, often used as a synonym for swearing, is a form of swearing distinguished by the fact that it invokes or calls down some evil upon its object.

Profanity, often used as a synonym for swearing and cursing, is the form of swearing in which the names or attributes of the figures or objects of religious veneration are uttered.

Blasphemy, often identified with cursing and profanity, is the act of vilifying or ridiculing the figures or objects of religious veneration. Although it has been identified by the Church, and in the past by the State, with profanity, it is better to distinguish between them on the ground that the profane swearer *intends* no blasphemy. It may be held that profanity *is* blasphemy, but most authorities—that is, profane swearers—will not agree. It is only in the opinion of a cleric, accustomed to the use of language having theological implications that profanity might be held to be identical with blasphemy. We shall not here treat of blasphemy as a form of swearing, although we do not deny that it may on occasion be so, but such occasions are extremely rare.

Obscenity, a form of swearing that makes use of indecent words and phrases.

Vulgarity, a form of swearing that makes use of crude words, such as *bloody*.

Euphemistic swearing, a form of swearing in which mild, vague, or corrupted expressions are substituted for the original strong ones.

Swearing may be abusive, adjurative, asseverative, ejaculatory, exclamatory, execratory, expletive, hortatory, interjectional, or objurgatory.

Abusive swearing is swearing in which words are hurled at another as one would hurl dirt. It is the lowest form of swearing.

Adjurative swearing is swearing closely akin to cursing, taking such forms as "You can go to hell if you won't believe it," or the self-adjurative form "May God blast my soul if I don't do as you say." It is a charge to the soul on pain of the wrath of the powers-that-be.

Asseverative swearing is swearing by solemn affirmative, which can hardly be distinguished from the adjurative form.

Ejaculatory and *Exclamatory swearing* is any form of swearing uttered in a single or a few words, such as *Damn!* and *God damn it*.

Execratory swearing is swearing in the form of a curse.

Expletive swearing is similar to ejaculatory and exclamatory swearing, but may be distinguished from them by the fact that the word used serves to act as a "filler," as "It's not so *damn* likely."

Hortatory swearing is swearing in the form of an appeal in the name of a venerated figure or an honored attribute, as in the expressions "For the love of Christ," "For pity's sake," "In the name of all that is good."

Interjectional swearing is practically identical with expletive swearing, differing only in that whereas the interjected word is one thrown in among others to lend the sentence greater emotional weight, the expletive may merely be a weak stopgap word.

Objurgatory swearing is chiding or berating swearing, having the purpose of administering a reforming rebuke.

Rather than consider in separate chapters the sources and forms of swearing that we have briefly outlined in this chapter, we shall treat them as they occur in the history of their use.

CHAPTER SEVEN

The History of Swearing: Before the Reformation

‹‹‹›››››››››››››››››››››››››››››››››››

He could nothing say without swearing.
DAN MICHAEL, *Ayenbite of Inwyt*, 1340

İN earlier chapters of this book something of the history of swearing in antiquity has been dealt with. In the present chapter we shall devote ourselves to a consideration of the history of English swearing from the earliest recorded evidences of it to the Reformation.

British swearing was probably greatly enriched by the Roman legionnaires after the Roman conquest of the first century A.D. But whatever new oaths the Britons acquired from the Romans cannot have matched either in quantity or in quality those which they were able to invent for themselves after the introduction of Christianity into their pagan islands. This event may be dated from Whitsunday, June 2, 597, when Ethelbert of Kent received Christian baptism at the hands of Augustine and was followed by thousands of his subjects.[1] Augustine was, it is of interest to note, an early opponent of profane swearing, summing up the view of the Church with unnecessary severity in the solemn passage, "Non minus peccant qui blasphemant Christum ambulantum in terris" ("They sin no less who blaspheme Christ the wanderer on earth"). It was Ethelbert who, doubtless due to the influence of Augustine, about the year 600 reduced to writing the old customary laws of the Cantwara and so gave us the first formal record of the laws of an English people. In these laws codes and penalties relating to swearing are to be found; the penalties were comparatively light.

The code governing the penalties prescribed for swearing in the northern districts of Britain were far more severe. By the statutes of Donald VI and Kenneth II the penalty of cutting out the tongue was inflicted upon swearers. Such a stringent penalty strongly suggests that swearing had already become something of an intolerable abuse.

With the Norman conquest of Britain in 1066 British swearing received a large addition of new words to its armory. The conqueror himself was said to have been a most accomplished swearer, his favorite oath being *By the splendor of God*. His son, William Rufus, preferred the oath *By the Holy Face of Lucca*, that is, by the wonder-working crucifix of that city. With such examples before them we can have no doubt that the conquered Saxon thanes and their erstwhile subjects would not lag far behind. The Normans sought to impose their language upon the subject people, and we may be sure that the words of the foreign language that left their most durable impression were the oaths and imprecations—in fact, most of the words expressing violence, frustration, and aggression.

Henry I (1068–1135), son of William the Conqueror, is said to have prescribed the following fines for swearing within the precincts of the royal residence: a duke, 40 shillings; a lord, 20 shillings; a squire, 10 shillings; a yeoman, 3s. 4d.; a page, a whipping.[2]

A Norman oath that soon became naturalized in England was *Datheit*. The original Merovingian French oath was *Deu hat (God's hate)*. The modern *dash it* is not the descendant of this oath, but the euphemistic form *damn it* is.

One of the most popular Norman oaths was the exclamation *Deus!* This was soon adopted by the English, and it has even been suggested that it today circulates among us as *deuce*,[3] but there is some reason to doubt this on historical and other grounds, of which more will be said later. That this expression was widely used throughout the land is attested by the fact that it occurs in miracle plays of the twelfth and thirteenth centuries and in the great metrical romance *Havelok the Dane*, of which the English version appeared in the thirteenth century. Here are some examples of its use in these works.

"Owe! what I am derworth and defte.—Owe! dewes! all goes downe!"[4]
Miracle Plays, I, 92

"'Deus!' quoth Ubbe, 'hwat may this be!'"[5]

Havelok the Dane

It should be observed that the word is not directly related to the Latin vocative, but derives immediately from the French *deus*.

To swear by the supreme deity, or by its medieval Christ, must already have been a common practice in England by the time of the Norman conquest, for in the earliest records we have of such expressions (from the eleventh, twelfth, and thirteenth centuries), they occur frequently. There can be very little doubt that in this practice English swearing received a tremendous fillip from the imported French forms. In France the problem of profane swearing during this period had already greatly exercised the ecclesiastical authorities, as is evident from the following discussion written by Petrus Cantor, Precenter of Notre Dame, in the middle of the thirteenth century.

Now, some oaths are spoken in careless haste, and others deliberately. Men plead that the first is a jesting word; yet it would seem to be a crime. For a plain word, spoken by itself would suffice to convey the jest; therefore the addition of an oath maketh it something more than a jest. Moreover the oath hath three concomitants; truth, judgment and justice; yet this nasty oath hath not such concomitants; wherefore it is perjury. Further, at the courts of certain princes it is forbidden under a standing penalty of five *sols*, to swear by the Lord's limbs. Yet some men are distinguished from their fellows and characterized, as it were, by their own particular and execrable oath.[6]

Here one may observe the age-old struggle between the judicial and the sporting oath, the reaction of each upon the other being the debasement of both.

A valuable source of information on medieval swearing is the English Dominican John Bromyard's *Summa Predicantium*, a compendium of the gathered fruits of mendicant preaching throughout the fourteenth century. The bulk of the material this work contains is drawn from the thirteenth century. The *Summa* was written some time between 1323 and 1350 and contains many pulpit satires on the swearer, among others.

When knighthood was in flower during the twelfth century, Peter of Blois, Archdeacon of Bath and later of London, had some scorching things to say of the knights of his day. Peter (*c.* 1135–1204) was the author of *Epistolae*, a favorite homiletic source for later generations. Quoting from Peter, Bromyard observes, "Forsooth, the order of Knighthood now is to observe no Order. For, his mouth is polluted with great foulness of words who swears the more detestably and fears God the less, who vilifies God's ministers and has no respect for the Church." It is a common accusation, among many others, against the knights who constantly crucified Christ with their every other word, as the preacher says, mocking Him of his garments, slaying and losing him afresh.

As for "ribalds and vile persons," says Bromyard, "If they chance to have seen some new vogue or eccentricity among any people, in any city or land, in the cutting of cloth, the wearing of large beards, or in oaths and so forth," they must at once adopt it for themselves. "These inventors of new oaths," Bromyard says, "who inanely glory in such things, and count themselves the more noble for swearing thus . . . just as they invent and delight in everything of the nature of outward apparel, so do they also in the case of vows and oaths. . . . Strange vows and swear-words invented by them are already so common that they may be found daily in the mouth of any ribald or rascal you please."

The attack on swearing is a conspicuous pulpit commonplace throughout medieval times. As G. R. Owst says, "In whatever sermon-collection the reader chooses to look, there he will find the preacher's expatiation on the wrongs of 'false swearing.'"[7]

The Englishman's fondness for strong words is not less ancient than his fondness for strong drink, and the swearer and his ways seem to have changed little through the centuries. Who is there who will not recognize those who, as Bromyard says, "scarce speak a few words without adding a vow or an oath." Friar John Waldeby, in a sermon, mourned:

Christ's blood, these days, is reckoned of little price amongst the greater part of the people. For, if one comes into the market-place or the tavern where these infernal dogs, that is to say, the swearers are, one will find Christ's blood held at so small a price and in such little reverence among them that scarcely a single word will escape their lips—be it true or false—without mention by name of the blood of Christ in an oath along with it. . . . And not only Christ's blood, but all the members of Christ.[8]

The swearer listened to the exhortations of his spiritual pastor with no more devotion than he has ever done, so that the way of his would-be reformers was always difficult and unrewarding.

The reformers never gave up, but continued to rebuke the swearer unremittingly and unrelentingly. *Virtute prevaelibit.*

Bromyard felt that it was not enough to bemoan the spread of this terrible vice of swearing. He suggested that this offense be visited with special penalties such as those decreed by Saint Louis of France, "who ordered such to be branded upon the face with a hot iron for a perpetual memorial of their crime, and later on, indeed, ordained that they should be set in a public place in the high stocks, which in their tongue are called *escale*, similar in form and in mode of punishment to that inflicted upon cut-purses in England." He adds that in the kingdom of Sicily the tongues of such swearers were ordered cut out, and he observes, "If princes and lords of the present day would now decree such penalties in every country against those giving vent to foul oaths, they would amend them quicker than the preachers. For the offenders would quit their evil habits more speedily for fear of punishments to be felt than for fear of those eternal punishments with which the preachers threaten them."

From the purely literary sources, I shall list examples of oaths in the name of the Supreme Being, his body and attributes. The Middle English works from which these examples are taken can only be dated approximately, but the century as given can generally be relied upon to be correct.

> God it wite, he shall ben ded,
> Wile I taken non other red
> > *Havelok the Dane*, 517, 8 (1250)

> "Goddot!" quoth Grim, "this is ure eir
> That shal ben lonerd of Denemark."
> > *Havelok the Dane*, 606, 7 (1250)

> "Goddoth!" quoth Lene, "Y shal the fete
> Bred and chese, butere and milk."
> > *Havelok the Dane*, 642, 3 (1250)

God it wite later became *God wight*, and *Goddot* and *Goddoth* are preserved in *God wot.*

> Be god, there wolde y fayne bee.
> > *Benes of Hamtoun* (1340)

God wet ssolle we do.

> *Dan Michel of Northgate* (1340)

"For gode," quoth Benes, "that ich do nelle!"

> *Benes of Hamtoun* (1340)

God a mercy, Symontt that thou wylt me knowe!

> *Miracle Plays*, 619

"So me helpe god!" quoth Benes tho,
"Hit were no meistri me to slo!"

> *Benes of Hamtoun* (1340)

Y name no truant, be godes grace!

> *Benes of Hamtoun* (1340)

"For godes love," she said nai!

> *Benes of Hamtoun* (1340)

Be godes name. I have for thee sofred meche schame.

> *Benes of Hamtoun* (1340)

As Havelok said:

> Soth is that men seyth and swereth:
> Ther God with helpen, nought ne dereth.
>
> *Havelok the Dane*, II, 686–687

The forms of Christ, Lord, and Jesus are all to be found in the literature of the fourteenth century. In *Benes of Hamtoun* we take, at random, *For Crystes ore, Lorde Jesu Cryst, Cryste*. In Chaucer's *Canterbury Tales* (1386), we have *For Cristes saule*. Some idea of the kind of oaths that were fashionable in Chaucer's day (1340–1400) may be obtained from the following passage from the *Canterbury Tales*. When the Man of Law had ended his pathetic tale of Dame Constance, then

> Oure Hoste upon his stiropes stode anon,
> And syde, "Good men, herkeneth, everichon!
> This was a thrifty tale for the nones!
> Sir Parish Prest," quod he, "for Goddes bones,
> Tell us a tale . . . by Goddës dignitee!"
> That Persone him answérde, "*Benedicte!*
> What eyleth the man, so sinfully to swere?"
> Our Hoste answérde, "O Jankyn, be ye there?
> I smelle a Loller in the wind," quod he.

"Nowe, good men," quod our Hostë, "herkeneth me,
Abydeth, for Goddës dignë passioun,
For we shul han a predicacioun;
This Loller here wol prechen us somewhat."
"Nay, by my fader soule, that shal he nat!"
Seyde the Shipman, "herë shal he nat preche;
He shal no gospel glosen herë, ne teche.
We leven alle in the grete God," quod he,
"We wolde sowen som difficulte,
Or sprengen cokkel in our clenë corn."

As G. G. Coulton, the distinguished medievalist, remarked upon this passage, it "might seem a mere caricature if we had not abundant corroboration from episcopal Registers and similar formal documents."[9] The Lollard was shocked and wished to preach a sermon on the evils of swearing, but the Shipman would have none of it. And even Chaucer could pretend to be shocked, as may be judged from the following verse:

Hir othes been so grete and so dampnable
That it is grisly for to heere hem swere;
Our blessed Lordes body they to-tere;
Hem thought that Jewes rente hum nought ynough,
And ech of hem at others synne lough.
                    "Pardoner's Tale," 472–476

And again he writes

And forther over, I wol thee telle, al plat,
"That vengeance shal nat parten from his hous
"That of hise othes is to outrageous,—
" 'By Goddes precious herte,' and 'By his nayles,'
"And 'By the blood of Crist that is in Hayles,'
"Sevene is my chaunce, and thyn is cynk and treye,
"By Goddes armes, if thou falsly pleye,
"This daggere shal thurghout thyn herte go!"
                    "Pardoner's Tale," 648–655

From these verses we see that *God, Lord* and *Christ* are indiscriminately employed to denote *Jesus.* Chaucer's vivid lines also indicate something of the dimensions to which the habit of swearing had grown in fourteenth-century England, and something of the disrepute into which it had fallen. This disrepute seems to have been brought about entirely by the clergy, who held that it was breaking the commandment of God, was profane, blasphemous, and perjurous. But the swearers held their own, and they could, when necessary, adduce biblical authority against the clergy and in support of swearing. For this purpose they were accustomed to appeal to I Cor., 15: 31, where Saint Paul wrote, "I protest by your rejoicing which I have in Jesus Christ our Lord, I die daily." As Petrus Cantor pointed out, they also adduced Heb. 6: 16, "For men verily swear by the greater: and an oath for confirmation is to them an end of all strife." They might further have cited, and probably did, the example of God himself swearing by himself, as in Heb. 6: 13, "For when God made promise to Abraham, because he could swear by no greater, he sware by himself."

In pre-Reformation England men no more swore because they were impious than they have ever done. The Englishman in that period was a rather more religious character than his modern counterpart. Stricken and toilworn, having no hope save in forbearance from the skies and no consolation but in the repose of the alehouse, drenched to the bone in superstition, he could be easily awed and subdued by the practiced masters in the arts of dreadful suggestion and ghostly terrorism. By dint of the monastic teaching, the Englishman had been brought to a state in which he experienced a keen personal realization of the actual sufferings and tortures of Christ. As Sharman remarks:

The fact is self-evident from every fragment of contemporaneous literature intended to react upon the fears and sympathies of uncultivated men. It was the constant presentment of the notion of the divine agony, the daily calling to remembrance of the thorns, the nails, and the hyssop, that was relied upon to keep alive in these poor agued souls some struggling flame of spiritual vitality. And so surely was the spark wont to kindle, and so reverently was the similitude of these priestly images treasured up, that they formed the mainstay of the ploughman's faith, the sum total of the poor man's theology.[10]

Thus, the medieval Englishman's passionate images draw largely upon the priestly language in which the life of Christ, and particularly his agony and sufferings, had been revealed to him.

It was in this manner that, laboring under the ban of priestly exaction and confronted on all sides by the ghostly emblems of wrath and condemnation, there descended upon England in the thirteenth and fourteenth centuries a torrent of abuse such as it has witnessed neither before nor since. Not mere words of intemperate anger came bubbling to the surface, but sullen and defiant blasphemies, execrations that proclaimed open warfare with authority and a lasting separation from everything that was gentle and decent in men's faith. Imprecations were contrived from every incident in the narrative of the crucifixion. Every limb and member and every wound and last drop of blood of the slain Christ was made the vehicle of the swearer's oaths.

> It is grisly for to heere hem swere,
> Oure blessed Lordes body they to-tere.

When Chaucer penned these lines the abuse was already more than a hundred years old, as was the opposition and resentment that it aroused. The modern reader can have no idea of the truly daring and, to a religious community of medieval England, horribly blasphemous nature of such an oath as *Zounds!* This oath, which has now been obsolete for more than a century, will remind the reader of Restoration plays and eighteenth-century comedies and novels, but in unreformed England—the England that still adored the *Genetrix incorrupta* and had earned among the devout the title of Our Lady's Dower—it was absolutely impossible to surpass in blasphemy the hideous import of the word or the moral degradation of the user. It was, in fact, nothing else than a rebellious and mutinous rendering of the once sacred oath taken by the wounds of the Redeemer. The legends relating to the five wounds in the body of Christ at this time occupied a conspicuous place in Catholic worship. In Church furniture, crucifixes, and stone carvings, in rosaries and Books of Hours, the monkish representations of the wounds found a universal motive of religious art. So holy had the conception of the wounds become that confraternities were formed in the Church for their greater veneration. There were occasions when papal absolution was specially extended to those worshipers who paid their devotions to the wounds in Christ's side. The so-called measurement of these was even preserved in families and was reputed to be a charm.[11] In the great northern revolt of 1536, following the carrying out of Henry's act of supremacy of two years earlier, which marked the beginning of the English Reformation, the Five Wounds was the badge under which the York and Lincoln farmers marched in their "Pilgrimage of Grace." The complete break with the Romanist faith was not, however, established until well into the reign of Henry's daughter Elizabeth—herself a good swearer in the Romanist tradition. But of these matters we shall speak further in due course.

Of the oaths most widely used in pre-Reformation England (that is, up to the year 1534) and that did not sensibly decline until the end of the sixteenth century, the following samples are culled from the contemporary literature.

By God's blessed angel, God's arms, God's limbs, God's body, God's bodykins, By God's precious bones, By God's bones, God's bread, By God's dear brother, By Godde's corps, By Godde's cross, God's death, By God's precious deer, By Goddes dignitie, By God's dentie, By God's dines (dignesse, or dignity), 'sdeins, By Goddy's dome, By God's fast, God's vast, God's fate, God's fish, By God's foot, For Godde's herte, By gode's grace, By God's guts, God's hat (heart?), By God's heart, God's precious Lady, God's lady, By God's lid, God's life, God's light, God's Lord, Godes love, God's malt, God's nails, God's good mercy, Be God's name, Godsnigs, By God's passion, For the passion of God, By God's pity, By Goddys pyne, By God's precious, God's sacrament, Sacrament of God, For God's sake, God's santy, By God's side, By God's soul, By God's will, God's word, God's wounds, By God's glorious wounds, God for his passion.[12]

God, it will be observed from the above partial list, was almost always used to signify Christ. The expressions for the most part explain themselves. *Bodykins* is formed from *body* after the pattern of *manikin* or *pipkin*, as a diminutive. *Dentie* is a corruption of *dygnitee*. *Lid* does service for *eyelids*, *light* for *lightning*, *santy* for *sanctity*, and *nigs* for *nails*.

An early corruption of *God* was *Gog* and also *Cock*. The forms *Gog* and *Cock* were all in use in pre-Reformation England with the same expressions as those given above. We have already noted the plural form *cokkes* used by Chaucer. It is unnecessary to give any further examples here.[13] The forms *Gad, Ged, Gud,* belong essentially to the seventeenth century, as do the forms *Cod, Cot,* and many others to which we shall return later.

To swear by the *Lord* was not uncommon in medieval England, but by no means was it as common as by *God* and its corruptions.

> Lorde, that wemen be crabbed aye,
> And non are meke, I dare well saye.
> *Miracle Plays*, II, 105, 106

Swearing by Christ and by Jesus was very common, and what are presumably corruptions of *Jesus*—*Jis, Gis*—seem first to have arisen in the early sixteenth century. It has been supposed that these corrupt forms originated from the letters IHS, but this seems extremely unlikely. The modern expression *Jeeze*, an obvious corruption of *Jesus*, is sufficiently like the medieval *Jis* and *Gis*, to account for the simple origin of these latter from the same source.

> Sheathe your whittle, or by Jis that was never born,
> I will rap you on the cotard with my horn.
>   *Hickscorner*, 168, 15

At the end of the sixteenth century Shakespeare makes use of this oath:

> OPHELIA: Indeed, la? without an oath, I'll make an end on't:
>   [*Sings*]
>   By Gis and By Saint Charity
>   Alack, and fie for shame!
>   Young men will do't, if they come to't;
>   By cock, they are to blame.
>   Quoth she, before you tumbled me,
>   You promised me to wed.
>   *Hamlet*, IV, v

Into these lines, it will be noted, Shakespeare has contrived to "compress" two oaths, *Gis* for *Jesus* and *cock* for *God*, both "compressed" or corrupted forms.

In the Middle Ages *Mary* and all the saints were frequently invoked, but after the Reformation *Mary* was corrupted to *marry*, and references to the saints were to a very large extent dropped; the patron saint of England, Saint George, was almost the only one honored in the swearer's calendar. By the end of the eighteenth century the form *marry* was already an archaism. To the modern reader it will probably be most familiar through the plays of Shakespeare.

By our Lady and all its corrupted forms—*By'r Lady, Berlady, Birladie, By Lady, Belakin, Byrlakyn, Berlaken, By'r Laken*—were in use before the Reformation and persisted for long after in various corrupt forms. It was reported in 1884 in the form *By'r Leddie* among the farmers, none of whom were Catholics, near Ludlow in Shropshire.[14]

Heaven, Hell, the mass, and the sacrament, of course, figured largely in the swearer's armamentarium, *mass* being retained after the Reformation in the form *mess*.

In the form of an expletive or interjection the devil also received his due, and we find the form *dickens* as early as Shakespeare's *Merry Wives of Windsor* (1598):

> I cannot tell what the dickens his name is.
>   III, ii

The form *deuce* is not recorded till 1651, when it occurs in Thomas Randolph's play *Hey For Honesty*:

> But a deuce on him, it does not seem so.
>   II, i

To swear by the *faith* and by the *troth* and by the variant forms of these attributes was very common. *Faith* appeared in the forms *fey, fay, fait, By the faith of my body, By faith, In faith, I'faith, My faith and truth, Good faith, Faith and troth, By my fackings, By my feckings, By my fac, By my feck, Faikins. Troth* took very similar forms: *Of troth, Bum troth (By my troth), a' my troth, By my truth.*

To swear by the parts of the body, the soul, and attributes such as humor and thriftiness was common practice in the Middle Ages, as the following examples will show.

Be min hore berd (By my hoary beard), Be my snowte (snout), Be me swere, By my hals, Heart o' me, By my head, By thy life, a my life, Body o'me, By this precious body, By this hand, By this hand, flesh and blood, By my blood, Beshrew your heart, By these bones, By these ten bones (i.e., the ten fingers), Man's bones and sides, By my father's soul, By the light, On my soul, Passion of my heart, Passion of me, On my honesty, By my virginity, Be my threft (thrift), Death of me, On mine honour, By this light, By this good light, By this day, By this fire.[15]

It will be observed that quite a good proportion of the pre-Reformation oaths listed in the preceding pages persisted in England up to very recent times; the majority of them, however, were already obsolete by the beginning of the seventeenth century. Long before this period there had appeared in England, in 1303, a moralistic work that dealt at great length with the abuse of swearing, Robert of Brunne's *Handlyng Synne*.[16] This work was

founded on the earlier thirteenth-century work of William of
Waddington, the *Manuel des Pechiez*. Since Robert of Brunne's
English would scarcely be understandable to the modern reader,
I have translated many of his words into a more readily com-
prehensible form.

Against Swearing Oaths

If thou were ever so foolhardy
To swear great oaths grisly,
As we foolish do all day,
Dismember Jesu all that we may.
Gentle man, for great gentry,
Deem that great oaths be courtesy,
Using, blood, feet and eyen
They scorn Jesu, and upbraid his pain.
Of his wounds he hath upbraid,
Our shame it is that it is said,
All that he suffered for our frame,
As in upbraiding we say him shame,
His flesh, his blood, he shed for thee;
Wounds he suffered to make thee free;
So much is our shame the more
That we oft pain him so sore.
And so men fall more in plight
That swear oaths false or right,
By any member of his manhood
Bynethyn the girdle, I thee forbid
For I have heard men swear such oaths
To think on them, forsooth I loathe.
A little tale I shall you tell
That I heard once a farar tell.

[The Tale of the Bloody Child]

It was once a rich man
That great oaths swore bygan;
For rich men use commonly
To swear great oaths grisly.
This rich man would not let
But that he swore ever oaths great.
An evil took him on a day,
That he sick on his bed lay;
A night, as he lay alone,
A woman he heard make her moan;

This woman came him before
With a child in her arms bore
Of the child that she bare in her arms
All to-drawn were the guts;
Of hands, of feet, the flesh off drawn
Mouth, eyes and nose, were all to-knawan,
Back and sides were all bloody.
This woman sorrowful was, and sorry.
This man for her wax sore agrysyn;
He spoke, when he was rising,
"What art thou woman, that makest such cry?
Who hath made thy child so bloody?"
"Thou," she said, "has him so shent,
And with thy oaths all to-rent.
Thus hast thou drawn my dear child,
With thy oaths wicked and wild;
And thou makest me sore too great
That thou thine oaths wilt not let.
His manhood, that he took for thee,
Thou painest it, as thou mayest see;
Thine oaths done him more grieviousness
Than all the Jews wickedness.
They pained him once, and passed away,
But thou painest him every day.
The pain, he suffered for thy good,
And thou upbraidest him of the rood;
All his flesh then thou tearest,
When thou falsely by him swearest;
And I am ever so in mind
For to pray for all mankind.
How should I longer pray for thee,
So ruly makest thou him to be,
And others many more than thou;
How should I then be meek to you?"
The caitiff that lay in his bed
For her seeing wax sore adread,
And said, "if it be thy will,
Help me, lady, that I not spill.
For all men see, O thou lady,
That thou art mother of mercy!"
She answered to the caitiff,
"In false oaths is all thy life;
What mercy mayst thou ask the right
When thou thus my son hast dight?"

"Lady, all my oaths great
From this forward will I let;
And preach to every man thy lore,
That they oaths swear no more."
"If thou wilt of oaths blynne
Then will I pray for thy sin,
That they may thee be forgive,
And do penance when thou art shryve
For all men that haunt great oaths,
To help them at need, certes I loathe;
And my son would not hear
For false oaths, any prayer;
For he commandeth to more and less
'Swear not his name in idleness.'"
This woman with her child away went;
Blessed be she without end!

For them that be of oaths bold
For them have I this tale told.
These gentlemen, these getters,
They be but God's tormentors;
They torment him all that they may,
With false oaths night and day.
But ye [who] love your false swearing,
Your unkind upbraiding,
Ye shall go a devil way
But ye amend ye, or ye die.
For every gadling not worth a pear
Takes example at you to swear,
So every man unto other—
The poor to the rich in brother—
In oaths and in wicked heed,
The toon the tother to hell I shall lead.

If thou ever swore by our lady,
In any time false or wickedly,
Hastily thee therefrom withdraw
Vengeance cometh for such that saw.
When thou swearest by her that he lied in,
He takes more to wrath that sin.
Than thou misdeedest against him
With word or deed never so grim.
And as much, he to him maketh
That her worshippeth or her beseecheth.

Thus saith Saint Anselme, that it wrote
To these clerks that well it wote.
More dread is, by her to swear,
Than is by him that she did bear;
Sooner he taketh for her vengeance
Than for any other chance:
That shall I show when we be went
Unto the third commandment.
If thou be at all right canst hear
Two things therein mayst thou lere:
The toon is, 'hold well thine holiday';
The tother, 'our lady thou worship ay.'
Now shall we have our oaths swearing,
And speak further of other thing,
We shall oft touch of this sin
When we be come further within.

Clearly, by the end of the thirteenth century swearing had in England, as in France, become a widespread habit seriously disconcerting to the clerical authorities. This is also to be inferred from another work that appeared in France during the thirteenth century and was translated into English toward the middle of the fourteenth century. This moralistic work, written in the Kentish dialect and completed in 1340[17] by the monk Dan Michel, a brother of the Cloister of Saint Austin, at Canterbury, contained an attack on the profane habit of swearing and provides us with an excellent insight into the contemporary habit of swearing and the prejudices that existed against it. Entitled *Ayenbite of Inwyt* (*The Again-Biting of the Inner Wit*, or *The Remorse of Conscience*), it is for the most part a literal translation of a French treatise entitled *Le Somme des vices et des vertues*, sometimes incorrectly styled *Le Miroir du monde*, composed in 1279 by Frère Lorens of the order of Friars Preachers for the use of Philip II of France. The *Ayenbite* is essentially a devotional manual. With swearing Dan Michel deals in a painstaking manner. There are seven modes of swearing according to our author: (1) bold swearing, (2) needful swearing, (3) light swearing, (4) habitual swearing, (5) foolish swearing, (6) swearing by God and his saints, and (7) false swearing.

The bold swearer is "him that likes to swear." The needful swearer is "the one that obeyeth saint Jacob 'ne swear nat: but when it is need." The light swearer is the one who swears "for

nought and without scale, that is forbidden in the other command of the laws that God wrote in the tables of stone with
his finger." The habitual swearer is one who swears

by habit [or custom], as at each word. For some are so evil taught that
they can say nothing without swearing. They hold God in great unworship
[contempt] when all day and for nought him call to witness of all that
is said, for swearing is no other thing but calling God to witness, and
his mother and his holy ones [halzen]. Again one may swear foolishly,
and that in many ways. Or when one swears in anger and suddenly,
whereof he repents afterwards. Or when one swears for things that one
may not keep without sin. Such oath one shall break: and do penance
for such foolish oath. Or when one swears confidently of things without
being certain of the truth. Or in promising what one cannot fulfil; and
swearing by the sun that shines, by the fire that burns, or by mine head,
or by mine father's soul, or other such like. Such oaths God forbids in
his Gospel. For that I shall make certain. I shall not draw to witness
but pane high truth which is God that al wot, not the pure sheep that
nothing buy but idleness. And when I swear by the thought: I bear to
them in worship what I should bear only to God. But when one swears
by the Gospel, one swears by him that the words bye and bye writ.
And when we swear by the holy relics and by the saints of Paradise:
we swear by them and by God what in them accustoms. Afterwards
when we swear villanously by God and his Saints, in this sin are the
Christians worse than the Saracens that would not swear in any manner
nor would endure that any one swear before them so wickedly by Jesu
Crist: as do the Christians. They be more worse than the Jewes who
crucified him. They broke none of his bones. But these him do break
smaller than one doth swine in butchery. These forbear nought our Lady,
and in pieces her do break more wickedly, and her and the other holy
ones, that it is a wonder how Cristendom bears it. Afterwards when one
swears falsely, or when one bears false witness, or one swears falsely
knowingly in such manner that one swears openly or stealthily by art
or by sophistry. For as the holy writ say, God loves meekness and truth
in such out of his wits receives the oath and understands nothing but
good, and that meekly and without strife it understands.

Exceeding great is God's mildness when such men swear of things
which he knows well are not true, that he will not esteem. That the
devil does not hastily strangle him. For when he says So God me help,
or So God me keep, and he lies, he puts himself out of the help and
the keeping of God.

In his section on blasphemy Dan Michel has much to say in
a similar mood, "as those players so wickedly break Jesus Christ's
body, and so wickedly missay of God and of his blessed mother

that it is dreadful and sorrowful to hear and list." In short, from Dan Michel's remarks we gather that save for the outward distinction of dress, the practice of swearing was much the same as it continues to be in our own day.

By the beginning of the fifteenth century the English were known throughout the length and breadth of France by what appears to have been the favorite oath of their soldiery—no less than the expression *God damn!* In the first quarter of the fifteenth century *Goddam* had become established in France as a synonym for the Englishman. Henry VI (1421–1471) during the days of Joan of Arc (1412–1431) was known to all Frenchmen as *petit roy godon*. A contemporary French song runs as follows: "Have no fear of getting to grips with these pea-stuffed Goddams! Any one of us is worth four of them, or at the least three. Come, let's make game of them, find all you can of them and hoick them up on the gallows."

D. B. Wyndham Lewis, who in his brilliant book on François Villon gives the words and melody of this song, shrewdly remarks, "I doubt very much, everything considered, if these sentiments, taken for all in all, can be said to echo that respectful affection which the English have always been accustomed to demand from foreign persons and the conquered."[18]

Joan herself almost always referred to the English as *Goddams*.[19]

It is of great interest to note that the expression *God damn* is not to be found anywhere in the literature or other records earlier than the last decade of the sixteenth century. Here it occurs for the first time, in Shakespeare's *Comedy of Errors*, written about 1591.

DROMIO OF SYRACUSE: Nay, she is worse, she is the devil's dam, and here she comes in the habit of a light wench; and thereof comes that the wenches say, "God damn me"; that's as much to say, "God make me a light wench." It is written, they appear to men like angels of light; light is an effect of fire, and fire will burn; *ergo*, light wenches will burn. Come not near her.   IV, iii

Thus, it will be observed that *God damn*, that favorite expression of the Englishman, though it is known to have been in common use at the beginning of the sixteenth century is not recorded in an English work until the end of that century. This clearly shows us how much older are many of the oaths with which we have dealt and shall have to deal than the date of their first written or printed appearance. But to the history and amenities of the British *damn* we shall have to devote a whole chapter, for it is a most engaging word. Here let us continue with our discussion of pre-Reformation swearing.

Margery Kempe, who wrote her autobiography about the year 1430, determined to wear white—for God, she was convinced, so willed it. The Bishop of Lincoln disapproved of this eccentricity in the color of her garments and bade her consult his brother of Canterbury, but God forbade this to Margery. The Mayor of Leicester suspected her of heresy and witchcraft. The Archbishop of York commanded his retinue to fetch a pair of fetters and said she should be fettered, for she was a false heretic:

And there came many of the Archbishop's retinue, despising her, calling her "Lollard" and "heretic," and swearing many a horrible oath that she should be burnt. And she, through the strength of Jesus, spoke back to them, "Sirs, I dread ye shall be burnt in Hell without end, unless ye amend in your swearing of oaths, for ye keep not the commandments of God. I would not swear as ye do for all the money in the world." Then they went away, as if they had been shamed.

This horror of oaths emerges repeatedly in Margery's pages. On one occasion Margery went to London, she says,

with her husband unto Lambeth, where the Archbishop lay at that time; and as they came into the hall in the afternoon, there were many of the Archbishop's clerks and other reckless men, both squires and yeomen, who swore many great oaths and spoke many reckless words, and this creature [as Margery calls herself in her autobiography in contradistinction to the Creator] boldly reprehended them, and said they would be damned unless they left off their swearing and other sins that they used.

Finding favor in the archbishop's eyes, this creature boldly spoke to him for the correction of his household, saying with reverence:

"My lord, Our Lord of all, Almighty God has not given you your benefice and great worldly wealth to keep His traitors and them that slay Him every day by great oaths swearing. Ye shall answer for them, unless ye correct them or else put them out of your service."

The archbishop "Full benignly and meekly suffered her to speak her intent, and gave her a fair answer, she supposing it would then be better."[20]

In Sir Thomas Malory's romance *Le Morte d'Arthur*, which was completed in 1469, we encounter the expression *fie on thee*. Sir Gawayne uses it upon the traitor Sir Mordred,

> Fals fostered foode, the feude have thy bonys!
> Fy one the, felone, and thy false werkys!
> > *Le Morte d'Arthur*, 11, 3776–3777

The expression *So God me rede* occurs frequently in this poem, as it did two centuries earlier in *Havelok the Dane*:

> For litel shal I do the lede
> To the galues, so God me rede!
> > *Havelok the Dane*, II, 686–687

It is highly probable that the oath *So God me rede* belongs to the tenth, or possibly ninth, century. It was a very popular oath during the Middle Ages, but by the end of the sixteenth century it had dropped out of use. *Rede*, or *Rood, Rude, Rode, Rod*, was a synonym for the cross, but both were sometimes used together, as in *Le Morte d'Arthur*:

> Madame, he said for crosse and rode.
> > *Le Morte d'Arthur*, I, 764

Another popular oath of the Middle Ages was *By cock and pie* or *pye*; that is, *By God and the ordinal* (of the Roman Catholic Church). Not only did this oath survive into Shakespeare's day, but we find it revived by Thackeray in 1853 in *The Newcomes*: "By cock and pye it is not worth a bender." *Pie* later became an expletive used by itself and was frequently also used as a curse, as in "Pyes take him!"

In John Myrk's *Instructions for Parish Priests*, written about 1450, the priest is enjoined:

> Of hande and mouthe thou must be true,
> And greate oathes thou must eschewe,
> In worde and deed thou must be mylde,
> Bothe to man and to chylde.[21]

Alexander Barclay (1475–1552) in his rather free adaptation of Sebastian Brant's *Narrenschiff* (1494), in *The Ship of Fooles*, published in 1509, writes:

It was once ordained by constitution,
As I have heard, that both simple men and high
Should only swear by that occupation
The which their Fathers did use and occupy;
But now each sweareth the Mass commonly,
Which is the priest's service and business,
So many oathes their Father's doth express.

Alas! no honour, laude, nor reverence
Is had now unto that blessed sacrement,
But boys and men without all difference
Tear that holy body of God omnipotent,
As it were Jews to his passion they assent,
In every bargain, in ale house, and at borde,
The holy Mass is ever the seconde worde.[22]

In the morality play *Hickscorner*, printed by Wynkyn de Worde about 1510, the oathiness of the play constitutes an obvious criticism of the wicked habit of swearing. Pity remarks:

We have plenty of great oaths,
And cloth enough in our clothes.

While Imagination can hardly utter a word without an imprecation: *Cock's body, Cock's passion, Cock's death, God's arms, God's wounds, God's sides, By God, By my troth, By the mass, What the devil, By Saint Typurn of Kent, By Christ, By Cock's hearth, By Cock's body, By Cock's bones.* By far the most frequent oath in the play, most probably reflecting the practice of the day, is *By God*, an oath that remains popular to this day.

The variety of pre-Reformation oaths is so great that it would require a Brobdingnagian volume merely to list them. It would be tiresome, if it has not already proven so, to do more than has been attempted here, which has been to give the reader a representative sampling of these oaths. In the next chapter swearing in Shakespeare's plays will be explored. These plays, though written after the Reformation, essentially present the swearing forms of the later pre-Reformation period. Before turning to that chapter, however, we may here consider some of the more pungent stories and events relating to swearing before the ascent of Elizabeth to the throne of England.

Although this chapter should properly terminate with the declaration of the first Act of Supremacy of 1534, pre-Reformation swearing obviously did not come to an abrupt end in that year. It continued to be as great an abuse for many years afterward. There were many who cried out against it, including Sir Thomas Elyot (1490–1546), who in his book on the ethics of government, *The Boke Named the Gouernour* (1531), is thoroughly disapproving of the besetting sin of swearing. He writes:

> In dayly communication the matter savoureth nat, except it be as it were seasoned with horrible othes. As by the holy blode of Christe, his wounds whiche for our redemption he paynefully suffred, his glorious harte, as it were numbles chopped in pieces. Children (whiche abhorrethe me to remembre) do play with the armes and bones of Christe, as they were chery stones. The soule of God, which is incomprehensible, and nat to be named of any creature without a wonderful reverence and drede, is nat onely the othe of great gentilmen, but also so indiscretely abused, that they make it (as I mought saye) their gonnes, wherewith they thunder out thretenynges and terrible manacis, whan they be in their fury, though it be at the damnable playe of dyse. The masse, in which honourable ceremony is lefte unto us the memoriall of Christes glorious passion, with his corporall presence in fourme of breade, the invocation of the thre divine persones in one deitie, with all the hole company of blessed spirites and soules elect, is made by custome so simple an othe that it is nowe all most neglected and little regarded of the nobilitie, and is only used among husbandemen and artificers, onelas some taylour or barbour, as well in his othes as in the excesse of his apparayle, will counterfaite and be lyke a gentilman.[23]

In a will dated 1535, Sir David Owen, a natural son of Owen Tudor, bequeathed a legacy of twenty shillings on condition that the legatee should desist from swearing.[24]

In 1540 the poet Stephen Hawes published in London a rhyming pamphlet entitled *The Conversyion of Swerers*, which was prefaced by a figure of the bleeding Christ. With awful realism Hawes depicts the sufferings that, as he believed, were daily being inflicted upon the body of Christ. In gory detail he describes how the hands and feet of Christ were being literally pierced anew and every member and portion of his body torn and lacerated by the imprecations of unheeding Christians.

This doctrine was one widely believed during the Middle Ages, as we have seen from the writings of Dan Michel and Robert of Brunne. It first appears to have been put forward in that encyclopedic work known as *Le Miroir du monde*, which was written in the middle of the thirteenth century. In England it was continually being revived, its last exponent being Thomas Becon (1512–1567), who in the year 1543 brought it forward again in his *An Invective Against Swearing*. Becon gives a colorful picture of peasant life, and he reminds us very much of Saint Bernardino of Siena (1380–1444) when he cries out upon the "dicer" who will swear rather than passively submit to the loss of a single cast or the "carder" who will tear God in pieces rather than lose the profit of one card. Compare this with Saint Bernardino's "When a gambler loses his money and his temper, then he eases himself by rending Christ limb from limb."

Becon writes:

How many swear continually, not only by God and all that ever he made—again, not only by his dearly beloved Son, our Lord and Saviour Jesus Christ, but also (with honour and reverence I speak it) by all the holy members of his most glorious body! How common an oath now-a-days is God's flesh, God's blood, God's heart, God's body, God's wounds, God's nails, God's sides, and all that ever may be rehearsed of God! O wickedness! O abomination! What parts of Christ's most blessed body do these wicked and abominable swearers leave unrent and untorn? They are much worse than the Jews, which cried *Tolle, tolle, crucifige eum.* Away, away, to the gallows with Him, crucify Him, torment Him, leave not one part of Him! For only they cried upon Pilate to have Him crucified, but these swearers themselves crucify Him, rent, and tear Him. The Jews crucified Him but once, and then their fury ceased; but these wicked caitiffs crucify him daily with their unlawful oaths, neither doth their malice and cruelness cease at any time.

Furthermore, this damnable use of swearing hath so greatly prevailed among them that profess Christ that it is also crept into the breasts of young children. It is not a rare thing now-a-days to hear boys and mothers tear the most blessed body of Christ with their blasphemous oaths, even from the top to the toe. What marvel is it then though they be abominable swearers when they come to age? But whence learn they this? Verily from their parents and such as bring them up.[25]

It was in Scotland, however, that the Parliament of Queen Mary in the year 1551, a full fifty years before the English passed such a measure, enacted an ordinance framed

in detestatioun of the grevous and abominabill aithis, sweiring, execrationnis and blasphematioun of the name of God, sweirand in vane be his precious blude, body, passioun and woundis; Devill stick, cummer, gor, roist or ryfe thame and sic uthers ugsume aithis and execratiounis aganis the command of God that the famin is cum in sic ane ungodlie use amangis the pepill of this Realme baith of greit and small Estatis that daylie and hourlie may be hard amangis thame oppin blasphematioun of Godis name and maiestie to the grete contemptioun thairof and bringing of the Ire and wraith of God upone the pepill heirfoir and for eschewing of sic inconvenientis in tymes cumming. It is statute and ordanit that quhatsumevir persoun or persounis sweiris sic abominabill aithis and detestabill execrationnis as is afoir reheirsit sall incur the panis efter following als oft as thay failthie respective. That is to say ane Prelate of Kirk Erle or Lord for everie fault to be committit for the space of thre monethis nixt tocum. That is to say unto the first day of Maij exclusive xij.d. [twelve-pence, or a shilling]. Ane Barrone or beneficit man constitute in dignite ecclesiastick iiij.d. Ane landit man, frehalder, wassal, fewar Burges and small beneficit men .ijd. Ane craftsman, yeoman, a seward man and all uthers .j.d. Item the pure [poor] folkis that hes na geir to pay the pane forsaid to be put in the stokis or presonit for the space of four houris and wemen to be weyit and considderit conforme to thair blude or estate of thair parteis that thay ar cuplit with. And this pane to be dowblit upone everie committar efter the outrinning of the saidis thre monethis for the space of uther thre monethis thairefter . . .[26]

It is worth observing here that though poets may be the unacknowledged legislators of the world, they are apparently also sometimes the inspiration of legislation. It would appear that this Scottish act was framed by the legislators with the verses of the national poet, William Dunbar (1465–1525?), before them, for the statute literally recites the "ugsume aithis" from Dunbar's poem "The Sweirers and the Devill" (1520?).

In this poem the Devil is made to assume human shape and to mix and converse with the traders in the Lowland market. As is usual in such episodes he invites them to join him in the use of the most toothsome oaths he can lay before them. The honest market folk are so taken by his allurements that the maltman, the goldsmith, the "sowter," and the "fleshor" try to outdo one another in their choice of oaths.

> The rest of craftis gryt aithis swair
> Thair wark and craft had na compair,
> Ilk ane into their qualitie;
> The Devill sayis thane, withouttin mair,
> "Renunce your God and cum to me."
>
> XVIII, 31

It need hardly be said that in this friendly contest, by reason of his superior knowledge of theology, the parish priest carries off the prize. Dunbar's successor, Sir David Lindsay (1490–1555), who will be familiar to readers of Scott—"Sir David Lindsay of the Mount/Lord Lion, king at arms"—similarly appears to have contributed to the impending legislation, but it is hardly likely, as Sharman suggests, that he may have been the immediate cause of it. His *The Satyre of the Thrie Estaitis*, performed at Coupar (which he represented in Parliament) in 1543, is a most swearingful poem. Many of the oaths that occur in it are of great interest and here is a list of them:

Be Cokis passion, Be God's passion, Be Cok's deir passion, Be Cok's tois, Be God's wounds, Be God's croce, Be God's mother, Be God's breid, Be God's gown, Be God himsell, Be greit God that all has wrocht, Be him that made the mone, Be the gude Lord, Be him that wore the crown of thorn, Be him that bare the cruel crown of thorn, Be him that herryit hell, Be him that Judas sauld, Be the rude, Be the Trinity, Be the haly Trinity, Be the sacrement, Be the haly sacrement, Be the messe, Be him that our Lord Jesus sauld, Be him that deir Jesus sauld, Be our Lady, Be Sainct Mary, Be sweit Sainct Mary, Be Mary bricht, Be Alhallows, Be Sanct James, Be Sanct Michell, Be Sanct Ann, Be Sanct Bryde, Be Bryde's bell, Be Sanct Geill, Be sweit Sanct Geill, Be Sanct Blais, Be Sanct Blane, Be Sanct Clone, Be Sanct Clune, Be Sanct Allan, Be Sanct Fillane, Be Sanct Tan, Be Sanct Dyonis of France, Be Sanct Maverne, Be the gude lady that me bare, Be my saul, Be my thrift, Be my Christendom, Be this day.

All these are perfectly ordinary pre-Reformation oaths, although one or two of them may have been peculiar only to Scotland.

The records of the local authorities from Glasgow to Aberdeen testify to the vigor and resolution with which the campaign against swearing was being prosecuted toward the latter part of the century.[27] The number of offenders who appeared before the presbyteries was something considerable. At Aberdeen, for example, in 1592 the attention of the council was specially engaged in repressing the swearing of "horrible and execrable oaths." Toward this end a system of fines was instituted. Heads of families were authorized to keep a box in which to place the fines they were empowered to levy on the members of their households. Servants' wages were liable to be taxed at the will of their masters and wives' pin money, at the instance of their lords. Several years later the presbytery went even further than the magistracy had seen fit to do and ordered the master of the house to keep a "palmer" (i.e., a cane) for inflicting pain, as a kind of bastinado, upon the palm of the hand.

In 1542 we find our good doctor Andrew Boorde writing in his *Dyetery of Health*, "Laudable mirth is, one man or one neighbour to be merry with another, with honesty and virtue, without swearing and slandering, and ribaldry speaking."

In 1544 a broadsheet entitled a *Supplycacion to Kynge Henry the Eyght*, published in London, set forth the evil of swearing as a national grievance; it was the forerunner of many others.

How lightly swearing was taken at this period is revealed in the story told of Henry's son Edward VI (1537–1553), who, when he ascended the throne in 1547 at the age of ten, is said to have delivered himself of a volley of the most sonorous oaths. It transpired that the young king had been given to believe by one of his associates that such language was both dignified and becoming in the person of a king. Upon being asked who had been so careful of the king's education, Edward instantly and innocently pointed to the culprit and was not a little astonished at the severe whipping that was there and then administered to his playful preceptor.[28]

Edward's sister Elizabeth (1533–1603), who succeeded to the throne in 1558, was old enough to take care of herself when she assumed the queenly dignity, for she swore profusely without let or hindrance all through her long and red-blooded reign. It is said that "she never spared an oath in public speech or private conversation when she thought it added energy to either."[29]

Since the Virgin Queen's oaths were neither rare nor diminutive, her example was not slow to be imitated. The ladies of the court, over their breakfasts of steak and beer, were not loath to interlard their words with choice and most elegant oaths.

At the very birth of English comedy blasphemy, ribaldry, and coarseness were so merrily wedded that it is, I believe, fair to state—especially in the case of the second of these comedies— the like has never since been equaled. The first English comedy, by general consent, is held to be Nicholas Udall's *Ralph Roister Doister*, written in 1550. It is a domestic farce, Plautine in its influences, amusing enough, no doubt, in its day but grown, with time, a trifle thin. However, what interests us here are the emphatics and expletives set within a context of unexceptionable propriety. These passionate particles are:

God save me, By Cock, By Goss [Jesus], In fay [In faith], By the Arms of Calais, In faith, So God me save, Go to, Avaunt losel [a pitiful worthless fellow], For the passion of God, By God's grace, For the paishe [passion] of God, By Gog's dear mother, By his lily wounds, For the pash of God, By the matt [mass], God save it, By Cock's precious, By Gog.

Gammer Gurton's Needle, first published in 1575 and the second comedy to have been written and acted in the English language, was performed about 1552 to 1563 at Cambridge University. It is said to be the first play ever acted within that institution. For many years the play was attributed to John Still of Christ's College, Cambridge, later Bishop of Bath and Wells. But subsequent research indicates that the author was William Stevenson, a Fellow of Christ's, who died the year his play achieved print.

The theme of the play is simplicity itself. Grandma Gurton has lost her needle. It is her needle, and the only needle in the village. The suspicion is planted in her mind that Dame Chat has stolen it. Crisis follows crisis, and there is a notable exchange of "hot words" between Grandma Gurton and Dame Chat that leads to violent fights between them. The parson, the bailiff, the doctor, and the cat, as well as Hodge, the odd-man whose breeches Grandma Gurton was sewing when the needle disappeared, were all involved in searching for the missing article. The needle, of course, finally declares its whereabouts following a loud and sudden howl from Hodge, whereupon it is rescued from the seat of Hodge's breeches. The whole rollicking farce has the flavor so beautifully preserved in some of the paintings of rustic scenes by the Breughels. Some idea of the fecundity and frequency of the oaths contained in this play may be gained from the following list:

What the devil, Gog's bones, Gog's soul, By the mass, Gog's sacrament, How a murrain, Gog's malison, A vengeance, Gog's death, Now God and good Saint Sithe, Whoreson, Gog's sides, What a devil, Go to, Fie shitten knave and out upon thee, By bread and salt [it was customary to take bread and salt before taking an oath], The pox, Gog's bread, God amercy, O gracious God, Jesus, By my conscience, A murrain, Avaunt, a bonable [abominable] whoreson, Jesus mercy, Fie on thee, Bawdy bitch, By m' father's soul, Dastard, I' faith, Faith, For God's Sake and Saint Charity, That dirty bastard, The whoreson dolt, O Christ, By Cock's mother dear, For God's sake, By my troth, By Saint Mary, By my faith, By God, By God's blest, Gog's blessed body, Thou shitten knave, By our lady, Old filth, By God's pity, Old witch, By God's cross, By God's mother, God's sacrament, That dirty shitten lout, By, all-Hallows, by my fay [faith], Thou liar lickdish, God's malt, For all the loves on earth, By sun and moon, By'r Lady, By our dear lady of Boulogne, Saint Dunstan, Saint Dominic, The Three kings of Cologne, By him that Judas sold, By Gis, By Saint Benet, By my truth, By my father's skin.

The adjuration *For all the loves on earth* is interesting. *For the love of God, of heaven,* of anything sacred were adjurations frequently used at this day. From the indiscriminate use of such adjurations it became customary on the properly earnest occasions to appeal to *all loves*, in various forms. For example, Shakespeare, in *A Midsummer-Night's Dream*, has Hermia say, "Alacke, where are you? speake an if you heare: Speake of all loves" (II, ii). *Gammer Gurton's Needle* undoubtedly faithfully reflects the manners of its day, when even the parson could feelingly describe another as "that shitten lout." The exchange between Grandma Gurton and Dame Chat after they fall to provides a good example of the becudgeling functions of certain words:

> GAMMER: Thou wert as good as kiss my tail,
>   Thou slut, thou cut [horse], thou rakes, thou jakes,
>   will not shame make thee hide thee?
> CHAT: Thou skald, thou bald, thou rotten, thou glutton, I
>   will no longer chide thee;
>   But I will teach thee to keep home.
>
> III, iii

Such exchanges between women can still be heard in the slums of English towns, but they would seldom, if ever, be encountered in a civilized English village in which the taboos upon "bad language" of any kind still remain Victorian in their rigor.

In *New Custom* (1573), a morality play of the period anonymously written to promote the Reformation, much the same expletives occur as in *Ralph Roister Doister* and *Gammer Gurton's Needle*, but there are a few oaths that occur in neither of the other two plays:

A God's name, Body of God, God's precious soul, God's soul, Whoremaster villain, Gramercy, Of my faith, God's precious wounds, A vengeance on them all and the devil break their necks, Heart of God, On my faith, By God's foot, By God's body, By God's guts.

In *Image of God* (1560), Roger Hutchinson wrote:

You swearers and blasphemers which use to swear by God's heart, arms, nails, bowels, legs and hands, learn what these things signify, and leave your abominable oaths. For when thou swearest by God's heart, thou swearest by God's wisdom; when thou swearest by God's arms, thou swearest by Christ; when thou swearest by his hands or legs, thou swearest by his humanity; when thou swearest by his tongue and finger, thou swearest by the Holy Ghost; and swearing by his head thou swearest by his divine and blessed nature; and swearing by his hairs, thou abusest his creatures, by which thou art forbidden to swear. When an oath is necessary we are bound to swear by God only, unto whom all honour is due; for we honour that thing whereby we swear. . . . But some will say, if we honour that thing whereby we swear, let us swear by God that we may honour him. Brother be not deceived: God is honoured by swearing, but how? Truly when thou swearest by him in a weighty matter of life and death, before an officer or in any other matters of importance, thou dost then honour and homage: but if in every trifle thou call him to witness, thou dishonourest him, and breakest his commandment, which saith: *Non assumes nomen Domini,* etc. "Thou shalt not take the name of thy Lord God in vain."[30]

CHAPTER EIGHT

Swearing in Shakespeare

‹‹‹

Who speak the tongue
That Shakespeare spake.

WILLIAM WORDSWORTH, *"It is not to be thought of,"* 1802

WILLIAM Shakespeare (1564–1616) was born some thirty years after the inception of those momentous changes that led to what we today call the Reformation. The middle-aged men and women of Shakespeare's youth all belonged to the earlier culture of Romanist tradition, and a large element of their ways and manners was characteristically of that period. Indeed, though the cleansing fires of the Reformation swept the monasteries away, many Romanist practices still continued, even though it was made a crime for a Catholic priest to be in England. Among the pre-Reformation habits that continued with unabated vigor in Shakespeare's time—by the good example of the queen herself—was the habit of swearing. An atmosphere of oaths hung not too heavily over the land. Men and women carried their swearing as lightly as they wore their cloaks. And since nothing that men did or said or were capable of doing or saying seems ever to have been lost upon Shakespeare, he displays an acquaintance with the forms of swearing and an insight into its various niceties and usages, that no writer before or since has ever equaled.

Picked up from the older men and women, the swearing of Shakespeare's plays belongs almost wholly to pre-Reformation days. This does not mean that in Shakespeare's day these oaths were already obsolete. That was by no means the case; on the contrary, most of these oaths were the oaths of Shakespeare's time—they formed the side arms ordinary of the queen, of her court, and of the populace. Although some were already obsolete when Shakespeare was writing his plays, they were not so obsolete that they failed to be understood by his audiences as belonging to the Romanist period, when they meant a good deal more to those who employed them.

Not all the swearing in the plays will be reproduced here, for the reason that many of the same oaths are repeated in several plays.

KING JOHN (1594)

KING PHILLIP: ... And by this hand I swear,
That sways the earth this climate overlooks,
Before we will lay down our just-borne arms ...

II, i

By this hand was a very common oath in the Middle Ages. From the same play we have a delightful passage, which has already been quoted in this book, as illustrative of the function of swearing as physical chastisement:

KING JOHN (1594)

PHILIP THE BASTARD: He speaks plain cannon fire, and smoke and bounce;
He gives the bastinado with his tongue:
Our ears are cudgell'd; not a word of his
But buffets better than a fist of France:
Zounds! I was never so bethumped with words
Since I first call'd my brother's father dad.

II, i

A MIDSUMMER-NIGHT'S DREAM (1595)

HERMIA: O hell! to choose love by another's eyes.

I, i

A Midsummer-Night's Dream is the most unswearingful of all Shakespeare's plays and is remarkable principally for the expression *O hell!* used as an expletive.

THE COMEDY OF ERRORS (1591–1592)

DROMIO OF SYRACUSE: By my troth.

I, i

.   .   .

DROMIO OF EPHESUS: A man may break a word with you, sir, and words are but wind;
Ay, and break it in your face, so he break it not behind.

I, ii

Earlier in the first act Antipholus remarks, "Stop in your mind Sir" (I, ii).

DROMIO OF SYRACUSE: Nay, she is worse, she is the devil's dam, and here she comes in the habit of a light wench, and thereof comes that the wenches say, "God damn me"; that's so much as to say, "God make me a light wench." It is written, they appear to men like angels of light; light is an effect of fire and fire will burn; *ergo*, light wenches will burn. Come not near her.

IV, iii

As I have already pointed out, this passage contains the first printed record of the expression *God damn me*. Here *damn* is also presented as a play on the word *dam*, that is, a copulable female. In the next scene the expression *whoreson* is hurled at Dromio:

ANTIPHOLUS: Thou whoreson, senseless villain!
IV, iv

Whoreson was not a common medieval epithet of opprobrium and seems to have come into fashion early in the sixteenth century. The word *whore* was commonly used in the Middle Ages to denote a prostitute. Today *whore* has become impolite, and *prostitute* only barely so. In Elizabethan times *whoreson*—that is to say, son of a female of high complexion and low morals—was a very common epithet and is to be found in the works of almost every Elizabethan dramatist. In the very next play of Shakespeare's there is a good example of the use of *whore*.

TITUS ANDRONICUS (1591–1592)

AARON [*to the* NURSE]: 'Zounds, ye whore! . . .
IV, ii

This line is of interest chiefly by reason of the presence of the expletive *'Zounds*, a corrupt contraction of the oath *God's wounds*. It has been said that the first swearer to use this latter oath was Sir John Perrot (1572?–1592), a natural son of Henry VIII; but, as we have seen, it was in use long before the time of Perrot, in the popular medieval oath *By Cokke's wounds* and in this and the other form in the play *Hickscorner* (1510):

God's wounds, who gave thee that counsel?
Hickscorner, 189

God's wounds was a favorite oath of Queen Elizabeth's and it is said that the corruption *'Zounds* first originated with the ladies of her court, who also used it in the form *zooterkins*.

In the following passage *damned* is used as an imprecation in its modern sense.

> TITUS: Reveal the damn'd contriver of this deed.
>
> IV, i

Although this represents one of the earliest records of the use of the word in this sense, there can be no doubt that it had already long enjoyed circulation before it was used by Shakespeare, but of this more will be said in Chapter Fourteen.

Young Lucius in taking leave of Aaron and his fellow conspirators remarks:

> And so I leave you both—[*Aside*] like bloody villains.
>
> IV, ii

The word *bloody* is discussed at length in Chapter Thirteen. Here we may remark that it is often difficult in Shakespeare to determine whether the word is used in its literal sense or in its objurgative colloquial sense. In most instances it is very clear that he used it in its literal sense as when in *Titus* Marcus exclaims:

> What, what! the lustful sons of Tamora
> Performers of this bloody deed?
>
> IV, i

In many other instances Shakespeare could be interpreted to be employing the word in both its literal and its colloquial senses, as when Bardolph in *Henry IV* (1598) says:

> in a theme so bloody-faced as this.
>
> Pt. II, I, iii

It would seem that Shakespeare employed *bloody* in this double sense in Young Lucius' aside, "like bloody villains." The only *apparently* clear-cut case of the use of the word by Shakespeare in its colloquial sense is when in *Henry V* (1599) Fluellen says

> . . . it is good for your green wound and your bloody coxcomb.
>
> V, i

But even here it is still doubtful.

When in the fourth act of *Titus Andronicus* the clown exclaims *By'r lady*, the expression is by no means an archaism, for it was in good use—by dramatists at least—way into the first half of the seventeenth century. It did not become altogether obsolete till the end of the eighteenth century, although here and there in small villages and hamlets, it persisted late into the nineteenth century.

The exchange between Lucius and Aaron in which Shakespeare reveals such acute insight into the psychology of belief has already been quoted, but it bears requoting here.

> LUCIUS: Who should I swear by? Thou believ'st no god:
>   That granted, how canst thou believe an oath?
> AARON: What if I do not? as, indeed, I do not;
>   Yet, for I know thou art religious
>   And hast a thing within thee called conscience,
>   With twenty popish tricks and ceremonies,
>   Which I have seen thee careful to observe,
>   Therefore I urge thy oath; for that I know
>   An idiot holds his bauble for his god,
>   And keeps the oath which by that god he swears,
>   To that I'll urge him; therefore thou shalt vow
>   By that same god, what god soe'er he be,
>   That thou adorest and hast in reverence.
>
>   V, i

LOVE'S LABOUR'S LOST (1594)

> BIRON: By yea and nay, sir, then I swore in jest. . . .
>
>   I, i

In this line Shakespeare echoes the Sermon on the Mount, in which Christ says, "Swear not at all . . . But let your communication be, Yea, yea; Nay, nay." (Matt. 5: 33–37).

> LONGAVILLE: Marry, that did I.
>
>   I, i

Marry, as we have already seen, is the popular rendering of *Mary*. In its various forms the expletive occurs frequently in Shakespeare's pages.

> COSTARD: . . . Go to; thou hast it *ad dunghill*, at the fingers' ends,
>   as they say.
>
>   V, i

This expression, *Go to*, recalls the remark in the schoolboy's essay on Shakespeare. "Shakespeare," he wrote, "was a very nice man, he often said 'go to' but he was too polite to finish the sentence." *Go to* was, of course, a perfectly innocent exclamation, though it was frequently combined with phrases that were far from innocent, as in Costard's comment.

Costard also swears *By my soul* and *O my troth* (IV, i).

Biron swears expletively *by heaven* (IV, iii), while the king swears very mildly by *Saint Cupid*.

> KING: Saint Cupid, then! and soldiers to the field!
> IV, iii

THE TAMING OF THE SHREW (1596)

> GREMIO: . . . "Ay, by gogs-wouns," quoth he . . .
> III, ii

This is, as we have seen, a corruption of *God's wounds*, a good pre-Reformation version, as is Petrucio's *O mercy God!* (IV, i) and Hortensio's *God-a-mercy!* (IV, iii), that is, *God have mercy*.

HENRY VI (1590–1592)

In this play, a most maledictory one, the Earl of Suffolk delivers himself of a profound soliloquy on the curse.

> A plague upon them! wherefore should I curse them?
> Would curses kill, as doth the mandrake's groan,
> I would invent as bitter-searching terms,
> As curst, as harsh, and horrible to hear,
> Deliver'd strongly through my fixed teeth,
> With full as many signs as deadly hate,
> As lean-faced Envy in her loathsome cave;
> My tongue should stumble in my earnest words;
> Mine eyes should sparkle like the beaten flint;
> Mine hair be fixt on end, as one distract;
> Ay, every joint should seem to curse and ban:
> And even now my burden'd heart would break,
> Should I not curse them. Poison be their drink!
> Gall, worse than gall, the dainties that they taste!
> Their sweetest shade a grove of cypress trees!
> Their chiefest prospect murdering basilisks!
> Their softest touch as smart as lizard's stings!
> Their music frightful as the serpent's hiss,
> And boding screech-owls make the consort full!
> All the foul terrors in dark-seated hell——
> Pt. II, III, ii

In this play *For God's sake* is used in much the sense as it is employed today.

> GLOSTER: For God's sake, take away this captive scold.
> Pt. III, V, v

And Queen Margaret exclaims in what would seem to be both the literal and colloquial sense:

> Butchers and villains, bloody cannibals!
> Pt. III, V, v

THE MERRY WIVES OF WINDSOR (1599–1600)

> FALSTAFF [*admonishing* PISTOL]: . . . and yet you, rogue, will en-sconce your rags, your cat-o-mountain looks, your red-lattice phrases, and your bold-beating oaths, under the shelter of your honour! . . .
> II, ii

The expression "red-lattice phrases" is a reference to talk in a manner appropriate to taverns of the lowest class, which were customarily distinguished by their red lattices.

In the third scene of this act, the Frenchman, Dr. Caius, swears *By gar! Gar* is, of course, the corrupted form of *God*, appropriate to "The clipped English of Dr. Caius," as Macaulay put it.

HAMLET (1601–1602)

Hamlet swears *Heaven and earth!* (I, ii), and *by Saint Patrick* (I, v). He also swears *'Sblood* (II, ii), and *'Swounds* (V, i), respectively the contractions of *God's blood* and *God's wounds*. Polonius swears *'Fore God* (II, ii), while the second clown ex-claims *Mass, I cannot tell* (V, i). And then Hamlet delivers him-self of the following soliloquy, which suggests to us something of the view that the person of quality took of swearing:

> HAMLET: . . . O, vengeance!
> Why, what an ass am I! This is most brave,
> That I, the son of a dear father murder'd
> Prompted to my revenge by heaven and hell,
> Must, like a whore, unpack my heart with words,
> And fall a-cursing, like a very drab,
> A scullion!
> II, ii

Finally, there is Ophelia's soliloquy.

OPHELIA: Indeed, la, without an oath, I'll make an end on't.
"By Gis, and by Saint Charity,
Alack! and fie for shame!
Young men will do't, if they come to't;
By cock, they are to blame.

"Quoth she, 'Before you tumbled me,
You promised me to wed. . . .'"

IV, v

La is the contracted form of *Lord. By Gis* is *By Jesus. By Saint Charity*—in the Middle Ages charity often mistakenly was taken to be a saint. *By cock* is, of course, *By God.*

RICHARD II (1595)

The only phrase, for our purposes, worth noting in this play is Richard's "Wrath kindled gentlemen" (I, i).

RICHARD III (1593)

RICHMOND: God and your arms be prais'd, victorious friends,
The day is ours, the bloody dog is dead.

V, v

Here *bloody* is probably used in both senses.

ALL'S WELL THAT ENDS WELL (1602)

FIRST LORD: A pox on't, let it go; 'tis but a drum.

III, vi

Pox here refers to the disease of syphilis, said to have been introduced into Europe from Haiti by the sailors returned from Columbus' first expedition, in 1492. The disease was, however, known in Europe at least two centuries before that time,[1] but its ravages appeared to have made great headway during the sixteenth century. The word *pox* for syphilis appears first to have been used in 1503, when it was identified as the "French pox."[2]

KING HENRY IV (1597)

This is a play most rich in the variety of its swearing, and several of the characters in it have favorite oaths. Falstaff's is *Zounds!*, while Mine hostess' is *O Jesu,* and Doll Tearsheets' specialty is versatility.

PRINCE: Why, what a pox have I to do with my hostess of the tavern?

Pt. I, I, ii

What a pox is, no doubt, not original with Shakespeare here, but in this form was probably at least half a century old, yet this is one of the earliest records of this later famous oath.

> FALSTAFF: . . . Thou whoreson mandrake . . .
>
> > Pt. II, I, ii

Falstaff here employs "mandrake" as a term of ridicule by reason of the resemblance of that root to a diminutive man, a "mannikin."

> FALSTAFF: Let him be damn'd like the glutton! Pray God his tongue be hotter! A whoreson Achitophel! a rascally yea-for-sooth knave! to bear a gentleman in hand, and then stand upon security! The whoreson smooth-pates . . .
>
> > Pt. II, I, ii

The next lines show *whoreson* in use as a simple intensive.

> FALSTAFF: And I hear, moreover, his Highness [the king] is fallen into this same whoreson apoplexy.
> CHIEF JUSTICE: Well, God mend him! I pray you, let me speak with you.
> FALSTAFF: This apoplexy, as I take it, is a kind of lethargy, an't please your lordship, a kind of sleeping in the blood, a whoreson tingling.
>
> > Pt. II, I, ii

> FALSTAFF: . . . A pox of this gout! or, a gout of this pox! for one or the other plays the rogue with my great toe. . . .
>
> > Pt. II, I, ii

> HOSTESS: . . . thou bastardly rogue . . . thou honey-suckle villain.
>
> > Pt. II, II, i

To have called a man a bastard or an adjectivally bastardly rogue was most probably an old imprecation by Shakespeare's time, yet instances of its use before the sixteenth century are wanting. The form *bastardly* followed the general rule in such cases and the *-ly* subsequently was dropped from the word.

And now let us to one of Doll Tearsheet's performances. Those who have walked o'nights to the old 43 Club in Gerrard Street or, better still, to the 1917 down the same street off Shaftesbury Avenue have, in their time, no doubt heard similar performances from the sulphurous lips of the three-pound-a-nighters plying their trade in that district. But let us to Mistress Dorothy.

> DOLL TEARSHEET: Charge me! I scorn you, scurvy companion. What! you poor, base, rascally, cheating, lack-linen mate!

	Away, you mouldy rogue, away! I am meat for your master.
PISTOL:	I know you, Mistress Dorothy.
DOLL:	Away, you cut-purse rascal! You filthy bung [sharper], away! By this wine, I'll thrust my knife in your mouldy chaps, an you play the saucy cuttle with me. Away, you bottle-ale rascal! you basket-hilt stale juggler, you! Since when, I pray you sir? God's light, with two points on your shoulder? Much!

Pt. II, II, iv

Of all the oaths in this passage, if there is one that is original with Shakespeare it is *you basket-hilt stale juggler*, which translated into modern English means "you worn-out practicer of sword tricks." If Shakespeare invented this piece of invective for the purposes of the play he but followed an already existing popular custom.

HENRY V (1599)

CONSTABLE OF FRANCE: *Dieu de batailles!* . . .

III, v

King Henry also swears this oath, *O God of battles* (IV, i). The Constable also swears by the devil, *O diable* (IV, v), while the Dauphin swears *By faith and honour* (III, v), and *Mort de ma vie!* (IV, v), and Katherine exclaims, "*O bon Dieu!*" (V, ii).

Fluellen, who does not have a very great command of the English tongue, can nevertheless swear volubly in it, as witness the following performances.

FLUELLEN: . . . the rascally, scald [scabby], beggarly, lousy, pragging [bragging] knaves . . .

. . .

God pless you Aunchient Pistol! you scurfvy, lousy knave, God pless you!

. . .

. . . it is good for your green wound and your ploody coxcomb.

V, i

We need remark here only that the adjectives seem here to be used in precisely the same sense as they are used as swearwords today.

ROMEO AND JULIET (1595)

> NURSE: Now, by my maidenhead . . .
>
> I, iii

The maidenhead (hymen) as always been prized as a symbol of virginity, hence its value as an expletive. *By my maidenhead* is a very old medieval oath and probably dates back to the ninth century if not earlier.

> FRIAR LAWRENCE: Holy Saint Francis! . . . Jesu Maria . . .
>
> II, iii

That is, Saint Francis of Assisi, and Jesus and his Mother.

> FRIAR LAWRENCE: . . . God's will . . .
>
> III, iii
>
> CAPULET: God's bread! . . .
>
> III, v

God's bread here, of course, refers to the bread of Christ—not to the Supreme Being's.

MUCH ADO ABOUT NOTHING (1598–1599)

Here we have a very fine example of refined swearing:

> BENEDICK [*referring to* CLAUDIO]: . . . He was wont to speak plain and to the purpose, like an honest man and a soldier; and now he is turn'd orthography; his words are a very fantastical banquet, just so many strange dishes.
>
> II, iii

By *orthography* in this passage Shakespeare means Benedick to say that Claudio has turned *euphuistical* in his speech.

> BENEDICK: By my sword, Beatrice, thou lov'st me.
>
> IV, i

By my sword is an early pre-Reformation oath that originated in the custom of taking one's oath on the sword. *By my halidome* is another form of the same oath. This device of oath taking upon the sword deserves a few words here. Half pagan, half barbarian in its origin, it was but slowly that this form of oath taking relaxed its hold upon Christian Europe. Julian Sharman conjectures that the oath came about in something like the following fashion.

In the terrors of an isolated death, remote from all the outward appliances of his faith, the stricken warrior found consolation in raising before his vision the hilt of his scabbardless sword. The tapering metal-hafted blade threw the shadow of a cross upon the dying soldier, and to this rude emblem the poor fevered lips would stammer out their last words of petition. The sword had become a revered symbol conveying to the departing the hope of divine favour and intercession. This thought so powerfully arrested the imagination that it did not relinquish its grasp when a period of security had succeeded a reign of bloodshed and danger.[3]

However this may be, it is certain that the sword came to be associated with the sense of honor—principally because it was the one weapon by which the ordinary man as well as the soldier could defend and avenge it. Upon the sword hilt the kingmaker would take his vows, and the custom lingered in effigy to the days of Shakespeare, when the fencing masters, practicing their calling at the Beer Garden, were required to take an oath upon their rapier's hilt to carry themselves honorably in their profession. In the British Museum there is a manuscript that, among other things, gives an account of this oath, which runs as follows: "First you shall swear, so help you God and halidome, and by all the christendome which God gave you at the fount stone, and by the cross of this sword which doth represent unto you which our Saviour suffered his most painful deathe upon . . ."[4]

In the traditions of Denmark the oath upon the sword hilt was preserved in a spirit of deep solemnity. Shakespeare probably knew this, for he makes Hamlet conjure Horatio "never to speak of this which you have seen, swear by my sword" (I, v).

In *Much Ado About Nothing* Dogberry swears *God's my life* (IV, ii), while Don Pedro exclaims *By my soul* (V, i), *By this light* (V, i).

JULIUS CAESAR (1599)

In this play there is not a word of swearing.

TROILUS AND CRESSIDA (1602)

PANDARUS: . . . by God's lid, it does one's heart good. . . .

I, ii

By God's lid, that is, God's eyelid, is an early medieval oath.

The first scene of the second act of this play opens with a splendid bout of swearing between Ajax and Thersites.

AJAX: Dog, . . . Thou bitch-wolf's son . . .

This is the forerunner of the modern American *son of a bitch*.

THERSITES: The plague of Greece upon thee, thou mongrel beef-witted lord. . . . A red murrain o' thy jade's tricks!
AJAX: Toadstool . . .
THERSITES: I would thou didst itch from head to foot and I had the scratching of thee. I would make thee the loathsom'st scab in Greece . . .
AJAX: Cobloaf! . . . You whoreson cur!

A cobloaf was a small loaf of rounded form. It is unique here as an expletive.

And so on, to good effect in blows and words, and with blows for words and words for blows, as in the following passage:

THERSITES: How now, Thersites! what, lost in the labyrinth of thy fury! Shall the elephant Ajax carry it thus? He beats me, and I rail at him. O, worthy satisfaction! would it were otherwise, that I could beat him, whilst he railed at me. 'Sfoot, I'll learn to conjure and raise devils, but I'll see some issue of my spiteful execrations. . . .

II, iii

In this speech Thersites recognizes the vicarious assaultive function of swearing and wishes that the beating could be real. Pulling himself out of the labyrinth of his fury, he vows, 'Sfoot— by God's foot—to "learn to conjure and raise devils"; that is, to make waxen defixive images so that he might see some real issue to his spiteful execrations. Some sign of his progress in this direction is one of the vivid curses he later utters: "a burning devil take them" (V, iii).

In the same scene Hector swears *By all the everlasting gods.*

MEASURE FOR MEASURE (1604)

Here we meet with two beautifully poetic lines, uttered by Angelo, that perfectly express the Christian view of the swearer's conduct:

> . . . [They] "that do coin Heaven's image
> In stamps that are forbid.
>
> II, iv

KING LEAR (1605)

> Thou whoreson zed!
> II, ii

That is, "Thou seed of a whore!"

There is an amusing exchange between Lear and Kent.

> LEAR: By Jupiter, I swear, no.
> KENT: By Juno, I swear, ay.
>
> II, iv

Lear curses his daughter, who, he declares, has

> struck me with her tongue,
> Most serpent-like, upon the very heart.
> All the stored vengeances of heaven fall
> On her ingrateful top! Strike her young bones,
> You taking airs, with lameness!
>
> . . .
>
> You nimble lightnings, dart your blinding flames
> Into her scornful eyes! Infect her beauty,
> You fen-suck'd fogs, drawn by the powerful sun,
> To fall and blast her pride!
>
> II, iv

Edgar, disguised as a madman, delivers himself of the following speech:

> EDGAR: Take heed o' the foul fiend. Obey thy parents; keep thy word justly; swear not; commit not with man's sworn spouse; set not thy sweet heart on proud array, Tom's a-cold.
>
> III, iv

It is a "madman" who must offer such admonishment!

Edgar, in the same scene, goes on to speak of "a servingman, proud in heart and mind" who "swore as many oaths as he spake words, and broke them in the sweet face of heaven."

MACBETH (1606)

> MACBETH [to SERVANT]: The devil damn thee black, thou cream-fac'd loon!
>
> . . .
>
> Go prick thy face, and over-red thy fear,
> Thou lily-liver'd boy. What soldiers, patch [fool]?
> Death of thy soul! Those linen cheeks of thine
> Are counsellors to fear. What soldiers, whey-face?
>
> V, iii

We recover the echo of this in the twentieth-century staff sergeant's speech (quoted earlier), which concluded with the words "You wooden stiffs with the paint sucked off your faces!"

PERICLES (1608)

> CERIMON: . . . O you most potent gods!
>
> III, ii

ANTONY AND CLEOPATRA (1607)

Here the oaths are naturally of the classical variety, suited to time, place, and character:

> CHARMIAN: O Isis!
>
> III, iii

Isis is the Egyptian goddess, mother of Horus, and the moon personified, sister and wife to *Osiris*, the sun.

> They [the priests] wore rich mitres shaped like the moon,
> To show that Isis doth the moon portend,
> Like as Osiris signifies the sun.
>
> Spenser, *Faerie Queene*, vii (1596)

> SCARUS: Gods and goddesses,
>   All the whole synod of them!
>
> III, x

This is a rather comprehensive expletive.

Antony swears *By Jove that thunders!* and *gods and devils!* (III, xiii).

THE TEMPEST (1611)

SEBASTIAN: A pox o' your throat, you bawling, blasphemous, uncharitable dog!

BOATSWAIN: Work thou, then.

ANTONIO: Hang, cur! hang, you whoreson, insolent noisemaker! We are less afraid to be drowned than thou art.

> I, i

There soon follows that notable passage in which the savage cries out to his tutor:

CALIBAN [*to* PROSPERO]: You taught me language; and my profit on't Is, I know how to curse. The red plague rid you For learning me your language.

> I, ii

CYMBELINE (1610)

CLOTEN: Was there ever man had such luck! When I kiss'd the jack, upon an up-cast to be hit away! I had a hundred pound on't: and then a whoreson jackanapes must take me up for swearing; as if I borrowed mine oaths of him and might not spend them at my pleasure.

FIRST LORD: What got he by that? You have broke his pate with your bowl.

SECOND LORD [*Aside*]: If his wit had been like him that broke it, it would have run all out.

CLOTEN: When a gentleman is dispos'd to swear, it is not for any standers-by to curtail his oaths, ha?

II, i

A banished rascal and *The south-fog rot him* are the worst oaths that Cloten actually utters.

It is in this play that Posthumus having sworn by *Jove* and Iachmo *By Jupiter*, that the Queen is moved to plead with them, as we have already noted on an earlier page, to

Forbear sharp speeches to her: she's a lady
So tender of rebukes that words are strokes
And strokes death to her.

III, v

"Words are strokes." Here once again the assaultive function of swearing is recognized.

Cymbeline herself exclaims *Heavens* (IV, iii), while Imogene makes it *good heavens!* (III, vi), and *'Ods pittikins* and *O gods and goddesses!* (IV, ii), *'Ods pittikins* being the corruption of *God's pity*.

TIMON OF ATHENS (1607)

FLAVIUS: O you gods!

I, ii

CORIOLANUS (1610)

VALERIA: O' my word . . . O' my troth . . .

I, iii

THIRD ROMAN: A murrain on't! . . .

I, v

Coriolanus swears *By Jupiter!* (I, ix), *O the gods!* (IV, i), and *You gods!* (V, iii).

VOLUMNIA: I would the gods had nothing else to do
But to confirm my curses! Could I meet 'em
But once a day, it would unclog my heart
Of what lies heavy to't.

IV, ii

Here again, the cathartic function of swearing is recognized.

OTHELLO (1611)

> IAGO: God bless the mark!
> I, i

> IAGO: By Janus . . .
> I, ii

> OTHELLO: Death and damnation!
> III, iii

> OTHELLO: O blood, blood, blood!
> III, iii

> OTHELLO: Damn her, lewd minx! O damn her! damn her!
> III, iii

> BIANCA: Let the devil and his dam haunt you!
> IV, i

HENRY VIII (1613)

Henry VIII's favorite oath was *By God's wounds!* but Shakespeare makes him swear *By my life* (I, ii).

Anne Boleyn swears *O, God's will!* and *By my troth and maidenhead* (II, iii).

From the above cross section of Shakespeare's mastery of the art of swearing, several facts emerge. In the first place, Shakespeare appears to have heard and noted practically everything that circulated in his day in the way of swearing. In the second place, it is obvious that he thoroughly understood the nature of swearing and its functions. In the third place, almost all the swearing that occurs in Shakespeare's plays is essentially that of the pre-Reformation period, with an occasional contemporary oath or one of his own invention introduced for good measure. Since all the plays refer to an earlier period than that in which he was writing, Shakespeare did not hesitate to make good use of Romanist oaths that in his own day were already obsolete or were fast becoming so. The audiences of his own time would fully have understood them and missed nothing of their meaning.

The freedom with which so many of Shakespeare's characters swear, the variety and vividness of their oaths, was not due to any immunity from censorship the plays enjoyed, for Shakespeare was no more able to escape the heavy hand of the censor than were his fellow playwrights. The swearing in Shakespeare's plays simply testifies to the firm hold that this habit had taken upon all classes of the English public. Under the sanction that happily descends upon most classics, Shakespeare's plays have long been performed upon the stage in unbowdlerized form. The modern playwright still experiences some difficulty in having a play performed in which "bad language" comparable to that employed by Shakespeare occurs. As his characters spoke, so spoke the people of the period he presented. Certainly in his own day people of all classes swore rather freely and were by no means averse to hearing the oaths of an earlier day brought to their remembrance. The spurious and hypocritical modesty of our own times forbids such faithfulness of presentation upon the stage— a bequest to us from the nineteenth century, during which values became so far sicklied o'er and prudery so hypertrophied that children were born but never made, piano legs were dressed in pantaloons, only "limbs" existed, and everyone undertook to become the keeper of his neighbor's morals.

From the freedom and luxuriance of the oaths in Shakespeare's plays, as well as from other sources, it is known that the habit of swearing was widespread in Elizabethan England. This was no new blossoming in the verbal spring of the Elizabethan Renaissance but the continuation of a long-established habit. We have earlier noted that in the thirteenth, fourteenth, and fifteenth centuries the habit was already well entrenched among all classes of people, and we have remarked that there were those who rebelled and cried out against the practice. With some of the complainants during the first half of the sixteenth century we have already dealt. The second half of the sixteenth century seems to have had few protesters who cared to rush into print with their remonstrances, but with the rise of Puritanism the torrential outpouring of printed protests—long and short—commenced. With these and the laws that were enacted against swearing we shall deal in the next chapter.

CHAPTER NINE

Swearing in the Seventeenth Century

‹‹›››

By This Good Day!
BEN JONSON, *Every Man in His Humour*, 1598

THE history of swearing in the seventeenth century is separable into two quite distinct phases falling within two very different periods, the first characterized by the growth of Puritanism, the second by the reaction against Puritanism expressed in the licentiousness of the Restoration.

The century began well with a 1600 production of Ben Jonson's homiletic comedy *Every Man in His Humour* (1598), produced at the Curtain Theatre, with Shakespeare in the cast. Ben Jonson himself disliked oaths and profanity, but as a conscientious monitor of his culture he held up the mirror to his times and faithfully made his characters talk as he had heard them. Possibly because of his aversion to swearing Ben Jonson makes fine sport of the habit in this play through a water bearer:

OLIVER COB: "By the foot of Pharaoh!" There's an oath! How many water-bearers shall you hear swear such an oath? O, I have a guest—he teaches me—he does swear the legiblest of any man christened: "By Saint George! the foot of Pharaoh! the body of me! as I am a gentleman and a soldier!" such dainty oaths! And withal he does take this same filthy roguish tobacco, the finest and cleanliest; it would do a man good to see the fume come forth at 's tunnels! Well, he owes me forty shillings—my wife lent him out of her purse, by sixpence at a time—besides his lodging; I would I had it! I shall ha' it, he says, the next action. Helter-skelter, hang sorrow, care'll kill a cat, up-tails all, and a louse for the hangman!

I, iii

The "legiblest" swearer is Captain Bobadill, who also swears *'Odso! What a plague! Body o' me! By the heart of valour in me!* and *Body o' Caesar!*

Stephen, a country gull, swears *By this light! By my fackins faith! 'Sfoot! By this good light! Upon my reputation! O' God's lid! By God's will! Whoreson coney-catching rascal! By gadslid! I'faith! 'Slid! Whoreson base fellow!*, and a most fetching oath, quite unique, *Whoreson Scanderbeg rogue!*

Scanderbeg was the Albanian hero George Castriota, who helped his people defeat the Turks during the wars of the mid-fifteenth century. Perhaps his original Moslem faith, worthy of all the opprobrium of which an Englishman of the time could think, accounts for his figuring in a sixteenth-century oath.

Downright, a plain squire, exclaims, "By this good day—God forgive me I should swear!—if I put it up so, say I am the rankest cow that ever pissed. 'Sdeins, an I swallow this, I'll ne'er draw my sword in the sight of Fleet Street again, while I live." Downright also swears *Fore George! 'Sdeath! Mass! Heart!* and *I'faith!*

Edward Knowell swears *'Slight! God's so'! I protest!* and *Hang it!*—still a common expletive in contemporary England.

Stephen, who greatly admires Captain Bobadill's way with an oath, sighs wistfully, "O, he swears admirably! By Pharaoh's foot! Body o' Caesar! No, I shall never do it, sure—Upon mine honour, and by Saint George!—No, I ha' not the right grace."

And finally, Knowell senior, satirizing the virtues of the day, remarks, "A witty child! Can't [can it] swear? The father's darling! Give it two plums."

Ben Jonson pokes gentle fun at the swearers of his time and quite clearly disapproves the habit, which in his day was epidemic.

Our epidemiological survey brings us chronologically to John Marston's play *Antonio and Mellida*, a tragedy printed in 1602 but probably acted two years earlier. Here Dildo delivers himself of a fine series of metaphors, catching the very essence of the swearer's state of mind: "The match of furie is lighted, fastnd to the linstock of rage, and will presently set fire to the touchhole of intemperance, discharging the double coulvering of my incensement in the face of thy opprobrious speech."

In Marston's comedy *The Malcontent*, printed in 1604, there is a very pretty exchange. Malvole says, "What though I call thee old oxe, egregious wittal, broken-bellied coward, rotten mummy?"

To which Bilisio replies, as a sound man would, "Words, of course, terms of disport" (I, v).

In *The Dutch Courtezan* (1605) Marston has Mulligrub swear, "For the love of God!" And Mary Faugh exclaims, "Thers a lustie *bravo* beneath, a stranger, but a good stale rascall. He swears valiantlie, kicks a bawd right vertuously, and protests an empty pocket right desperately."

Cocledemoy, in the same play, swears by *The bread of God!* and Tisefan exclaims, "'Sdeath a virtue! what a damd things this! Whole trust fair faces, teares, and vowes? 'Sdeath! not I."

In this year, 1605, Marston together with George Chapman and Ben Jonson staged their play *Eastward Ho*. The following passage, held to be derogatory to the Scots, landed all three in gaol:

You shall live freely there [in Virginia] without sergeants, or courtiers, or lawyers, or intelligencers, only a few industrious Scots, perhaps, who are indeed dispersed over the face of the whole earth. But as for them there are no greater friends to English men and England. And for my part I would a hundred thousand of 'em were there, for we are all one country men now, ye know; and we should find ten times more comfort of them there than we do here.

III, iii

These were rather bold words, for upon the death of Elizabeth in 1603 James VI of Scotland had ascended the throne, and he was known to be sensitive to comments reflecting upon the Scots. James had showered his Scottish friends with favors, and this had rightly disgusted most Englishmen. James was aware of this, and what gave him equal umbrage were the references in the play to "my thirty-pound Knights," of whom James had created many. The words that gave offense seem utterly harmless to us, but they did not appear so to the king, who was infuriated and ordered the offending playwrights cast into jail. For a while the imprisoned playwrights were threatened with the direst punishments. But James' fiery temper tantrum was like a summer squall; it soon blew over, and the jailbirds were finally released. At a dinner given to celebrate their release from jail Ben Jonson's mother distinguished herself with a noble speech in which she told how she was ready to take a philter of poison to her son, had he not been released, which she would have consumed with him.

The theater has traditionally been the arena in which new and revolutionary ideas have been tried out, and almost from the earliest days of the English stage, playwrights have not infrequently been made to pay for their frowardness. During the seventeenth century the stage was increasingly to come under attack not only from without but also from within its own ranks. The chief grounds of complaint were abuse, impiety, and immorality.

James had come to England from a land that had long been engaged in the fruitless attempt to outlaw swearing. We have already had occasion to refer to the Scottish law against swearing of 1551 (pp. 129–130), which was further supplemented by others in 1561 and 1567. The Scottish legislation was known to have achieved no more positive results than to secure a very small sum from the fines levied on swearers.

Across the border in England those who sought to imitate the legislative example of the Scots met with as little success as the latter in enforcing it. In 1601 a measure "against usual and common swering" was introduced into the House of Commons, but it was dropped after the first reading in the House of Lords. This would appear to have been the first attempt at Parliamentary legislation upon the subject in England, and when James ascended the throne of England in 1603 it might have been supposed that he would look favorably upon the enactment of such laws in England. But James was himself too uncontrollable a swearer to do so; moreover, his early years as king were far too beset with difficulties for either James or Parliament to pay much attention to such legislation. The inauspicious beginning of James' reign and the consequences of the Gunpowder Plot of 1605 served to concentrate attention upon the more serious business of the land, but this did not prevent the Puritans from pressing through a piece of legislation that made it an offense for any person in any interlude, pageant, or stage play to use jestingly or profanely the name "of God, or of Christ Jesus, or the Holy Ghost, or of the Trinity." This was the Act of 1606 (3 Jac. I. c. 21).

In the same year Marston's play *The Parasitaster; or the Fawne* appeared. Here, Herod, a vicious braggart, exclaims, "As for my weake-raind brother, hang him! He has sore shinnes. Dam him, Heteroclite, his braine's perished." And again, he swears *By even truth!* (IV). Gonzago, Duke of Urbino, swears *Death a discretion!* (V).

The next year Marston renounced the drama and took holy orders, becoming incumbent of Christchurch, Hampshire. As any reader will observe, Marston's plays are singularly free of objectionable swearing.

In that other nonswearer's play, Ben Jonson's *Epicene, or The Silent Woman*, first acted in 1609, the swearing in general is most unremarkable, except for a very elegant series of curses. Sir John Daw does swear *By this picktooth!*—which is, at least, original. But the curses are the thing in this comedy. Morose, the egoistic old bachelor, swears at his barber, and Truewit humors him:

TRUEWIT: 'Tis very well, sir. If you laid on a curse or two more, I'll assure you he'll bear 'em. As that he may get the pox with seeking to cure it, sir? Or that, while he is curling another man's hair, his own may drop off? Or, for burning some male bawd's lock, he may have his brain beat out with the curling-iron?

MOROSE: No, let the wretch live wretched. May he get the itch, and his shop so lousy, as no man dare come at him, nor he come at no man!

TRUEWIT: Ay, and if he would swallow all his balls for pills, let not them purge him.

MOROSE: Let his warming-pan be ever cold!

TRUEWIT: A perpetual frost underneath it, sir.

MOROSE: Let him never hope to see fire again!

TRUEWIT: But in hell, sir.

MOROSE: His chairs be always empty, his scissors rust, and his combs mould in their cases.

TRUEWIT: Very dreadful that! And may he lose the invention, sir, of carving lanterns in paper.

And so Truewit goes on, cursing away, until even Morose can bear it no longer and cries out, "I beseech you, no more. . . . I will forgive him rather than hear any more. I beseech you, sir."

Such, are sometimes the happy results of the strategy of excess.

In 1609 also the Scots again bestirred themselves and by special act (103. Parl. 7. Jam. 6) ratified the act of 1551:

Against Cursing and Swearing, and not delating, or neglect to Prosecute, the same,

Abominable Oaths, and detestable Execrations, particularly Swearing in vaine by God's Blood, Body, Passions, and Wounds; saying Devil Stick, Gore, Rost, or Rieve them; and such other Execrations; are Punished as in Act 16. Parl. 5. Q. M. which is Ratified: The Penalties Augmented: And Censors appointed in the Mercat places of Burrows, and other publick Fairs, with power to put the Delinquents in ward till Payment, and Surety for abstaining in time coming: And that by Direction and Commission of the Judges Ordinary. And that all House-Holders Delate Transgressors within their Houses, under pains of being punished as offenders themselves. And if the said Majistrates be remiss, they shall be called before the Council, Committed to ward during pleasure, and fined surety for exact diligence thereafter.

As we have earlier noted, the Act of 1551 seems to have been directly inspired by William Dunbar's poem *The Sweirers and the Devill*, which he had composed early in the century and which had enjoyed considerable popularity. The very same "ugsome oaths" that were used by Dunbar's characters are recited one by one in the statute. Dunbar, who had been the Scottish national poet, was a man of great character, imagination, and Rabelaisian humor. The harshness of the Act of 1551 would have outraged him, for it specified that "a prelate of kirk, earl or lord," shall be fined twelvepence for the first offense, but shall be imprisoned or banished for a year for the fourth offense. It is hard to say which was worse, the English or the Scottish penalty, for by the Act of 1606 an Englishman was liable to a fine of fifty shillings! And so the ratified Act of 1609 continued to represent one of the few legal documents in history that embodied the phrases of a poet.

During the first decade of the seventeenth century the Puritans began their attacks on the citadels of the swearers, and there began to issue from pulpit and press an increasing volume of adjurative literature, not to mention sermonizing, against the practice of swearing. The printed works against swearing published between 1601 and 1650, from broadsides to books, numbered many hundreds. Some of the writers were men of considerable distinction, although most of the authors of these productions were as undistinguished as their writings, which were for the most part tiresomely similar. The authors were usually clergymen, the larger number of whom were Puritans.

The Dean of St. Paul's, Alexander Howell, took the field in 1611 with a tract entitled *A Sword Against Swearers*, which is in the usual pious vein and contains not a sentence that is remarkable.

The year 1611 saw the production of Beaumont and Fletcher's romantic drama *A King and No King*. Here, within the conventions relating to such matters, the swearing comprises a mixed bag of original and unoriginal traditional expressions. Bessus swears *Let me not live!* Mardonius, *I'll be sworn!* Lignes, *By my hand!* and Bacurius, *'Sfoot!* The king, Arbaces, as befits a king, swears *Oh, my temper! By all the world! By heaven and earth!* and the simple *Puft!*

In the following year, 1612, appeared one of the earliest protests against swearing on the stage. What was remarkable about this was that it was written not by a Puritan remonstrancer but by a fellow actor and fellow dramatist of Shakespeare, the sweet-natured Thomas Heywood (1574?–1641). The tract, entitled *An Apology for Actors*, gently deplored the growing tendency to scurrility on the stage. Even in the depth of passion Heywood retained his temperate mood, gently chiding his fellow dramatists for their forgetfulness and enjoining them to mend their ways.

Heywood's own plays are singularly free of swearing, except for an occasional *Pox* and such an innocuous expletive as *Heavens!* In *The Fair Maid of the West*, acted in 1617 and perhaps earlier, the kitchen maid swears at Roughman, "The devil take your ox-heels, you foul cods-head!" In the first act Spencer swears, "Go, let your master snick-up." The term is used as if to say, "Go, be hanged!" Its origin is obscure, but Shakespeare used it: "We did keep time, sir, in our catches. Snecke up!" (*Twelfth Night*, II, iii). The earliest record of the expression occurs in Henry Porter's *The Two Angrie Women of Abington* (1599). The expression is still or was until recently in use in some parts of western Yorkshire.

In 1612, too, Ben Jonson's comedy *The Alchemist* appeared. First acted in 1610, this play contains very little swearing, and what there is of it is unoriginal. Subtle, the alchemist, swears *I fart at thee! By heaven! A plague of Hell!* and *Pox on it!* There is a pretty passage in which Subtle says to Face, the housekeeper, "Giv'n thee thy oaths, thy quarrelling dimensions" (I, i). Dapper swears *By this hand and flesh! I'fac! By Gad!*

Face challenges Dapper, a clerk, about his being born with a caul over his head, "Come, you know it well enough," he says, "though you dissemble it." And Dapper replies, "I'fac, I do not. You are mistaken." "How!" says Face,

> Swear by your fac, and in a thing so known
> Unto the Doctor? How shall we, sir, trust you
> I' the other matter? Can we ever think,
> When you have won five or six thousand pound,
> You'll send us shares in 't, by this rate?

And Dapper declares, "By Gad, sir, I'll win ten thousand pound, and send you half. I'fac's no oath." And, indeed, while at one time to swear by one's faith may have been a legal oath, it no longer was so in Ben Jonson's day.

Bartholomew Fair, Jonson's next play, was produced in 1614 and printed in 1616. This farcical comedy, the plot of which is very slight, presents with much sport and drollery the scenes of a London fair, with all its colorful characters, language, and their singularities. In his Prologue, addressed to the king, Jonson, prepares his majesty for the language he "must expect" at such a place and speaks of the "rage" and "petulant ways/ Yourself have known, and have been vexed with long." Not quite sure of himself, but desirous of ensuring the pleasure of his temperamental monarch, Jonson addressed the king once more in

> The Epilogue
> Your Majesty hath seen the play, and you
> Can best allow it from your ear and view.
> You know the scope of writers, and what store
> Of leave is given them, if they take not more,
> And turn it into license: you can tell
> If we have used that leave you gave us well;
> Or whether we to rage or license break,
> Or be profane, or make profane men speak?
> This is your power to judge, great sir, and not
> The envy of a few. Which if we have got,
> We value less what their dislike can bring,
> If it so happy be t' have pleas'd the King.

Having at least once before fallen foul of the king, Jonson was careful to avoid the repetition of such a contingency. *Bartholomew Fair* is adorned with an occasional conventional but unobjectionable oath. Even Wasp's imprecations—*Turd i' your teeth! Shit o' your head!*—are no exceptions. Ursula, the pig woman, is a valiant curser, whose "quarrelsome dimensions" are unlimited. Quarlous, a gamester, is the recipient of a splendid blast:

Do you sneer, you dog's head, you trendle-tail!* You look as if you were begotten atop of a cart in harvest-time, when the whelp was hot and eager. Go, snuff after your brother's bitch, Mistress Commodity,† that's the livery you wear, 'twill be out at the elbows shortly. It's time you went to't, for the tother remnant.

In the year 1615 Sir John Harington's posthumously published *Epigrams* appeared. Harington (1561–1612), a godson of Queen

---

* A dog with a curled tail, hence, no thoroughbred.
† A whore.

Elizabeth, a courtier, a robust Rabelaisian with a flair for society and a witty pen, spoke thus "Against Swearing":

> In elder times an ancient custom was,
>   To sweare in weighty matters by the Masse.
>   But when the Masse went down (as old men note)
>   They sware then by the crosse of this same grote.
>   And when the Crosse was likewise held in scorne,
> Then by their faith, the common oath was sworne.
> Last, having sworne away all faith and troth,
> Only God damn them is their common oath.
>   Thus custome kept *decorum* by gradation,
>   That losing Masse, Crosse, Faith, they find damnation.

God damn me! we have already noted (p. 138) occurs for the first time in Shakespeare's *The Comedy of Errors* (1591).

Thomas Middleton and William Rowley's comedy *A Faire Quarrell*, published in 1617, which one would have thought presented many opportunities for fiery particles, is surprisingly almost wholly devoid of them. In the most quarrelsome scene of all Captain Ager calls the colonel *a foul-mouth'd fellow*, and the colonel replies by calling him *the son of a whore*, and that is all. Similarly, in Nathan Field's *Amends for Ladies*, of 1618, there is very little swearing, except for the too frequent iteration of *Damn-me*.

The combined effects of the Puritan offensive, the concern of the Crown, and the criticism from within their own ranks had begun to be felt. Playwrights were now cautious in the use of "language." They did not fail to record in good faith the life about them, but they willy-nilly resolved that, for the time being at any rate, discretion was indeed the better part of valor. Swearing, for the next several years, virtually disappeared from the stage.

Finally, in the year 1623 Parliament passed an act (21 Jac. I. c. 20) declaring:

For as much as all profane Swearing and Cursing is forbidden by the Word of GOD, be it therefore enacted, by the Authority of the then Parliament, that no Person or Persons should from thenceforth profanely Swear or Curse, upon the Penalty of forfeiting one Shilling to the use of the Poor for every Oath or Curse.

If any refuse to pay, upon Conviction, the Money is to be levied by Distress. And in defeet of Distress, the Offender is to be set in the Stocks if above twelve Years old, if under that Age he is to be whip'd by the Constable, or by the Parent, or Master if present.

This act was continued and ratified by the Parliament of Charles I in 1627 (3 Chas. I. c. 4).

Bishop John Earle's *Microcosmographie*, a book of characters full of wisdom and acute observations also appeared in 1623. One of the characters described is "A Prophane Man":

A Prophane Man is one that denies God as farre as the Law gives him leave, that is, only does not say so in downright Termes, for so farre hee may goe. A man that does the greatest sinnes calmly, and as the ordinary actions of life, and as calmely discourses of it againe. He will tell you his businesse is to breake such a Commandment, and the breaking of the commandment shall tempt him to it. His words are but so many vomitings cast up to the loathsomenesse of the hearers, onely those of his company loath it not. He will take upon him with oathes to pelt some tenderer man out of his company, and makes good sport at his conquest o're the Puritan foole. The Scripture supplies him for jests, and hee reades it of purpose to be thus merry. He will proove you his sin out of the Bible, and then ask if you will not take that Authority: He never sees the Church but of purpose to sleepe in it: or when some silly man preaches with whom he means to make sport, and is most jocund in the Church. One that nick-names Clergymen with all the terms of reproch, as *Rat, Black-coate*, and the like which he will be sure to keep up, and never calls them by other. That sings Psalmes when he is drunk, and cryes God mercy in mockery; for hee must doe it. Hee is one seemes to dare God in all his actions, but indeed would out-dare the opinion of him, which would else turne him desperate; for Atheism is the refuge of such sinners, whose repentance would bee onely to hang them selves.

It is in this last sentence that Earle exhibits the keynote of the seventeenth-century indictment against swearing. Profanity constitutes a threat to religion; therefore, it must be put down. And as the Puritans saw it, where persuasion fails, the application of the law must take its place. From the outset Puritans were devotedly good men of business, and they did not fail to perceive that a means of increasing the revenues of the church lay in the possibility of taxing the financial resources of the swearer. Not only was wealth considered to be an evidence of divine grace, but its instrument, business acumen, was also so esteemed.

Philip Massinger's play *The Parliament of Love*, written in 1624, is most well aired and free of wordy pollutants. Indeed, the new spirit in the air is clearly conveyed by the manner in which the noble lady Bellisant chides the courtiers:

> Whereas, now
> If you have travelled in Italy, and brought home
> Some remnants of the language, and can set
> Your faces in some strange and ne'er-seen posture,
> Dance a lavolta, and be rude and saucy;
> Protest, and swear, and damn (for these are acts
> That most think grace them) . . .
>
> I, v

In 1625 James I died and was succeeded by his son Charles I. Charles was a shy and dignified figure, a religious man who soon after his ascent to the throne came into conflict with Parliament. In the bitter struggle for supremacy that was to terminate in his death on the scaffold, Charles did not fail to enjoin upon his subjects that they conduct themselves as they ought.

In 1627 the Act of 1623 was ratified, with the clearest intimations of the direst penalties to all offenders.

During the year 1628, while the nation was engaged in fighting an unsuccessful war with France, John Taylor, the water poet, produced a poem entitled "A Dog of War," in which there were some pleasant stanzas on swearing. In this performance we may again perceive the disapproval into which the comminative habit had fallen. In his poem Taylor attempted to ridicule the habit.

A Dog of War

> Some like *Dominicall* Letters goe,
> In Scarlet from the top to toe,
> Whose valour's talke and smoake all.
> Who make (God sink 'em) their discourse,
> Refuse, Renounce, or Dam, that's worse,
> I wish a halter choake all.
>
> Yet all their talke is Bastinado,
> Strong Armado
> Hot Scalado,
> Smoaking
>   Trinidado.
> Of Cauvasado,
> Pallizado,
> Of the secret
> Ambuscado,
> Boasting with
>   Bravado.

> If Swearing could but
>   make a Man,
> Then each of these is one
>   that can
> With Oathes, an Army
>   Scatter:
>
> If Oathes could conquer
>   Fort, or Hold,
> Then I presume these
>   Gallants could
> With Braggs, a Castle
>   Batter.

Although the situations in Massinger's *The City Madam*, performed in 1632, are provoking enough, there is no swearing whatever. The self-censorship continued until the performance in this same year of Ben Jonson's *The Magnetick Lady, or The Humours Reconciled*. Ben Jonson once more found himself in trouble. The playwright, who was ill in bed, was at a complete loss to understand why a charge of blasphemy should be preferred against him, for his play was completely free of all profanity. The charge was brought in consequence of the rigor with which the ratified Act of 1623, now of date 1627, was being enforced. Hard swearing in the refined world of Charles I had become unfashionable, and the unrelenting attacks of the Puritans combined to make it less than tolerable. The King's Reader was therefore kept busily engaged expunging or attenuating such expletives as the more hard-mouthed writers permitted themselves. At this period the Master of the Revels was Henry Herbert, brother of poet George Herbert. It was Henry Herbert who had licensed the script of Ben Jonson's play and therefore given it official approval. He and the actors were summoned to appear before the ecclesiastical court; Jonson was excused from appearing because of his illness. Before the high commission of the court the actors at first claimed that they were not responsible, for they had merely uttered the words that had been in the original script. For a time things looked serious for the dramatist, until the actors changed their minds and confessed that they had themselves supplied the objectionable expletives. The dialogue had been too tame for their liking, so they had freely larded it, where they thought they ought, with oaths. No less a person than the Archbishop of Canterbury himself solemnly handed down the judgment that the playwright was guiltless of any offense.[1]

In the poem that opens *The Temple* (1633), his book of poems sacred and private, George Herbert writes:

The Church Porch

Take not his name, who made thy mouth, in vaine.
It getts thee nothing, and hath no excuse.
Lust, and wine plead pleasure; avarice gaine:
But the cheap swearer through his open sluce
  Lets his soule runne for nought, as little fearing;
  Were I an *Epicure*, I could bate swearing.

When thou doest tell anothers jest, therein
Omitt the oathes, which true witt cannot need.
Pick out of tales the mirth, but not the sinne.
He pares his apple, that will cleanely feed.
  Play not away the vertue of that name,
  Which is thy best stake, when greifes make thee tame.

Nowhere is the ridicule of swearing more clear than in Shackerley Marmion's comedy *A Fine Companion* (1633). The play is completely free of swearing, and poor Lackwit remarks, "An' they would but learn me to swear and take tobacco! 'tis all I desire. . . . Now do I want some two or three good oaths to express my meaning withall." It is all very laughable, and even the comments made on the noxious habit of smoking were designed to have the same effect: to satisfy the censorious as well as the censored on the assumption that virtue is so much more dangerous than vice because it is not subject to the constraints of the conscience. Thus, the culminating effects of the king's virtues and the Puritans' passions are to be seen in the special announcement that accompanied the production of James Shirley's play *The Young Admiral*, in which it was stated that the play was "free from oaths, profaneness, and obsceneness."

In 1633 a devastating attack on the stage was launched by the Puritan William Prynne in his *Histriomastix*. Had it not been for a supposed aspersion on the king and his queen, the book would have been well enough received. For the affront to their majesties, Prynne was fined £5,000 by the Star Chamber and was sentenced to have his ears cut off in the pillory and to imprisonment for life.

In July, 1635, letters patent were granted for the establishment of a public department charged with enforcing the laws against swearing. One Robert Lesley was appointed to the office of chief inquisitor and was authorized to take all the necessary steps in every parish of the land. It was stipulated that whatever money might be realized from the enforcement of the law against swearers was to be paid over to the bishops for the benefit of the deserving poor. From this sum the deputies, appointed by Lesley to each parish, were at liberty to deduct two shillings and sixpence for their pains.[2]

In 1640 the Acts of 1623 and 1627 were again ratified by Parliament, the last of Charles' parliamentary years. In 1642 civil war broke out, and the Puritan armies under the command of Oliver Cromwell took the field for Protestantism against the king, "popery, prelacy, superstition, heresy, schism, and profaneness." Soon Cromwell could boast of his Ironsides, "Not a man swears but pays his twelve pence." But under the military law of Cromwell, soldiers often paid with more than twelvepence for their profanity, as witness the case of the quartermaster Boutholmey, who was tried by council of war for uttering impious expressions. Found guilty in March, 1649, he was condemned to have his tongue bored with a red-hot iron, his sword broken over his head, and himself ignominiously dismissed the service. In the following year a dragoon was similarly sentenced by court-martial to be branded on the tongue.[3] The common citizenry was dealt with more leniently. From the records of the contemporary quarter sessions we learn that they were mostly punished by heavy fines. John Huishe of Cheriton in Somerset was convicted for swearing twenty-two oaths. Humfrey Trevitt, for swearing ten oaths, was ordered to pay 33s.4d. for the use of the poor, that is, at the rate of 3s.4d. per oath, three and a third times the ordinary penalty of twelvepence. William Harding of Chittlehampon in Devon was held to be within the act of swearing for saying, "Upon my life," and Thomas Buttand was fined for exclaiming, "On my troth!"[4]

As an example of the literature that was composed at this time and too frequently printed, the work of Walter Powell, "Preacher at Standish, neer Gocester," may serve as a sample for most. This work was printed in 1645 at London at the press of Matthew Simmons in Aldersgate Street. It is an octavo volume containing no less than 384 closely printed pages—all devoted to swearing. Its title page runs as follows:

A SUMMONS FOR SWEARERS, AND A Law for the Lips in reproving them: Wherein the chiefe Disswasives from Swearing are proposed, the sleight objections for swearing answered, The strange judgments upon Swearers, For-swearers, Cursers, *That take Gods Name in* vain, related. Which may be a terror to the wicked for swearing, and a preservative for the godly from Swearing. With sundry Arguments to prove the verity of the Scriptures, and excellencie of the Decalogue, against all prophane and Atheisticall deniers thereof.

Here we may observe once more that swearing is taken to be a "prophane and Atheisticall" denial of the faith.

Some notion of the style of this book, which is full of learning and ingenious argumentation, may be gathered from the following passages, the first from the Preface (which runs to twenty-four pages) and the second from the text.

What powder is to bullets, a clapper to the Bell, fire to wood, wings to a bird, wind to sailes, sailes to a ship, an edge to a razor, wine to the spirits, metall to a horse, a soul to the body, vivacity to any creature, that is zeale to a Christian, it acts his soul, it moves his affection. . . . "I will keep my mouth with a bridle, I will take heed unto my way, that I offend not in my tongue" [Ps. 39:1].[5]

.   .   .

Swearing hath been punished by men; by God. By men, heathen and Christians.

It was punished of the Romans with throwing down from the rock *Tarpeius*: Therefore when they did sweare, they held a stone in their hand and protested; If I lie or swear ought but truth, cast me down from the hill violently, as I fling this stone from me.

Of the Egyptians with loss of head, of the Grecians with loss of ears, of the Scythians with loss of goods, of the Turks with no admission of government, of *Maximilian* the Emperour with forfeiture of money, of *Justinian* the Emperour with putting to death, of *Lewis* King of France with searing the lips, of *Henry* the first King of England, with a payment to the poore for every oath vainly uttered, who caused within his palace a Duke to pay 40 shillings, a Lord 20 shillings, a Knight or Gentleman ten shillings, a yeomen three shillings fourpence, a Page or Servant to be scourged. . . . A good law to banish oathes out of a Land, Court, Citie, Countrey, lest oathes banish men out of all.[6]

Citing every religious and secular argument and authority against the swearer, Powell attacks him from every side. It is an overwhelming besiegement.

No less remarkable than this treatise is a work penned in 1647 by a twenty-year-old youth. This young man, who was already a scientist and who later became one of the outstanding savants of his age, was the Honorable Robert Boyle (1627–1691), a younger son of the Earl of Cork. However, this work was not published until April, 1695, four years after the death of its author, when it was considered as "seasonable" as it was "for those Times of Uncontroul'd Liberty and Confusion in which it was wrote." Throughout his life Boyle was a most conscionably pious Christian and composed and published more religious tracts than he did scientific ones. Of his gentle nature and nobility of character there are many records, and few of his later works reveal more of his character than this early composition. Entitled *A Free DISCOURSE AGAINST Customary Swearing AND A DISSUASIVE FROM CURSING*, the work was edited and prepared for the press and "Published by John Williams, D.D.," who also contributed the Dedication, to Boyle's eldest brother, the Earl of Cork, and to Sir Henry Ashhurst, Boyle's executors.[7]

The first part of the work is written in the form of "pleas" and "answers," and the following excerpt should convey some idea of the style and scope of the work:

Plea V

Nor will it avail the Oathmonger to reply, But I do not take God's Name in vain; for I swear not by God, or by Christ, or other Oaths of the like nature, but only by the Creatures, as by this Light, by this Bread, by Heaven, and the like; and the Creatures name I hope it is no sin to take in vain.

Ans. For sure if we will allow our Saviour to be best Interpreter of his Father's Commandments, he will teach us a very different Lesson, in those (already twice alledged) words of St. Matthew Matt. 5:34; for doubtless he that forbids to swear by Heaven, the noblest, or by Earth, the meanest Ingredients of this vast Fabrick of the World, intended that Prohibition should reach all other Creatures; which is as clear as light, in the ensuing words of the 37th verse of the same chapter; where Christ's express Injunction is, *But let your communication be yea, yea; nay, nay; for whatsoever is more than these, cometh of evil.*

Besides, either by the thing you swear by, you mean God, or no; if the former, your guilt is evident in the breach of God's Commandment; and if the latter, remember what the Spirit says in Jeremy 5:7, *How shall I pardon thee for this? Thy children have forsaken me, and sworn by them that are no gods.*

And so on to the end of the answer. The answer to the next plea is not unamusing.

Plea VI

Ally'd to this plea, is theirs that will not flatly swear by God, but by certain fictitious terms and abbreviatures, as by Dod, etc. and by the like disguising of them believe to justify their Oaths; as if they cared not, so (like *Saul* to the Witch of *Endor*) they may go mask'd to Satan.

Ans. To These I shall only answer with the Apostle, *Be not deceived, God is not mocked*; since (as the same Apostle elsewhere says) *He taketh the wise in their own craftiness.* Well may this childish Evasion cheat our own Souls, but never him, who judgeth as well as he discerns Intents; and regards not so much the precise signification of your words, as what they are meant and understood for; which (in such cases) is usually an Oath, since the same credit is both given and expected upon these mongrel Oaths, that is paid to those they mean, but would not seem. These people bring into my mind the Bloody Persecuters of our first Christians, who clothed them in the skins of savage beasts, that it might seem no crime to worry them; for so these Hypocrites disguise God's Name, to give themselves the license to dishonour it.

'Tis a very pretty flight of these Gentlemen, to cozen the Devil to their own advantage, and to find out By-ways to Damnation, and descend to Hell by a pair of backstairs; and methinks argues a Cunning much about the size of his, that pleaded he was innocent of falsifying the King's Coin, because he had displac'd some Letters in the *Motto.* But to Hell, as to Towns, these singular By-paths (tho less frequented) may read directlier than the broad Highways: And to these Gentlemen, and those that rely upon the last answer'd Objection, I shall at present only recommend the serious pondering of that passage of the Wise-man in the *Proverbs: All the ways of a man are clean in his own eyes, but the Lord weigheth the spirits.*

In the second section Boyle offers a series of well-reasoned directions calculated to assist the swearer in breaking himself of the habit. And in an "Advertisement," which follows this first part, Boyle makes it quite clear "that in no part of this Discourse my intention was to justify that plausible Error of our Modern Anabaptists, that indiscriminately condemn all Oaths as absolutely and indispensibly prohibited and abolished by the Gospel."

The second part of the work, *A Dissuasive from Cursing*, "For Mr. W. D. to Sir G. L.," is believed by the editor to be from Boyle's pen. In it the writer attempts to persuade his friend Sir G. L. of the iniquity of cursing, here too basing his argument entirely upon the teaching of the Scriptures.

During the period when Boyle wrote his essays on swearing (1647), the Scottish Parliament was doing its utmost to dissuade the people from the habit. In 1645 Parliament ordered that whoever should curse or blaspheme should upon a second conviction be "censurable" in the manner prescribed—that is, a nobleman should pay twenty pounds Scots; a baron, twenty marks; a gentleman, ten marks. The Act anticipates the case of a minister of religion coming under its provisions, in which case the punishment was the forfeit of the first part of his year's stipend. In 1649 a further enactment was passed (the previous one being admittedly too lenient), and in the same session the offense of cursing a parent was made punishable by sentence of death. In 1650, when the country was in a state of great excitement and men were rushing to arms to resist the invasion of Cromwell, an Act of Parliament was prepared that disqualified for command all officers who were addicted to swearing.

It may be remarked here that the interdiction of swearing to the troops in campaigns likely to be over in a few days is not without ingenuity, for the accumulated aggressiveness can be expended upon the enemy. But where the campaign is likely to be of considerable duration, prohibiting swearing would not only be likely to breed maladies but to be self-defeating. We shall speak of this later in connection with such ill-advised prohibitions among modern fighting forces.

As we have seen, the seriousness with which the Scots attacked swearing was no less than that with which the English approached the problem, hence the fact that battles were won and lost must be attributed to other causes.

The period of Puritan supremacy following the beheading of Charles I in 1649 served to consolidate the steady gains they had been making in the preceding years, and in 1642 playwriting virtually ceased, except for the bookshelves. On September 2, 1642, the blow was delivered, the following edict becoming the law of the land:

Whereas the distressed Estate of Ireland, steeped in her own Blood, and the distracted Estate of England, threatened with a cloud of Blood, by a Civill Warre, call for all possible meanes to appease and avert the Wrath of God appearing in these Judgements; amongst which Fasting and Prayer have been often tried to be very effectual, have been lately, and are still enjoyned, and whereas publicke Sports doe not well agree with publicke Calamities, nor publicke Stage-playes with the seasons of Humiliation, this being an exercise of sad and pious solemnity, and the other being Spectacles of, too commonly expressing lascivious Mirth and Levitie. It is therefore thought fit, and Ordeined by the Lords and Commons in this Parliament Assembled, that while these sad Causes and set times of Humiliation doe continue, publicke Stage-playes shall cease, and bee foreborne. Instead of which are recommended to the people of this Land, the profitable and seasonable Considerations of Repentance, Reconciliation, and peace with God, which probably may produce outward peace and prosperity, and bring again Times of Joy and Gladness to these Nations.[8]

The blackout was virtually complete. A few plays, however, under the pretext of a sacred or classical revival did manage to get produced, mostly as a consequence of the enterprising Sir William D'Avenant.

◖ *Swearing During the Restoration*

On May 28, 1660, Charles II entered London; he was crowned king April 23, 1661. After the return of the monarchy, no more was heard of the dominance of Puritanism. Hundreds of Puritans and as many Quakers were thrown into prison. John Bunyan, the village pastor of Bedford, spent eleven years in the village gaol, and it was during this period that he sent forth his *Pilgrim's Progress* to comfort and direct his fellow sufferers on their way to the Celestial City. The populace needed but the example of its profligate king for the full reaction to set in against Puritanism and the Commonwealth. The king wasted no time. He surrounded himself with a group of courtiers whose principal qualifications for the king's favor were wit and profligacy. It was no uncommon thing for these gentlemen to appear upon a public balcony drunk and nude or to amuse themselves by urinating into the bottles the encouraging contents of which they had just emptied down their throats and hurl them at the crowds assembled below to urge them on. This was one of the diversions of that remarkable man Sir Charles Sedley, who, among other things, contributed to the amusement of the king by presenting to him his daughter as a mistress. As for Charles' mistresses, these were numberless and notorious. To those that he kept about him for any length of time, and to such other ladies of the court as were willing, it was his habit to teach the most obscene oaths, as if they were parrots, and great was his delight to hear them repeat them out of as well as *in* season.

Charles II, perhaps the most amiable scoundrel who ever sat upon a throne, took the lead in ruling what could or could not be allowed upon the stage. An opportunity was afforded him early in his reign. In 1663, when Sir William D'Avenant submitted the manuscript of his play *The Wits* to the licenser previous to its production on the stage at Blackfriars, that dignitary saw fit to expunge all expressions that according to the new act were forbidden. But one who claimed Shakespeare for his father, as D'Avenant seriously did, would not accept the judgment of the licenser and took his complaint directly to the king. After reading the play, Charles found himself at variance with his licenser, ruling that the words "s'death," "s'light," and such kindred terms were asseverations merely, not oaths. Sir Henry Herbert, the licenser, had, of course, to submit to this ruling, but in his office book he has left a note maintaining his own judgment. This note reads: "The king is pleased to take 'Faith,' 'Death,' and 'S'light' for asseverations and no oaths, to which I do humbly submit as my master's judgment; but under favour conceive them to be oaths, and enter them here to declare my opinion and submission."[9] The play was returned to D'Avenant, and with the full sanction of the king it was produced in its uncensored state, the king taking the boat to Blackfriars to witness the first performance.

The licentiousness of the period took its cue from the court, and nowhere was this libertinism more freely exhibited than in the drama of the period. Neither before nor since has such freedom of expression been allowed upon the stage, and it need hardly be said that practically nothing by way of swearing was prohibited. The very first words of a play were apt to be a full-rounded oath. For example, *The Soldier's Fortune*, a play by Thomas Otway (1652–1685) produced in 1679, opens with these words, spoken by Beaugard: *A pox o' Fortune!*

In this play all the old oaths are aired—Beaugard's favorite being *By this light!* He also swears the following: *Igad, 'Sdeath,* and *Death and the Devil.* He can swear very gently, too, as when he says, "Sir, if you were to go to the Devil, I should think you very well disposed of."

Sir Jolly swears *Odd, Odd's life, Odd's fish, Odd's so (God's soul), A dad (Afore God), Udd's-bud (God's blood), 'Sbud (God's blood),* and *Gemeni* (probably a euphemism for *Jesus*).

In this play the third whore swears *O crimine,* a euphemism for Christ.

In the second part of this play, entitled *The Atheist*, which was first performed in 1684, Beaugard swears a new oath, *Ah dear damnation!*, and then *Hell and the devil!*

Courtrine swears *By this good day, Let me be hanged and quartered*, and curses *Clusters of poxes on ye*, and *no hospitals pity ye*.

Daredevil, who swears *Faith and troth, Pox on me, Rot me*, surprises Courtrine when he exclaims *Dam'me*. The following exchange takes place:

COURTRINE: Dam'me Sir? Do you know what you say? You believe no such thing?
DAREDEVIL: Words of course, Child, mere Words of course. We use a hundred of 'em in conversation, which are indeed but in the nature of Expletives, and signifie nothing: as *Dam'me, Sir; Rot me, Sir; Confound me, Sir*, which purport no more than *So, Sir; And, Sir;* or *Then, Sir*, at the worst; For my part, I always speak what I think; no Man can help thinking what he does think: So if I speak not well, the Faults not mine.

This explanation perfectly describes the Restoration view of swearing as a quite harmless means of expression "expletives [that] signifie nothing"—"Sound and fury," as Shakespeare said in another connection, "signifying nothing."

If we are to judge by the plays of Otway and others, various forms of the expression *Hang* were very popular at this period. Thus, in Otway's play *Friendship in Fashion*, produced in 1678, we have *Hang money, Hang't, Hang me*. Here, too, occur *Hell and confusion, Odds heart, 'Fore George, Before George, 'Ounds (God's wounds), Death and Destruction, Soul of my Honour, Blood! Fire! and Daggers!*

Oaths like *Hell and confusion, Death and Destruction, Blood! Fire! and Daggers!* were apparently innovations of the Restoration.

One of the first new plays to be acted after the accession of Charles II was *The Parson's Wedding*, by Thomas Killigrew (1612–1683), which was produced in 1663. Among the older oaths such as, *Faith! As I live, Cuds body, God's nigs, Jesus, By this hand*, and *By this light*, we also find *By sire and damn, Thou son of a thousand fathers! Son of a batchelour! The Devil he does, A pox forbid it! How the pox, A pox of a good husband, A pox, Paxat. Thou son of a thousand fathers!* is a somewhat surprising oath and at this time probably represented a new importation into England. In the play it is uttered by the Captain. Actually, the oath is a very ancient Eastern expression, and in the East today it is also encountered in the form of *Thou son of a thousand dogs*. *Son of a batchelour* also seems new and suggests *son of a bitch*, a favorite modern American oath. All these oaths are, of course, euphemistic expressions for *bastard*.

As for the forms of *pox*, there is actually nothing unusual in any of them, except possibly *paxat*, for they are all found in plays of the sixteenth century, while *paxat* (poxed), at least in the spelling *pax*, occurs in Thomas Middleton's *A Trick to Catch the Old One* (1605)—*Pax on't, I can ne'er hit of that place either* (II, i).

Here it may be remarked that the pronunciation *a* for *o* was common during the sixteenth century. The word *not*, for example, was frequently pronounced *nat* and written so (as may be seen from the quotation from Elyot, p. 128). Queen Elizabeth, for instance, pronounced *shop* as *shap*. A survival of this old form of pronunciation is seen in the word *strap*, of which the old form *strop* is now preserved only by the barber. And while *toffee* is more popular than *taffee* the latter is often preferred to the former. *Drat it* for *God's rot*, *Gad* for *God*, and *Stap* for *Stop* are additional examples. But in the seventeenth century *pax* was no longer an archaism or a survival but a flourishing affectation.

On February 5, 1663, John Dryden's first play, *The Wild Gallant*, was produced before the king at the Theatre Royal. The king, it is recorded, was bored—as well he might have been, for the play, despite its title, was not very exciting. It is worthy of note here because in the very first scene the word *bloody* occurs in a colloquial sense, when Bibber, the tailor remarks, "Well, in short, I was drunk; damnably drunk with Ale: great Hogen Mogen bloody Ale: I was porterly drunk; and that I hate of all things in Nature."

Here the use of *bloody* is in its perfectly respectable colloquial sense, before the word had fallen into disrepute, which we shall be concerned with later. The rest of the play is peppered with *I gad, I vow to god, I'faith, By this hand, By this good light, Gramarcy ifaith, Pox on't, I'll be hanged.*

We run through half a dozen of Dryden's plays before we encounter one that contains any notable swearing: *The Tempest*, first produced November 7, 1667.

The exchanges during the storm at sea are reminiscent of Friar John's volleys aimed at Panurge and the jolly tars.

MUSTACHO: O Master! six foot Water in Hold.
STEPHANO: Clap the helm hard aboard. . . .
TRINCALO: Overhaul your fore-boling.
STEPHANO: Brace in the Lar-board. [*A great cry within.*]
TRINCALO: A curse upon this howling, they are louder than the weather. [*Enter* ANTONIO *and* GONZALO]. Yet again, what do you here! Shall we give O're, and drown? ha' you a mind to sink?
GONZALO: A pox o' your throat, you bawling, blasphemous, uncharitable dog.
TRINCALO: Work you then.
ANTONIO: Hang, Cur, hang, you whoreson insolent noise-maker, we are less afraid to be drown'd than thou art."

I, i

"This wide chopt rascal" Antonio calls Trincalo, the boatswain; then there is a clap of thunder capable of shivering the timbers of the most hardened sailor.

Dryden's *The Assignation*, appropriately dedicated to Sir Charles Sedley and produced in the winter of 1672, contains a conventional quantity of swearing, but nothing very remarkable.

The plays of Sir Charles Sedley and those of William Wycherley, perhaps the two lewdest writers of Restoration comedies, are surprisingly deficient in swearing. The little swearing their works contain calls for no particular comment here.

Thomas Shadwell's comedy *The Virtuoso*, produced at the Duke's Theatre in May, 1676, pokes fun at the shallow pedants who had rushed headlong and ill equipped into the study of natural history, experimental philosophy, and other sciences, after the fashion of the fellows of the Royal Society, then only little more than ten years old. Sir Samuel Hearty, a character described as "the most amorous coxcomb" who "has never made Love where he was not refus'd, nor waged War where he was not beaten," is full of *I'faith, I'gads, Pox*, and *I vow to gad*. Old Snarl swears by *'Sdeath! 'Ounds!* and *By the Mass*; Sir Formal Trifle, *Upon my sincerity* and *By my integrity*.

There exists a curious tract of four folio pages printed in 1681 at London "for N. T." entitled *The Swearing-Master: Or, A Conference Between Two Country-Fellows Concerning the Times*. The two "Country-Fellows" are Ned and Will. The latter draws the attention of Ned to "a Swearing-Master . . . come down into our Country here to set up a Swearing-School." Says Ned, "Hang 'em, they'l do no good on't here in the Country; they were better e'en go back again to *London*, and there they may fairly put out Printed-bills of their Mystery. But what do such clumsie Bumkinly Fellows as thou an I care for *swearing*, except it be at the Alehouse, or at the 'sizes? and there we can do it without the help of a *Master*."[10]

The persiflage, such as it is, and the meaning of the whole performance escapes me. But there it is. There really were no Swearing-Masters, any more than there ever existed any Roaring-School Masters. One could have wished them a more substantial being than the imagination of their creators.

In one of the most unswearingful plays of the period, Nathaniel Lee's *Constantine the Great* (1684), there is so much oath taking, foreswearing, and beswearing that it surely must rank as one of the most be-oathed plays of all time. Almost everyone takes an oath at one time or another in the play, and the most popular exclamation, which, again, almost everyone uses, is *By heaven!* It is in this play that one character so memorably remarks of another, that he

> Vows with so much passion, swears with so much grace
> That 'tis kind of heaven to be deluded by him.

Dudley Bradstreet, the contemporary adventurer, tells how, as a soldier, he "learned, when at a Loss for Words, to swear pretty gracefully." And, indeed, vulgar swearing is one thing, but to swear with delicacy, grace, propriety, and judgment is quite another. It is not given to everyone to understand the sublimity of the accomplishment of a proficient swearer. This is, doubtless, due to the premature judgment that the art is a pejorative one. But is it not possible that, as an art, swearing can be as skillful as any other? If our censorious contemporary judges could bring themselves to the state of candor of a Lackwit, who in abject and deserving admiration declares to the Captain, "I desire, sir, to incorporate you into my acquaintance," and express themselves equally openly toward swearing, they would not be given over in their gray hairs to that lack of sympathy that characterizes those who have never known what they have missed. It is, in such matters, no consolation to reflect that there are some who cannot even see a hole through a ladder—it is one of those elemental facts of nature with which we must all learn to live.

On February 6, 1685, the sovereign lord Charles II shuffled

off this mortal coil with the words, addressed to his assembled courtiers, "Gentlemen, I'm sorry to be so unconscionably long a time adying." Having been some fifty-five years unconscionably long aliving, Charles contrived to leave no legitimate descendants, though his illegitimate children were innumerable. He was succeeded by his tactless and unfortunate brother James II. Deposed three years later, James was succeeded in 1689 by William III and Mary II, a joint reign that came to an end without issue with William's death in 1702, when the throne passed to Anne, the daughter of James II.

In 1694 a new act was passed (6 and 7 Wm. III. c. 2), entitled *An Act for the More Effectual Suppressing Profane Cursing, and Swearing*, wherein it is appointed

That any Person or Persons who should Swear or Curse, in the Presence, or Hearing of any Justice of Peace, Mayor, Bailiff, or other head Officer; or should be convicted before any of these, by the Oath of our Witness (provided, the Information be within ten Days after the Offence committed) that such should forfeit and pay to the Use of the Poor the respective Sums after mentioned; that is to say, every Servant, Day Labourer, common Soldier, and common Seaman, is, for every Offence, to pay one Shilling. Every other Person is to pay two Shillings. And, if after Conviction, such Persons offend a second Time, they are to pay double. And if a third time, treble to what was paid for the first Offence.

The Money to be levied by Distress. And in defect of Distress, the Offender is to be set in the Stocks, if above sixteen. If under that Age to be whip'd by the Constable, or by the Parent, Guardian, or Master of such Offender in the presence of the Constable.

Magistrates that wilfully and willingly omit their Duty in the Execution of this Act, are to forfeit five Pounds; the one Moiety to the use of the Informer, to be recovered by Suit in any of His Majesty's Courts of Westminster.

[But] . . . if any Action or Suit be commenced against any Person, for doing, or causing to be done any thing in pursuance of this Act, treble Costs shall be allowed to such in Defense of themselves.

This Act is appointed to be read in Churches four Times every Year, immediately after Morning Prayer.

In 1696 a broadside appeared, *The Character of the Beaux*, by an anonymous satirist delightfully capturing the mannerisms of that fop. Attending the theater,

while the *Play's* Acting, he turns his Back to the Stage, as disregarding such *Nonsense*; and crying, *Damme*, here's a dam'd Play; then speaking to a *Masque Madam*, says he, *How can your ladyship sit it?* Why, Sir, *says she?* Methinks 'tis very tolerable; *O ged Madam! no, the Devil take me if I cou'dn't write a more tolerable one* ex Tempore: But if she still persists to commend it, and will needs confute him, as O dear Sir! I'm sure you wrong your Judgment now, this *Scene* is very pretty, and witty; then the *Fop* complies a little, and, with a simple Grimace, He! He! *Why faith*, Madam, *this is indifferent, though if such a thing had been out or in, 'twou'd ha' been much better;* still criticising, and pretending to amend what he does not understand: When an Hour or two's spent there, he goes to the *Park*, and creeping to a Lady, O Madam, *I'm almost suffocated; stop my Vitals! the Smoak of* London *is insufferable: How does your Ladyship find it?* yet, not permitting her to Answer; *O Madam, renounce me, if I am not ready to expire; your Ladyship's most humble Servant*: Then the same Stuff to another, always endeavouring to speak Fine, and Unintelligibly.[11]

This is the year of the comedy *The Relapse* by Sir John Vanbrugh (1664–1726), in which "the nice, affected Beau" is Lord Foppington himself, down to his very oaths. *The Relapse*, one of the most enchanting of comedies, contains some pretty swearing. Young Fashion, Lord Foppington's brother, swears, " 'Sdeath and Furies! Why was that Coxcomb thrust into the World before me? O Fortune—Fortune—thou art a Bitch by Gad—"(I, ii).

Lord Foppington swears *Strike me Dumb, Stap my vitals, Death and Eternal Tartures, By all that's Great and Powerful, Gad's curse, O Lard, Far Gad's sake, Before Gad, Strike me speechless.*

Vanbrugh's *The Provok'd Wife*, produced in 1697, contains the proper sprinkling of *pox, oons, damn, devil.* " 'Tis a damn'd Atheistical Age, wife," exclaims Sir John Brute to his spouse. Lady Brute assures Bellinda that women are as wicked as men, "but our Vice lies another way: Men have more Courage than we, so they commit more Bold, Impudent Sins. They Quarrel, Fight, Swear, Drink, Blaspheme, and the like. Whereas we, being Cowards, only Backbite, tell Lyes, Cheat at Cards, and so forth" (V, ii).

These two plays were soon to be the subject of a bitter attack, largely because of the alleged profanities contained in them. But let us go on to one more play before we turn to this.

In George Farquhar's play *Love and a Bottle*, first produced about mid-December, 1698, a beggar comments upon the charity of soldiers as compared with the clergy in the following words: "Ay, Sir, A Captain will say Dam'me, and give me Six-pence; and a Parson shall whine out God bless me, and give me not a farthing: Now I think the Officer's Blessing much the best" (I, i).

Young Squire Mockmode, just down from the university, desires to "bind himself 'prentice to a beau. Cou'd I but dance well, push well, play upon the Flute, and swear the most modish Oaths, I wou'd set up for Quality with e're a young Nobleman of 'em all, —Pray what are the most fashionable Oaths in Town? *Zoons*, I take it, is a very becoming one."

RIGADOON: Zoons is only us'd by the disbanded Officers and Bullies: but Zauns is the Beaux pronunciation.
MOCKMODE: Zauns—
CLUB [SERVANT *to* MOCKMODE]: Zauns—
RIGADOON: Yes, Sir, we swear as we Dance; smooth, and with a Cadence. Zauns! 'Tis harmonious, and pleases the Ladies, because 'tis soft.—Zauns, Madam,—is the only Compliment our great Beaux pass on a Lady.

Mockmode, having taken some "snush," finds he must sneeze.

MOCKMODE: Zauns I must sneeze—[*Sneezes*]—Bless me.
RIGADOON: Oh fie, Mr. *Mockmode!* what a rustical expression that is.— Bless me!— you should upon all such occasions cry Dem me. You wou'd be as nauseous to the Ladies, as one of the old Patriarks, if you us'd that obsolete expression.

II, ii

But for all his *Zauns*es and *Dem me*s Mockmode's favorite oath remains, as he begun, *By the Universe!*

Some months before the production of this play there issued from the pen of Jeremy Collier (1650–1726), a nonjuring clergy-man, a scathing attack upon the plays of the day, *A Short View of the Immorality and Profaneness of the English Stage*.[12] Pub-lished in March, 1698, it was widely read and sold out as many as three editions in as many months. Collier's criticism was symp-tomatic of the growing dissatisfaction of the public with the loose-ness of the theater.

Collier devotes the first 55 pages of his book to the immorality of the stage, the next 40 pages deal with cursing and swearing on the stage, and the remaining 192 pages deal both more gen-erally and more particularly with aspects of these offenses. What appears to be a disproportionately large part of the work deals with vulgar swearing and profane and blasphemous language. Collier asks:

What is more frequent than their Wishes of Hell and Confusion, Devils and Diseases, all the Plagues of this World, and the next, to each other?

And as for Swearing, 'tis used by all Persons, and upon all Occasions: By Heroes, and Paltroons; by Gentlemen, and Clowns; Love and Quarrels; Success and Disappointment; Temper and Passion, must be varnish'd, and set off with *Oaths*. At some times, and with some *Poets*, Swearing is no ordinary Relief. It stands up in the room of Sense, gives Spirit to a flat Expression, and makes a Period Musical and Round. In short, 'tis almost all the Rhetorick, and Reason some People are masters of: The manner of performance is different. Sometimes they mince the matter; change the Letter, and keep the Sense, as if they had a mind to steal a Swearing (*Gad* for *God*), and break the Commandments without Sin. At another time, the Oaths are clipt, but not so much within the Ring, but that the *Image and Superscription* are visible. These Expedients I conceive are more for variety, than Conscience: For when the fit comes on them, they make no difficulty of swearing at length. Instances of all these kinds may be met with in the *Old Batchelour, Double Dealer*, and *Love for Love*. And to mention no more, *Don Quixot*, the *Provok'd Wife*, and the *Relapse*, are particularly Rampant and Scandalous.

Writing at boiling point, Collier often detects salacious allusions and profanity where none was intended. He attributes the immorality of the age to the corrupting influence of the stage. The truth was quite otherwise; the immorality was due to totally different causes, of which the contemporary drama was but one expression. Dryden, referring to Collier, puts the matter more justly:

> Perhaps the Parson stretched a point too far,
> When with our theatre he urged war.
> He tells you that this very moral age
> Received the first infection from the stage;
> But sure a banisht Court, with lewdness fraught,
> The seeds of open vice, returning, brought.[13]

The immorality of the age was largely due to the pattern of reaction to the Puritan Commonwealth set by the profligate Charles II and his cronies—a design for living that they openly encouraged dramatists to represent and improve upon the stage. But on the whole Collier had a sound case, and he argued it well and wittily.

Thomas D'Urfrey, William Congreve, and John Vanbrugh all made replies to the attack upon them. D'Urfrey and Congreve were rather surprisingly lusterless, and Vanbrugh was not much better.

Vanbrugh urged in his own defense:

whether such Words are entirely justifiable or not, there's this at least to be said for 'em; That People of the Nicest Rank both in their Religion and their Manners throughout *Christendom* use 'em.

In France you meet with *Par Die, Par Bleu, Ma Foy,* &c., in the constant Conversation of the Ladies and the Clergy, I mean those who are religious up to Bigotry it self; and accordingly we see they are always allow'd in their Plays: And in England, we meet with an Infinity of People, Clergy as well as Laity, and of the best Lives and Conversations who use the Words *I-God, I-faith, Cods fish, Cot's my Life,* and many more, which all lye liable to the same objection.

Now whether they are right or wrong in doing it, I think at least their Example is Authority enough for the Stage; and shou'd have been enough to have kept so good a Christian as Mr. *Collier* from loading his Neighbour with so foul a Charge as Blasphemy and Prophaneness, unless he had been better provided to make it good.[14]

Vanbrugh was perfectly right in this defense for, as he said, he was merely reflecting the manners of his time. Collier, on the other hand, wrote out of hatred of the theatre, and went to great pains to support his hostility by quoting freely from the writings of the Ancients on the same score.

In 1699 Collier replied in *A Defense of the Short View* to both Congreve and Vanbrugh, and the effect was telling.[15] In 1700 Collier published *A Second Defense,* and in 1701 he issued a tract entitled *Maxims and Reflections Upon Plays.* Collier, off to a good start, was nothing loath to make the best of his advantage, and it must be said that his attacks did a great deal to decrease swearing and bawdiness on the stage. This was not altogether due to Collier's writings, but certainly he precipitated a very general feeling that during the next century succeeded in carrying its influence through the public taste to the dramatists who were willing to cater to it.

George Farquhar made a more effective riposte by writing a comedy taking up the gauntlet that Collier had thrown down. This was *The Twin-Rivals,* produced at the Theatre Royal on December 14, 1702. In the Preface Farquhar wrote:

The Success and Countenance that Debauchery has met with in Plays, was the most Severe and Reasonable Charge against their Authors in Mr. *Collier's short View*; and indeed this Gentleman has done the *Drama* considerable Service, had he Arraign'd the Stage only to Punish it's Misdemeanours, and not to take away it's Life; but there is an Advantage to be made sometimes of the Advice of an Enemy, and the only way to disappoint his Designs, is to improve upon his invective, and to make the Stage flourish by vertue of that Satyr, by which he thought to suppress it.

I have therefore in this Piece, endeavour'd to show, that an *English* Comedy may Answer the strictness of Poetical Justice. . . . I thought indeed to have sooth'd the Splenetick Zeal of the City, by making a Gentleman a Knave, and Punishing their great Grievance—A *Whoremaster*; but a certain Virtuoso of that Fraternity has told me since, that the Citizens were never more disappointed in any Entertainment, for (said he) however Pious we may appear to be at home, yet we never go to that end of the Town, but with an intention to be Lewd.

The result was that the galleries were unusually thin during the run of the play to the mortification of the author and to the delight, no doubt, of Collier.

In 1697 Daniel Defoe in *An Essay Upon Projects* proposed the establishment of an Academy that would preside over the uses of the English language. In this dissertation Defoe delivers himself of a fusillade against the intemperate habit of swearing, which typifies the reaction that had set in against the licentiousness of the preceding period.

Defoe urges as a principal purpose of the Academy the polishing and refining of the English tongue and the purging from it of "all the irregular Additions that Ignorance and Affectation have introduced." In that connection, he writes:

I ask leave here for a Thought or two about the Inundation Custom has made upon our Language and Discourse by *Familiar Swearing*; and I place it here, because Custom has so far prevail'd in this foolish Vice, that a man's Discourse is hardly agreeable without it; and some have taken upon them to say, *It is pity it shou'd not be lawful, 'tis such a Grace in a man's Speech, and adds so much Vigour to his Language.*

I desire to be understood right, and that by Swearing I mean all those Cursory Oaths, Curses, Execrations, Imprecations, Asseverations, and by whatsoever other Names they are distinguish'd, which are us'd in Vehemence of Discourse, in the Mouths almost of all men more or less, of what sort soever.

I am not about to argue any thing of their being sinful and unlawful, as forbid by Divine Rules; *let the Parson alone to tell you that*, who has, no question, said as much to as little purpose in this Case as in any other: But I am of the opinion, that there is nothing so Impertinent, so Insignificant, so Sensless and Foolish, as our vulgar way of Discourse, when mix'd with Oaths and Curses; and I wou'd only recommend a little Consideration to our Gentlemen, who have Sense and Wit enough, and wou'd be asham'd to speak Nonsense in other things, but value themselves upon their Parts; I wou'd but ask them to put into Writing the Common-Places of their Discourse, and read them over again, and examine the *English*, the *Cadence*, the *Grammar* of them; then let them turn them into *Latin*, or translate them into any other Language, and but see what a *Jargon* and Confusion of Speech they make together.

Swearing, that Lewdness of the Tongue, that Scum and Excrement of the Mouth, is of all Vices the most foolish and sensless; it makes a man's Conversation *unpleasant*, at least to those who do not use the same foolish way of Discourse; and, indeed, is an Affront to all the Company who swear not as he does; for if I swear and Curse in Company, I either presume all the Company likes it, or affront them who do not.

Then 'tis *fruitless*; for no man is believe'd a jot the more for all the Asseverations, *Damnings* and Swearings he makes: Those who are us'd to it themselves, do not believe a man the more, because they know they are so customary, that they signify little to bind a man's Intention; and they who practise them not, have so mean an opinion of those that do, as makes them think they deserve no belief.

Then, they are the Spoilers and Destroyers of a man's Discourse, and turn it into perfect *Nonsense*; and to make it out, I must descend a little to Particulars, and desire the Reader a little to foul his Mouth with the Bruitish, Sordid, Sensless Expressions, which some Gentlemen call Polite *English*, and speaking with a Grace.

Some part of them indeed, tho' they are foolish enough, as Effects of a mad, inconsiderate Rage, are yet *English*; as when a man swears he will do this or that, and it may be adds, *God damn him he will*; that is, *God damn him if he don't*: This, tho' it be horrid in another sense, yet may be read in writing, and is *English*: But what Language is this?

Jack, *God damn me* Jack, *How do'st do, thou little dear Son of a Whore? How hast thou done this long time, by God?*—And then they kiss; and the t'other, as lewd as himself, goes on;

Dear Tom, *I am glad to see thee with all my heart, let me dye. Come, let us go take a Bottle, we must not part so; prithee let's go and be drunk by God.*—

This is some of our new florid Language, and the Graces and Delicacies of Stile, which if it were put into *Latin*, I wou'd fain know which is the principal Verb.

But for a little further remembrance of this Impertinence, go among the Gamesters, and there nothing is more frequent than, *God damn the Dice*, or *God damn the Bowls*.

Among the Sportsmen 'tis, *God damn the Hounds*, when they are at a Fault; or *God damn the Horse*, if he bau'ks a Leap: They call men *Sons of Bitches*, and Dogs, *Sons of Whores*: And innumerable Instances may be given of the like Gallantry of Language, grown now so much a *Custom*.

'Tis true, Custom is allow'd to be our best Authority for Words, and 'tis fit it should be so; but Reason must be the Judge of Sense in Language, and Custom can never prevail over it. *Words*, indeed, like Ceremonies in Religion, may be submitted to the Magistrate; but *Sense*, like the Essentials, is positive, unalterable, and cannot be submitted to any Jurisdiction; 'tis a Law to it self, 'tis ever the same, even an Act of Parliament cannot alter it.

Words, and even Usage in Stile, may be alter'd by Custom, and Proprieties in Speech differ according to the several Dialects of the Countrey, and according to the different manner in which several Languages do severally express themselves.

But there is a direct Signification of Words, or a *Cadence in Expression*, which we call speaking *Sense*; this, like Truth, is sullen and the same, ever was and will be so, in what manner, and in what Language soever 'tis express'd. *Words* without it, are only Noise, which any Brute can make as well as we, and Birds much better; for *Words* without *Sense* make but dull Musick. Thus a man may speak in *Words*, but perfectly unintelligible as to *Meaning*; he may *talk* a great deal, but *say* nothing. But 'tis the proper Position of *Words*, adapted to their Significations, which makes them intelligible, and conveys the Meaning of the Speaker to the Understanding of the Hearer; the contrary to which we call *Nonsense*; and there is a superfluous crowding in of insignificant Words, more than are needful to express the thing intended, and this is *Impertinence*; and that again carry'd to an extreme, is *ridiculous*.

Thus when our Discourse is interlin'd with needless Oaths, Curses, and long *Parentheses* of Imprecations, and with some of very indirect signification, they become very *Impertinent*; and these being run to the extravagant degree instanc'd in before, become perfectly *ridiculous* and *Nonsense*; and without forming it into an Argument, it appears to be *Nonsense* by the Contradictoriness; and it appears *Impertinent*, by the Insignificancy of the Expression.

After all, how little it becomes a Gentleman to debauch his Mouth with Foul Language, I refer to themselves in a few Particulars.

This Vicious Custom has prevail'd upon Good Manners too far; but yet there are some degrees to which it is not yet arriv'd.

At first, The worst Slaves to this Folly will neither teach it *to*, nor approve of it *in* their Children: Some of the most careless will indeed negatively teach it, but not by reproving them for it; but sure no man ever order'd his Children to be taught to curse or swear.

. . . The Grace of Swearing has not obtain'd to be a Mode yet among the Women; *God damn ye*, does not sit well upon a Female Tongue; it seems to be a Masculine Vice, which the Women are not arriv'd to yet; and I wou'd only desire those Gentlemen who practice it themselves, to hear a Woman swear: It has no Musick at all there, I am sure; and just as little does it become any Gentleman, if he wou'd suffer himself to be judg'd by all the Laws of Sense or Good Manners in the world.

'Tis a senseless, foolish, ridiculous Practice; 'tis a Mean to no manner of End; 'tis Words spoken which signify nothing; 'tis Folly acted for the sake of Folly, which is a thing even the Devil himself don't practice: The Devil does evil, we say, but it is for some design, either to seduce others, or, as some Divines say, from a Principle of Enmity to his Maker: Men Steal for Gain, and Murther to gratify their Avarice or Revenge; Whoredoms and Ravishments, Adulteries and Sodomy, are committed to please a vicious Appetite, and have alluring Objects; and generally all Vices have some previous Cause, and some visible Tendency; but this, of all Vicious Practices, seems the most Nonsensical and Ridiculous; there is neither Pleasure nor Profit; no Design pursued, no Lust gratified, but is a mere Frenzy of the Tongue, a Vomit of the Brain, which works by putting a Contrary upon the Course of Nature.

Again, other Vices men find some Reason or other to give for, or Excuses to palliate; men plead Want, to extenuate Theft; and strong Provocations, to excuse Murthers; *and many a lame Excuse they will bring for Whoring*; but this sordid Habit, even those that practice it will own to be a Crime, and make no Excuse for it; and the most I cou'd ever hear a man say for it, was, That *he cou'd not help it*.

Besides, as 'tis an inexcusable Impertinence, so 'tis a Breach upon Good Manners and Conversation, for a man to impose the Clamour of his Oaths upon the Company he converses with; if there be any one person in the Company that does not approve the way, 'tis an imposing upon him with a freedom beyond Civility; as if a man shou'd *Fart* before a Justice, or *talk Bawdy* before the Queen, or the like.

To suppress this, Laws, Acts of Parliaments, and Proclamations, are Bawbles and Banters, the Laughter of the Lewd Party, and never had, as I cou'd perceive, any Influence upon the Practice; nor are any of our Magistrates fond or forward of putting them in execution.

It must be Example, not Penalties, must sink this Crime; and if the Gentlemen of *England* wou'd once drop it as a Mode, the Vice is so foolish and ridiculous in it self, 'twou'd soon grow odious and out of fashion.

This Work such an Academy might begin; and I believe nothing wou'd so soon explode the Practice, as the Publick Discouragement of it by such a Society. Where all our Customs and Habits both in Speech and Behaviour, shou'd receive an Authority. All the Disputes about Precedency of Wit, with the Manners, Customs, and Usages of the Theatre wou'd be decided here; Plays shou'd pass here before they were Acted, and the Criticks might give their Censures, and damn at their pleasure; nothing wou'd ever dye which once receiv'd Life at this Original: The Two Theatres might end their Jangle, and dispute for Priority no more;

Wit and Real Worth shou'd decide the Controversy, and here shou'd be the *Infallible Judge*.

> *The Strife wou'd then be only to do well,*
> *And he alone be crown'd who did excell.*
> *Ye call'd them* Whigs, *who from the Church withdrew,*
> *But now we have our* Stage-Dissenters *too;*
> *Who* scruple Ceremonies *of Pit and Box,*
> *And very few are Sound and Orthodox:*
> *But love Disorder so, and are so nice,*
> *They hate* Conformity, *tho' 'tis in Vice.*
> *Some are for* Patent-Hierarchy; *and some,*
> *Like the* old Gauls, *seek out for Elbow-room;*
> *Their Arbitrary Governors disown,*
> *And build a* Conventicle-Stage o' *their own.*
> *Phanatick Beaus make up their gawdy Show,*
> *And Wit alone appears* Incognito.
> *Wit and Religion suffer equal Fate;*
> *Neglect of both attends the warm Debate.*
> *For while the Parties strive and countermine,*
> *Wit will as well as Piety decline.*[16]

This was a perceptively topical disquisition, in which Defoe sensibly recognized that penalties would continue to be utterly ineffectual to suppress men's desire to swear and that worthy example would be more likely to succeed. Defoe's observation on the want of "Musick" in the swearing of women was already probably old in his time (see Mark Twain's observation on the subject, p. 68), though "to swear like a Billingsgate scold" or "fishwife" was an expression that in his own day testified to the subleased skills, at least, of some women.

This account of the history of swearing in the seventeenth century may be appropriately concluded with Sir Christopher Wren's injunction to the workmen employed upon the building of St. Paul's Cathedral during the years 1675 to 1710. The bills he ordered posted read as follows:

Whereas, among labourers and others, that ungodly custom of swearing is too frequently heard, to the dishonour of God and contempt of authority; and to the end that such impiety may be utterly banished from these works, which are intended for the service of God and the honour of religion, it is ordered that profane swearing shall be a sufficient crime to dismiss any labourer.

CHAPTER TEN

Swearing in the Seventeenth Century:

As Observed in the Urquhart and Motteux Translation of Rabelais

◄◄◄◄◄◄◄◄◄◄◄◄◄◄◄◄◄◄◄◄◄◄◄◄◄◄◄◄◄◄◄◄‹›►►►►►►►►►►►►►►►►►►►►►►►►►►►►►►►►►

> *There is then in the abbey a claustral monk*
> *called Friar John.*
>
> Françqis Rabelais, *Gargantua* and *Pantagruel*, 1532

W ITHOUT the slightest question the most notable collection of swearers and their performances to be found in any of the literatures of the world is contained in *Gargantua*[1] and *Pantagruel*,[2] by François Rabelais (*c*1495–1553). While these works were first published in France in 1532–1533 and 1546, an English translation did not become available until more than a century later. Sir Thomas Urquhart (1611–1660) issued the first three Books in 1653, while Peter Motteux (1660–1718) published the last two Books in 1694.[3] Both Urquhart and Motteux translated the greater part of Rabelais' swearing from the original French into the English forms current in their own as well as in an earlier day. In these translations the swearing of the first three Books is representative of that of the first half of the seventeenth century, while that of the last two represents that of the second half of the seventeenth century.

An adequate commentary on Rabelais' swearing would require a huge treatise in itself. We can therefore here offer no more than the briefest explanation necessary, wherever that is possible, of the terms used in the English translation of Rabelais.

BOOK I

"You would not have given the beard of an onion for him [i.e., the root of an onion, a thing of as little value as anything one could name]."

"A turd for him. Thou filthy collier toad. Withdraw yourselves unto the serpent's brother, [i.e., Go to the devil]. I wish your bum-gut may fall out. By my figgins." This is the diminutive or euphemistic form of *By my fig*, that is, *By my vulva*. "*By the belly of Sanct Buff. By St. John. By God. By my sweet Sanctesse.*"

It perhaps is not necessary to mention that Rabelais' frolicsome burlesque is nothing more than that. Rabelais tells us that the city of Paris actually acquired its name during a burst of swearing, cursing, and laughter. Since Urquhart has omitted several words from the original French, I have restored them within square brackets [ ].

When Gargantua arrived at the city,

seeing so many about him, he said with a loud voice, I believe that these buzzards will have me to pay them here my welcome hither, and my Proficiat. It is but good reason. I will now give them their wine, but it shall be only in sport. Then smiling, he untied his fair braguette, and drawing out his mentul into the open air, he so bitterly all-to-be-pissed them, that he drowned two hundred and sixty thousand four hundred and eighteen, besides the women and little children. Some, nevertheless, of the company escaped this piss-flood by mere speed of foot, who, when they were at last at the higher end of the university, sweating, coughing, spitting, and out of breath, they began to swear and curse, some in good hot-earnest, and others in jest. Carimari carimara [By the wounds of God! There is no God! God's blood! Look at that, will you? Mother of God! By the head of God! May God's passion confound you! Holy mackerel! St. Quenet's Belly! In God's name! St. Fiacre of Brie! St. Treigman! I make a vow to St. Theobald! Crucified Christ! Holy Sunday! May the devil take me! On the word of a gentleman! St. Sausage! St. Godegrain, who was made martyr with *pommes cuites*! St. Photin, the apostle! St. Vitus! St. Mamie!], we are washed in sport, a sport truly to laugh at, in French, *Par ris*, for which that city hath been ever since called Paris.

In the above passage Rabelais was endeavoring to convey the sophisticated cosmopolitanism of Paris as reflected in its swearing. It is therefore somewhat surprising to discover that scholars have spent much fruitless time attempting to interpret the meaning of "carimari" or "carymary," when it is clearly the Italian expletive *Caro Maria!*—that is, *Dear Mary!* Saint Mamie, the virgin and martyr Mamyca, was the patron saint of mistresses.

An amusing instance of corruption occurs when Janotus, the cleric, says "Vultis etiam pardonos? Per diem vos habetis et nihil payabitis" ("Do you want pardons? By God, you shall have them, and pay nothing"). Janotus swears *Per diem, by day*, not daring to swear *Per Deum, By God*.

Reason, said Janotus? We use none of it here. Unlucky traitors, you are not worth the hanging. The earth beareth not more arrant villains than you are. I know it well enough; halt not before the lane. I have practised wickedness with you. By God's rattle [*ladre*, really, "spleen"] I will inform the king of the enormous abuses that are forged here and carried underhand by you, and let me be a leper, if he do not burn you alive like bougres, traitors, heretics, and seducers, enemies to God and virtue.

God's rattle is Urquhart's own substitution for Rabelais' own invented oath *God's spleen (ladre)*.

Bougres (i.e. *buggers*) occurs in the double sense here of heretic *and* sodomist, which, it is said, the masters of the Sorbonne frequently were.

Forgier is made to swear *by his zounds*, a deliberately weak and disguised oath after what the cake-makers annexed to the poor shepherds who had wished to purchase their cakes, calling them such defamatory epithets as:

prattling gabblers, licorous gluttons, freckled bittors, mangy rascals, shite-a-bed scoundrels, drunken roysters, sly knaves, drowsy loiterers, slapsauce fellows, slabberdegullion druggles, lubbardly louts, cozening foxes, ruffian rogues, paultry customers, sycophant-varlets, drawlatch hoydons, flouting milksops, jeering companions, staring clowns, forlorn snakes, ninny lobcocks, scurvy sneaksbies, fondling fops, base loons, saucy coxcombs, idle lusks, scoffing braggards, noddy meacocks, blockish grutuols, doddi-poljolt-heads, jobbernol goosecaps, foolish loggerheads, flutch calf-lollies, grouthead gnat-snappers, lob-dotterels, gaping changelings, codshead loobies, woodcock slangams, ninnie-hammer fly catchers, noddiepeak simpletons, turdy-gut, shitten shepherds.

And now, at least, as an act of piety, let the reader—if he has not already met him—be introduced to that most heroic of all swearers, the most mellifluous Friar John.

There was then in the abbey a claustral monk, called Friar John of the funnels and gobbets, in French, des Entomeures, young, gallant, frisky, lusty, nimbly, quick, active, bold, adventurous, resolute, tall, lean, wide-mouthed, long-nosed, a fair dispatcher of morning prayers, un-bridler of names, and runner over vigils; and, to conclude summarily in a word, a right monk, if ever there was any, since the monking world monked a monkery: for the rest, a clerk even to the teeth in matter of breviary.

Observing the gathering of the grapes, Friar John returns to the church where he hears the monks intoning the litany "Ye shall not fear the onslaught of enemies." He is outraged and exclaims, "It is well shit, well sung, said he. By the virtue of God, why do not you sing, Panniers farewell, vintage is done? The devil snatch me . . . By the belly of Sanct James, what shall we poor devils drink the while? Lord God? da mihi potum" [Give me drink].

From this point on Friar John swears his way, steadily, and without repeating himself once, all through the pages of Rabelais' chronicle.

Virtue God, says Friar John, what could that gouty limpard have done with so fine a dog? By the body of God, he is better pleased, when one presents him with a good yoke of oxen.

How now, said Ponocrates, you swear, Friar John.

It is only, said the monk, but to grace and adorn my speech. They are colours of a Ciceronian rhetoric.

Friar John had evidently read his Longinus *On the Sublime* (Longinus, XVI, 3–4), holding that a good oath on occasion served to grace a man's speech. Cicero's rhetoric was frequently colored with an oath (see p. 32).

The following oaths may be noted.

By the faith of a Christian. God and Sanct Benedict be with us! If I had strength answerable to my courage, by's death, I would plume them for you like ducks. By cock's death. By St. Rhenian. By the body of God. By the Lord God. By God [*da jurandi*, i.e., pardon my swearing].

BOOK II

By St. John. By St. Anthony's belly. By St. Adauras. By mine oath. By St. Quenet's belly. God confound him that leaves you. The devil take these sink-holes, if, by God, I do not bumbast some one of them. For God's sake. By Mahoom [Mahommet]. By Golfarin the nephew of Mahoom. Cotsbody. The pox take you. Jesus. Good God.

Book III

By my good forsooth. Cops body. A plague take 'em. By the holy Saint Babingoose. In the name of God. In God's name. By the Belly of Saint Buff. By the virtue of Acheron.

And further to the point:

Upon my conscience. God save thee and shield thee. Pox take that fashion. A plague rot that base custom! By the hook of God. God's bodikins. Copsody. By the body of a fox new slain. Before God. What the devil. The devil roast me. Cancro. Ho the pox! O Lord God. This devilish, hellish, damned, fool. In the devil's name. What the devil. By St. Rigomé. By the thirst of my thropple. By the kibes of thy heels. The devil hale it. What a pox to thy bones dost thou mean. By the worthy wrath of God. By the body of a hen. By the raking pace of my mule. By the haven of safety [these two oaths were said to have been sworn by William Rondelet, a physician contemporary with Rabelais]. Ods fish. By cocks-hobby. By cod.

Panurge's consultation with the slippery noncommittal ephectic and pyrrhonian philosopher Trouillogan on whether he should marry or not proves so frustrating that Panurge is moved to swear. Says he:

By the death of a hog, and mother of a toad, O Lord, if I durst hazard upon a little fling at the swearing game, though privily and under thumb, it would lighten the burden of my heart, and ease my lights and reins exceedingly. A little patience, nevertheless, is requisite.

Panurge can get nothing out of the unyielding Trouillogan, and hardly being able to contain himself, he turns to a page to swear for him vicariously.

PANURGE: Page, my little pretty darling, take here my cap—I give it to thee. Have a care you do not break the spectacles that are in it. Go down to the lower court. Swear there half an hour for me, and I shall in compensation of that favour swear hereafter for thee as much as thou wilt. But who shall cuckold me?

TROUILLOGAN: Somebody.

PANURGE: By the belly of the wooden horse at Troy, Master Somebody, I shall bang, belam thee, and claw thee well for thy labour.

TROUILLOGAN: You say so.

PANURGE: Nay, nay, that Nick in the dark cellar, who hath no white in his eye [the devil was supposed to have eyes of fire], carry me quite away with him . . .

TROUILLOGAN: Talk better.

PANURGE: It is *bien chien, chié chanté*, well cacked, and cackled, shitten, and sung in matter of talk. Let us resolve on somewhat.

TROUILLOGAN: I do not gainsay it.

PANURGE: Have a little patience. Seeing I cannot on this side draw any blood of you, I will try, if with the lancet of my judgment I be able to bleed you in another vein. Are you married, or are you not?

TROUILLOGAN: Neither the one nor the other, and both together.

PANURGE: O the good God help us! By the death of a buffle-ox, I sweat with the boil and travail that I am put to, and find my digestion broke off, disturbed and interrupted; for all my phrenes, metaphrenes, and diaphragms, back, belly, midriff, muscles, veins, and sinews, are held in a suspense, and for a while discharged from their proper offices, to stretch forth their several powers and abilities, for incornifistibulating, and laying up into the hamper of my understanding your various sayings and answers.

. . .

Come on, in the name of God. I vow by the burden of Saint Christopher, that I had rather undertake the fetching of a fart forth of the belly of a dead ass, than to draw out of you a positive and determinate resolution. Yet shall I be sure at this time to have a snatch at you, and get my claws over you. Our trusty friend, let us shame the devil of hell, and confess the verity. Were you ever a cuckold? I say you who are here, and not that other you, who playeth below in the tennis-court?

TROUILLOGAN: No, if it was not predestinated.

PANURGE: By the flesh, blood, and body, I swear, reswear, forswear, abjure, and renounce: he evades and avoids, shifts and escapes me, and quite slips and winds himself out of my gripes and clutches.

Panurge has tried everything. He is completely frustrated.

This concludes the account of the swearing in Rabelais as translated into English by Sir Thomas Urquhart. It may be noted here that Urquhart was a Scot and that some of his swearing was perhaps a little more Scots than English, but on the whole it adheres strictly to the forms of swearing that were prevalent in England during the first half of the seventeenth century.

With Book IV, the translation by Peter Motteux, who was English, begins.

BOOK IV

Ods-bodikins. What a devil. Codszooks, By the mass. With a pox to them. I vow and swear by the handle of my paper lantern. Adzookers. Zwoons. A pox on it. A murrain seize thee for a blockheaded booby . . . by the worthy vow of Charroux. By St. Winifred's pocket. By St. Anthony's hog. By St. Ferreol of Abbeville. By St. Patrick's slipper. By our Lady of Riviere. By St. Bridget's troth. By St. Bennet's sacred boot. Od zoons!

Panurge and Friar John are on board ship when a fearful storm overtakes their fragile craft. Panurge whimpers like an invertebrate coward, while Friar John swears as only Friar John can.

Holos, bolos, holas, alas! cried Panurge, this devilish wave (*mea culpa Deus*), I mean this wave of God, will sink our vessel. Alas, Friar John, my father, my friend, confession. Here I am down on my knees; *confiteor*; your holy blessing. Come hither and be damned, thou pitiful devil, and help us, said Friar,—who fell a swearing and cursing like a tinker,— in the name of thirty legions of black devils, come; will you come? Do not let us swear at this time, said Panurge; holy father, my friend, do not swear, I beseech you; tomorrow as much as you please. Holos, holos, alas, our ship leaks. I drown, alas, alas! I will give eighteen hundred thousand crowns to anyone that will set me on shore, all bewrayed and bedaubed as I am now. If ever there was a man in my country in the like pickle. *Confiteor*, alas! a word or two of testament or codicil at least. A thousand devils seize the cuckoldy cow-hearted mongrel, cried Friar John. Ods belly, art thou talking here of making thy will, now we are in danger, and it behoveth us to bestir our stumps lustily, or never? Wilt thou come, ho devil? Midshipman, my friend; O the rare lieutenant; here, Gymnast, here on the poop. We are, by the mass, all beshit now, our light is out. This is hastening to the devil as fast as it can. Alas, bou, bou, bou, bou, alas, alas, alas, alas, said Panurge, was it here we were born to perish? Oh! ho! good people, I drown, I die. *Consummatum est*. I am sped—*Magua, gna, gna*, said Friar John. Fye upon him, how ugly the shitten howler looks. Boy, younker, see hoyh. Mind the pumps, or the devil choke thee. Hast thou hurt thyself? Zoons, here fasten it to one of these blocks. In this side, in the devil's name, hay—so my boy. Ah, Friar John, said Panurge, good ghostly father, dear friend, do not let us swear, you sin. Oh ho, oh ho, be be be bous, bous bhous, I sink, I die, my friends. I die in charity with all the world. Farewell *in manus*. Bohous, bohous, bhousowauswaus. St. Michael of Aure! St. Nicholas! now, now or never, I here make you a solemn vow, and to our Saviour, that if you stand by me this time, I mean if you set me ashore out of this danger, I will build you a fine large little chapel or two, or between Candé and Monsoreau, where neither cow nor calf shall feed. Oh ho, oh ho. Above eighteen pailfuls or two of it are got down my gullet; bous, bhous, bhous, bhous, how damned bitter and salt it is! By the virtue, said Friar John, of the blood, the flesh, the belly, the head, if I hear thee again howling, thou cuckoldy cur, I will maul thee worse than any sea-wolf. Ods fish, why do we not take him up by the lugs and throw him overboard to the bottom of the sea? Here, sailor, ho, honest fellow. Thus, thus, my friend, hold fast above. In truth here is a sad lightning and thundering; I think that all the devils are got loose; it is holiday with them; or else Madame Proserpine is in child's labour: all the devils dance a morrice.

This is a splendid natural commotion to accompany this homily on cowardice and courage, the coward whines and abandons all hope, and the man of courage swears and acts.

The account continues:

Oh, said Panurge, you sin, Friar John, my former crony! former, I say, for at this time I am no more, you are no more. It goes against my heart to tell it you: for I believe this swearing doth your spleen a great deal of good; as it is a great ease to a wood cleaver to cry hem at every blow; and as one who plays at nine-pins is wonderfully helped if, when he hath not thrown his bowl right, and is like to make a bad caste, some ingenious stander by leans and screws his body halfway about, on that side which the bowl should have took to hit the pin. Nevertheless you offend, my sweet friend . . . He doats, he raves, the poor devil! A thousand, a million, nay, a hundred million of devils seize the hornified dod-dipole. Lend us a hand here; hoh, tiger, wouldst thou? Here, on the starboard side. Ods me, thou buffalo's head stuffed with relics, what ape's paternoster art thou muttering and chattering here between thy teeth? That devil of a sea-calf is the cause of all this storm, and is the only man who doth not lend a helping hand. By G——, if I come near thee, I'll fetch thee out by the head and ears with a vengeance, and chastise thee like any tempestative devil. . . . Ods fish, the beak-head is staved to pieces. Grumble, devils, fart, belch, shite a turd on the wave. If this be weather, the devil is a ram . . .

And to the whining Panurge, "Help, here, in the name of five hundred thousand millions of cart-loads of devils, help! may a shanker gnaw thy moustachios, and the three rows of pock-royals and cauliflowers cover thy bum and turd-barrel, instead of breeches and cod-piece. Codsooks our ship is almost overset. Ods death . . ."

"If ever thou taste a drop of it, let the devil's dam taste me, thou ballocky devil," says Friar John to Panurge. "Pork and peas choke me," exclaims Panurge when the storm is over and he begins to play the brave fellow. He turns to the pilot.

Hark you me, dear soul, a word with you—but pray be not angry. How thick do you judge the planks of our ship to be? Some two good inches and upwards, returned the pilot, don't fear. Odskilderkins, said Panurge, it seems then we are within two fingers' breadth of damnation . . . By the pavilion of Mass, I fear nothing but danger.

By this dignified frock of mine, said Friar John to Panurge, friend, thou hast been afraid during the storm, without cause or reason . . . By the tufted tip of my cowl I am even resolved to become a scholar before I die . . . May I never be damned . . . In the name of Belzebub, cried Panurge . . . Shankers and bubos stand off, godzooks, let us make the best of our way. May I be pelled like a raw onion, exclaims Friar John. Old Nick take me, cries Panurge . . . Odds-belly . . . when the devil would you have a man be afraid . . . Odd's fish.

When the Pantagruelists got ready for a fight Panurge decided to be off.

By this worthy frock of mine, quoth Friar John, thou hast a mind to slip thy neck out of the collar, and absent thyself from the fight, thou white-livered son of a dunghill! upon my virginity thou wilt never come back. By my thirst, swears Rhizotomus . . . By St. Christopher's whiskers, swears Friar John . . . Odd's belly . . . a God's name. By the helmet of Mass, cries Gymnast . . . I swear to you, by the celestial hen and chickens, says Pantagruel . . . By the old woman of Pope-Figland, adds Peter Motteux . . . 'S blood and 'ounds, cries Friar John . . . Odd's-boddikins, quoth Friar John, it frets me to the guts . . . By our body, says Homenas . . . Egad, returns Panurge. The devil boil me like a black pudding, swears Friar John. Sansorain the Elder's greatest oath was By hard figs!

Rhizotomus swears, Now by the virtue of God— Hold, interrupted Homenas, what God do you mean? There is but one, answered Rhizotomus; but on my soul I protest I had quite forgot it. Well then, by the virtue of God the Pope . . .

Gad judge me, exclaims Friar John . . . By jingo, quoth Panurge.

In what hierarchy of venemous creatures do you place Panurge's future spouse? asked Friar John. Art thou speaking ill of women, cried Panurge, thou mangy scoundrel, thou sorry noddy-peaked shaveling monk? By the cenomanic paunch and gixie, said Epistemon . . .

Friar John was all for landing on the island of thieves, Pantagruel was disinclined to.

Believe me, said Friar John, let's rather land, we will rid the world of that vermin, and inn there for nothing. Old Nick go with thee for me, quoth Panurge. This rash hair-brained devil of a friar fears nothing but ventures and runs on like a mad devil as he is, and cares not a rush what becomes of others; as if everyone was a monk, like his friarship. A pox on grinning honour, say I. Go to, returned the friar, thou mangy noddy-peak! thou forlorn druggle-headed sneaksby! and may a million of black devils anatomize thy cockle brain. The hen-hearted rascal is so cowardly that he bewrays himself for fear every day. If thou art so afraid, dung-hill, do not go, stay here and be hanged, or go and hide thy loggerhead under Madam Proserpine's petticoat.

Pork and peas choke me! exclaims Panurge . . . By Beelzebub's bumgut, swears mine host . . . By this packsaddle, swears the ass . . . Odd so . . . Catso . . . May I never stir.

In Chapter 10 of Book V Rabelais writes his indictment of gaming: "How Pantagruel arrived at the Island of Sharping (or Gaming)." Here the relation between gaming and swearing is shrewdly described.

We left the island of Tools to pursue our voyage, and the next day stood in for the Island of Sharping, the true image of Fontainebleau: for the land is so very lean that the bones, that is the rocks, shoot through its skin. Besides, it is sandy, barren, unhealthy, and unpleasant. Our pilot showed us there two little square rocks, which had eight equal points in the shape of a cube. They were so white that I might have mistaken them for alabaster or snow, had he not assured us they were made of bone.

He told us that twenty-one chance devils very much feared in our country, dwelt there in six different stories, and that the biggest twins or braces of them were called sixes, and the smallest amb's-ace; the rest cinques, quatres, treys, and duces. When they were conjured up, otherwise coupled, they were called either sice cinque, sice quatre, sice trey, sice duce, and sice ace; or cinque quatre, cinque trey, and so forth. I made there a shrewd observation: would you know what it is gamesters? It is that there are very few of you in the world, but what call upon and invoke the devils. For the dice are no sooner thrown on the board, and the greedy gazing sparks have hardly said, Two sixes, Frank; but six devils damn it! cry as many of them. If amb's-ace, then, A brace of devils broil me, will they say. Quarter duce, Tom, The duce take it, cries another. And so on to the end of the chapter. Nay, they do not forget sometimes to call the black cloven-footed gentleman by their christian names and surnames: and what is stranger yet, they use them as the greatest cronies, and make them so often the executors of their wills, not only giving themselves, but everybody, and everything, to the devil, that there is no doubt but he takes care to seize, soon or late, what is so zealously bequeathed him. Indeed, it is true, Lucifer does not always immediately appear by his lawful attornies, but, alas! it is not for want of good-will: he is really to be excused for his delay; for what the devil would you have a devil do? He and his blackguards are then at some other places, according to the priority of the persons that call on them: therefore pray let none be so venturesome as to think that the devils are deaf and blind.

Catch me there and hang me! exclaims Panurge, Damme, let us march off! . . . By gold. . . . May my bauble be turned into a nut-cracker, quoth Friar John . . . May the devil be damned. Virtue of the frock, quoth Friar John, what kind of voyage we are making? A shitten one, on my word: the devil of anything we do, but fizzling, farting, funking, squattering, dozing raving, and doing nothing. Odd's belly, it is not in my nature to lie idle; Damn it, did you then take me along with you for your chaplain, to sing mass and shrive you? By Maundy Thursday, the first of ye all that comes to me on such an account shall be fitted. Mahomet's tutor, swallow me body and soul, tripes and guts . . . Come, he that would be thought a gentleman, let him storm a town, well, then, shall we go? I dare swear we will do their business for them with a wet finger; they will bear it, never fear; since they could swallow down more foul language that came from us, than ten sows and their babies could swill hogwash. Damn them, they do not value all the ill words or dishonour in the world at a rush, so they but get the coin into their purses, though they were to have it in a shitten clout . . . Hell and damnation, cried Friar John . . . May I never sup . . . The devil be damned! . . . By my oriental barnacles [spectacles] cried Panurge.

A squincy gripe the cods-headed changelings at the swallow [epiglottis], and eke at the cover-weesel; we shall make them—But the deuce take them; They flatter the devil here, and smoothify his name, quoth Panurge, between their teeth.

May I be gutted like an oyster, cries Friar John . . . Bounce tail and God have mercy guts . . . A plague rot it . . . May I never piss! . . . Buttock of a monk! . . . May I ride on a horse that was foaled by an acorn . . . Spare your breath to cool your porridge . . . By Priapus . . . By the oath you have taken . . . By Pluto . . . On the faith of true lanterners . . . By St. Bennet's boot . . . Cat so . . . May the devil's dam suck my teat . . . Cripes.

But to all good things, alas, there must come an end. The reader who has any feeling for swearing at all will fully appreciate, in perusing this Rabelaisian commination of oaths in seventeenth-century vernacular English, that in Panurge, Pantagruel, and most notably in that right monk Friar John, he has savored something more than mere competence. No one had sworn with quite such distinction before Rabelais chronicled their words, and no one has equaled that achievement since.

Distinguished poetry and memorable prose are justly admired as among the nobler of the arts. Surely, Rabelais showed, some 400 years ago, that swearing can be no less so regarded as a creative product of the imagination.

When Rabelais, who had himself been a religious, made the most accomplished of all his swearers a monk, he was faithfully reflecting the conditions prevailing in sixteenth-century France. Not all monks swore, but many did. Friar John is presented as an eminent representative of those who did. It was early in the sixteenth century that a work condemning the monkish habit of swearing was issued by a Parisian press. This work was entitled *Moralité des blasphemateurs.* More than a hundred years later a similar work was published at London. This work, by Sir Edward Dering, appeared in 1641 and was entitled *The Fower Cardinall-Vertues of a Carmelite-Fryar, Fraud, Folly, Foul-Language, Blasphemy.*[4] Its popularity was such that it was many times reprinted.

CHAPTER ELEVEN

Swearing in the Eighteenth Century

<<<<<<<<<<<<<<<<<<<<<<<<<<<<<<< < > >>>>>>>>>>>>>>>>>>>>>>>>>>>>>>

To be magnificently passionate.
RICHARD STEELE, *The Tatler*, No. 137

THE eighteenth century appropriately opens with the publication of a fifty-nine-page volume by Sir Francis Grant, Lord Cullen, published at Edinburgh in 1700. The title of this work is *A Discourse Concerning the Execution of The LAWS Made Against Prophaneness, &c.* The title page further describes its contents, reading:

Which contains some Account of, The *Reasons* and *Tendency* of these *Laws*; The *Occasions*, which, tell of late, *obstructed* their Execution; The *Manner* in which, *Now*, they may be legally and easily made effectual; *The Obligations* in *Duty, Honour,* and *Interest,* of all *Ranks,* in their Respective *Stations,* to promote this *necessary* Work; the *Sin* and *Misery,* both as to *Private* and *Publick,* which will be the Consequences of a *Neglect* thereof, And the *Spiritual* and *Temporal Happiness,* that will ensue on setting about it, without further *Delay* in the same.

A portion of the Preface from this work is well worth quoting:

Its a main Design, and the Natural Tendency, of Religion, to procure the Private and Publick Happiness of Mankind; and restrain them from whatsoever would make them Miserable in themselves, and Troublesome to the world.

Hence the open Violations thereof, as they are the Follies and Deformities of Humane Nature in the Vitious themselves: So the Malignant blasts of their Example do nip the Buds of Piety, Honesty and Sobriety in others, which going on, without Restraint by the means that are competent to private Persons in the Body of the People, and to Judges who have the Executive Authority of the Law; these by such Omission not only become Partakers in the Sins of those, But also the Guilt becomes National, Imputable to the Community as such: And consequently Divine Justice is concerned (GOD being the Great Governour of the Earth) to Vindicate this Combination against Heaven, by Ruine.

That it is thus, Especially when the Tolerance is so Supine, that many dare reckon it Breeding to Swear, Gallantry to be Lewd, Good humour to be Drunk. Abjectness to be Serious, Witt to despise Sacred things, or Fanaticism, to observe the Sabbath &c. Can be made plain, For, in the Nature of the thing, he who forbids not, as he may and ought, is a Constructive Doer: In the Law, if a Soul Sin and hear the voice of Swearing and is a Witness, whether he hath seen or known of it, if he do not utter it, then he shall bear his iniquity (Deut. 13:8; Lev. 5:1). Thou shalt not hate thy Brother in thy Heart, thou shalt in any ways Rebuke thy Neighbour: That thou bear not Sin for him (Lev. 19:17. As the last words are on the margins of our Bibles). And the Hands of the Witnesses were to be first, and then the Hands of the rest of the People, on the Malefactor, That they might put evil away from among them. (Deut. 7:13 and 21:15, 20:21). In the Gospel, he who layes up his Talent in a Napkin, is an Unfaithful Servant; when the Royal Command of Charity and Love obliges to this Imployment of it: And in Experience, the Histories of all Ages and Nations import, that Guilt hath been thus imputed both to private Men and *Societies*, Deficient in their duty.

To Prevent this, we have Laws and Proclamations against Immoralitys, more full and better Calculate, than most other Nations: But these, no more than the best Medicines, Operate nothing, because they want Application.

The King, Parliament and Council, having thus put it in the Subjects power to be Happy, and Safe by an orderly Execution of these Laws against the Prophane, who mak a continual *Theomacy* that contributes more to the Publick Calamities, than the most resined Traitors or open Enemies could do: Therefore Our Destruction is of ourselves, if all Ranks, in their Respective Stations, do not speedily set about doing their outmost that they lawfully can, for their Religion and Country, in freeing us from these *Regicids* and *Murderers* who lurk in our bosome, without either sense or Guilt, or Punishment.

It seems that three things, which are Legal and Easy, could not, having GOD's Blessing, miss of Success herein. Namely, Imo. That there be a Judge in each Parish for Executing the Laws made against Vice. 2do. That there be Informers appointed within the same Parishes for bringing before him, delations of Delinquents without Excluding discoveries made by his own observation, or others. 3tio. That for promoving so Noble a work, especially as to both these, there be such Societies as those (which

have had so Glorious Success against the Subjects of Satan, and thereby
Enemies of the Nation, yea of all Mankind) in England and Ireland.[1]

The "Societies" referred to in the last passage were those remarkable institutions that came into existence in the late seventeenth
century and called themselves the Societies for Reformation of
Manners &c. in England and Ireland.

The principal burden of Grant's book, apart from the schemes
for the suppression of swearing that he puts forward, is that the
existence of swearing constitutes a threat to Government and
Religion and must therefore be put down. In all seriousness he
argues at length that by the act of informing against a swearer
a person becomes so much the nobler. It will be seen that the
good Judge would, if he had had his way, have set up a sort of
Gestapo for the suppression of swearing. His Preface has been
somewhat fully quoted here because it immediately set a pattern
of thinking in these matters that was followed by many imitators
in the next century. The idea of every man as his own informer
struck a note that, in an age that had been full of political informers, was at once seen to be a very useful one.

It is not to be wondered at that Cullen's work was immediately
followed by another work of a similar sort—a pamphlet of four
pages, almost certainly by John Woodward, Doctor of Divinity,
published in 1701, and entitled *A Letter from a Minister to his
Parishoners Shewing the Indispensable Duty Incumbent on All
Persons to Give Informations to the Magistrate as Well Against
Prophane Swearing and Cursing, as Against Other Crimes and
Misdemeanours*. Here, once again, Scripture and the Law are invoked as authority for the necessity, the obligation, to inform. But
there are affectingly additional reasons, for "he who makes a
Swearer pay [the penalty prescribed by law] does a real and
double Act of Charity. To the *poor*, who receive it without dispute; and I think, the greatest to the Offender; it being the like-
liest Means to put a stop to his impious Practices, and perhaps
(for who knows how far it will work) to prevent his damnation."[2]

It is likely that Woodward was also responsible for a pamphlet
of three pages published in the following year, 1702, entitled
*A Disswasive From Prophane Swearing and Cursing, Offered to
Such Unhappy Persons as Are Guilty of Those Horrid Sins, and
Are Not Past Counsel*.[3] Here, too, much the same arguments as
were used by Cullen are rehearsed. The writer makes his appeal

with remarkable force and obvious sincerity, but he might as well have been addressing the supersonic layers of the atmosphere for all the effect his words had upon the swearers of the eighteenth century.

At the conclusion of this pamphlet the following note is appended: "This Disswasive from Prophane Swearing and Cursing is printed in half a Sheet of Paper, that it may be made up in the Form of a Letter, and directed to any Persons when they are informed against, or are brought to Punishment for this Sin by the Magistrate, at which times the giving or sending of it to them may be most likely to promote their Reformation."

Indeed, the Reverend Doctor Woodward seems to have been a Society for the Reformation of Manners all unto himself, and a most energetic one, for in this same year he published another reformatory tract the title of which will sufficiently indicate its nature: *The Oath of a Constable, so Far as It Relates to His Apprehending Night-Walkers, and Idle Persons, and His Presenting Offences Contrary to the Statutes Made Against Unlawful Gaming, Tipling, and Drunkenness, and for the Suppressing of Them."*[4]

In 1705 Woodward appeared with two additional pamphlets, the first entitled *The Obligations of a Justice of the Peace, to Be Diligent in the Execution of the Penal Laws Against Prophaneness and Debauchery, for the Effecting of a National Reformation. In a Letter to a Friend,*[5] and the second entitled *A Kind Caution to Prophane Swearers. By a Minister of the Church of England.*[6]

If seriousness of purpose could have won the day Woodward would have stamped out all vice in England. But even if you drive nature out with a pitchfork. . . . The truth is that Woodward had overlooked the fact that the men of his day were true hogs of Epicurus' herd, delighting in what they regarded as the pleasure of free speech and reciprocal billingsgate.

In 1704 Colley Cibber's play *The Careless Husband* was performed at the Theatre Royal. In the dedication of this comedy to the Duke of Argyle Cibber makes reference to the fact that

the best Criticks have long and justly complain'd that the Coarseness of most Characters in our late Comedies, have been unfit Entertainments for People of Quality, especially the Ladies: And therefore I was long in hopes that some able Pen (whose Expectations did not hang upon the Profits of Success) wou'd generously attempt to reform the Town into a better Taste than the World generally allows 'em: but nothing of that kind having lately appear'd, that would give me an Opportunity of being wise at another's Expense, I found it impossible to resist any longer the secret Temptation of my Vanity, and so even struck the first Blow myself . . .

and so on in the same vapid strain.

Cibber's comedy, which is a lusterless imitation of Vanbrugh's *The Relapse*, has for its main character the inimitable Lord Foppington, the shrewd and heartless coxcomb whose oaths are of the most acceptable piety:

Sun-burn me if I wou'd, Curse catch me, Strike me blind, Who the Devil, Stop my Breath, As I got my title, Let me Blood, By all that's Infamous, Stap my Breath, Run me through, Strike me stupid, By all that's Handsome, Knock me down, May the eternal Frowns of the whole sex doubly demme . . .

The mounting attacks on profanity, especially on the stage, were not without effect upon the license that playwrights permitted themselves in the theater. A careful reading of the plays of this century will show that, with few exceptions, that effect was a very considerable one and endures to the present day.

George Farquhar, a playwright of the end of the seventeenth and the beginning of the eighteenth century, wrote comedies that provide one situation after another in which the full-bodied swearing of the Restoration could have found an appropriate place. Instead, however, the playwright manifestly felt constrained to keep a check not alone upon the quantity but also upon the quality of the swearing he permits his characters to indulge. In *The Stage-Coach*, acted February 2, 1704, at Lincoln's Inn Fields, there are not more than a dozen oaths. Fetch, the servant, exclaims *E'gad*, Macahone the Irishman *Be me shoul*, Squire Somebody *Odszookers*, *I'fath*, *E'cod*, and *What a Devil*, the Captain *You dog*, Tom Jolt, the coachman, *Adzooks, the damn'd Jade* and *Odsnigs*. Indeed, the swearing is pale and utterly debilitated, hardly the language one would expect on the occasions presented. There is one passage in which the Captain says, "*Basil*, I know him, bloody Rogues he leads, indeed" (II, i). But the *bloody* describes their sanguinariness and is not the swearingful *bloody* of later usage.

In *The Recruiting Officer*, a comedy produced April 8, 1706, at the Theatre Royal, which really called for soldierly language, Farquhar could not be more restrained. There are a few of the euphemisms of *God's wounds*, as *Oons, Wauns, Odso* and *Flesh*

(*God's Flesh*), *I'cod, Death and Fire, The Devil take me, 'Sdeath, Faith, 'a Dog, Hang You plaguy Harrydan, Mort de ma vie*, and *Thou art a bloody impudent fellow*, in which the *bloody* is still a respectable emphatic, and there is *You're a son of a whore*.

In that most popular of all his comedies, *The Beaux Strategem*, first acted at the Queen's Theatre March 8, 1707, the swearing is almost conspicuously absent, being limited to a *'Sdeath, Oons*, a *By Jupiter, The Devil hang you*, and a *damn's Son of a Whore of Babylon*.

In *The Tatler* (No. 137, Thursday, February 23, 1710) Richard Steele reflects upon the habit of swearing. He is clearly—though he pretends otherwise—not indifferent to the art:

Of all persons who add elegancies and superfluities to their discourses, those who deserve the foremost rank are the swearers; and the lump of these may, I think, be very aptly divided into the common distinction of *High* and *Low*. Dullness and barrenness of thought is the original of it in both these *sects*, and they differ only in constitution: The *Low* is generally a phlegmatic, and the *High* a choleric coxcomb. The man of phlegm is sensible of the emptiness of his discourse, and will tell you, that, "fackins," such a thing is true: or if you warm him a little, he may run into a passion, and cry, "Odsbodikins, you do not say right." But the *High* affects a sublimity in dullness, and invokes "Hell and damnation" at the breaking of a glass, or the slowness of a drawer.

I was the other day trudging along Fleet-street on foot, and an old army-friend came up with me. We were both going towards Westminster; and, finding the streets were so crowded that we could not keep together, we resolved to club for a coach. This gentleman I know to be the first of the order of the choleric. I must confess, were there no crime in it, nothing could be more diverting than the impertinence of the *High* juror: for whether there is remedy or not against what offends him, still he is to shew he is offended; and he must, sure, not omit to be magnificently passionate, by falling on all things in his way. We were stopped by a train of coaches at Temple-bar. "What the devil!" says my companion, "cannot you drive on, coachman? D——n you all, for a set of sons of whores; you will stop here to be paid by the hour! There is not such a set of confounded dogs as the coachmen, unhanged! But these rascally cits—— 'Ounds, why should there not be a tax to make these dogs widen their gates? Oh! but the hell-hounds move at last." "Ay," said I, "I knew you would make them whip on, if once they heard you"—"No," says he, "but would it not fret a man to the devil, to be paid for having carried slower than he can walk? Look'ye! there is for ever a stop at this hole by St. Clement's church. Blood, you dog! Hark'ye, sirrah!—Why, and be d——d to you, do you not drive over that fellow?—Thunder, furies, and damnation! I will cut your ears off, you fellow before there—Come hither, you dog you, and let me ring your neck round your shoulders." We had a repetition of the same eloquence at the Cockpit, and the turning into Palace-yard.

This gave me a perfect image of the insignificancy of the creatures who practise this enormity; and made me conclude, that it is ever want of sense makes a man guilty in this *kind*. It was excellently well said, "that this folly had no temptation to excuse it, no man being born of a swearing constitution." In a word, a few rumbling words and consonants clapped together without any sense, will make an accomplished swearer. It is needless to dwell long upon this blustering inpertinence, which is already banished out of the society of well-bred men, and can be useful only to bullies and *ill* tragic writers, who would have sound and noise pass for courage and sense.

If Steele was a little premature in saying that swearing was no longer permitted in the society of well-bred men, his mainsail had nonetheless picked up the full force and direction of the wind that was blowing swearing no good and keeping him and the others on the Ship of Fools straight on course to the age of Victoria.

In No. 13 of *The Tatler*, Tuesday, May 10, 1709, Steele told how seated on a bench in Lincoln's Inn walk, his bench companion mentioned how he had gone to "a common Swearer," and how never was a creature so puzzled as he when he came first to view his brain:

half of it was worn out, and filled up with mere expletives, that had nothing to do with any other parts of the texture; therefore, when he called for his cloaths in a morning, he would cry, "John?"—John does not answer. "What a plague! nobody there? What the devil, and rot me, John, for a lazy dog as you are!" I knew no way to cure him, but by writing down all he said one morning as he was dressing, and laying it before him on the toilet when he came to pick his teeth. The last recital of what I gave him of what he said for half an hour before was, "What, a pox rot me. Where is the wash-ball? call the chairmen! damn them, I warrant they are at the alehouse already! zounds, and confound them!" When he came to the glass, he takes up my note—"Ha! this fellow is worse than I: what, does he swear with pen and ink?" But, reading on, he found them to be his own words. The stratagem had so good an effect upon him, that he grew immediately a new man, and is learning to speak without an oath, which makes him extremely short in his phrases: for, as I observed before, a common swearer has a brain without any idea on the swearing side; therefore my ward has yet mighty little to say, and is forced to substitute some other vehicle of nonsense, to supply the defect of his usual expletives. When I left him he made use of "Odsbodi-kins! Oh me! and Never stir alive!" and so forth; which gave me hopes of his recovery.

But the point here is the very opposite of the one Steele would wish to make. Steele is in favor of elegant and eloquent language, and as he himself shows, the bencher's ward from prolixity fell into perplexity as hardly knowing what to say without the customary carriers of his meanings. We may rather more than suspect that Steele's intention was not altogether what it overtly appears to be and that if he seems to be moralizing in favor of the non-swearer, he is not, in fact, out of sympathy with the swearer. Steele, himself, was not a swearer.

Joseph Addison, writing at about the same time, mentions one of the rules of a certain club, which provided that "if any member swears or curses, his neighbor may give him a kick upon the shins." One would have thought that such a rule would have had an effect exactly opposite to that it was intended to produce— and for that reason, if for no other, it is very unlikely that it was much practiced.

On May 6, 1712, in *The Spectator* (No. 371) Addison tells how a well-meaning gentleman took occasion

to bring together such of his Friends as were addicted to a foolish habitual Custom of Swearing. In order to shew them the Absurdity of the Practice, he had Recourse to the Invention . . . an *Amanuensis* in a private Part of the Room. After the second Bottle, when Men open their Minds without Reserve, my honest Friend began to take Notice of the many sonorous but unnecessary Words that had passed in his House since their sitting down at Table, and how much good Conversation they had lost by giving way to such superfluous Phrases. What a Tax, says he, would they have raised for the Poor, had we put the Laws in Execution upon one another? Every one of them took this gentle Reproof in good Part: Upon which he told them, that knowing their Conversation would have no Secrets in it, he had ordered it to be taken down in Writing, and for the Humour sake would read it to them if they pleased. There were ten Sheets of it, which might have been reduced to two, had there not been those abominable Interpolations I have before-mentioned. Upon the reading of it in cold Blood, it looked rather like a Conference of Fiends than of Men. In short, every one trembled at himself upon hearing calmly what he had pronounced amidst the Heat and Inadvertency of Discourse.

And again, in No. 531 of *The Spectator*, for November 8, 1711, Addison writes

Every one knows the Veneration which was paid by the *Jews* to a Name so great, wonderful, and holy. They would not let it enter even into their religious Discourses. What can we then think of those who make use of so tremendous a Name in the ordinary Expressions of their Anger, Mirth, and most impertinent Passions? of those who admit it into the most familiar Questions and Assertions, ludicrous Phrases and Works of Humour? not to mention those who violate it by some Perjuries. It would be an Affront to Reason to endeavour to set forth the Horror and Prophaneness of such a Practice. The very mention of it exposes it sufficiently to those in whom the Light of Nature, not to say Religion, is not utterly extinguished.

It was a time for the mending of manners, and these light bantering essays of Addison and Steele were not, it is thought, without effect upon the gentlemen who regularly read *The Tatler* and *The Spectator*. In satire and in more serious mood their plea was ever in behalf of the amenities of a more civilized morality.

In the midst of the excitement of the South Sea madness, during the second decade of the eighteenth century, the penurious and occasionally profane Jonathan Swift produced a broadside in which he satirized both the frenzy of monetary speculation and the addiction to "bad language." The prospectus shall be given in the dean's own words. It was printed in 1720 and entitled:

The Swearer's Bank;
OR,
Parliamentary Security for Establishing a New Bank
in Ireland.
Wherein the Medical Use of Oaths Is Considered

It is very well known, that by an act of parliament, to prevent profane swearing, the person so offending, on oath made before a magistrate, forfeits a shilling, which may be levied with little difficulty.

It is almost unnecessary to mention, that this is become a pet vice among us; and though age renders us unfit for other vices, yet this, where it takes hold, never leaves us but with our speech.

So vast a revenue might be raised by the execution of this act, that I have often wondered, in a scarcity of funds, that methods have not been taken to make it serviceable to the public.

I dare venture to say, that if this act were executed in England, the revenue of it, applied to the navy, would make the English fleet a terror to all Europe.

It is computed by geographers, that there are two millions in this kingdom [of Ireland], of which number there may be said to be a million swearing souls.

It is thought there may be five thousand gentlemen; every gentleman, talking one with another, may afford to swear an oath every day, which will yearly produce one million eight hundred twenty-five thousand oaths; which number of shillings makes the yearly sum of ninety-one thousand two hundred and fifty pounds.

The farmers of this kingdom, who are computed to be ten thousand, are able to spend yearly five hundred thousand oaths, which give twenty-five thousand pounds; and it is conjectured that, from the bulk of the people, twenty or five-and-twenty thousand pounds may be yearly collected.

These computations are very modest, since it is evident that there is a much greater consumption of oaths in this kingdom, and consequently a much greater sum might be yearly raised.

That it may be collected with ease and regularity, it is proposed to settle informers in great towns, in proportion to the number of inhabitants, and to have riding-officers in the country; and since nothing brings a greater contempt on any profession than poverty, it is determined to settle very handsome salaries on the gentlemen that are employed by the bank, that they may, by a generosity of living, reconcile men to an office that has lain under so much scandle of late, as to be undertaken by none but curates, clerks of meeting-houses, and broken tradesmen.

It is resolved, that none shall be preferred to those employments, but persons that are notorious for being constant churchmen, and frequent communicants; whose piety will be a sufficient security for their honest and industrious execution of their office.

It is very probable, that twenty thousand pounds will be necessary, to defray all expenses of servants, salaries &c. However, there will be the clear yearly sum of one hundred thousand pounds, which may very justly claim a million subscription.

It is determined to lay out the remaining unapplied profits, which will be very considerable, toward the erecting and maintaining of charity schools. A design so beneficial to the public, and especially to the Protestant interest of this kingdom, has met with so much encouragement from several great patriots in England, that they have engaged to procure an act to secure the sole benefit of informing, on this swearing act, to the agents and servants of this new bank. Several of my friends pretend to demonstrate, that this bank will in time vie with the South Sea Company; they will insist that the army dispend as many oaths yearly as will produce one hundred thousand pounds nett.

There are computed to be one hundred pretty fellows in this town, that swear fifty oaths a-head daily; some of them would think it hard to be stinted to a hundred: this very branch would produce a vast sum yearly.

The fairs of this kingdom will bring in a vast revenue; the oaths of a little Connaught one, as well as they could be numbered by two persons, amounted to three thousand. It is true, that it would be impossible to turn all of them into ready money; for a shilling is so great a duty on swearing, that if it was carefully exacted, the common people might as well pretend to drink wine as to swear; and an oath would be as rare among them as a clean shirt.

A servant that I employed to accompany the militia their last muster day, had scored down, in the compass of eight hours, three hundred oaths; but, as the putting of the act in execution on those days would only fill the stocks with porters, and pawn-shops with muskets and swords; and as it would be matter of great joy to Papists, and disaffected persons, to see our militia swear themselves out of their guns and swords; it is resolved that no advantage be taken of any militiaman's swearing while he is under arms; nor shall any advantage be taken of any man's swearing in the Four Courts, provided he is at hearing in the exchequer, or has just paid off an attorney's bill.

The medicinal use of oaths is what the undertaker would by no means discourage, especially where it is necessary to help the lungs to throw off any distilling humour. On certificate of a course of swearing prescribed by any physician, a permit will be given to the patient, by the proper officer of the bank, paying no more than sixpence. It is expected that a scheme of so much advantage to the public will meet with more encouragement than their chimerical banks; and the undertaker hopes, that as he has spent a considerable fortune in bringing this scheme to bear, he may have the satisfaction to see it take place for the public good, though he should have the fate of most projectors, to be undone.

It is resolved that no compositions shall be made, nor licenses granted, for swearing, under a notion of applying the money to pious uses; a practice so scandalous, as it is fit only for the see of Rome, where the money arising from whoring licenses is applied *ad propagandum fidem*: and, to the shame of Smock-alley, and of all Protestant whores (especially those who live under the light of the gospel-ministry), be it spoken, a whore in Rome never lies down, but she hopes it will be the means of converting some poor heathen or heretic.

The swearing revenues of the town of Cork, will be given for ever, by the bank, to the support of poor clergymen's widows: and those of Ringsend will be allowed to the maintenance of sailor's bastards.

The undertaker designs, in a few days, to appoint time and place for taking subscriptions; the subscribers must come prepared to pay down one-fourth on subscribing.

P.S. The Jews of Rotterdam have offered to farm the revenues of Dublin at twenty thousand pounds *per annum.* Several eminent Quakers are also willing to take them at that rent; but the undertaker has rejected their proposals, being resolved to deal with none but Christians.

Applications may be made to him about them any day, at Patt's coffee-house, where attendance will be given.[7]

Patt's or Pat's was a well-known coffee house in High Street, Dublin. There is no record that it was at any time besieged by applicants itching to invest in Swift's company. It was a splendid idea persuasively presented, but it appears to have had no takers.

In Elizabeth's day a similar proposal had been put before Lord Burghley by a Monsieur Rodenberg. He proposed to add to the royal coffers the sum of 20 million crowns annually, part of which was to be secured by a rigorous levy of fines on swearing. This proposal is recorded in the *State Papers (Domestic)* for 1595,[8] but it, too, enjoyed no better fate than that of Swift's, though Swift's was satiric and Monsieur Rodenberg's serious.

In a later work, *Polite Conversation,* published in 1738, designed to ridicule cant words and expressions, Swift anticipates the possibility that some critics may accuse him of a defect in his system of polite conversation—to wit, that there is one great ornament of discourse whereof he has not produced a single example. But this, he says, he purposely omitted. The defect referred to is not having inserted into the body of his book all the oaths then in fashion for embellishing discourse; "especially since it could give no Offence to the *Clergy,* who are seldom or never admitted to these polite Assemblies. And it must be allowed, that Oaths, well chosen, are not only very useful Expletives to Matter, but great Ornaments of Style." In extenuation Swift pleads that the inclusion of oaths would have doubled not only the bulk of the book but also its cost. Second, he had been assured that certain ladies have been known to take offense at cursing and swearing, "even when that Kind of Ornament was not improperly introduced; which, I confess, did startle me not a little; having never observed the like in the Compass of my own several Acquaintance, at least for twenty Years past."

Thirdly, as this most useful Treatise is calculated for all future Times, I considered, in this Maturity of my Age, how great a Variety of Oaths I have heard since I began to study the World, and to know Men and Manners. And here I found it to be true what I have read in an antient Poet.

For, now-a-days, Men change their Oaths,
As often as they change their Cloaths.

In short, Oaths are the Children of Fashion, they are in some sense almost Annuals, like what I observed before of Cant-Words; and I my self can remember about forty different Sets. The old Stock-Oaths I am confident, do not mount to above forty five, or fifty at most; but the Way of mingling and compounding them is almost as various as that of the Alphabet.

Sir JOHN PERROT was the first Man of Quality whom I find upon Record to have sworn by *G*——'s *W*——s. He lived in the Reign of Q. *Elizabeth*, and was supposed to have been a natural Son of *Henry* the Eighth, who might also have probably been his Instructor. This Oath indeed still continues, and is a Stock-Oath to this Day; so do several others that have kept their natural Simplicity; But, infinitely the greater Number hath been so frequently changed and dislocated, that if the Inventors were now alive, they could hardly understand them.

Current oaths would soon be out of fashion and would grow as useless as an old dictionary.

I, therefore, determined with my self to leave out the whole System of Swearing; because, both the male and female Oaths are all perfectly well known and distinguished; new ones are easily learnt, and with a moderate Share of Discretion may be properly applied on every fit Occasion. However, I must here, upon this Article of Swearing, most earnestly recommend to my male Readers, that they would please a little to study Variety. For, it is the Opinion of our most refined Swearers, that the same Oath or Curse, cannot, consistent with true Politeness, be repeated about nine Times in the same Company, by the same Person, and at one sitting.

.   .   .

It may be objected, that the Publication of my Book may, in a long Course of Time, prostitute this noble Art to mean and vulgar People: But, I answer; That it is not so easy an Acquirement as a few ignorant Pretenders may imagine. A Footman can swear; but he cannot swear like a Lord. He can swear as often: But, can he swear with equal Delicacy, Propriety, and Judgment? No, certainly; unless he be a Lad of superior Parts, of good Memory, a diligent Observer; one who hath a skilful Ear, some Knowledge in Musick, and an exact Taste, which hardly fall to the Share of one in a thousand among that Fraternity, in as high Favour as they now stand with their Ladies; neither hath one Footmen in six so fine a Genius as to relish and apply those exalted Sentences comprised in this Volume, which I offer to the World.[9]

Of course, Swift is quite right. Swearing is a noble art in its upper reaches and requires as much imagination, fancy, and sensibility—not to mention skill—as accomplishment in any other art. This was already recognized long before Swift's time, as may be judged from the remarks on the subject uttered by various characters in the plays of the preceding century. In the comedies of that century swearing was considered an ornament without which no gentleman could adequately express himself.

George II had ascended the throne in 1727 and reigned until his death in 1760. But even prior to his coronation there had been some improvement in the manners of the court and in what were esteemed to be the standards of good breeding. In part reaction to the profligacy and the freedom of the Restoration, in part the consequence of Puritan ardor, and in part attributable to the politeness and good humor of such writers as Addison and Steele, there had developed a distinct distaste for the inveterate swearer. And as with any form of behavior that appears to have gotten out of hand, there was a very general reaction among the "higher" if not among the "lower" orders of Englishmen against the excrescences that had grown like so many disfiguring sores upon the language.

Playwrights and writers felt compelled to restrain their language, and even to apologize for it when forced by the demands of their plots to resort to oaths and expletives and other means of asseveration. It became unfashionable for a gentleman to swear—even though some gentlemen, not to mention some ladies, continued to do so. This reforming spirit passed the "lower orders" wholly by. They continued to swear until the relapse brought about among the "higher orders" by the Jacobite disturbances enabled them to swear more freely than ever. By 1745 things had reached such a pass that Parliament enacted the most stringent of the statutes designed to put an end to "the offence of profane and common *swearing* and cursing." This act (19 Geo. II. c. 21) is discussed by Sir William Blackstone, in his *Commentaries on the Laws of England* (1765–1769):

By the last statute against which, 19 Geo. II. c. 21, which repeals all former ones, every labourer, sailor, or soldier profanely cursing or swearing shall forfeit 1s.; every other person, under the degree of a gentleman, or person of superior rank, 5s., to the poor of the parish; and, on the second conviction, double; and for every subsequent offence, treble the sum first forfeited, with all charges of conviction: and in default of payment shall be sent to the house of correction for ten days. Any justice of the peace may convict upon his own hearing, or the testimony of one witness; and any constable or peace officer, upon his own hearing, may secure any offender and carry him before a justice and there convict him. If the justice omits his duty he forfeits 5£., and the constable 40s. And the act is to be read in all parish churches and public chapels the Sunday after every quarter-day, on pain of 5£., to be levied by warrant from any justice. Besides the punishment for taking God's name in vain in common discourse, it is enacted, by Statute 3 Jac. I. c. 21 [1606], that if, in any stage-play, interlude, or show, the name of the Holy Trinity, or any of the persons therein, be jestingly or profanely used, the offender shall forfeit 10 £., one moiety to the king, and the other to the informer.[10]

In Book IV Blackstone clearly specifies the reasons underlying the negative sanctions placed upon such immoralities as profanity.

I proceed now to consider some gross impieties and general immoralities which are taken notice of and punished by our municipal law; frequently in concurrence with the ecclesiastical, to which the censure of many of them does also of right appertain; though with a view somewhat different: the spiritual court punishing all sinful enormities for the sake of reforming the sinner, *pro salute animae*; while the temporal courts resent the public affront to religion and morality on which all governments must depend for support, and correct more for the sake of example than private amendment.

The fourth species of offences, therefore, more immediately against God and religion, is that of *blasphemy* against the Almighty by denying his being or providence; or by contumelious reproaches of our Saviour Christ. Whither also may be referred all profane scoffing at the holy scripture, or exposing it to contempt or ridicule. These are offences punishable at common law by fine and imprisonment, or other infamous corporal punishment; for Christianity is part of the laws of England.

Such immoralities are simply subversive of existing institutions, and therefore the state must protect itself by law against the subverters. In this the church was at one with the state, and a great part of the hostility that has existed toward profanity in civilized societies has been conditioned through the pressures of these agencies.

Serious attempts were made to enforce this Act of George II's, but they had no more effect upon the practice and popularity of swearing than a few stinging nettles would have against a charging regiment of foot soldiers.

For the eighteenth century the novels of Tobias Smollett (1721–1771) afford a treasure-trove of the swearing characteristic of the century. He had served in the British Navy, lived in the Caribbean, traveled much on the Continent, and known all sorts and conditions of men; all his novels draw heavily upon his own experiences, especially for the embellishments with which so many of his characters decorate their speech.

Roderick Random, Smollett's first published novel, appeared in 1748. In the Apologue the reader is at once greeted with some very pretty swearing, the best of which reflects Smollett's medical training, as when he makes a learned physician swear *By the beard of Esculapius!* Almost immediately upon entering the life of Roderick Random we are treated to some fine examples of nautical swearing. Roderick's maternal uncle, Lt. Tom Bowling, cusses Roderick's wicked cousin for loosing his dogs upon them, "Lookee, you lubberly son of a w——e, if you come athwart me, 'ware your gingerbread work; I'll be foul of your quarter, d——m me." The lieutenant also swears *By the Lord, Odds fish, Odds bob, Zounds, Egad,* and *I'faith.* The captain swears *Damn my blood, Hell and the devil confound me, Blood and thunder, God's fury, Blood and oons, By G——d, Zauns, God's curse.* Rifle swears *Hell and damnation,* the soldier *'Sblood, Jenny 'Sdeath,* the lodger *Blood and wounds,* Joey *Odds bodikins,* Strap *Ecod,* Strap's friend *Ch——st,* Jackson *Blood,* the parson *Gad so* and *By gad,* the robber *Damn that son of a bitch,* while Betty, the chambermaid, exclaims *Ods bobs, I'll be hanged* and a very ladylike *Good lack-a-daisy.* The female traveling in the coach waggishly says to Isaac, the usurer, "You doting rogue. Speak, you old cent. per cent. fornicator." And Isaac appropriately vows *Upon my credit.* At the inn Miss Jenny, the other female traveler, has an altercation with the captain. She had called his wife "Creature." "D——me, madam, what do you mean by that?" "D——n you, sir, who are you?" replied Miss Jenny, "who made you a captain, you pitiful, trencher-scraping, pimping curler? . . . 'Sdeath! the army is come to a fine pass, when such fellows as you get commissions . . ." and so on.

Morgan exclaims, *The devil and his dam, Splunter and oons, Got pless my soul, Cot is my life, Passion of my heart,* and *By the soul of my grandsire.* The doctor exclaims *Upon my integrity,* Rattlin *Damn my heart, Odds heart.* The sentinel tells Roderick how Captain Oakum woke Lieutenant Bowling and "swore woundily at the lieutenant, and called him lousy Scotch son of a whore."

The use of *lousy* here is of interest because there are some authorities who claim that its usage dates to the late nineteenth century. Clearly this is not so.

In the coach there is a son of Mars, a lieutenant, a most arrant coward who swears with virulence and volubility to give the appearance of blood and thunder. There is a long silence, whereupon this gentleman of the sword avows that he had got into a meeting of Quakers.

"I believe so, too," said a shrill voice at my left hand, "for the spirit of folly begins to move." "Out with it, then, madam," replied the soldier. "You seem to have no occasion for a midwife," cried the lady. "D——m my blood!" exclaimed the other, "a man can't talk to a woman, but she immediately thinks of a midwife." "True, sir," said she, "I long to be delivered." "What! of a mouse, madam?" said he. "No, sir," said she, "of a fool." "Are you far gone with a fool?" said he. "Little more than two miles," said she. "By Gad, you are a wit, madam!" cried the officer. "I wish I could with any justice return the compliment," said the lady. "Zounds, I have done," said he. "Your bolt is soon shot, according to the old proverb," said she.

Switching his culverin the contentious lieutenant began to boast of his exploits with salvo after salvo of expletives, too tiresome to repeat here, and as dreary dull, and as dissembling as their fuseless fuselier.

The squire exclaims *Odds* and *Odds niggers*, and Mr. Melopyn swears *Upon my sincerity*.

In *Peregrine Pickle*, published in 1751, Commodore Trunnion swears *Damn my eyes, Blood, Damn my heart, Damn my limbs, Damn ye, Damn my heart and liver, Blood and thunder, You bitch's baby, 'Sblood, By the Lord, Odds my timbers, Odds heartlikins*, and a variety of other not unfamiliar nautical oaths. Mrs. Trunnion's attempts to reform her husband out of his profane and brutal way of talking had no more effect upon that noble seaman's behavior than a zephyr upon the course of a full-masted eighty-gun brig. Trunnion's apostrophes and execrations were "vented with such rapidity, that he left himself no time to breathe, and [often] had almost been suffocated with his choler."

Peregrine himself learns to swear by *Hell and the devil* and *gads zooks*, while the publican, among other oaths, swears *Add rabbit him*. Mr. Pallet, the young traveler making the Grand Tour, produces some elegant oaths: *Gadzooks! and the devil and all that, Gadsbodikins, By the Lard, By this light*, and *Fire and Fagots!*

Hatchway, the sailor, swears most nautically: *Smite my crossways, Hector*, and *By Hell and brimstone*; and the Aggressor exclaims *Stap my breath!*

In 1753, when *The Adventures of Count Fathom* was published, Smollett felt it necessary to mollify the critics and vindicate himself in the eyes of the reader for once again dealing with "the objects of low life." In the first chapter of a book that, but for an occasional *damn, Heaven and earth, Sacred powers, Stuff*, and *Rabbit him*, is singularly free of swearing, Smollett writes:

Have a little patience, gentle, delicate, sublime critic; you, I doubt not, are one of those consummate connoisseurs, who, in their purifications, let humour evaporate, while they endeavour to preserve decorum, and polish wit, until the edge of it is quite worn off . . . who, when Swift or Pope represents a coxcomb in the act of swearing, scruple not to laugh at the ridiculous execrations; but, in a less reputed author, condemn the use of such profane expletives;—who eagerly explore the jakes of Rabelais, for amusement, and even extract humour from the dean's description of a lady's dressing-room; yet in a production of these days, unstamped with such venerable names, will stop their noses, with all the signs of loathing and abhorrence, at a bare mention of the china chamber-pot.

It is a spirited defense, but it is notable that in the book of which it is part of the first chapter there is the least amount of swearing to be found in any of Smollett's works.

Smollett's next novel, *The Adventures of Sir Launcelot Greaves*, was published in 1762. There is very little swearing in it, but what there is of it is not uninteresting. The squire swears *Adzooks, Wounds*, and *Go and teach your grannum to crack filberds*. In various guises this polite objurgation persists in New England, where its most popular form is *Go teach your grandmother to suck eggs*.

Captain Crowe swears *By the L——d, Adad, Odds firkin, Split my matchlock, Splice my old shoes, Smite my timbers, Body o' me, What apize, Adds buntlines, Odds heartlikines*, and *'Noint my block*.

In Smollett's last book, *The Expedition of Humphrey Clinker* (1771), the swearing is also noticeably restrained. Instead, for example, of giving a sonorous word-for-word account of the expletives used at the party at Bath, Smollett circumspectly writes of it as follows: "Some cried, some swore, and the tropes and figures of Billingsgate were used without reserve in all their native zest and flavour; nor were those flowers of rhetoric unattended with significant gesticulation. Some snapped their fingers, some forked them out, some clapped their hands, and some their backsides." The "significant gesticulation" represents some good examples of gesticulatory swearing (see p. 344).

In *Humphrey Clinker* Smollett's hero turns moralist and descants upon the wickedness of profane swearing. At dinner he tells his host, the squire, that he had given "a word of advice to my fellows in servitude and sin."—"Advice! Concerning what?"—"Concerning profane swearing, an' please your honour; so horrid and shocking, that it made my hair stand on end."—"Nay, if thou canst cure them of that disease, I shall think thee a wonderful doctor indeed."—"Why not cure them, my good master? the hearts of those poor people are not so stubborn as your honour seems to think. Make them first sensible that you will listen with patience, and easily be convinced of the sin and folly of a practice that affords neither profit nor pleasure." At this remark our uncle changed color and looked around the company, conscious that *his own withers were not altogether unwrung.* "But, Clinker," said he, "if you should have eloquence enough to persuade the vulgar to resign those tropes and figures of rhetoric, there will be little or nothing left to distinguish their conversation from that of their betters."—"But then, your honour knows, their conversation will be void of offence; and at the day of judgment, there will be no distinction of persons."

May one, perhaps, detect in this disquisition something of a change of heart in Smollett himself in respect to swearing? Quite clearly he had been affected by the criticism to which he and other contemporary writers had been subjected, principally from the pulpit, on the viciousness of the profane swearing contained in their writings. The worst oath in *Humphrey Clinker* is the footman's *Damn nasty son of a bitch and them he belongs to;* for the rest, the swearing is very lean. There is a *Foregad*, an *Odso, Faith and troth*, a *Jesus, By Christ*, and a *By Heaven.* Indeed, whenever he possibly can, Smollett seems to avoid the actual tropes and figures of rhetoric, as he so amiably called them, and either uses some conventionally innocuous expletive like '*sdeath* or *Good God*, or else merely refers to the performances of his characters in general terms, as when he describes a certain declaration as opening "the floodgates of Tabby's eloquence, which would have shamed the first-rate oratress of Billingsgate. The footman retorted in the same style . . ."

Perhaps the most sympathetic commentary on swearing in the whole range of English literature is to be found in the works of Laurence Sterne (1713–1768). There is the magnificent scene in *Tristram Shandy*, in which Uncle Toby was whistling *Lillibullero*, "which was the usual channel thro' which his passions got vent, when anything shocked or surprized him," and "Dr. Slop was stamping, and cursing and damning Obadiah at a most dreadful rate.—It would have done your heart good, and cured you, Sir, for ever of the vile sin of swearing, to have heard him." Tristram then explains how the maid and Obadiah had tied the strings of Dr. Slop's green baize bag, containing his instruments designed to assist in the delivery of Mrs. Shandy, into untieable knots, and how Dr. Slop having cut his thumb to the bone in the unsuccessful attempt to cut the knots, swore most pungently at his assistant Obadiah:

I wish the scoundrel hang'd!—I wish he was shot!—I wish all the devils in hell had him for a blockhead!—

My father had a great respect for Obadiah, and could not bear to hear him disposed of in such a manner:—he had, moreover, some little respect for himself,—and could as ill bear with the indignity offered to himself in it.

Had Dr. Slop cut any part about him but his thumb,—my father had pass'd it by—his prudence had triumphed:—as it was, he was determined to have his revenge.

Small curses, Dr. Slop, upon great occasions, quoth my father (condoling with him first upon the accident), are but so much waste of our strength and soul's health to no manner of purpose.—I own it, replied Dr. Slop.—They are like sparrow-shot, quoth my uncle Toby (suspending his whistling) fired against a bastion.—They serve, continued my father, to stir the humours—but carry off none of their acrimony:—for my own part, I seldom swear or curse at all—I hold it bad;—but if I fall into it by surprize, I generally retain so much presence of mind (right! quoth my uncle Toby) as to make it answer my purpose;—that is, I swear on till I find myself easy. A wise and a just man, however, would always endeavour to proportion the vent given to these humours, not only to the degree of them stirring within himself,—but to the size and ill intent of the offence upon which they are to fall.—'injuries come only from the heart,' quoth my uncle Toby.—For this reason, continued my father, with the most Cervantic gravity, I have the greatest veneration in the world for the gentleman, who, in distrust of his own discretion in this point, sat down and composed (that is at his leisure) fit forms of swearing suitable to all cases, from the lowest to the highest provocations which could possibly happen to him;—which forms being well considered by him,—and such, moreover, as he could stand to, he kept them ever by him on the chimney-piece, within his reach, ready for use. —I never apprehended, replied Dr. Slop, that such a thing was ever thought of,—much less executed.—I beg your pardon! answered my father: I was reading, though not using, one of them to my brother Toby this morning, whilst he pour'd out the tea:—'tis here upon the shelf over my head;—but if I remember right, 'tis too violent for a cut of the thumb.—Not at all, quoth Dr. Slop—the devil take the fellow!—Then, answered my father, 'tis much at your service, Dr. Slop,—on condition you read it aloud.—So rising up and reaching down a form of excommunication of the Church of Rome, a copy of which my father (who was curious in his collections) had procured out of the ledger-book of the church of Rochester, writ by Ernulphus the bishop,—he put it into Dr. Slop's hands.—Dr. Slop wrapt his thumb up in the corner of his handkerchief, and with a wry face, though without any suspicion, read aloud, as follows,—my uncle Toby whistling Lillibullero as loud as he could, all the time.

Dr. Slop then proceeds to read Bishop Ernulphus' curse (given in all its pristine purity in Chapter Four), with interjections by himself and his two listeners.

Upon the concluding of the reading of this terrible curse Uncle Toby declares, "My heart would not let me curse the Devil himself with so much bitterness."

He is the father of curses, replied Dr. Slop.—So am not I, replied my uncle.—But he is cursed and damned already, to all eternity, replied Dr. Slop.

I am sorry for it, quoth my uncle Toby.

Dr. Slop drew up his mouth, and was just beginning to return my uncle Toby the compliment of his *Whu-u-u-*, or interjectional whistle,— when the door hastily opening in the next chapter but one,—put an end to the affair.

Now don't let us give ourselves a parcel of airs, says Tristram, and pretend that the oaths we make free with in this land of liberty of ours are our own; and, because we have the spirit to swear them,—imagine that we have had the wit to invent them too.

I'll undertake this moment to prove it to any man in the world, except to a connoisseur;—though I declare I object only to a connoisseur in swearing, as I would do to a connoisseur in painting, &c., &c., . . . to anyone else I will undertake to prove that all the oaths and imprecations which we have been puffing off upon the world for these two hundred and fifty years last past, as originals,—except *St. Paul's thumb,—God's flesh* and *God's fish*, which were oaths monarchical, and considering who made them, not much amiss; and as king's oaths, 'tis not much matter whether they were fish or flesh;—else, I say, there is not an oath, or at least a curse amongst them, which has not been copied over and over again out of Ernulphus a thousand times: but, like all other copies, how infinitely short of the force and spirit of the original!—It is thought to be no bad oath,—and by itself passes very well,—"G——d damn you!" —Set it beside Ernulphus's,—"God Almighty the Father damn you! God the Son Damn you!—God the Holy Ghost damn you!"—you see 'tis nothing.—There is an orientality in his we cannot rise up to: besides, he is more copious in his invention,—possess'd more of the excellencies of a swearer,—had such a knowledge of the human frame, its membranes, nerves, ligaments, knittings of the joints, and articulations,—that when Ernulphus cursed,—no part escaped him.—'Tis true, there is something of a *hardness* in his manner,—and, as in Michael Angelo, a want of *grace*;—but then there is such a greatness of *gusto!*

My father, who generally look'd upon everything in a light very different from all mankind, would, after all, never allow this to be an original.—He considered rather Ernulphus's anathema as an institute of swearing, in which, as he suspected, upon the decline of swearing in some milder pontificate, Ernulphus, by order of the succeeding pope, had with great learning and diligence collected together all the laws of it;—for the same reason that Justinian, in the decline of the empire, had ordered his chancellor Tribonian to collect the Roman or civil laws all together into one code or digest—lest, through the rust of time,— and the fatality of all things committed to oral tradition,—they should be lost to the world for ever.

For this reason, my father would oftentimes affirm, there was not an oath, from the great and tremendous oath of William the Conqueror ("By the splendour of God!") down to the lowest oath of the scavenger ("Damn your eyes!") which was not to be found in Ernulphus.—In short, he would add,—I defy a man to swear out of it.

When, in concern for his brother officer, Uncle Toby exclaimed *He shall not die, by G——d!* "The *accusing spirit*, which flew up to Heaven's chancery with the oath, blushed as he gave it in;— and the *recording angel*, as he wrote it down, dropp'd a tear upon the word, and blotted it out for ever."

Mr. Shandy calls Dr. Slop *a son of a w——*. Mr. Shandy, indeed, was capable of quite paroxysmic behavior, and writes Tristram that in such a state

my father was all abuse and foul language, approaching rather towards malediction;—only he did not do it with as much method as Ernulphus's; —he was too impetuous; nor with Ernulphus's policy;—for though my father, with the most intolerant spirit, would curse both this and that, and every thing under heaven, which was either adding or abetting to his love,—yet he never concluded this chapter of curses upon it, without cursing himself in at the bargain, as one of the most egregious fools and coxcombs, he would say, that ever was let loose in the world.

"G—— help my father!" writes Tristram somewhat later, "he pish'd fifty times at every new attitude, and gave the Corporal's stick, with all its flourishings, and danglings, to as many Devils as chose to accept them."

Pish was a favorite eighteenth-century exclamation of both sexes and probably represents a contraction of *God's fish*. Tristram had a very low opinion of some ejaculations, such as *Heaven have mercy upon us*, of which, for a reverend gentleman, he irreverently remarks he would not give a groat for what the world thinks of that ejaculation.

Tristram Shandy was published between 1760 and 1767, and as befits the work of a cleric, it is largely free of profane swearing. *A Sentimental Journey Through France and Italy*, which appeared in 1768, except for *Mon Dieu, Psha, Good God, My God, I'll be shot, May I perish, The deuce take it*, has no tint of indelicate words that in the least would spot the snowy mantle of this enchanting travelogue. It is a pity Sterne never met Voltaire during his travels in France, for they would have rejoiced in each other. It was in 1773 that Voltaire published in his *Letters Concerning The English Nation*, an account of his stay in England. In Letter 1 he writes of an interview with a Quaker: "My dear sir, says I, were you ever baptiz'd? I never was, replied the Quaker, nor any of my brethren. Zouns, says I to him, you are not Christians then. Friend, replies the old man in a soft tone of voice, swear not."

Voltaire at one point exclaims, "Heavens!" and is again gently admonished not to swear. "We never swear," says the Quaker, "not even in a court of justice, being of opinion that the most holy name of God ought not to be prostituted in the miserable contests betwixt man and man."

Voltaire, who was a quite competent swearer in both French and English (see p. 283), was not much impressed by the Quaker's views and continued to swear to the end of his days.

In 1786, James Fordyce, in his *Poems*, reflected something of the conventional view of swearing in the eighteenth century when he wrote:

It chills my blood to hear the blest Supreme
Rudely appeal'd to on each trifling theme.
Maintain your ranks, vulgarity despise:
To swear is neither brave, polite, nor wise.
You would not swear upon the bed of death:
Reflect! your Maker now could stop your breath.

The sermonizing and publication of tracts against profane swearing during the eighteenth century undoubtedly represented a reaction against the undisciplined license of the preceding century. A typical example is a tract by Joseph Moser, *Reflections on Profane and Judicial Swearing*, published at London in 1795:

There are two bodies of men, and those very large ones, that it is said, and I fear with truth, are more addicted to a wanton profanation of God's holy Name; to swearing for amusement, and blaspheming for want of better conversation, than most others taken in general; I mean our *Soldiers* and *Sailors*; And this sinful propensity is the more to be wondered at, as one would think, that the dangers to which both professions are, or may daily, nay hourly be exposed, would render them more attentive to their religious duties.

.   .   .

In the vice which he [the profane swearer] practices, he can find no gratification of his passions; it can afford him no amusement; from it he can derive no profit; it will supply no want; nor will his repeated oaths and curses draw down the vengeance of the Almighty upon any head but his own.

Alas!

CHAPTER TWELVE

Swearing in the Nineteenth Century

‹‹›››››››››››››››››››››››››››››››››››››››

Swear not at all; for, for thy curse
Thine enemy is none the worse.

ARTHUR HUGH CLOUGH, *The Latest Decalogue*, 1862

S WEARING in the nineteenth century presents a not unexpect-
edly ambivalent picture. One perceives the effects of two
opposing forces at work: on the one side, the fettered
human spirit is seeking to escape the bonds that bind it and
express itself freely; and on the other side, the oppressive spread
of a canting hypocritical morality is observed to be gradually
enveloping the English-speaking world in the depressing fog of
ultrarespectability, which came to be known as Victorianism. It
was an age in which Mrs. Grundy set the standards of propriety,
in which lower extremities were concealed from view and never
referred to as "legs"—but at the most daring as "limbs"—and
when even the "legs" of pianos in some fastidious establishments
were dressed in pantaloons or otherwise obscured. Children, of
course, were neither "born" nor "made," but "sent," and never
"breast-fed," but merely "nursed."[1] Nothing in any way connected
with sex or reproduction could ever be directly referred to, and,
indeed, ladies and gentlemen agreed that some things were all
the better for not being mentioned at all.

In an atmosphere so genteel no lady, of course, ever swore, except euphemistically, nor did a genuine gentleman ever employ
so much as a *damn*, except in certain occupationally hazardous
professions, such as the armed forces.

So strong was the taboo on swearing during the Victorian period that there were probably more frustrated swearers who never used a swearword in their entire lives during this period than at any other in the history of civilized man. Many of us who were raised in an environment of elders all of whom were born in the nineteenth century can vouch for the fact that we never heard the slightest approach to an unadulterated swearword emerge from the lips of most of them, unless, of course, these elders were members of the lower classes or in some respect exceptional.

The men of the army and navy swore, and so did their officers upon occasion. But this was expected behavior, for an indispensable part of the equipment of a fighting man was a good assortment of fiery particles. Choleric squires and similar types might be allowed their quota of oaths, but for the most part pure and impious swearing flourished in this bleak age among the lowest classes. But even among these profane creatures the pressures of Victorian morality did not fail to exert their restraining influences, for those who appeared to swear without restraint were not uncontaminated by the euphemisms of those who swore with circumspection.

As Dr. Abraham Myerson has pointed out, "The taboo of certain words is merely part of the caste stratification of society and should really be opposed by all believers in democracy."[2]

Ladies might exclaim *Oh, Fudge, Fiddlesticks, Oh, Pshaw, Gracious, Goodness,* or *Goodness me, Rats, Lordy, Lord's sakes, Lan sakes, Mercy me, For Heaven's sake, Good Heavens, Great ghosts, Great Scott, Oh Bosh,* and even an occasional *Jimminy Cricket, Jehovah,* or *By Jove, Gosh, Gee, Gad, By Gorry, Jeepers,* and the like.

Such innocuous expressions were merely exclamatory, permissible in a lady, and hardly to be considered oaths. Indeed, many who customarily used such expressions would have been appalled to learn that strictly speaking they were engaged in swearing.

As we have said, the inveterate swearers did not escape the euphemizing influences of Victorianism, but though to some extent yielding to the constraints they continued to swear as vigorously as before. While words like *Jesus, Christ,* and *God* were more than ever firmly rooted in the swearer's vocabulary, it was in this period that their euphemistic forms really began to flourish.

A sampling of euphemisms common in this period are, for

Jesus Christ: Jimminy Cricket, Jimminy Cracket, Gee Whiskers
Christ: Cripes, Crikey, Crimey, Criminey, Christopher, For Tripe's sake,
   For Crying out loud
Jesus: Gee, Jeeze, Jimminy, Jerusalem, Jehosephat, Geraniums
God: Cor, Coo, Gaw, Gawd, Gosh, Gol, Golly, Jolly, George

Such expletives as *Cor love a duck, Gaw-blimey*, and the euphemistic forms of *God*, as well as a good many others, are mostly of cockney origin and are largely though not exclusively in usage restricted to those estimable groundlings.

Euphemistic asseverations lost all touch with their original meanings and so provided outlets for strong expressions that were socially perfectly acceptable. Who could possibly be offended by a *Goodness gracious me* or a *My, my*? As Franz Boas has pointed out, the disuse into which profanity fell during the nineteenth century was first due to a religious reaction, and then came to be simply a matter of good manners.[3]

"From the beginning of the nineteenth century," wrote Henry Cecil Wyld in 1920, "it would seem that nearly all the old oaths died out in good society, as having come to be considered, from unfamiliarity either too profane or else too devoid of content to serve any purpose. It seems to be the case that the serious oaths survive longest, or at any rate die hardest, while each age produces its own ephemeral formulas of mere light expletive and asseveration."[4]

Clifford Gessler, commenting on the absence of swearwords among the Polynesians, remarks that "most four-letter words are less indecent than the prudish euphemisms and circumlocutions that replace them."[5] Gessler is, of course, quite right. However, to those who resort to euphemisms, it is the euphemized term that is indecent; for them it represents a mild or vague substitute for a blunt or unacceptable expression. It is of the nature of such euphemisms that their origins are soon forgotten, and more often than not, except for the antiquary in such matters, no one in the least cares.

Some period examples of euphemistic swearing may be given here.

In that splendid anonymously published 1852 Oxford irony *Phrontisterion* (actually by Mansel, later Waynflete Professor and Dean of St. Paul's), Pheidippides-Johnny, "the Model Minister, a compound, as his name implies, of parsimony and chivalry, a great public benefactor, but [who] prefers doing it at other people's expense," swears *Odds Dos and Dodges!*[6] A magnificent piece of transmogrificatory circumnavigation around the forbidden words.

Southey, in his miscellany *The Doctor*, which he wrote and published between 1834 and 1847, tells how he swore by the great decasyllabon *Aballiboozobanganovribo.* "In my use of it, however," he writes, "I observed this caution,—that I do not suffer myself to be carried away by an undue partiality, so as to employ it in disregard of ejaculatory propriety or to the exclusion of exclamations which the occasion may render more fitting."[7] It is rather a mouthful, but evidently served its employer well on the appropriate occasions.

Leigh Hunt (1784–1859), in his *Autobiography*, published in 1850, tells how his mother had produced in him "such a horror, or rather such an intense idea of even violent words, and of the commonest trivial oath, that being led one day, perhaps by the very excess of it, to snatch a 'fearful joy' in its utterance, it gave me so much remorse that for some time afterwards I could not receive a bit of praise, or a pat of encouragement on the head, without thinking to myself, 'Ah! they little suspect that I am the boy who said, 'd—n it!'"

Hunt goes on to say

I may here mention, as a ludicrous counterpart of this story, and a sample of the fantastical nature of scandal, that somebody having volunteered a defence of my character on some occasion to Mr. Wordsworth, as though the character had been questioned by him—the latter said he had never heard anything against it, except that I was "given to swearing."

I certainly think little of the habit of swearing, however idle, if it be carried no further than is done by many gallant and very good men, wise and great ones not excepted. I wish I had no worse faults to answer for. But the fact is, that however I may laugh at the puerile conscience of the anecdote just mentioned, an oath has not escaped my lips from that day to this.

I hope no "good fellow" will think ill of me for it. If he did I should certainly be tempted to begin swearing immediately, purely to *vindicate* my character. But there was no swearing in our family: there was none in our school (Christ Church); and I seldom ever fell in the way of it anywhere except in books; so that the practice was not put into my head. I look upon Tom Jones, who swore, as an angel of light compared with Blifil, who, I am afraid, swore no more than myself. Steele, I suspect, occasionally rapped out an oath, which is not to be supposed of Addison. And this, again, might tempt me into a grudge against my own nonjuring turn of colloquy; for I must own that I prefer open-hearted Steele with all his faults to Addison with all his essays. But habit is habit, negative as well as positive. Let him that is without one cast the first sarcasm.

After all, swearing was once seriously objected to me, and I had given cause for it. I must own that I even begged hard to be allowed a few oaths. It was for an article in a magazine (the *New Monthly*), where I had to describe a fictitious person, whose character I thought required it; and I pleaded truth to nature, and the practice of the good old novelists; but in vain. The editor was not to be entreated. He was Mr. Theodore Hook. Perhaps this is what gave rise to the poet's impression.

What a gentleman in mid-nineteenth-century England thought of "strong" language may be gathered from Walter Savage Landor's comment to William Wetmore Story. "Old Wheler the counsellor dined often with my father and swore horribly. Vulgar habit it is —that's luckily done away with. I could see my aunt jump in her chair when he came out with his horrid words. At last he said something very bad, and I burst out laughing to see her. 'What the devil in hell are you laughing at?' says he, naming not only the *padrone*, but the locality too."[8]

The event that Landor was describing took place toward the end of the eighteenth century. Landor again reverts to the "vulgar" habit of swearing in his poem "The Modern Idyll" in his *Dry Sticks Fagoted* (1858).

> LADY: Now I declare to god.
> POLICEMAN: Pray don't!
>   Or he may think it an affront.
>   Ten times you've made that declaration
>   Since I have been upon the station.
>   At our most gracious Queen's expence,
>   Thousand and thousand of miles from hence
>   Some have been sent for change of air
>   By swearing; so mind what you swear.[9]

Henry Fuseli (1741–1825), the Anglo-Swiss painter and draughtsman, was an accomplished swearer. Joseph Farington and Sir Thomas Lawrence both agreed that Fuseli was an impossible person, whose manners rendered him beyond the pale. John Flaxman had often been outraged by Fuseli's language, and on one occasion asked William Blake what he did when Fuseli swore. "What do I do?" asked Blake. "Why, I swear again! and he says, astonished, 'Vy, Blake, you are svaring!' but he leaves off himself!"[10]

Bliss Perry, in his charming book *And Gladly Teach* (1935), writes that though his father actually never swore, he could load the most ordinary language with profane implications. *"Fish to Bungtown!* was a favorite expletive which he had brought from Lyme."[11] Pierrpont Noyes tells that his uncle Abram would occasionally deliver himself of a *By Jolly!*[12]

In the early nineteenth century, before Victoria's ascent to the throne, quite well brought up boys of "respectable" families were often permitted a certain latitude in the language they used. For example, Charles Darwin, whose family was Unitarian and upper middle class, writing of himself as he was in 1819 at the age of ten, says, "I was at that age very passionate (when I swore like a trooper) and quarrelsome. The former passion has, I think, nearly wholly but slowly died away."[13]

Herbert Spencer, in his *Autobiography*, confesses that he was once betrayed into uttering an oath:

While out fishing one breezy morning, I got my line into a tangle, which I could not unravel; and at length, losing all patience, I vented an oath. The man in the boat with me, who, as I afterwards learned, was precentor at some neighbouring village kirk or chapel, reproved me: perhaps thinking himself called upon to do so by his semi-ecclesiastical function. I suppose it was the oddity of this incident which drew my attention to the fact that, being then thirty-six years of age, I had never before been betrayed into intemperate speech of such kind.[14]

And in the next sentence, Spencer characteristically puts the escape of the intemperate word down to "the irritability produced by my nervous disorder." As Tyndall once remarked of Spencer, he would have been a much better fellow had he indulged in a good swear now and then. But that is purely theoretical, and as Thomas Henry Huxley said, Spencer's idea of a tragedy was a beautiful theory killed by an ugly fact.

As a substitute for *Damn it* a certain nineteenth-century clerical scholar used to exclaim *Therewith!* This being a translation of the German word *damit*, the punning relationship suggesting this curious English substitution and affording some indication of the lengths to which men would go in attempting to mitigate the odium of the prohibited words.

A "judicious imprecation," as Leigh Hunt termed it, popular with persons of gentility in the nineteenth century was *Confound it!* In one form or another the oath goes back at least to the sixteenth century, but in the form quoted constituted a favorite expletive with gentlemen of the nineteenth century. It was exclusively a class oath and seldom was used by members of the lower classes, although Huckleberry Finn, in *Tom Sawyer* (1876), employs a euphemized form of it when he exclaims *Consound it!* In the same work Huck swears *By jings* and Tom swears *Dad fetch it.*

A popular oath in America during the nineteenth century was *I don't give a continental!* This oath constitutes an illuminating example of the manner in which words assume an emotional charge and become adapted to the uses of the swearer. During the War of Independence the Continental Congress issued its own money. This continental currency gradually depreciated in value until it became almost worthless. Hence, as a symbol for worthless or discredited things the continental dollar was a swearword that could be uttered with genuine feeling.

In one of Mark Twain's works one of the characters remarks, "He didn't give a continental for anybody. Beg your pardon friend, for coming so near saying a cuss word."

The "cuss word" persisted right into the twentieth century, though it is less frequently heard now than formerly.

Mark Twain, himself an accomplished swearer and a great admirer of the art in others, in his *Autobiography* tells of Captain Ned Wakeman, with whom he had made two voyages at sea: "He was a liberal talker and inexhaustibly interesting. In the matter of a wide and catholic profanity he had not his peer on the planet while he lived. It was a deep pleasure to me to hear him do his stunts in this line. He knew the Bible by heart and was profoundly and sincerely religious."[15]

Twain had spoken much of Captain Wakeman and of his prowess as a swearer to his friend the Reverend Joseph Twichell. The latter some time afterward had occasion to take a Pacific mail-boat south for the Isthmus. There was only one other passenger aboard. "After that passenger had delivered himself of about six majestically and picturesquely profane remarks Twichell (alias Peters) said 'Could it be, by chance, that you are Captain Ned Wakeman of San Francisco?"[16]

It could, and it was.

The forty-second chapter of Twain's *Autobiography* is wholly devoted to an account, told in Twain's own inimitable style, of an encounter with a swearer the like of whom has probably many times been heard but seldom if ever so well recorded—not the words, so much as the *stimmung*. And so the whole chapter is given here.

The world loses a good deal by the laws of decorum; gains a good deal, of course, but certainly loses a good deal. I remember a case in point. I started to walk to Boston once with my pastor*—pastor and old familiar friend in one. At nine that night, twelve hours out, we had tramped nearly thirty miles and I was nearly dead with fatigue, cold, pain and lameness; skin mostly gone from my heels, tendons of my legs shortened by a couple of inches, each and every limp a sharp agony. But the Reverend was as fresh as ever; and light-hearted and happy to a degree that was not easy to bear. There were small farm-houses at intervals but the occupants all fled down cellar whenever we hailed or knocked, for the roads were alive with murderous tramps in those days.

By ten at night I had dragged myself another half mile and this, to my unutterable gratitude, brought us to a village—call it Duffield, any name will do. We were soon in the bar of the inn and I dropped at once into a chair behind the big hot stove, full of content, happy to the marrow and desiring only to be left unmolested. But the Reverend did not care to sit down; he was brimming with unexpended vigors, his jaw was not tired with twelve hours' wagging, he must stir about, he must ask some questions.

The room was about twelve by sixteen, a snug little place—unpainted counter at one end, four or five feet long, three unpainted white-pine shelves behind it with ten or twelve bottles scattered along them, containing liquor and flies; no carpet, no decorations except a lithograph on the wall—horse race in a hailstorm, apparently; hail turns out to be flyspecks. Two men present: No. 1, the old village bummer, seated and hovering over the stove, opposite side from me—expectorating on it occasionally, where he could find a red-hot spot; No. 2 was a young and vigorous man, in a chair tilted back against the white-pine partitions; chin buried in his breast; coonskin cap on, its natural tail sticking down past left ear; heels propped on round of chair; breeches rolled to boot tops. Now and then *he* shot at the stove, five feet away, and hit it without breaking up his attitude.

These men had not moved since we entered, nor made utterance except to answer our greeting, in the beginning, with a grunt, courteously meant. The Reverend browsed around, now here, now there, plying me with remarks which I did not disturb my bliss to respond to; so, at last he was obliged to apply elsewhere. He is an observer. He had observed signs and smelt smells which suggested that although these men seemed so dumb and dead, the one tilted against the wall might possibly be coaxed into a state of semi-interest by some reference to horses:—an

* Joseph Twichell. The walk occurred in 1874.

ostler, the Reverend guessed and was right, as transpired later. So he said, "Well, ostler, I suppose you raise some pretty fine breeds of horses around here?"

The young fellow unbent right away; and his face, which was a good face, lighted pleasantly, eagerly in fact. He untilted, planted his feet on the floor, shoved his coon tail around to the rear, spread his broad hands upon his knees, beamed up at the tall Reverend, and turned himself loose:

"Well, now, I tell *you!*—*pretty* fine ain't the word!—and it don't *begin!*"

Evidently he was as goodhearted a young fellow as ever was, and as guiltless of wish or intent to offend; yet into the chance chinks of that single little short sentence he managed to wattle as much as two yards and a half of the most varied and wonderful profanity! And that sentence did not end his speech—no, it was the mere introduction; straight after it followed the speech—a speech five minutes long, full of enthusiastic horse statistics; poured out with the most fluent facility, as from an inexhaustible crater, and all ablaze from beginning to end with crimson lava jets of desolating and utterly unconscious profanity! It was his native tongue; he had no idea that there was any harm in it.

When the speech ended there was a mighty silence; the Reverend was in a state of stupefaction—dumb, he was, for once. The situation was unique, delicious. The bliss which I had been feeling before was tame to what I was feeling now. Skinned heels were nothing; I could have enjoyed this thing if I had been skinned all over. I did not laugh exteriorly, for that would have been indecorous. I made no motion, gave no sign; simply sat still and slowly died with joy. The Reverend looked at me appealingly, as much as to say, "Don't desert a friend in heavy trouble—help me out of this." I did nothing—was too near dissolution to be useful—and the ostler turned himself loose once more—once more he oozed eloquent profanity and incredible smut from every pore; and all so naturally and sweetly and innocently that it would have been flattery to call it a sin.

In desperation the Reverend broke in with a question about some other matter—mild, commonplace, less exciting than horse affairs; something about the roads and distances thence to Boston; hoped and believed that this cold topic would furnish no chances for lurid language. A mistake; the ostler sailed into that subject, rained, hailed, blew great guns and thundered and lightened over it, under it, around it and through it, with all the profane splendor which had distinguished his horse talk.

The Reverend rushed to the front again, pulled the ostler loose from the roads and got him to tackle the crops. Another failure. He went into the crops with as fresh a zeal as ever and drove his dialectic night cart through it at as rattling a gait and with as fragrant effect as in the beginning. In a sort of pathetic despair the Reverend fled, as a refuge, to the ancient bummer at the stove and uncorked him with a most innocuous remark, a colorless and unincendiary remark, about my lame and sore condition; whereupon the bummer, a pitying and kindly creature, turned *him*self loose with a perfectly Vesuvian eruption of charitable dirt and blasphemy concerning the healing properties of "Karosine" externally applied; appealed to the ostler to confirm the almost miraculous excellence of Karosine for bruises and abrasions; the ostler responded with mephitic enthusiasm; and for five minutes the Reverend stood speechless there while the unutterable tides from these two sewers swept over him.

At last a saving thought slipped into his brain. He sauntered to the counter, got a letter out of his pocket, glanced through it, returned it to its envelope, laid it on the counter, ciphered aimlessly upon it with a pencil; then presently sauntered away and left it there with a sinful pretense of having forgotten it. There was a pale joy in his jaded eye when he saw the bait take; saw the ostler loaf toward the counter; saw him take up the envelope and drop his eye on it. There was a pause, and silence! then the ostler broke out with glad surprise:

"What!—you are a preacher?"

(Prodigious and long-continued thunderpeal of improprieties and profanities.)

"Why didn't you *tell* a body so! *I* didn't know you was anybody!"

And straightway he flew around with loving alacrity, routed the cook out of bed, chambermaid likewise, and in two minutes these people were hard at work in our behalf. Then the delightful and delighted orator seated the Reverend in the place of honor and told him all about the state of church matters in Duffield: a flowing, masterly, goodhearted, right-purposed narrative which was fifteen minutes passing a given point, and was torch-lighted with indelicacies from end to end, which flickered lambent through a misty red hell of profanity rent and torn at four-foot intervals all down the line by sky-cleaving rocket explosions of gorgeous blasphemy! Admirable artist!—all his previous efforts were but lightening-bug-and-glowworm displays compared to this final and supreme conflagration!

As we turned in, in a double-bedded room, the Reverend remarked, with subdued gratefulness:

"Well, as to this thing, there is one comfort, anyway—such as it is: You can't *print* it, Mark."

He was right about that, of course. It was extravagantly funny. But only because those men were innocent of harmful intent. Otherwise it would have been barren of fun and merely disgusting. Next morning the warm-blooded ostler bounded into the breakfast room, perishing with laughter, and told the grave and respectable landlady and her little daughter how he had found the geese frozen fast in the pond; and his language was just as terrific as it had been the night before. These persons showed great interest in the geese but none at all in the language —they were used to that and found no offense in it.[17]

So sensitive was Mark Twain to the world about him that he could animistically endow inanimate objects with the ability to swear. William Dana Orcutt tells of a visit with his wife to Twain when the latter and his family were living at the Villa di Quarto in Florence. Twain delivered himself picturesquely on the banality of the villa and its appointments. About the landlady responsible for the furnishings he remarked, "Less said about her the better. You never heard such profanity as is expressed by the furniture and the carpets she put in to complete the misery. I'm always thankful when darkness comes on to stop the swearing."[18]

If it was considered good manners to refrain from every kind of violence in speech, it was esteemed even more so on the stage and in the novel. One may search through the plays of the nineteenth century without encountering a serious imprecation. The fuss that was made about Gilbert and Sullivan's *Ruddygore* when the comic opera was staged in January, 1887, showed how strongly the prejudice against questionable words had become entrenched. The objections were many and fierce—not to the play but to the title. *Ruddy* was taken to be a euphemism for *bloody*, the very thought of which was too much for Victorian public and critical fastidiousness. As we shall see in the chapter on *bloody*, Gilbert was ready to change the title, but Sullivan would not have it. Another quarter of a century was to elapse before such a word was permitted on the stage, in Bernard Shaw's *Pygmalion* (1914) (see pp. 256–257).

In the literature of the nineteenth century, swearing, save of the mildest kind, is conspicuously rare. Even in a private letter Swinburne could not bring himself to write the word *damn* (see p. 295).

Cecil Torr, in *Small Talk at Wrayland* (1932), writes of his maternal aunt, Emma King, author of the widely read *Questions in Church History* (1848), who found time "to expurgate the *Ingoldsby Legends*, thus rendering them presentable at Penny Readings. I have her copy with her pencillings. 'There's a cry and a shout and a deuce of a rout'—*for* deuce of *read* terrible. 'The Devil must be in that little Jackdaw'—*for* the Devil *read* A Demon. And so on."[19]

Expurgation of the *Ingoldsby Legends* was surely an example of supererogative piety, if ever there was one, for Richard Barham, the author, had himself striven to render the work as inoffensive and moralistic as—he apparently mistakenly thought—he possibly could. The work, published in 1840, apropos of swearing enjoined the reader in the following words:

> And now, gentle reader, one word ere we part,
> Just take a friend's counsel, and lay it to heart.
> Don't use naughty words, in the next place, and Ne'er in
> Your language adopt a bad habit of swearing.
> Never say, "Devil take me!"
> Or "shake me!" or "bake me!"
> Or such-like expressions: Remember, Old Nick
> To take folks at their word is remarkably quick.[20]

This sort of thing undoubtedly contributed to the ill-repute into which the habit of swearing increasingly fell during the next sixty years. It was a text upon which Victorians never tired of preaching. Firmly ensconced in their citadels of fortified respectability they felt that no impropriety of this kind could be tolerated in any form, and at the very beginning of the nineteenth century a wealthy Edinburgh physician, Thomas Bowdler (1754–1825), a man eminently devoted to good works, set himself the task of purging from the works of such writers as Shakespeare and Gibbon every word that he considered improper. In 1818 appeared his ten-volume *The Family Shakespeare*, "In which nothing is added to the original text; but those words and expressions are omitted which cannot with propriety be read aloud in a family." The verb "to bowdlerize" was a very active one during this century, and Dr. Bowdler's example was widely followed.

There were others who, like James Plumtre,[21] not only bowdlerized but rewrote the classics, with sometimes surprising effects. This was the age of every man his own censor, with official censorship so rigidly enforced that while "strong language" virtually disappeared from speech, it flourished illicitly in the forbidden literature of pornography as never before. Indeed, pornography flourished as a subculture with a life of its own as a covert complement to the hypocritical overt aspects of the culture to which it was the reaction, the "negative analogue," as Steven Marcus has put it.[22] The only effect of censorship upon the publication of such works was to ensure their proliferation. If only the censorious had paid some attention to the words of John Marston, who wrote in his play *The Dutch Courtezan* (1605): "I love no prohibited things, and yet I would have nothing prohibited by policy, but by vertue; for as in the fashion of time, those books that are cald in are most in sale and request, so in nature those actions that are most prohibited are most desired" (III, i).

When George Colman the Younger, playwright, reformed rake, and friend of the Prince Regent, became Examiner of Plays in 1824, he deleted with red ink all oaths and expletives from the plays submitted to him. "I think," he solemnly declared before a Royal Commission in 1832, "nobody has gone away from the theatre the better for hearing a great deal of cursing and swearing." Hence, references to God, heaven, hell, providence, thighs, virgins, and the damned were adjudged either profane or indecent or both.

The egregious E. F. Smyth Pigott, who was Examiner of Plays from 1874 till his death in 1895, wrote in the margin of a play submitted to him (*London Life*) against a passage in which the hero ordered a steak and beer, "During Lent it would be better if the order were for a boiled egg and a glass of water."

The trouble with the Victorians was not a want of virtue but an excess of it, wantonly applied. Victorian virtue represented the public expression of private vice, not merely a private torment but, what was worse, an intolerable public nuisance. Looking back upon the Puritan spirit, which found so perfect an embodiment in Victorian mores, we can appreciate the truth of the dictum that virtue is so much more dangerous than vice because it is not subject to the constraints of the conscience. The evil that good men do has never been more disastrously attested than by the consequences of the canting, hypocritical morality of the Victorians. Of the typical Victorian it may be remarked, as someone once said of William Ewart Gladstone, that he was a "good" man in the worse sense of the word. As Bertrand Russell once put it, "We all know what we mean by a 'good' man. He neither drinks nor smokes, avoids bad language, and in the presence of men converses only exactly as he would if there were ladies present."[23] With the battering ram of his own moral standards, which he conceives to be *absolutely* right, he self-righteously invades the privacy of others, just as Gladstone used to do when he nightly prowled the streets of London determined to save the souls of fallen women, who, of course, he considered would be better employed washing away their sins in workhouse laundries.

Ernest Weekley recounts that when he was ten he lent a copy

of Ballantyne's *Coral Island* to a friend. One of the characters is a repentant pirate named Bloody Bill. When the book was returned to Weekley the offensive adjective had been penciled out wherever it occurred by a disapproving aunt.[24]

The puritanizing blight extended to the farthest corners of the earth. Mrs. W. J. Tobey tells what happened when her father, captain of a clipper ship, visited Pitcairn Island in the 1860s. The captain, on being introduced to one of the young girls, said, "Bless my soul, my dear, I am glad to meet you." Whereupon the girl's scandalized mother broke in, "Captain, that is very strong language."[25] What the lady would have said to "Shiver my timbers," or "Split my timbers," can scarcely be thought upon. It is fortunate that the captain did not take the name of the Lord in vain.

Thomas Henry Huxley, the great evangelist of evolution, Darwin's "bulldog" as he called himself, in a letter addressed to Darwin, dated February 3, 1880, with reference to Samuel Butler's intemperate attack on Darwin, almost brings himself to write the words that he "would kill any son of a bitch," but stops short of the final word and substitutes a drawing of the animal![26] Huxley was a very unstuffy forward-looking "Eminent Victorian," but one is still surprised to find even so emancipated a thinker daring to write so boldly to his friend, that other "Eminent Victorian," Charles Darwin. It is *not* surprising to find that Huxley's son Leonard (the father of Aldous and Julian) omitted this letter from his *Life and Letters of Thomas Henry Huxley* (London, 1901).

At the end of the nineteenth century two of the greatest students of the English language, James Bradstreet Greenough and George Lyman Kittredge, both of Harvard, as authorities on the subject, in their book on *Words and Their Ways in English Speech* (1901), took the view that "the propensity to curse and swear is deep-seated."[27] Hence, the singular compromise of euphemistic expressions. I cannot speak for Greenough, who died in 1901, but Kittredge himself was no resorter to euphemisms. He could use good Chaucerian English to noble effect. But his belief in the deep-seated nature of the propensity to swear is, as we have seen, untenable. Nevertheless, that belief may have served some swearers as an excuse in mitigation of this execrable habit.

During the nineteenth century the ideals of gentility and good manners that the rising mercantile classes sought to imitate left the working classes and the intermittently employed quite untouched. Swearing was not only part of their daily communication, but also an easement to the much besieged spirit. Those who suffer great frustrations are likely to be considerable swearers. It is principally for this reason, we may suppose, that the oppressed classes of mankind, nautical men and soldiers, have so excelled in the art.

CHAPTER THIRTEEN

Bloody: The Natural History of a Word

‹‹‹‹‹‹‹‹‹‹‹‹‹‹‹‹‹‹‹‹‹‹‹‹‹‹‹‹‹‹‹‹‹‹ ‹ › ›››››››››››››››››››››››››››››

> *Among tragic downfalls from high to lowest place, the unfortunate and familiar adjectives* blooming *and* bloody *are deserving of sympathetic attention.*
>
> LOGAN PEARSALL SMITH

O F all the words in the English swearer's vocabulary one has probably been worked harder than all the rest put together. It is the word *bloody*. In 1884 Julian Sharman wrote:

Dirty drunkards hiccup it as they wallow on ale-house floors. Morose porters bandy it about on quays and landing-stages. From the low-lying quarters of the towns the word buzzes in your ear with the confusion of a Babel. In the cramped narrow streets you are deafened by its whirr and din, as it rises from the throats of the chaffering multitude, from besotted men defiant and vain-glorious in their drink, from shrewish women hissing out rancour in their harsh querulous talk.[1]

Sharman refers principally to conditions as they prevailed in London, and it is evident from what he says that already in the nineteenth century *bloody* was being badly overworked. The cloud of ill fame and ill favor that clung to the word when Sharman wrote caused him to reserve its discussion for the last dozen pages of his book. The assumption, no doubt, was that by the time the reader had proceeded thus far he would not be unwilling to advance further, even though it might necessitate the devotion of ten minutes' attention to a word that had previously been permitted none whatever.

Sharman deserves to be well remembered by all good men for

the service that he performed for *bloody*, for this gentle man had the courage, at the most frigidly self-righteous period of the age of Victoria, to attempt to strip the term of its infamous significance and dispel from it something of the unsavory reputation that had overtaken it. How the term came to fall into disrepute and suffer an almost total eclipse among the respectable is part of the story we have to tell in this chapter. The word is itself of the most spotless origin. This, however, is a fact unknown to those who are still inclined to look with disfavor upon it. To them the term is an illegitimate word of obscure parentage—it being taken for granted that its genitors were neither good nor careful. In the eminently respectable age of Victoria it need hardly be said that a word of such doubtful repute was doomed to become a social outcast, a poor orphan with no one to take it in or care for it but the "horrid poor." And, in order to adorn their speech and lend greater force to what they were saying, the poor naturalized it among themselves, peppering their speech with it as a hunter scatters birdshot. And so much force did they lend to their words by the use of it, and with such imagination, or lack of it, the word soon began to flourish and to be elevated to new functions, from a mere intensive to an adjective, from an adjective to an adverb, and from an adverb to a noun. Eventually it was to migrate all the way from Poplar to Park Lane, from Hampstead Heath to Zanzibar. The word proved to be so useful that it went through, for the first time in the history of a language of the Indo-European family, a grammatical and syntactical process that is known only to several American Indian languages and to one or two others. This is the process of infixing, in which a particle, or a part of a word, or a whole word, is placed in the middle of another word, as we commonly add particles in the form of prefixes and suffixes to the beginning and end of words. We shall deal with such linguistic niceties later in this chapter.

Though its career has been truly checkered, *bloody* has today come fully into its own. It is now heard upon stage and screen. Even *Punch* admitted it some years ago into its pages, and newspapers generally no longer give it the quietus of a dash or a scattering of asterisks but print in bold unblushing type every full letter of the word. Pukkah gentlemen utter it before ladies without apology, and miracle upon miracle, not only do ladies no longer blush to hear the word, but appreciable numbers of English women work it no less hard than their men do.

How has all this come about? The answer to this question is a most beguiling one. But let us begin at the beginning.

([On the Origin of the Word "Bloody" and Its Popularity

Few words have given rise to greater philological and etymological ingenuity than the word *bloody*. Of the etymological attempts to explain it I am acquainted with eight. Here they are.

1. *Bloidhe*. According to Charles Mackay, writing in 1888, the word *bloody* is derived from the old British root *bloidhe*, meaning *rather*.[2] But since this is merely a conjecture based upon no more evidence than a superficial resemblance between the words, it cannot be taken seriously. All that *can* be said is that there does not at present exist the slightest evidence in support of this explanation.

2. *By'r Lady*, that is, the contracted form of *By our Lady*. This theory holds that *bloody* represents the final form of the further contracted *By'r Lady* through the elision of the "yr" in *Byr*, to form *blady* and so *bloody*. Very ingenious, but it won't do since both *By'r Lady* as an interjection and *bloody* as an adjective and adverb occur in Shakespeare. Thus, in Part III of *Henry VI* Queen Margaret exclaims, "bloody cannibals" (V, v.). In *Richard III* Richmond exclaims:

> God and your arms be praised, victorious friends;
> The day is ours, the bloody dog is dead.
>
> V, v

And Derby immediately afterward refers to the "bloody wretch." In Shakespeare the term is almost invariably used as an adjective referring to the sanguinary qualities of the persons to whom it is applied. *By'r Lady* is always employed as an interjection, as for example when Lucius, in Titus Andronicus refers to the three "bloody villains" (IV, ii) Aaron, Demetrius, and Chiron, while the clown in the same play swears "by'r lady" (IV, iv). Similarly, in the following instances the word serves the same functions:

> PRINCE: Benvolio, who began this bloody fray?
> *Romeo and Juliet*, III, ii.

> FIRST CITIZEN: O most bloody sight!
> *Julius Caesar*, III, ii

DUNCAN: What bloody man is that?
                                   Macbeth, I, ii

Macbeth, indeed, contains more *bloody*s than Masefield's dramatic poem of 1912, *The Everlasting Mercy*.

With so excellent a store of *bloody*s to choose from it is most unlikely that anyone ever transmuted a *By'r Lady* into a *bloody*. We may therefore dismiss this most popular of the attempted explanations.

3. *S'blood*, that is, the contracted form of *God's blood*. This theory holds that from *s'blood* to *bloody* is but an easy step. Maybe it is, but there is no evidence that it was ever taken. Indeed, the same kind of objections that apply to *By'r Lady* apply with equal force to *s'blood*.

4. *Blood* in its ordinary physiological sense but especially as it relates either to menstruation or "the bloody flux," the old name for dysentery. But the objection here is that the special sense and reference of the word is far too limited to have fathered a term of so many uses. Furthermore, evidence in support of it is entirely wanting.

5. *A blood*, a rich, and usually young, roisterer. According to this theory, put forward by no less an authority than *The Oxford English Dictionary*, the term probably first referred to the habits of the "bloods," or aristocratic rowdies who flourished toward the end of the seventeenth and the beginning of the eighteenth centuries. The phrase "bloody drunk," it is suggested, apparently meant to be "as drunk as a blood." This theory is so obviously far-fetched that its cause was lost from the beginning. It is significant that it emanated from Oxford.

6. *Blütig*, the exact German equivalent of *bloody*. According to this theory, which was first put forward by Sharman, *bloody* probably originated from the German *blütig* at the very end of the sixteenth century, when Englishmen were fighting in the Low Countries under Vere and Stanley. *Blütig* is an inconsequential sort of particle that was employed in all the dialects of Germany to denote a sense of the emphatic. The word was especially favored among the lower classes and soon came to serve a reprobate soldiery as the most popular makeweight with which to balance their assertions. Sharman writes:

It will be at once seen that this alien growth was capable of being readily transplanted to our soil in the shape of its literal counterpart.

The circumstance of the words being so nearly identical is sufficient to account for the work of transposition being swiftly and effectually done. But beyond the mere accident of the respective tongues being an exact literal equivalent, there was nothing in common between the German "blütig" and the English correlative term.[3]

It is difficult to understand what Sharman means in his last sentence, for *blütig* was and still is a fairly polite word. Perhaps what Sharman *does* mean is that whereas *blütig* was a respectable word, *bloody* was far from being so, for he remarks in his next sentence, "As evidenced by the purity of its antecedents, the latter derives nothing of the opprobrium that has devolved upon it by reason of any hereditary defects, far less on account of any of its inherent properties."[4]

This explanation of the origin of the use of the word *bloody* in the English language in its modern sense has a great deal to recommend it. In the first place, both the Dutch and the German languages still make use of the literal equivalents, *een bloedige beleediging* (a bloody insult) or *een bloedige hoon*. And we have in German, *Ich habe keinen blütigen Heller mehr* (I haven't a bloody bean, or, less slangily, I have not even a penny left). In compounds the form *blüt* is used, as in *blütarm* (miserably bloody poor); and as Weekley, who cites these examples, states, "'Das ist mein blütiger Ernst' is fairly polite German for 'I seriously (Shavian *bloodywell*) mean what I say.'"[5]

In the second place, the first recorded use of the word *bloody* occurs in a work published soon after the return of the English armies from the Low Countries. This was John Marston's *The Parasitaster; or the Fawne*, a comedy published in 1606. Nymphadoro, a young courtier and designing "common lover," says to the braggart Herod:

Speak till thy lungs ake, talke out thy teeth; here are none of those cankers, these mischiefs of societie, intelligencers or informers that will cast rumor into the teeth of some Laelius Baldus, a man cruelly eloquent and bluddily learned.

I, ii

Later in the same play Don Zuccone, "a causelessly jealous Lord," cries out upon that same Herod:

Doe not anger me, least I most dreadfully curse thee, and wish thee married! Oh, Zuccone, spitte white, spitte thy gall out, The only boone

I crave of Heaven is—But to have my honors inherited by a bastard I will be most tirranous—bloodily tirranous in my revenge, and most terrible in my curses.

II, i

Interestingly enough, *bloodily* does not occur in any of Marston's earlier or later plays, a fact that would suggest that Marston had but recently made its acquaintance when he was writing *The Parasitaster*. Weekley has shown that the rendering *bloody* for *bloodily* is due to a very general tendency to drop -*ly* from a word already ending in *y*, as for example, in *very, pretty, jolly*.[6] It seems, then, very likely that Marston picked up the word from some of the warriors who had recently returned from the Low Countries. Ben Jonson, who fought in these campaigns, does not use the word, but there was a good reason for this. In 1606, the very year of the publication of Marston's *The Parasitaster*, swearing in plays was strictly forbidden, and Ben Jonson, himself no swearer, could afford to take no chances with a new word that might be stupidly misunderstood.[7] Shakespeare, one of the greatest exponents of the art of swearing, wrote his plays between the years 1590 and 1610, when the English form of *blütig* had not yet taken root in its new home. Yet it is by no means certain that Shakespeare always used the word *bloody* in its literal sense. Thus, Shakespeare almost certainly employed the word in its modern sense when in *Henry V* the Frenchman Fluellen says, ". . . it is good for your green wound and your bloody coxcomb" (V, i).

However, it may be that *bloody* was originally a thoroughly respectable word, to which no breath of tainted odor could possibly be attached and that it remained so well into the eighteenth century.

During the Restoration *bloody* became popular in its present form. The relish of the word had "caught on" and was received with a sort of éclat. For a time it enjoyed a certain degree of esteem and even patronage, being adopted by men of civility and refinement as an article of adornment. Playwrights put it on the stage.

John Dryden was the first playwright to do this; moreover, he put *bloody* into his very first play, *The Wild Gallants*, presented before the king at the Theatre Royal on February 5, 1663. The gallants were not, in fact, very wild, and the play was rather a bore, but in it occurs the following line, spoken by Bibber the tailor: "Well, in short, I was drunk, damnably drunk with Ale: great Hogen Mogen bloody Ale. I was porterly drunk; and that I hate of all things in Nature" (I, i).

Thirteen years elapsed before the word made another appearance in a play.

Sir George Etherege, in his comedy *The Man of Mode*, played for the first time in 1676 and received by society with unbounded approval, makes one of his characters say, referring to the importunities of a tipsy vagrant, "Give him half-a-crown!" To which the other replies, "Not without he will promise to be bloody drunk!" In George Farquhar's first play, *Love and a Bottle*, performed in mid-December 1698 at the Theatre Royal, Mockmode, in an aside, remarks, "I knew he was some damn'd bloody dog." The *bloody* here is clearly no more than an ordinary intensive. In the same author's *The Recruiting Officer*, played at the Theatre Royal on April 8, 1706, Captain Plume says to the disguised Silvia, "Thou art a bloody impudent fellow" (I, i), in a context in which it is evident that the word is no more intended to be offensive than "very." In this same sense the word is, in the eighteenth century, used by Swift and Richardson. Thus, Swift, writing to Stella on May 28, 1714, informs her that "it was bloody hot walking to-day." In 1727 he describes himself as "bloody sick," and later, "It grows bloody cold." All these *bloody*s in letters to a gentlewoman. In 1742 the proper Samuel Richardson says of a character in *Pamela*, "He is bloody passionate."

It may be seen, then, that up to the middle of the eighteenth century *bloody* was a perfectly respectable word that performed the function of an intensive no stronger than "awfully," "very," "fearfully," "exceedingly," "terribly."

7. *Bliudi.* Walter Duranty thought that the Russian word *bliudi* (dirty, obscene, improper) may have been picked up by the British forces during the Crimean War (1854–1856) and that the use of the word in the sense of *bliudi* brought *bloody* into disrepute.[8] There are several strong objections to this theory. In the first place, there is no evidence whatever that the Russian word was ever adopted by any English soldier; and second, contrary to H. L. Mencken's statement that this intensive aroused no indignation among English prudes until long after the middle of the nineteenth century,[9] the word was in fact regarded as offensive by many before that.

8. *Blood* as physiological blood in general. This theory is best given in the words of its able proponent Eric Partridge.

In "a man cruelly eloquent and bluddily learned," *cruelly* may retain something of the sense "severely," "distressingly," but this adverb early became an intensive meaning little more than "very" as in "cruelly cold"; likewise *bluddily*, as it is there spelt, may preserve some connotation of "vividly," "spiritedly," "heatedly" or "enthusiastically." But, all in all, both words connote little more than "exceedingly." It is, however, notice-able that the root-idea of blood as something vivid or distressing or both still colours the use of the adjective, which is, as it has always been, stronger and less "polite" than the adverb: but then adverbs in general lose their original signification more rapidly than adjectives in general do theirs. There is no doubt that *bloody* has been chosen as an expletive "for its grisly and repellant sound and sense" and that its frequent asso-ciation with battle, murder, wounds, outrage, insult and kindred facts has strengthened its appeal to those who like a violent word: at first, these were the rougher members of the lower classes. Its use is similar to that of terrible, devilish, damned, beastly, filthy, and their adverbs.[10]

In the annals of swearing I have been able to find one case that gives direct support to Partridge's theory: when Othello utters the triple oath "O blood, blood, blood!" (*Othello* [1611], III, iii).

Clearly Partridge's theory of the cause of the popularity of *bloody* is a most probable one, and it will be seen that it fits our discussion of the origin of the word most satisfactorily, for it is in the sense referred to by Partridge that *blütig* was and still is used in the Germanic languages, as well as in medieval and modern French. Thus, in a fourteenth-century report of a marital dispute, we read that "elle l'appela sanglant sourd et lui l'appela sanglante ordure" ("she called him a bloody clod and he called her a bloody stinker").[11] Earlier than that, in 1270, there is a record of the "vigier" of Béziers addressing the recalcitrant taxpayers in terms which the chronicler renders in Latin as follows: "*O rusticis sanguinolenti, vos dabitis, velitis vel non.*" In the eighteenth century Voltaire wrote: "La Princesse Henriette joua un tour bien sanglant affront [a bloody trick] à Corneille . . ."[12] In modern French *un sanglant affront* (a bloody affront), *un sanglant outrage* (a bloody outrage), and *la sanglante raillerie blesse et ne corrige pas* (a bloody joke hurts and doesn't improve things) are examples of the use of the French equivalent of *bloody* in a perfectly legitimate sense. Indeed, the French word enjoys an even wider sphere of application than our own adjective, never for a moment having fallen upon such evil days as the latter. Thus, it is seen that the word in all other languages but English serves the function of a perfectly respectable intensive. Partridge has pointed out that the Latin adjective *cruentus* and, still more significantly, the adverb *cruente* served the same function; that is, as an intensive meaning nothing more than "severely."

Blütig, bloedige, and *sanglante* because of their strong emotional association with blood and injury are almost predestined for service as intensives, and it is in view of this prepotent quality of the word that we need seek no further for an explanation of its popularity as an intensive.

We have now, I believe, seen that there is nothing either in the origin or in the inherent properties of the word *bloody* that accounts for the degraded and debased position into which it fell during the nineteenth century. The word has a good and estimable ancestry and until the middle of the eighteenth century was a perfectly blameless and uncorrupted expression that an Englishman could use without the least impropriety. In 1933 Partridge noted: "It is in some ways a pity that *bloody* has been thus debased, despite the vigour of its expletive use, for the debasement has been so general that, in serious contexts, we are now, in order to avoid a titter, forced to use severe, cruel or sanguinary instead of an excellent word."[13]

Partridge was unable to foresee that it would not be long before the word would be fully rehabilitated and restored to service.

Now that we have traced the origin and indicated something of the rise to popularity of *bloody*, let us endeavor to trace and inquire into the causes, the downfall, and the prolonged disrepute of this most "excellent word."

❨ *The Fall, but Not the Eclipse, of "Bloody"*

Up to the middle of the eighteenth century, as we have seen, *bloody* was in perfectly good standing. In fourteenth-century England we find it employed by William Langland in *Piers Plowman*, when he says, "They are my blody brethren" (VI, 210). Here the term is used as a reference to kinship by blood. We have seen how innocently it was employed in the sixteenth and seventeenth centuries in the examples cited from Shakespeare, Marston, and Etherege; and in the eighteenth century in the examples cited from Swift and Richardson. When, then, did the fall from grace of *bloody* occur? *The Oxford English Dictionary* tells us that the word was in good standing till about 1750, having become popular during the Restoration, but that the low English usage of the word as "an epithet expressing detestation," and not merely as an intensive, may be dated from about 1840.

I am for various reasons inclined to think that this puts the date of the use of *bloody* as a swearword rather later than it should. Unfortunately among the classes in which such words luxuriate earliest and most profusely, chroniclers are rarely found. They propagate their ballads but rarely write them down, and hardly ever do they date them. Hence, the first printed reference to the use of a word is likely to postdate its actual currency by a good many years. Furthermore, it does not seem likely that the acceptance of *bloody* could have become so widespread in a generation, as Sharman stated. Some forty-four years after the time when the *Oxford English Dictionary* presumes its first low usage to have commenced, Sharman, in the 1880s, wrote: "It is so widespread in its influence, and so powerful in its dominion, that it has been rung out and has reverberated probably more than any other in the great 'fisc and exchequer' of abuse."[14] By 1884 the word was already the "great standby" of the lower classes. While it is conceivable that *bloody* grew to its present supremacy in a period of no greater duration than forty years, it seems to me improbable that it in fact did so. However, forty years is about the lifetime of a human generation, and it is quite possible that the *O.E.D.* is near enough to the truth, but I should myself be inclined, on not altogether purely a priori grounds, to date the commencement of the usage of *bloody* as a swearword at the very beginning of the nineteenth century. For this certain facts may be adduced. Early in the nineteenth century the common appellation by which Adm. James Gambier (1756–1833) was known to the sailors of the British navy was "old bloody Politeful." Here the reference is very definitely to the well-known swearing habits of the admiral. Thus, as early as the first and second decades of the nineteenth century *bloody* was already well-established among sailors as a swearword. Sharman also tells the story of "a once famous (or infamous) *bon mot* that passed current in a fashionable club where a certain learned and witty serjeant was wont to repair for his nightly rubber. One evening, after meeting with a stranger at the card-table who held a remarkable number of trumps, he had impatiently inquired who had been his antagonist. On being told that the player was Sir So-and-So, Bart, the serjeant is reported to have at once rejoined that 'he might have known the fellow to have been a baronet by his bloody hand!' "[15]

Now the point of this story as evidence for the greater age of *bloody* as a swearword is that Sharman refers to it as "a once famous (or infamous) *bon mot*." In such a context it would seem most probable that the words "once famous" refer to a story that enjoyed a certain currency about a generation before—which would put us very near the year 1840. And if such a word could have been used in a London club at such a date then it is certain that it was in wide use long before that time.

We conclude then, that the use of *bloody* as a swearword most likely dates from the beginning of the nineteenth century, and probably earlier. But when did it embark on the career that led to this enlargement of its domain? How did it come to fall into so deep a disrepute?

Partridge suggests that the beginning of the decline may be traced to a line in the play *The Englishman in Paris*, by Samuel Foote (1720–1777), produced in London on March 24, 1753. Here is the exchange in which the line occurs:

MR. BUCK: . . . I wanted to talk about Miss Lacinda.
MRS. SUBTLE: What of her?
MR. BUCK: She's a bloody fine girl; and I should be glad to——
                                                                II, i

This, according to Partridge, marks the transition of *bloody* from respectability to indecency. But it is difficult to see why. The word is used in no salacious or indecent context, but merely as an adverbial makeweight exactly equivalent in meaning to "exceedingly" or "very." Partridge seems to have missed the bus, for it is in this very play that Mr. Buck actually does use the word in its modern vulgar sense.

The periwig-maker arrives to do up Mr. Buck's wig in the Parisian style.

MR. BUCK: Well, what must I do?
BARBER [*Places him in a chair*]: To the right, sir:—now to the left;—
                 now your full;—and now, sir, I'll do your business.
MR. SUBTLE: Look at yourself a little; see what a revolution this has
                 occasioned in your whole figure.

MR. BUCK: Yes! a bloody pretty figure indeed! But 'tis a figure I am
damnably ashamed of: I would not be seen by Jack Wild-
fire or Dick Riot for fifty pounds, in this trim, for all that.
I, i

It is from about this time that *bloody* began to grow in popularity with the "masses," that a perfectly respectable word began
to do yeoman service among the "vulgar." And it is because of
its popularity among the "vulgar" that it principally began to fall
into disrepute among the gentler classes. To the strength of the
ban on the score of vulgarity was added the addled notion that
the expression bore the savor of irreligion, of profanity. It was
generally, and erroneously, assumed to represent a juggled form
of the old oath by the *blood and wounds* of the Savior. By many,
as we have seen, it was believed to be a contraction of *By'r Lady*.
It thus came to be considered as both a vulgar and a blasphemous
expression, a more than sufficient reason for completely banish-
ing the word from the vocabulary of all worthy people.

This, briefly is the story of the decline and fall, though not
of the eclipse, of *bloody*. It was a reaction of class consciousness.
The outrageous Lord Byron, true to the characters of his dramatis
personae, in 1824, in the eleventh canto of *Don Juan*, makes the
footpad exclaim, "Oh Jack! I'm floor'd by that 'ere bloody Frenchman!" That, however, represents one of the rare examples of the
word in print in the period. We next find it in Dana's *Two Years
Before the Mast* (1840), in which a character remarks, "You'll
find me a bloody rascal."[16] But this *bloody*, like Byron's, remained
for many years one of the few specimens of its kind both in American and in English literature. It had no imitators, except in one
purely accidental case when in August, 1869, the government of
Paraguay instructed its Resident at London that the presence
of Francisco López on Paraguayan soil was "a bloody sarcasm to
civilization." Obviously the official who penned this document
possessed an unusually broad if not altogether accurate knowledge of the English language.

The factor chiefly responsible for the disrepute into which *bloody*
fell is the fact that the word had come to be associated with the
lower classes, the poor and the sordid, the illiterate and the
uncultivated. In a class-conscious society in which the social barriers are maintained not only by the possession of money and
titles, but by distinctive cultural norms of behavior of every kind,
the use of certain grammatical forms of speech and accent identify

the class to which a man belongs, as do the words he uses. *Bloody* was preeminently a lower class word. A "horrid word," as the *Oxford English Dictionary* says, "on a par with obscene or profane language, and usually printed in the newspapers (in police reports, etc.) 'b——y.'" Hence, all those who were in any way attempting to escape from the lower classes, and all those who were without its ranks, would shut themselves off from any possible contamination or association with the expression. This, added to the fact that it was considered indecent and irreligious, kept the word in the nineteenth century out of the vocabulary of all the respectable classes. And it is this combination of factors that to some extent still keeps it outside the portals of the respectable.

Writing early in the nineteenth century, Charles Lamb, in his "Christ's Hospital Five-and-thirty Years Ago,"goes so far as to make a "town-damsel" utter the first two letters of the word, but no more. Speaking of one of the masters of Christ's Hospital, he writes, "in the days of the maturer waggery, thou didst disarm the wrath of infuriated town-damsel, who, incensed by provoking pinch, turning tigress-like round, suddenly converted by thy angel-look, exchanged the half-formed terrible 'bl——,' for a gentler greeting—'bless thy handsome face!'"

It is evident, then, that already in the first quarter of the nineteenth century *bloody* could be referred to by the gentle Elia as a "terrible" word, characteristically the first oath of a lady of low morals and high complexion.

But the nineteenth century must not go down in this chapter as having been altogether without any defenders of *bloody*. There were probably many, but most of these paid it no more respect than an unwritten lip service. Curiously enough, it was a woman, a great poet, who came to its defense. Elizabeth Barrett Browning, in a letter to R. H. Horne, insists on embracing and cherishing this ill-starred word as a long lost acquaintance. In the letter, which begins, "Oh—you are a gnasher of teeth in criticism, I see!" she defends her rhyming schemes, and after ragging him a good deal, she concludes: "You are a bloody critic, nevertheless."[17]

What "Orion" Horne thought of this has not, so far as I have been able to discover, been recorded. But this was a brave word for a gentle lady to write in a letter addressed to a gentleman in the doldrums of the reign of Queen Victoria.

In America *bloody* seems never to have possessed the connotation given it by Englishmen. H. L. Mencken has recorded that *bloody* "is entirely without improper significance in America."[18] This is not altogether true, although it may have been so in 1919, when Mencken made the statement. The fact is that the word never appears to have enjoyed any degree of popularity in America and that as an intensive in the speaker's vocabulary it was simply nonexistent. This difference in the attitude of Americans and Englishmen toward the word is well brought out by J. Brander Matthews at the turn of the century. He wrote:

Every American traveler in England must have remarked with surprise the British use of the Saxon synonym of *sanguinary* as an intensive, the chief British rivals of *bloody* in this respect being *blooming* and *blasted*. All these are held to be shocking to polite ears, and it was with bated breath that the editor of a London newspaper wrote about the prospects of "a b——y war"; while, as another London editor declared recently, it is now impossible for a cockney to read with proper sympathy Jeffrey's appeal to Carlyle, after a visit to Craigenputtock, to bring his "blooming Eve out of her blasted paradise."[19]

In America the word has always been regarded as peculiarly English, and has never been naturalized upon American soil. American attitudes toward the word before World War I remained unchanged after the war. And the same was true after World War II. More Americans became aware of the existence of *bloody* as a swearword frequently used by the English, but somehow a word that did not easily fit into the American vocabulary.

In the late 1930s I asked a number of Americans from representative classes what they thought of the word *bloody*. Two answers are typical of most I received: The headmaster of a well-known private school stated that he had never heard the word used as a swearword or in the adjectival or adverbial senses in which the English used it. To him it was "a good earthy word and quite proper." His wife, of good New York State stock like her husband, was quite unaware of the fact that even so much as a suspicion of bad odor attached to the word either in America or in England.

Several New Yorkers stated that they were aware of the fact that *bloody* was a swearword of English origin, but they had never heard it used by Americans. Similar answers were obtained from a good sampling of Bostonians.

The answers to the same question in the sixties were not significantly different.

Bloody has simply never "taken" in America. Why?

Perhaps because Americans have no roots in the emotional background of the word and its place in the English ethos, they simply find it too feeble for their purposes. Semper, writing in 1929, remarked, "The American is frankly puzzled by the attitude of the refined Englishman to this word, and inquiry generally elicits the information that the word is frightfully vulgar, not because of any hidden meaning attached to it, but because it is used by frightfully vulgar people."[20]

Recognizing the innocent Adam's inappreciation of certain English words, in keeping with Bernard Shaw's observation that England and America are two countries separated by the same language, the United States War Department in 1942 issued a booklet to American soldiers destined for duty in England, offering the following advice: "The British have phrases which may sound funny to you. You can make just as many boners in their eyes. It isn't a good idea, for instance, to say 'bloody' in mixed company in Britain—it is one of their worst swear words."

The War Department need not have feared. *Bloody* has simply never caught on among Americans. Its freighted use has never formed part of the language, and it is as foreign to the American ethos as it is indigenous to the English. For Americans *bloody* has no *mana* whatever and is therefore less than feeble for the purposes that a good intensive should serve. As an intensive *bloody* is utterly without oomph for Americans, and in a language in which there are so many more efficient words available, *bloody* has no appeal whatever. When Dana made one of his characters use the word *bloody*, he was depending upon his knowledge of its use among English sailors—to Americans of the early nineteenth century a very esoteric form of knowledge.

As we have already seen, by the second half of the nineteenth century *bloody* was thoroughly established in the English swearer's vocabulary as his most serviceable arm; but it was still, for the most part, an unprintable word.

In 1882 Walter Besant in his novel *All Sorts and Conditions of Men* was forced to leave the printed word to the imagination. Lord Jocelyn, exploring the East End of London, questions a passing workman as to the object of a new building. "The man replied that he did not know the object of the building, and, to make it quite manifest that he really did not know, he put an adjective before the word 'object,' and another, that is, the same, before the word 'building.'"

Ernest Weekley tells of a most economically illuminating use of the adjective, which he overheard outside Hampstead Heath station in 1890. The driver of a four-wheeler, large and beery, was exhorting a taciturn and unconvinced opposite number at the reins of his hansom: "An' where d'yer s'pose they got their bloody money from? Why, robbed it aht o' the bloody people." "I submit," remarks Weekley, "that the Marxian theory of wealth has never been more ably or succinctly summarized. It is put, so to speak, in a nutshell."

It was not until 1892, seventy-two years after Byron had done so, that an English poet and novelist had the courage to print the word, albeit in euphemistic form, in the exact context in which it belonged. Rudyard Kipling dared, in *Barrack-Room Ballads*, to make the soldier in India talk as British soldiers everywhere talked:

> Shillin a day
> Bloomin' good pay—
> Lucky to touch it shillin a day.

It need hardly be said that Kipling's "language" in *Barrack-Room Ballads* was heartily condemned in many quarters of English society, and until very recently the book was excluded from many public, private, and school libraries. Kipling's remark that the English private's vocabulary consisted of "three hundred words and the adjective," was a linguistically accurate statement of the facts. Nonetheless, Kipling could not bring himself to write the "adjective" uneuphemized.

The mild sensation created by a few words in a printed book is nothing compared to what happened when the same words, even in a dissimulated form, were spoken upon the stage or even hinted at in the title of a play. Nothing illustrates the uproar caused better than the reception given to Gilbert and Sullivan's new opera *Ruddygore*, which opened at the Savoy Theatre on January 22, 1887. The title created something of a sensation among a certain faction of the British public. The press fastened upon the fact that *ruddy* was really a synonym or euphemism for *bloody*, and *that* would certainly not do. The weekly London *Graphic*, in its issue of January 29, 1887, commenting upon the "not very happily selected title," said: "The sterner and less mealy-mouthed sex, safe in the club smoking-room, might pass such a name with a smile. But it is different in the case of ladies, to whom Savoy operas largely appeal, and on whose lips such a title would scarcely sound pretty."

It is recorded that when a forward young lady reproached Gilbert for his choice of a title, saying that it was a quite obvious disguise for an objectionable word, he replied, "My dear young lady, you are quite wrong. For example, when I say 'I like your ruddy cheek,' I do not refer to your bloody cheek!"

The Savoy management did everything in its power to appease the public wrath, going so far as to substitute *i* for *y* in the title, but the shocked grumblings continued.

In one of the several answers he gave to correspondents Gilbert wrote: "I do not know what there is to complain of. *Bloodigore* would have been offensive, but there can be no offense about *Ruddygore*. *Ruddi* is perfectly harmless; if, for example, I were to talk of your *ruddy* cheek you could not be angry with me, but if I were to speak, as well I might, about your—well—." But Mrs. Grundy was not to be so easily appeased. Not only were the first two syllables of the title found to be offensive, but so was the last. In response to this new development Gilbert wrote on January 26, 1887:

To object to a title in which the syllable "gore" occurs is a new develop-ment of critical fastidiousness. The houses of Kensington Gore have com-manded high rents for many years past. Gore House, once the residence of the Countess Blessington, became a restaurant under Voger's manage-ment, & people eat with an appetite in spite of its horrible name. It is true that the novels of Mrs. Gore are not as widely read as they used to be, & this may, perhaps, be due to the recent discovery that her name is not to be mentioned without a shudder.[21]

Let it be recorded, however, that Gilbert was sufficiently moved by the outcry against the title of the new operetta to be willing to yield to the clamor and change it. He wrote to a friend: "When the Press shuddered with horror, as it did, at the title, I endeav-oured to induce my collaborator to consent to the title being changed to 'Kensington Gore, or Robin and Richard were Two Pretty Men.' But Sullivan wouldn't consent."[22] This would seem to throw something of a new and favorable light upon the char-acter of Sullivan.

It is a pity that there were no good Spenserians courageous enough to come to the defense of *ruddy*, for the word had been in perfectly good literary standing since the year 1590, when

Edmund Spenser, in *The Faerie Queene*, caused Sir Guyon to give the name *Ruddymane* to the babe rescued from Amavia, who had stabbed herself in grief at the death of her husband. Ruddymane was so called because

> . . . in her streaming blood he did embay
> His little hands.
>
> II, i, 3

Ruddy was a perfectly good euphemism for *bloody*, but the status of the latter had come to such a pass in Victorian England that anything admitting of the slightest resemblance to the abhorred word could not be allowed. But *Ruddygore* had done its work, and it now remained only to put the word upon the stage in all its ruddy nudity. This it was left for George Bernard Shaw to do. In his delightful comedy *Pygmalion*, produced in London at His Majesty's Theatre on April 11, 1914, Shaw's cockney heroine, Liza Doolittle, played by Mrs. Patrick Campbell, on being asked by Freddy whether she will be walking across the park, exclaims, "Walk! Not bloody likely. I am going in a taxi" (III). The tremor that this word sent through the audience was felt throughout the whole of the English-speaking world. St. John Ervine, a contemporary, gave a vivid account of the performance:

The theatre world was full of gossip about the shocking word Mrs. Patrick Campbell would have to utter; and a vast amount of windy argument was heard on the subject. Some people, ignorant of the fact that *bloody* had been heard in other plays, especially in one by Lennox Robinson, without any member of the audience appearing to be in the least perturbed by it, assured all who would listen to them that the Lord Chamberlain would ban it or that Beerbohm Tree would forbid Mrs. Patrick Campbell [to whom she was under contract, and hence the miscasting of Tree in the role of Henry Higgins] to say it. It was also foretold that if the word were used, there would be a frightful scene in the theatre, the performance might be stopped, and the play would probably be withdrawn.

None of these prophecies was fulfilled; and the astonishing fact is that although every member of the audience at the first performance appeared to know that Mrs. Campbell would say "Not bloody likely," the whole audience behaved as if it had not had the slightest idea that such a phrase would be uttered. As the words came off Mrs. Campbell's lips, there was a great gasp, followed in a few minutes by an extraordinary roar of laughter, a brief silence, and then by what is technically known as the double laugh: a renewal of the laughter even stronger than the first. G. B. S. had taken the colour and vigour out of the word *bloody* by making it a term no more awful than *dash* or *bother*. To-day genteel girls use it without turning a hair or suffering any rebuke.[23]

Reporting on the London production of *Pygmalion*, the dramatic critic of *The New York Times* wrote on April 14, 1914 that much of the interest in the first English performance of the play lay in "the heroine's utterance of this banned word. It was waited for with trembling, heard shudderingly, and presumably when the shock subsided, interest dwindled."

Contrary to St. John Ervine and E. M. Forster, *Pygmalion* did no more to devitalize *bloody* and reestablish it in polite society than did the jocular euphemisms that at the time enjoyed a brief currency—*Not Bernard Shaw likely!* and *Not Pygmalion likely!* But the impact had been so great that for some years afterward the word was referred to as "the Shavian adjective."

In 1912 John Masefield published his great religious poem *The Everlasting Mercy*, in which one of the poet's drunken yokels declares, "I'll bloody him a bloody fix, I'll bloody burn his bloody ricks." This scarcely caused a raised eyebrow, which perhaps only goes to show that what cannot be said can often be sung.

In 1913 in *Fifty Caricatures*, parodying Wordsworth and referring to Masefield's propensity for such words, Max Beerbohm captioned one of his cartoons:

> A swear-word in a rustic slum
> A simple swear-word is to some,
> To Masefield something more.

And then came the Great War of 1914–1918, when *bloody* saw more service as a word-of-all-work than in all its previous history. To the British soldier everything was *bloody*. As W. V. Tilsey has said, "Snow was bloody, khaki was bloody, green envelopes were bloody."[24] Everything was bloody. Eric Partridge accurately says, "Bloody was their favourite adverb and adjective: all other 'swear words,' frequently as some were used, might be described as 'also-rans.' It even served as an intersyllabic or intervocative word, as in 'im-bloody-possible' or 'too bloody right.'"[25]

Partridge quotes a favorite British marching song of the Great War, sung to the melody of the hymn "Holy, Holy, Holy" that begins:

> Raining, raining, raining,
> Always bloodywell raining.
> Raining all the morning,
> And raining all the night,

and ends

> Marching, marching, marching,
> Always bloodywell marching;
> When the war is over
> We'll bloodywell march no more.[26]

This is probably a correct transcription of one of the versions of this song, but when the present writer was a cadet in the Officers Training Corps of an English university in 1922, the ending was sung as follows:

> Marching, marching, marching,
> Always bloodywell marching,
> When we are dead and gone
> We'll still go marching on.

The soldier at the front obviously preferred the prospect of a living marchless world to the cadet's prospect of a world of eternal ghostly marching, for there was that other marching song of the British soldier that begins:

> When the bloody war is over
> No more soldiering for me.

This was sung to the tune of *What a Friend We Have in Jesus*. And there were several others in which *bloody* figured prominently.

Edward Thompson, in his novel *These Men Thy Friends*, has a passage that conveys some idea of the manner in which *bloody* could be overworked during World War I.

Adams—a chubby boy, with incredibly insolent face and exasperatingly exaggerated "Oxford" tones . . . asked, "Lambert, you funny old thing, would you mind passing the bloody bread?"

Now Adams had already worked a reform that many padres would have attempted in vain—because they would not have known how to set about it. To him every creature in the universe was so monotonously bloody that he drained swearing of all its value. Men began to drop it, except when with overstrained courtesy they asked him, "Adams, would you be so good as to pass the bloody knife as well as the bloody bread, and the bloody jam and the bloody butter at the same time?" But he was impervious to sarcasm, and these things passed idly by him. He remained as he was; it was the rest of the mess who from sheer weariness of certain words fell back on the colourless English which is all that convention approves.[27]

If the British Tommy swore horribly in France, it was nothing compared to such feats by the Australian forces, who were inveterate and uncontrollable swearers and who have, if anything, improved with the years. Their swearing, however, was of a rather unimaginative and adjectivally limited variety, *bloody* being the great standby and employed with regular and monotonous frequency on every occasion. As long ago as 1899 this fact was satirized by the Australian wit W. T. Goodge in a poem entitled "———(The Great Australian Adjective)," which appeared in the *Sydney Bulletin*, following a prolonged correspondence on the word in its pages. During World War I the version then current was known simply as "The Australian Poem." This version is rather better than the original, and so it is given here:

The Australian Poem

A sunburnt bloody stockman stood,
And in a dismal, bloody mood
Apostrophized his bloody cuddy:
"This bloody moke's no bloody good,
He doesn't earn his bloody food.
Bloody! Bloody! Bloody!"

He leapt upon his bloody horse
And galloped off, of bloody course.
The road was wet and bloody muddy:
It led him to the bloody creek;
The bloody horse was bloody weak,
Bloody! Bloody! Bloody!

He said "This bloody steed must swim
The same for me as bloody him!"
The creek was deep and bloody floody
So ere they reached the bloody bank
The bloody steed beneath him sank—
The stockman's face a bloody study
Ejaculating Bloody! Bloody! Bloody![28]

The genesis of this poem is rather amusing. For several years, in the last decade of the nineteenth century, there had been much discussion of the great Australian adjective. In 1898 the University of Melbourne conferred the honorary degree of Doctor of Literature on Edward E. Morris, author of the rather unsatisfactory *Austral English: A Dictionary of Australian Words, Phrases and Usages* (London, 1898). The work was quite severely criticized in the Australian press, for the word *bloody*, the crowning glory of the Australian language, was prudishly entirely omitted from the dictionary. The students at Melbourne, outraged by its university's conduct, staged a burlesque of the degree-conferring ceremony, presenting a solemnly gowned candidate carrying under his arm a huge tome entitled "The Great Australian Adjective." It was in the following year that "The Australian Poem" made its appearance in the *Sydney Bulletin*.

During World War II Australian troops stationed in Newfoundland sang a song to the following refrain:

> No bloody sports; no bloody games;
> No bloody fun with bloody dames;
> Won't even tell their bloody names;
> Oh, bloody, bloody, bloody.

We shall return to the Australian's use of *bloody* later in this chapter. Meanwhile, let us continue our chronicle of the history of *bloody*.

The freedom with which the word was used during World War I and its open circulation among the fighting men for more than four years made the word familiar to every English adult as the favorite intensive of the soldier. A population for whom no sacrifice was too great to make for "the heroes at the front," could, in the spirit of the times, afford to be indulgent where mere words were concerned. And so *bloody* for the first time in its late history received a sort of quasi-sanction. People no longer pretended not to have heard it or overlooked it, but actually produced a smile of sympathy or tolerant acquiescence. Its common use generated a certain camaraderie. Those were the great days of *bloody*. Officers returning from the front, where they had *bloody*ed the Boche, the rain, the mud, the food, the men, the brass hats—everything —found it difficult to expurgate the word from their conversation when restored to the bosom of their families. The men of the lower ranks for the most part did not try. They had always used it, and what did it matter if they indulged in it a little more frequently than formerly?

The women who had come into a new freedom with the war and had signaled their acquisition of it by raising their skirts, cutting their hair, and taking to the smoking of cigarettes did not stop at an occasional oath. And, of course, their choice was *bloody*. To the women at home the oath was transmitted by the WAACs, the members of the Women's Army Auxiliary Corps, who had acquired it from the men of the regular army. In this way the word became a sort of token of good fellowship, of camaraderie, an icebreaker, a leveler of all classes, a warmer-upper. It was *the* great word of World War I—and if the grateful nation had had a proper sense of its indebtedness to those who had served it so valiantly and so well it would have bestowed a red ribbon upon the word that had served it far more faithfully and ably than most of the generals and admirals in the services.

From being frowned upon, the word now came to be looked upon almost with affection, sentimentally, as the password among all those who were hoping and striving toward the same end. Jokes such as the following were now being told with gusto and listened to with appreciation in Mayfair and Belgravia:

Bishop coming down from Salisbury in the same compartment with a Tommy, third-class. Language seemed a bit strong to bishop. Bishop remarks, "I see, my man, you believe in calling a spade a spade."
Says Tommy, "That's right, a bloody shovel."
Peals of "naughty" laughter. "How utterly utter!" "You're bloody right," adds the narrator, producing further freshets of laughter.

Thus it was that *bloody* found its way into "high society," into the open. In this manner it became possible to utter the word where formerly it had never been heard. It had penetrated to every class and was no longer the exclusive property of the lower classes.

In 1924, with the publication of R. H. Mottram's *The Spanish Farm*, the flood of war books began, the autobiographies and the novels: C. E. Montague's *Rough Justice* (1926), Edward Thompson's *These Men Thy Friends* (1927), Edmund Blunden's *Undertones of War* (1928), Richard Aldington's *Death of a Hero* (1929),

Robert Graves' *Goodbye to All That* (1929), Siegfried Sassoon's *The Memoirs of an Infantry Officer* (1930), and Frederic Manning's *Her Privates We* (1930).

In most of these books *bloody* occupied an honored place, for it did service side by side with honorable and heroic men and lightened the burden that they had to carry through every moment of each day. In the tragic novel *Rough Justice*, its author, C. E. Montague, whose *Disenchantment* is probably the best chronicle of the temporary soldier's estimate of war, obliquely attempts to defend the use of *bloody* by the British soldier, when he makes one of his characters declare that "All the little different emphasizing particles in Greek mean what an English workman means by bloody."[29]

The war books kept going the good work that the war itself had started, so that a sizable part of the older generation of England today, which was then in its late teens and twenties, is familiar with *bloody* as a perfectly unobjectionable and valuable intensive, which they occasionally delight to use. It continues, among the stuffy and very proper, to be a banned word, and as late as 1920, H. C. Wyld could still write of *bloody*, without naming it in his text or his indexes, as "a certain adjective, most offensive to polite ears. . . . In an age like ours, where good breeding as a rule, permits only exclamations of the mildest and most meaningless kind, to express temporary annoyance, disgust, surprise, or pleasure, the more full-blooded utterances of a former age are apt to strike one as excessive."[30] In the same year the Lord Chamberlain's office (the state censor of all written works published in England) disallowed the use of the words "Not B—— Likely" for the title of an English revue.[31] In 1930 The Very Reverend W. R. Inge, D.D., Dean of St. Paul's, could only permit himself to refer to the word as "the working man's favourite adjective," which he correctly described as "just a warning that a noun is coming."[32] Such reticence in a dean is commendable, but Dr. Inge, who was an outspoken realist and therefore was known as "the gloomy Dean," in his article, which was entitled "We Swear To-day —and Mean No Harm," was not quite so reticent when it came to Latin and foreign swearing.

Arnold Bennett, in a review of Leon Gordon's *White Cargo*, produced at The Playhouse (London) on October 11, 1924, exactly places the date when *bloody* emerged once more into a licensed respectability. Bennett tells us that "in the 3rd act, at perhaps the most tragic moment of the play, a character has to say to another, 'Poor bloody fool!' Roars of laughter. Why? The censor has only just begun to allow the word 'bloody' on the stage."

In this same period Frederick Lonsdale's popular comedy *Aren't We All?* was allowed a single *bloody* by the Lord Chamberlain in the final curtain scene. The insufferable parson Ernest Lynton is badly put out because his brother-in-law Lord Grenham has called him something nasty. Lord Grenham can't remember. You called me a bloody old fool, says the parson. Come, says the noble Lord, aren't we all? Whether or not the audience fully agreed, no one protested either the word or the sentiment.

But fifteen years later there was still a limit on the number of times one could use the loaded word on the stage. Sir Lawrence Jones tells in the third volume of his enchanting reminiscences, *Georgian Afternoon*, how upon receiving news that the Lord Chamberlain had made more than sixty cuts in the manuscript of his play, he made an appointment to see the censor at Windsor. "Apart from some perfectly loyal references to Queen Victoria, who, with God, is unmentionable upon the stage, and a third 'bloody' (the allowance is two), all the cuts were restored." This was late in 1939.

Ten years later the ban was still in force. Ted Willis, speaking in the House of Lords in 1966, said, "I think that in 1948 or 1949 one of my first plays went to his [the Lord Chamberlain's] office, and it came back with a long list of words which had to be omitted, including the word 'bloody,' which it was requested should be removed, I think, fourteen times. Subsequently, of course, in 1956–57, I went to see a play called *Billy Liar*, which had that same word in it 249 times. I do not quite know what this proves: either I was ten years ahead of my time or the Lord Chamberlain was ten years behind it."

On the afternoon of May 31, 1916, the German High Seas Fleet, for which the British had been lying in wait for two years, was finally encountered and engaged off the coast of Jutland. This major naval engagement of World War I was hailed at the time, by the British, as a great victory. It was hardly that. The German fleet, inferior in numbers and in guns, sank ten English vessels and lost eleven, but also inflicted heavy damage upon many other English vessels. The English lost some 6,100 men, while the Germans lost 2,550. Under cover of darkness the German High Seas Fleet made its way safely to home base, while the British admirals were left wondering what was going on. During the course of the engagement Admiral Beatty signaled to one of his captains, "There must be something wrong with our bloody ships, Chatfield." This, at least, exhibited a somewhat more realistic view of the situation than that of the commander of the Grand Fleet, Admiral Jellicoe, who apparently had no idea at all that anything was wrong. After the cessation of hostilities the noble services of the two admirals, surpassed only by those of the commanders in the field, were rewarded with Earldoms and other substantial perquisites. Admiral Scheer, the German commander, merely received some cheers. His account of the battle, generous and restrained, sank the reputation of the British navy for most students of naval warfare even more effectively than his guns and logistics. Twenty years after the event, when the debate about the battle was once more revived, English newspapers timidly represented Beatty's intensive with a dash.[33]

The reluctance of English book publishers to print the word *bloody* in their books as late as the mid-1920s is documented by the statement of Nevil Shute in an interview reported in *Time* on January 25, 1960, that all he could recall of his first novel, *Marazan*, published in 1926, "was a brief interchange with the publisher ('The House of Cassell does not print the word bloody')." Shute changed *bloody* to *ruddy*, and the book was printed.

Twenty years earlier James Joyce had the same difficulty with *Dubliners*, and in 1916 with *A Portrait of the Artist as a Young Man*. He could not find a printer willing to set the latter in England at all. It was that splendid American Ben Huebsch who published the book in New York, late in 1916. Mary Colum tells us that Grant Richards from 1906 to 1914 refused publication of *Dubliners* after signing a contract, but he finally published the book. "The printers had objected to the contents of *Dubliners* and refused to set it up; they objected to whole stories, to passages in others, and to the use of the word 'bloody.' It was a genteel age and printers were very refined. When the Egoist Press in London wanted to publish *Portrait of the Artist* different firms of printers went on the same sort of rampage." A succession of seven different printers, in fact, declined to set it.

Those who had been in the midst of things during the Great War by 1927 took *bloody* very much for granted. This can be seen clearly from the manner in which Robert Graves treats the word in his delightful little volume *Lars Porsena, or the Future of Swearing*, which appeared in January, 1927. A few words in passing and the quotation of "The Australian Poem" are all he devotes to it. It was not until 1933 that a serious scholarly essay smiled upon *bloody*. This was Eric Partridge's "The Word Bloody," published in his *Words, Words, Words*.

September, 1936, is a stellar month in the history of *bloody*, for in that month a fascist open-air speaker was fined by the Bath magistrates for using the word in a speech. Upon appealing the verdict, Mr. Justice Humphreys laid it down that the word was neither indecent nor obscene. In spite of this, shortly after the commencement of World War II William Dobbie, a Labour M.P., referring to the government's failure to pay soldiers' wives their allowances, said that this was "a bloody disgrace to the whole government." Pressure was brought to bear upon him to apologize, and the next day he did so.

May 6, 1941 was, however, the red-letter day in the history of *bloody*, for it was on that day that *The Times* (London) printed a poem with the word unasterisked, undashed, and in its full naked six letters. The occasion was properly celebrated by D. B. Wyndham Lewis in the *Tatler and Bystander* (May 21, 1941):

Clashing her wiry old ringlets in a kind of palsied glee at her own audacity, Auntie *Times* has printed a little poem containing the line "I really loathe the *bloody* Hun," and all Fleet Street stands aghast. . . . "Bloody" ("————," or "the Shavian adjective") is one of the hardest-worked words in current speech and in constant use by duchesses and dustmen alike, but to find Auntie *Times* spelling it in full is a shock.

It marked the beginning of the end, although not quite the end, for as late as May, 1962, Post Office officials refused permission to the Crime Club to print on the club's own envelopes an advertisement for a book called *Bloody Instructions*, even though this *Bloody* had no connection whatever with the intensive! The reason offered for the refusal was that "the words . . . may offend quite a number of people."

We have seen, then, how originating in the sixteenth century in the perfectly harmless and proper *blütig*, *bloody* became naturalized in England as an intensive. Used in the sense of "awfully" or "very" the word was in polite usage until the middle of the eighteenth century, when it began to fall into disrepute, owing to its newly acquired disrespectability. By the beginning of the

nineteenth century the word was current coin among the lower
classes only, being strictly banned by all other classes. The word
was considered to be indecent, irreligious, and vulgar. It was not
until the advent of World War I that the ubiquitous and continuous usage of the word by the fighting forces and those associated with them brought about a change in attitude toward
bloody. In England today the generation that grew to manhood
during the first decade of the postwar period is acquainted with
the word as a rather useful and even friendly intensive. Even
when it is "torn from its home and suddenly implanted in the
wrong social atmosphere," it no longer "chills the blood and raises
gooseflesh," as Wyld, in 1920, suggested it did.[34] But rather, as
Eric Partridge has stated, "it is frequently employed to warm
the conversation, and it has become one of the tricks of the best-
selling—and other—novelists."[35] Indeed it might be said that just
as it was at one time held that the word was the peculiar pride
and property of the lower classes, it is today one of the "indispen-
sables" of the "best-selling—and other—novelists." But this is for
the most part an artificial growth, a "trick," as Partridge says.
There is no virtue in it, and the practice is, on the whole, doing
the word a disservice. Good writers will not need to be told that
words are no substitutes for ideas and that the bad use of good
words tends to reduce the value of the latter. Let those whom
the plume fits remember Sir John Davies' description of the gull
("Of a Gull," 1590):

> A gull is he which wears good handsome cloathes,
> And stands in Presence stroaking up his haire,
> And fills up his imperfect speech with oaths,
> But speaks not one wise word throughout the yeare.

Good oaths will always be abused because man is an abusing
animal. But let us not dwell on that unhappy trait, but proceed
now to the presentation, in practical examples, of the uses to
which *bloody* has been put.

❲ *On the Uses of Bloody*

We have already seen that *bloody* is used as an adjective, an
adverb, and as an intersyllabic, such as in the example "im-bloody-
possible," or "of-bloody-course." The fact is that *bloody* may be

used to modify every verb, noun, adjective, and adverb in the English language. H. C. Wyld has stated that the word may be employed by the same speaker to mean absolutely nothing and also to mean a great deal. One may question the "absolutely nothing" part of Wyld's statement, for whatever may be true of other words *bloody* has seldom or never been used meaninglessly. The word has always added meaning to what it qualified. *Bloody* often serves the function of a particle. This particle-meaning function of *bloody* is well illustrated in the following story, which dates from the latter part of the nineteenth century. Two miners are contemplating an election poster. "What's all this mean," asks Bill, "'one man one vote'?" "Why," answers his companion, "one bloody man one bloody vote." To which Bill replies, "Then why the hell don't they bloody well say so?"

The chronic and inveterate use of *bloody* among some sections of the lower classes and the linguistically acrobatic feats that the word has been made to perform have actually bestowed upon it the sort of particle function illustrated in the above story. The story is usually told as a joke, but it happens to constitute a perfect example of the function the word serves among large sections of the lower classes. When used in this sense the word ceases to have any swearing value at all and becomes part and parcel of a significant grammatical process. Chronic adjectivitis—that is, the inveterate use of highly inflamed adjectives—generally goes together with this particle use of *bloody*. When employed in this particle sense the word is in adjectival adverbial form, but it is not, properly speaking, an adjective or an adverb since it serves neither to qualify nor to modify whatever may follow it. It is a particle—but not a meaningless particle that from force of habit persists in cropping out in every sentence in which the active adjective would normally occur when its user is swearing. This constitutes, in its way, an enrichment of the English language, although it must be confessed that it is not a wholly necessary one. The truth is that those given to adjectivitis generally exhibit the condition from a poverty of linguistic resources, but not necessarily from a lack of imagination. "The Great Australian Poem" was designed to exemplify this.

In no part of what was once the British Empire has *bloody* established itself more fully and become a more indispensable part of the national vocabulary than in the Commonwealth of Australia. Alexander Marjoribanks, writing in 1847, in his book *Travels in New*

South Wales, tells us that the favorite oath in that settlement was *bloody*. "One may tell you that he married a bloody young wife, another, a bloody old one; and a bushranger will call out, 'Stop, or I'll blow your bloody brains out.'" Marjoribanks records that he heard a bullock driver use *bloody* twenty-seven times in a quarter of an hour. He calculated that at this rate, allowing eight hours a day for sleep and six for silence, and assuming that the bullock driver had become an established swearer at twenty and died at seventy, in the course of those fifty years he would have uttered "this disgusting word no less than 18,200,000 times."[36] It is not surprising the atmosphere in Australia is said to possess a certain crispy quality.

Sidney J. Baker, in his admirable book *The Australian Language*, has some interesting remarks on the Australian's profanity in general and upon *bloody* in particular. He writes: "It has been part of the national destiny of Australia that profanity should have provided an accompaniment, or at least an undertone, to our social growth. It is not only that our original settlers were convicts and the sweepings of English backstreets well-versed in vulgar speech, but that the country itself was one to stir exasperation and helpless fury in even the most patient soul."[37] The country, in short, was so difficult that it acted as a whetstone upon which the mostly unwilling settlers, transported from their homeland, could sharpen their profane skills. *Bloody*, of course, arrived with the earliest settlers from England and was made to do such frequent labor as an adjective that by the end of the nineteenth century it came to be known as "the great Australian adjective." As an editorial in the *Sydney Bulletin*, August 18, 1894, put it "The 'Bulletin' calls it the *Australian adjective* simply because it is more used and used more exclusively by Australians than by any other allegedly civilised nation."

Dr. Thomas Wood, who spent the first three years of the 1930s traveling in Australia provides an example of the use of *bloody* that shows what, in skilled hands, can be done with the word. He writes:

It seems impossible that strong men, to whom strong language is as necessary as strong meat, could be hard-up for swear words. Yet they are, in Australia. Swearing is not an act as it is in Spain, it is a habit. The serious student finds little that is new to him. The material used for censure, comparison, or emphasis consists chiefly of standbys he has heard before. In short, most situations are met by the Big Five. These, however, from much use, have gained a suppleness which recalls the imaginative subtlety of the Latins. I can give no better example than this, founded on the most popular and most printable of the Five.

"It's bloody high, Bill," said an admirer from the back-blocks, gazing up at the tower of Brisbane's City Hall.

"Aw," said Bill, "not so bloody."

"That, I think," remarks Dr. Wood, "shows an economy of means which approaches Art."[38]

The first syllable of *bloody*, reduced to a particle, is combined with particles from other words to form new ones. Thus, *bloody* and *bugger* are combined to form *bludger*—a term originally applied to a prostitute's pimp. *Bludger* is regarded as an indecent word, whereas *bloody* and *bugger* are not and are as freely used by women as by men. As a participle *bludging* is often employed adjectivally. A recent development is a synonym for *bloody*. This is *dirty big*. In Xavier Herbert's magnificent novel of the Northern Territory, *Capricornia* (1938), *blunny* and *burry* are not seldom employed as synonyms for *bloody*.

Blanky is yet another Australian synonym for *bloody*.

Bludger has become somewhat disrespectable, and by way of softening it a compromise between *bludger* and *parasite* has been evolved, namely, *bludgasite*. This term was first used in the Australian army journal *Salt* in March, 1943.

In 1939 *bloody* was still regarded as a swearword, as is evidenced by the fact that in January, 1939, in Newtown Court, Sydney, a man was charged with having used indecent language, having used the word *bloody*. The magistrate held that the word might be sometimes offensive, but not indecent. The charge was therefore altered to one of offensive language and a fine of £1 was imposed. But by June, 1942, the word had altogether been freed of any taint of crimson and admitted to the open forum of common parlance. On June 22, 1942, Mr. Justice Halse Rogers held, in the Sydney Divorce Court, that "the word *bloody* is so common in modern parlance that it is not regarded as swearing."

The infixes of *bloody* are well developed in Australia, as for example, in such expressive terms as *transconti-bloody-nental, abso-bloody-lutely, inde-bloody-pendent, imma-bloody-material, umber-bloody-ella, hippo-bloody-crite, hoo-bloody-rah*. Australians are clearly by no means as uninventive swearers as they have been alleged to be.

The children who live out in the bush or back-blocks in Australia early learn to become proficient swearers. Francis Ratcliffe, who traveled as a naturalist in Australia in 1936–1937, recounts that when he was at Cairns in Queensland two young boys were told to show him the fox camps in which he was interested. Of the swearing of these two lads Ratcliffe remarks:

I doubt, however, whether in their worst moments Mark Twain's heroes Huck Finn and Tom Sawyer would have used the words with which these two young rips garnished their every sentence. The barefooted one was the worse. Once when a particularly purple expression had befouled his lips, the other seemed to think that some apology was due to an hotel guest, for he turned to me and said with great seriousness, "He swears bloody terrible, that bastard."[39]

Evidently this was nothing more than plain English to these young gents. A good deal of the "plain English" that the aborigines acquire is of this variety. When Sir Hubert Wilkins gave Johnny, his aboriginal helper, a liberal supply of food the latter exclaimed, "By cripes! you plenty too much good for me. Me thinket me come back live longa you. No mind em wife or clothes."[40]

Jack McLaren tells how when a Gulf of Carpentaria aboriginal was apprised of an honor that had been conferred upon him, he exclaimed, "Well—I bloody!"

In the matter of intersyllabic *bloodys*, the English *im-bloody-possible, abso-bloody-lutely* and its *abso-bloomin-lutely* (which is to be found in that marvelous song "Wouldn't It Be Loverly" in *My Fair Lady*), as well as other forms, have long been established in England. A charming intersyllabic occurs in John Wain's novel *Living in the Present*, when Mr. Charley, indicating the door to the object of his wrath, remarks, "Outside mister . . . Out bloody *side*."

In Alan Sillitoe's novel *Saturday Night and Sunday Morning*, it is a female who squeals, "Christ All-bleedin'-mighty!"

For sheer virtuosity it would be difficult to beat the following performance, recorded by a New York reporter in England, when a stout Englishman recognizes an old American friend: "Blimey! May I bloodywell be struck dumb, blind and bloodywell dead if it isn't me bloody Yank ally. At last you've come back to the only friends you absobleedinglutely have got bloodywell left."[41]

In an unpublished letter dated January 22, 1935, we find Ezra Pound writing to C. K. Ogden, editor of the Psyche Miniature Series and of the International Library of Psychology, Philosophy and Scientific Method, "Only *set* of books issued in Eng that shows ANY interest in thought whatsobloodyever."

A magnificent example of the interpolative use of *bloody* is produced by Col. Rodney Savage in John Master's novel *Bhowani Junction.* "And now," he says, "when does the next bloody train on the Delhi bloody Deccan bloody Rail-bloody-way bloody well leave for Bho-bloody-wani?"[42]

This may be overdoing it a bit, but it does indicate the possibilities to which the intersyllabic uses of *bloody* can be put by an imaginative user.

A quite unexpected user of *bloody* was Sigmund Freud. Dr. Joseph Wortis tells of a conversation with Sigmund Freud during an analytic session. Wortis had remarked that he expected to study later and perhaps learn more when he did his own analyzing. "But you have no right to analyze," said Freud emphatically. "You know nothing about it—you are just a *bloody beginner*" (italics in original).[43]

It is known that Freud had an excellent command of English, but this expertise in demotic English is quite surprising. It is not reported that Freud was in his own native German tongue given to swearing.

For use of the word as a superlative Hugh Walpole must be credited with a rare usage of *bloody.* In a letter to Henry James, written from Moscow on November 12, 1914, Walpole writes: "Well, I had the bloodiest six weeks of my whole life first."[44]

Years later Dylan Thomas, in a letter written March 18, 1953, makes an even more original use of the superlative; after ungratefully having referred to "Margaret bloody Taylor," he again petulantly refers to her as "Margaret bloodiest Taylor."

Poets have always been the most sensitive to the uses of the *mot juste.* It is, therefore, gratifying to find Tennyson, as related by E. F. Benson in *As We Are,* correcting a friend who had remarked of something or other that it was "awfully fine." "Don't say 'awfully,'" replied the poet, "say 'bloody.'" As Tennyson suggested, in such a context "awfully" is effete compared to the full-bodied *bloody.*

J. W. Robertson Scott gives us a good example of the effective use of the word. A literary group in a Fleet Street tavern was accosted by a gentleman who claimed to be descended from Addison. This pretension elicited from one of the company (James Hannay of the *Pall Mall*) the comment, "Sir, since the only descendant of Addison was a daughter, who died before the age of puberty in a lunatic asylum, my respect for facts compels me to address you as a bloody liar."[45]

It is an excellent story, and while it is true that Addison is not known to have left any descendants other than his daughter, the truth is that she lived to a relatively advanced age. Women, furthermore, have been known to become pregnant and to give birth to children in lunatic asylums, and finally, conception is quite possible before the age of puberty. So while Hannay was probably and practically right (except for the age at which Addison's daughter died), he was not on as safe ground theoretically as he supposed himself to be.

A. S. Neill, in *A Dominie Dismissed*, tells how, when teaching in Scotland, a certain verse from "The Ancient Mariner" presented the boys with a challenge they never failed to take up. The verse was

> All in a hot and copper sky
> The bloody sun at noon
> Right up above the mast did stand,
> No bigger than the moon.

The boys used to emphasize the adjective in the second line, "but that is perhaps natural," remarks Neill (subsequently of *Summerhill* fame), "in a community in which strong language is the prerogative of grown-ups."[46]

Of the uses of *bloody* and its various forms a splendid example is provided in a poem recited to me by my old friend Vilhjalmur Stefansson. I forgot to ask him where he got it, and it would be interesting to know how old it is—probably not older than the middle of the nineteenth century.

> There was a bloomin' sparrer
> Flew up a bloody spout,
> An' then the bloomin' rain came down
> An' washed the bleeder out;
> But when the bloomin' sun came out
> An' cleared the bloomin' rain
> The bloomin' bloody sparrer
> Flew up the bloody spout again.

The enrichment of *bloody* with its own variant *bloomin'* in the penultimate line is masterly.

As Julian Franklyn says in his book *The Cockney*, the words *bloody* and *bleeding* are the very nails that hold a cockney sentence together. Without them the cockney could hardly verbalize.

Bleeding and its variants *bleedin'*, *bleed'n'*, *bleet'n'*, *bleen*, and, when giving special emphasis, *ber-leed-in* are all variants of *bloody* and are ecologically perhaps exclusively cockney. *Ruddy* as a euphemism for bloody is scarcely ever used by cockneys.[47]

In some circles the most frightful of foreign imprecations are considered genteel and ineffectual compared with the good work that *bloody* is capable of doing. For example, Bruno Werner in *The Slave Ship*, has the following exchange:

"*Merde!*" George nodded and slapped Heinrich on the back.
"Oh, to hell with *merde*," Heinrich said. "It's all the most utter bloody shit."

Which makes the point much more effectively.

Mrs. Grundy continued to lecture navvies and others for using the resilient *bloody*, but without the least success. She was fighting a hopeless and a losing battle. By 1940 the word was so much rehabilitated, indeed revitalized, that a newspaper, the *Daily Mirror*, could blazon the successful evacuation of some 350,000 men from Dunkirk, with the banner headline BLOODY MARVELLOUS. As, indeed, it was.

Several new meanings for *bloody* have developed since the early 1930s, when the word *bloody-minded* came into use to mean feeling rather blue, as in "I couldn't get any work done last week because I was feeling rather bloody-minded."

Subsequently the term developed the meaning of ornery, despicable, or difficult, and the latest meaning, developed in the late fifties, is deliberately obstructive, noncooperative, as when reference is made to the workers' bloody-mindedness. Or, "He would not repair my car—he was just feeling bloody-minded." In the sense of violent-minded Shakespeare uses the term when Suffolk says to Whitmore, "Yet let not this make thee be bloody-minded" (II *Henry VI*, IV, i).

The contemporary meaning of *bloody-minded* may be achieved by the simple use of *bloody*, as in Robert Ruark's novel *Something of Value* (1955), in which Johnston inquires of Peter McKenzie what his clients are like. "What sorts are they? Bloody?" and Peter replies, "Very unbloody, at first glance."

Here, too, we may note, as in the last sentence, the occasional use of *unbloody*, in the sense of "all right," or passing muster.

In the same book by Ruark Bsana John swears, by "My bloody oath!"

A peculiar meaning for *bloody-minded* appears to have been developed by Australian fighting men during World War II. Sidney Baker reports that the term described "the good-natured tomfoolery in which bored soldiers indulged while waiting for action at tropical bases."[48] But later, it came to be used as a synonym for *troppo*, "to describe a peculiar mental lethargy suffered by men on tropical service."[49]

The employment of *bloody* in the sense of "despicable" is more clearly defined in the following passage, from a review of Gwyn Griffin's novel *Shipmaster*, written by Simon Raven appearing in *The Spectator* November 17, 1961: "A disreputable liner is taking an assortment of working-class emigrants (both British and Italian) and upper-class escapists to Australia. Some of the ship's crew, in particular the Neapolitan chief officer, are quite nice, everyone else is bloody; rich and poor alike, they are a whining and embittered crowd of race-haters, shirkers and toadies, and the British are the worst of all."

Bloody is employed in a similar sense in the following passage from an article entitled "Roman Scandals," by Anthony Carson, published in the *New Statesman* February 12, 1955. Describing a visit to Rome, where he shared a room with a photo-reporter, he says, "One night he woke me up and asked me what I thought of Mussolini. I gathered my thoughts together, and replied that Mussolini was, as far as I knew, bloody."

As meaning frightful, beyond description, ghastly, *bloody* does good service, as is illustrated in the following passage from Fred Majdalany's *The Monastery*:

"It must be bloody awful getting a bomber back through heavy flak with two of the engines out."
"Absolutely bloody. I agree."[50]

And finally, there is the London *Daily Mirror* again, admonishing Khrushchev—this time for his intemperate behavior during the Summit crisis of May, 1960. A square box headline, in the issue of May 16, 1960, read as follows: "Mr. K! (If you will pardon an olde English phrase) Don't be so bloody rude!"

That in good English society *bloody* has come to serve as a perfectly *good* adjective to which no suspicion of anything objectionable attaches when it is used in certain contexts is illustrated by such a phrase as "Yes, he's a bloody fine fellow," which is the exact equivalent of "Yes, he's an awfully fine fellow." The same speaker might, however, draw the line at using the word simply as a swearword, although most would not. Thus, we perceive that there is today a polite sense, in which the word may be used as an intensive, and an impolite sense, in which it would not be used by the same speaker.

Of the various forms of *bloody*, *blinker*, pejorative for chap, fellow man, is the further corruption of *bleeder*. *Blasted* is often employed as a euphemism for *bloody* and sometimes achieves even greater force than *bloody*. *Blessed*, as in "It's no blessed good," frequently serves as a polite euphemism for *bloody*, as does *bally*, with its intersyllabic *absoballylutely*.

Yet another rare euphemism for *bloody* occurs in Masefield's poem "The Yarn of The *Loch Achray*." This sailor's poem is reasonably well sprinkled with *bloodys*, and in two stanzas *blushing* serves to reduce the monotony of *bloody*, as in the following stanza:

> Ere the watch below had time to dress.
> She was cluttered up in a blushing mess.

I have not found this stand-in for *bloody* elsewhere, but doubtless it occurs.

Finally, there is *perishing*, as in "It's perishing cold," which sometimes does service for *bloody*. *Blistering* performs a similar service.

Other euphemisms for *bloody* are *blurry*, which, as Partridge points out when used in newspapers and books is a euphemism, but in actual speech is more often than not a slurring of the original, and *blinking*. The latter is probably not directly a euphemism for *bloody*, but is indirectly so by way of *blanking—bleeding—bloody*: "Take the blinking thing away." The relationship is seen more clearly in the pejorative for fellow or man, namely, *blinker*. The cognate *bleeder*, also for pejorative *bloke* ligatures in origin with *bleeding* and the obsolete usage of *bleed*, as in "I'll have his bleed."[51]

George Orwell, in *Down and Out in Paris and London*, quite rightly states that "swear words also change—or, at any rate, they are subject to fashions." But he was surely somewhat premature in saying that the London working classes have now utterly abandoned the use of *bloody*. Writing in 1933, Orwell states that no born Londoner any longer uses *bloody* unless he is a man of education. "The word has, in fact, moved up in the social scale and ceased to be a swear word for the purposes of the working classes."[52] Certainly the word has moved up in the social scale, but it has not been abandoned by the London working classes.[53]

Bloody, in its various forms, is linguistically and psychologically one of the most interesting words in the English language. Certainly it is the most popular weighted adjective in English English. Linguistically, as we have seen, during the course of its evolution it has developed many somewhat different meanings. In its various semantic forms the word has exhibited an adaptive radiation akin to that observed in living organisms that have developed somewhat different morphologic forms in adaptation to different environmental challenges. This diversification of function has enriched both spoken and written English. In several of its forms the word retains its status as a swearword, while in some of its forms the word has assumed the function of an ordinary adjective. Although as an adjective *bloody* is not acceptable to everyone, it is widely used among those who are not inhibited by outworn conventions or premature psychosclerosis.

Bloody constitutes the remarkable example of a word that in the course of its history accumulated so much magic that it provided an unfailing source of energy for use in all sorts of refined meanings. It is perhaps no exaggeration to say that *bloody* is now fairly on its way toward becoming the most versatile word in the English language. Certainly there is no other capable of so many meanings or of performing so many services.

Because it was for so long a forbidden word it accumulated a prodigious quantum of talismanic potency that could be drawn upon for every kind of service. No other word would have done in the ethos within which it has flourished—in the English-speaking world, with the exception of the United States and Canada. It is curious that *bloody* has no more meaning for Canadians than it has for Americans, a fact that indicates how much greater the influence has been of the United States upon Canadian manners than that of the Mother Country—if, indeed, it ever was the Mother Country.

Another fact that probably played a significant role in determining the popularity of *bloody* is to be found in the psychophysics of the word. *Bloody* consists of two consonants and two vowels, each vowel following a consonantal sound, *bl-u-d-ee*. A phonetic analysis of these sounds suggests that as a complex, they are eminently suited to the purposes they are called upon to serve. Almost any word beginning with *b* has the makings of a good intensive, since to sound it, one must close the air passages, press both lips to one another, and then quickly push them, as it were, apart. Phonetically such a sound is called a bilabial stop. It is an effective assaulting sound. It explodes, so to speak, with speed, and releases the pent-up air or "steam" with some force. In *bloody* not only the lips push but the tongue also, the curled anterior part of which rolls off the top of the palate forward with some force, allowing, at the same time, a lateral escape of air. The short vowel *u* assists in the full expulsion of air by the necessity that it imposes upon the speaker of having to open his mouth fairly widely in order to release the additional air that has been called into service in operating the vocal cords. A word like "Blah!" with its strong suggestion of contempt is not without interest here because of its phonetic resemblance to the first two sounds of *bloody*, and its not dissimilar function. The *d* in *bloody* is a sound made with the tongue pushing off the back of the upper front teeth, again, a propulsive muscular motion on a falling succeeding pneumatic vowel *e*.

It is very likely that the actual physical assaultative character of these rhythmically easily pronounced sounds (consonant-vowel-consonant-vowel) contributed, in addition to the word's already enhanced associations, to the popularity that *bloody* has so long enjoyed, and will undoubtedly long continue to enjoy, as an intensive.

CHAPTER FOURTEEN

Damn!

〈〈〈〈〈〈〈〈〈〈〈〈〈〈〈〈〈〈〈〈〈〈〈〈〈〈〈〈〈〈〈〈〈〈〈〈〈 〈〉〉〉〉〉〉〉〉〉〉〉〉〉〉〉〉〉〉〉〉〉〉〉〉〉〉〉〉〉〉〉〉〉〉

Pantagruel then asked what sorts of people dwelled in that damn'd island.
> FRANÇOIS RABELAIS, *Pantagruel*, Bk. IV, chap. lxiv, 1532

I am damned in hell for swearing . . .
> WILLIAM SHAKESPEARE, *The Merry Wives of Windsor*, (II, ii), 1596

THE following dialogue occurs in a famous scene in Sheridan's *The Rivals* (1775):

ACRES: If I can find out this Ensign Beverley, odds triggers and flints! I'll make him know the difference o't.

ABSOLUTE: Spoken like a man! But pray, Bob, I observe you have got an odd kind of a new method of swearing.

ACRES: Ha! Ha! you've taken notice of it—'tis genteel, isn't it?— I didn't invent it myself though; but a commander in our militia, a great scholar I assure you, says that there is no meaning in the common oaths and that nothing but their antiquity makes them respectable—because, he says, the ancients would never stick to an oath or two, but would say, by Jove! or by Bacchus! or by Mars! or by Venus! or by Pallas! according to the sentiment; so that to swear with propriety, says my little major, the oath should be an echo to the sense; and this we call the *oath referential* or *sentimental swearing*—ha! ha! 'tis genteel, isn't it?

ABSOLUTE: Very genteel, and very new, indeed!—and I daresay will supplant all other figures of imprecation.

ACRES: Ay, ay, the best terms will grow obsolete. Damns have had their day.

(II, i)

This was in the Augustan age, when *damns* had far from had their day, but which was unequivocally the age during which swearing had reached its high watermark. But *damns* suffered no eclipse from the shower of new stars that appeared in the swearer's firmament, and the best terms do not grow obsolete, simply because they are the best—and *damn* stands among the first of these. *Damns* have not had their day, but *oaths referential* or *oaths sentimental* have. *Damn* remains the great English shibboleth, the most widely used of intensives, and the one most likely to steer the swearer clear of the Scylla of profanity and the Charybdis of vulgarity—that is, in certain circles; in others *damn* is still considered either profane or vulgar or both.

In 1947 I wrote an article in which I quoted Percy W. Bridgman, the distinguished Harvard physicist, as having said that science was doing one's damndest with one's mind. The journal in which the article appeared, read almost exclusively by technical men and scientists, printed the statement as "doing intensely the very best with one's mind." Ten years later the word was still objectionable, for in a book in which I again quoted Bridgman, published in 1957, *damndest* was softened to "utmost." It was the editorial opinion that the presence of the word would cause parents and schoolteachers to discourage children from reading the book. The journal was *Technology Review*, published by the Massachusetts Institute of Technology, and the book was *Man: His First Million Years*. I daresay both editors were right, although in 1957 I drew the attention of my book editor to the fact that in 1952 a book had been published in New York by a respected author, a professor of philosophy, Elijah Jordan, entitled *Business Be Damned*. But that, it was pointed out to me, was a book unlikely· to be read by anyone but the adults to whom such a title might appeal.

During World War II the Reverend Dr. Norman Vincent Peale, pastor of the Marble Collegiate Reformed Church in New York, preached a sermon (reported in *The New York Times*, November, 1942), in which he said:

It seems that we are developing quite an aggregation of "tough boys" in American public life today. I refer to the fact that it is scarcely possible to read a newspaper any more that does not contain the explosive "damns" of public figures. There was a time when the newspapers preserved a very high grade of decorum in the public print, and I think it is rather unfortunate that the papers feel now that they have to lower the standard.

For example, a leading public figure arrives from a trip and leaps from his plane shouting, "I am damn glad to be back." This, of course, may reveal a certain nonchalance, but it is a little bit hard on parents who are trying to bring their children up to exercise cultivated speech. Just today one of our officials in Washington, speaking of a certain board's policy, said, "It would be pretty damn tough."

I certainly do not want to mark myself as a mossback, but whereas a few years ago newspapers and magazines maintained a high standard of language, I notice today a tendency to let down into this commonplace talk. The public men of other years may have cussed plenty in private, but they had the good taste to keep it out of public address. As a minister it is certainly none of my business what a man wishes to make his private life, but I think it is incumbent upon somebody to raise his voice in a word of kindly protest on this subject.

It is understood, even comprehensible, that a man of the cloth may not swear under any circumstances, but the smoke and sulfur has long vanished from the word *damn* for ordinary men, even though it may not have done so for most clergymen. The man who imitates those chimneys that swallow their own smoke is in danger, like them, of accumulating so much soot as to precipitate a consuming conflagration. The smoke and sulfur of his fulminations should be allowed free access to the open air, to the pollution index of which he is unlikely to make any significant contribution. Better a harmless pyrotechnical disport of words than a consuming destructive internal combustion, the outcome of passion repressed and mettlesomeness internalized. In the age of Freud even clergymen have come to understand these things a little better, even though they may continue in their unwillingness to condone the swearer's *damns*.

If theologians would inquire seriously into the nature of swearing before condemning it out of hand, they might find that there is a certain practical ethic or morality to swearing, especially in the low *damns*, which should be allowed as a prescriptive right, an indulgence, because they serve to reduce the amount of entropy that would otherwise be available for expression in more destructive forms. Surely, it is better to *damn* innocuously than to act in other ways more destructively. So, at least the whole of the English-speaking world has thought, with the exception, for the most part, of its ecclesiastical moiety.

How, then, did this simple four-letter word, *damn*, come to occupy the prominent place it does in the swearer's vocabulary?

The English word *damn* is derived from the Latin *damnare* or *dampnare*, meaning to inflict damage or loss upon, to condemn, doom to punishment. In the Christian theology, *to damn* meant to condemn to eternal punishment in the world to come, to condemn to hell.

The damnation of man was the exclusive prerogative of the Deity, and no mortal man could presume to usurp it without endangering his immortal soul unto eternity. For any mere mortal to assume the power of the Deity was in itself a sacrilege of the most awful kind, but what was worse was the iniquity of treating that power irreverently. Any man who *damned* another might merely be exhibiting outraged reverence; but that is profane, and profanity is the homage that disillusion pays to faith. The impiety of such men is blasphemous, frivolous, irreligious, profane, and subversive, for they would become as the Deity, assuming to themselves the functions that belong only to him.

Drawing its power from such a profoundly holy and solemn source, the holy and the forbidden, with all the imagery of hell and damnation to call upon, the power to *damn* has had an irresistible appeal. The fire and brimstone, the smoke and sulfur, and all the tormenting devils that populate the nether regions provide the conditions most fitting to that realm to which one may satisfyingly consign one's enemies. With one magically omnipotent monosyllabic word one may achieve, in imagination at least, the perpetual perdition of the victim of one's sorcery.

William Maginn, the early nineteenth-century writer, in his story "Bob Burke's Duel," conveys the effect nicely, when he makes Burke say, " 'I will,' said I at once, and left the house in the most abrupt manner, after consigning Ensign Brady to the particular attention of Tisiphone, Alecto, and Megaera, all compressed into one emphatic monosyllable."[1]

Since the three ladies mentioned are the Furies that sit at the gates of hell, it is the latter monosyllable that Bob Burke may have uttered, but the effect is the same as if he had *damned* Ensign Brady.

Damn and *hell* draw their power from identical sources, and what may be said of the one applies with equal force to the other. As Browning says in "Soliloquy of the Spanish Cloister,"

> There's a great text in Galatians,
> Once you trip on it, entails
> Twenty-nine distinct damnations,

One sure if another fails;
If I trip him just a-dying,
Sure of heaven as sure can be,
Spin him round and send him flying
Off to hell, a Manichee.

And as Paul says in Gal. 1:8, "But though we, or an angel from heaven, preach any other gospel unto you than that which we have preached unto you, let him be accursed."

G. C. Lichtenberg, the German philosopher and satirist, who was in England in the 1770s, goes so far as to say that if towns were to be called after the first words that greeted a traveler on arrival, London would be known as "Damn it."

The impious particle is recorded in the *Oxford English Dictionary* as early as the year 1300 in the manuscript *Cursor Mundi*, where it is written, in the Middle English of the day, "For suilk he dampned theim of lijf." But in common speech the usage of the word undoubtedly dates back much earlier. By the next century the oath, especially when coupled with the name of the Deity, was known throughout France as the synonym for an Englishman. The dauphin, kept from the throne by the English in the Hundred Years' War, had almost been forced to yield the last jewel from the diadem of France to the arms of the Earls of Shrewsbury and Bedford, when the daughter of a farmer of Lorraine, Joan of Arc, persuaded him of her divine mission to stem the English advance. In 1429 she raised the siege of Orléans, conquered other posts on the Loire, and defeated the Goddams at Patay. Rising from her sleep and encasing herself in armor to direct the memorable assault on Tournelles, a soldier produced for her consumption a repast of fish. "Joan," said he, "let us eat this shad-fish before we set out." But Joan declined. "In the name of God," said she, "it shall not be eaten till supper, by which time we will return by way of the bridge, and I will bring you back a Goddam to eat it with." That day the redoubtable Tournelles was taken by the French under Joan's command, and Joan brought back with her not one but many Goddams as condiment for her shad. Shortly afterward, with Joan at his side, the dauphin was crowned king, and Joan proceeded to the unsuccessful siege of Paris. The following spring she went to relieve Compiègne, was captured by the Burgundians, and was sold by them to the English. In prison, she was visited by the Earls of Warwick and Stafford, who held out hope of a ransom to her. Irritated by the specious language of the noble lords, Joan turned upon them sharply. "I know you well," she cried, "you have neither the will nor the power to ransom me. You think, when you have slain me, you will conquer France; but that you will never bring about. No! although there were one hundred thousand Goddams in this land more than there are!"[2]

Beaumarchais, in his *Le Mariage de Figaro* (1784), makes one of the characters say, "The Devil! what a beautiful language is this English; with just a little bit of it one can go far; with Goddam one cannot fail anywhere in England . . . In conversation the English merely add some other word here and there; but it is easy to see that Goddam is the basis of the language" (III, v). And in 1804, Evariste Parny, a poet of no mean ability, published in Paris his celebrated work *Goddam! Poëm en quatre chants, par un french-dog.*

Has any word been so celebrated in a foreign tongue? It is doubtful.

Voltaire, who had lived in England for a time, acquired a most excellent armamentarium of English swearwords. Thomas Pennant, in a manuscript account of a "Tour on the Continent," now in the National Library of Wales, gives an account of a visit at Ferney on May 6, 1765 with Voltaire:

We were at first introduced to his niece Mademoiselle Dennis, a sedate worthy looking woman about fifty. Voltaire made his appearance out of an adjacent study and came into the room with more affectation of bodily infirmity than was requisite; not but that he really was as meagre and as arid a figure as ever I saw, his dress was a sky blue ratteen coat lapelled, a blue turned up cap over a long flowing brigadeer grey wig, his knees without buckles; his stockings coarse, his shoes thick and large. After a short address on the honour we did a weakly old man, his countenance brightened, his eyes, which were the most brilliant I ever saw, sparkled with pleasure, at the attention paid to his fame. He repaid with interest our flattering visit: spoke in our language which he seemed almost to have forgotten; except our imprecations; which he denounced most liberally on himself if he did not love the English better than his own countrymen. "By G—— I do love the Ingles G—— dammee, if I dont love them better dan de French, by G——!" Our victories had made a full impression on the old man.

After Waterloo, it was scarcely possible for an Englishman to appear upon any French street without being pursued by the cry "Goddam."

The persisting tradition among the French of characterizing the English as "goddams" is reflected in W. S. Gilbert's Bab Ballad "Lorenzo de Lardy" (1869):

> Mademoiselle De La Sauce Mayonnaise
>   Was a witty and beautiful miss,
> Extremely correct in her ways,
>   But her English consisted of this:
>
> "Oh my! pretty man, if you please,
>   Blom boodin, biftek, currie lamb,
> Bouldogue, two franc half, quite ze cheese,
>   Rosbif, mi spik Angleesh, godam."
>
> (1819–1824)

Byron, in the eleventh canto of *Don Juan*, describes how Don Juan on his first arrival in England is rudely awakened from the innocent belief that their shibboleth Goddamn is the usual salutation.

> —he was interrupted by a knife,
> With—"Damn your eyes! your money or your life!"—
> · · · · · · · · · · · ·
>
> Juan, who did not understand a word
> Of English, save their shibboleth, "God damn!"
> And even that he had so rarely heard,
> He sometimes thought 't was only their "Salām,"
> Or "God be with you!"—and 't is not absurd
> To think so: for half English as I am
> (To my misfortune), never can I say
> I heard them wish "God with you," save that way.

And on *damn* Byron has this to say in another stanza of the same canto:

> Man
> In islands is, it seems, downright and thorough,
> More than on continents—as if the sea
> (See Billingsgate) made even the tongue more free.
>
> And yet the British "Damme" 's rather Attic;
> Your continental oaths are but incontinent,
> And turn on things which no aristocratic
> Spirit would name, and therefore even I won't anent
> This subject quote; as it would be schismatic

In politesse, and have a sound affronting in 't;—
But "Damme" 's quite ethereal, though too daring—
Platonic blasphemy, the soul of swearing.

Byron was savagely attacked for the freedom of his language in *Don Juan*. William Hone, the author and bookseller, made a stinging allusion to Byron's irreverent use of the "unutterable Name, with a profane levity unsurpassed by any other two lines in the English language."[3] The lines complained of were

Tis strange—the Hebrew noun which means "I am,"
The English always use to govern d——n.

Damme, the shortened form of *Damn me* is first recorded in print in 1645 in James Howell's "My Lord Powis . . . said, dammy, if ever he come to be King of England, I will turn rebel" in *Epistolae Ho-Elianae. Familiar Letters Domestic and Forren*.[4] And in 1652, in *Commonwealth Ballads*, we have:

Hee's not a gentleman that wears a sword,
And fears to swear dammee at every word.

The Elizabethan dramatists put the adjective to wholesome use, and it is frequent enough in Shakespeare, but not as popular with his period as it later became.

In February, 1933, at the Oxford University Dramatic Society performance of *King John*, a man in the audience rose and protested against the use of the word "damnation" in the lines:

O, when the last account 'twixt heaven and earth
Is to be made, then shall this hand and seal
Witness against us to damnation.

Now, Oxford, which is proverbially the home of lost causes, and which Adam Smith described as "A sanctuary in which exploded systems and obsolete prejudices find shelter and protection after they have been hunted out of every corner of the world," seemed at that moment to be the very incarnation, or at least, the man in the audience did, of everything Adam Smith had said of it. *Damnation* was being used by Shakespeare in its strict and literal sense. The interrupter called it "swearing." He might with equal irrelevance have protested against the use of the name of the Deity because the name is sometimes taken in vain.

But if Oxford sometimes harbors quaint notions as well as quaint chaps, it is not to be held responsible for the eccentrics that occasionally appear at the excellent productions of the O.U.D.S. As reference to any concordance of Shakespeare will show, the word so unpalatable to some appears in the plays in the following proportions:

Damn 15	Damnation 14
Damnable 11	Damned 105
Damnably 1	Damned'st 1

Hamlet and *Othello* are the most frequent users. *Othello* is richer in objurgation, while *Hamlet* employs both the theological as well as the colloquial usages.

Julian Sharman traced the origin of the British shibboleth to a decidedly French source. His etymological ecology of the word has, so far as I know, gone entirely unnoticed. I shall, therefore give his discussion of it in his own words. After pointing out that the similarity with the numerous derivatives of the verb *damno* have probably obscured the true derivation of the word, he goes on to say:

For its real parentage we must have recourse to the Latin *dominus* or *domina* which produced the Gallic *dame*. This again was used equally to denote a potentate of either sex, until at last we find the interjection *dame!* applied in the same sense as *Seigneur!* or our own *Lord!* When, therefore we go still further, and meet with *dame Dieu!* occurring frequently in ancient texts we are helped at once to the source of our adopted expletive. By one of those combinations so often to be found where there is a confusion or admixture of tongues, the English soldiery rendered their *dame!* or *dame Dieu!* in the way we have seen, and a hybrid term was thus produced which has not even yet been found waning in popularity. The derivation we have here suggested is sufficient of itself to account for the amusement that was displayed by laughter-loving Frenchmen, who twitted the invader in that he was unable to pronounce the irrepressible *Dieu*, and was forced to anglicise it to fit it to the remainder of the oath.[5]

The first occurrence of *dame* in English is recorded by the *Oxford English Dictionary* as the fifteenth and sixteenth centuries. This coincides with the English occupation of France, and the first occurrence of the phrase is in Shakespeare's *The Comedy of Errors* (1591–92): "*God damn me!* that's as much as to say, God make me a light wench." This distinctly has the ring of an interpolated newly coined catchword.

Dame Dieu! translated as *Goddamn!* is a very natural transition from one language to the other, and the evidence indicates that such a transition occurred.

That the optative *damn* and the imprecative *Goddamn me* had entered the language about this time is suggested by Sir John Harington's remarks in his *Epigrams* (1615), published in London some three years after his death.

Against Swearing

In elder times an ancient custom was,
To sweare in weighty matters by the Masse.
But when the Masse went downe (as old men note)
They sware then by the crosse of this same grote.
And when the Crosse was likewise held in scorne,
Then by their faith, the common oath was sworne.
Last, having sworne away all faith and troth,
Only God damn them is their common oath.
   Thus custome kept *decorum* by gradation,
   That losing Masse, Crosse, Faith, they find damnation.

Harington, a courtier of noble birth, a robust Rabelaisian, with a flair for society, picked upon the newest and most fashionable oath and so recorded for us the fair promise of its establishment. This suggestion receives even stronger support from Nathan Field's *Amends For Ladies*, which was produced at Blackfriars in 1618. Nathan is not to be confused with his brother Nathaniel, an error that has led more than one silverfish in the bookstacks to the most desperate comminations. A newfangled oath could provide the means of considerable amusement in the hands of a skillful playwright, and in the following excerpt from the play we find several graduates of the Academy for the art and mystery of roaring or bullying, so divertingly portrayed in the pretended roaring school of Thomas Middleton and William Rowley's *The Faire Quarrell*, which was staged a year earlier, in 1617.

WELLTRIED: Why, Monsieur Whore-bang? I am no play maker, and for pledging your healths, I love none of the four you drank so well.

SPILL-BLOOD: Zounds! you shall pledge on this.

WELLTRIED: Shall I?

FEESIMPLE: What's the matter? do'st hear, master Welltried, use thine own discretion; if thou wilt not pledge him, say so, and let me see, if e'er a damn-me of 'em all will force thee.

SPILL-BLOOD: Puff! will your lordship take any tobacco? you lord with
the white face.
BOTS: 'Heart! he cannot put it through his nose.
FEESIMPLE: Faith, you have ne'er a nose to put it through, d'ye hear?
blow your face, sirrah.
TEAR-CHAPS: You'll pledge me, sir?
WELLTRIED: Indeed, I will not.
FEESIMPLE: Damn-me he shall not then.
TEAR-CHAPS: Lord, use your own words, damn-me is mine: I am known
by it all the town o'er, d'ye hear?
FEESIMPLE: It is as free for me as you, d'ye hear, Patch? [fool]
TEAR-CHAPS: I have paid more for't.

There are several things of interest in this exchange: The user
of the oath is referred to as a *damn-me*, which at once suggests
characterization by a distinctive trait, and in this case a novel one.
This is strongly confirmed by Tear-chaps' claim that the oath is
his very own. "I am known by it all the town o'er, d'ye hear?"
And clearly Tear-chaps would be known by *damn-me* only if it
were uncommon enough for anyone to be recognized by it, unless,
of course, he was making a false claim. In 1618 Geffray Mynshull,
in his *Certaine Characters and Essayes of Prison and Prisoners*,
wrote: "Though he steale his band of tenne thousand Dam-mees."[6]
Damne it occurs in the anonymously published *Pappe* 1589, and
damnedly in Cyril Tourneur's *The Revenger's Tragedie* (1607).

In Phillip Massinger's play *The Parliament of Love* (1624) the
noble lady Bellisant chides the courtiers:

> Whereas, now,
> If you have travelled Italy, and brought home
> Some remnants of the language, and can set
> Your faces in some strange and ne'er seen posture,
> Dance a lavolta, and be rude and saucy;
> Protest, and swear and damn . . .

"Protest" in this passage represents a newly fashionable oath.
It raised the presumption of quality in the user. In Ben Jonson's
Every Man Out of His Humour, first acted at the Globe Theatre
in 1599, the playwright holds up to ridicule various absurd characters and fashions of the day. Here Carlo Buffone, "a public
scurrilous profane jester," perhaps intended to designate John
Marston, is made to say, "Ever, when you can, have two or three
peculiar oaths to swear by, that no man else swears, and above

all protest." This fashionable eccentricity is also noted by Shake-speare in *Romeo and Juliet* (1595):

ROMEO: Nurse, commend me to thy lady and mistress. I protest unto thee—
NURSE: Good heart, and i'faith, I will tell her as much: Lord, Lord, she will be a joyful woman.
ROMEO: What wilt thou tell her, nurse? thou dost not mark me.
NURSE: I will tell her, sir,—that you do protest; which, as I take it, is a gentlemanlike offer.

II, iii

The moment Romeo utters, "I protest," the nurse is instantly won over, for she knows he is a gentleman. She is so taken with the expression that she takes the part for the whole of the message, indeed, is so overcome by the word, that Romeo makes her repeat what he has said to her, "thou dost not mark me." It is clearly a piece of banter at the expense of the gallants of the day who sported their new oaths as they did their fine clothes.

In a contemporary play, *Sir Gyles Goosecappe* (1606), we are afforded an insight into the special estimation in which the term was held, when one of the characters says, "There is not the best duke's son in France dares say *I protest* till he be one-and-thirty years old at least, for the inheritance of that word is not to be possessed before."

The point of all this is that the bracketing by Massinger of *protest* and *damn* in the context in which he does so strongly indicates the recency of *damn* in acceptable English conversation. We may, then, fairly accurately pinpoint the establishment of this imprecatory element in its various forms—*God damn me, damn-me* or *dammy*, and *damn it*—about the end of the sixteenth and the beginning of the seventeenth centuries.

While *Goddamn* was already well established among the English soldiery in France in the early fifteenth century, it would appear that almost three-quarters of a century was to elapse before this mercuric particle's true versatility was to be fully appreciated.

The Puritans, who swore not at all, nevertheless referred to the Cavaliers as the *God-dammees*. As Thomas Peyton wrote in 1652, "The Courtiers garnished their mouths with God-dammes, as if they desired Damnation rather than Salvation."[7] And there is much else to the like effect. However, as Abraham Cowley in 1643 pointed out in his satire *The Puritan and the Papist*, there were Puritans of elevated status who were not beyond this favored oath:

> Nay, though *Oaths* be by you so much abhorr'd
> Ye allow *God damne me* in your *Puritan Lord.*

Essentially a soldier's oath originating in France, the various forms of *Goddamn* did not become established at home until well into the first third of the seventeenth century.

In Richard Brome's play *The Covent-Garden Weeded*, posthumously published in London in 1658, there is much game with *Dammy*, and a gentlewoman, Damaris, is so nicknamed by some of the young gallants. Mun Clotpoll, a foolish gull, is admitted into the Brotherhood of the Philoblatici, yet another of the roaring associations of insolent bloods and vaporers whose delight was to annoy well-behaved citizens. The Captain of the Philoblathici, Driblow, speaks to his young gentlemen:

CAPT: I have given you all the rudiments, and my most fatherly advices withal.

CLOT: And the last is that I shall not swear, how make you that good? I thought now I was sworne into this Brotherhood, I might have sworne what and as much as I would.

CAPT: That's most unnecessary, for look you son, the best and even the leudest of my sons do forbear it, not out of conscience, but for very good ends; and in stead of an Oath furnish the mouth with some affected Protestation. As I am honest, it is so. I am no honest man if it be not. Ud take me, if I lie to you. Nev'rgo, nev'stirre, I vow, and such like.

CLOT: Or never credit me, or let me never be trusted.

CAPT: O take heed of that, that may be spoken in so ill an houre, that you may run out of reputation, and never be trusted indeed; the other will gaine you credit and bring you into good and civil estimation with your Hostesses; and make 'em terme you a fair conditioned Gentleman if he had it; and truly I never heard worse word come out of his mouth.

CLOT: Nev'r go, nev'r stir, I vow. I'le have, I vow then.

ANT [Another member of the Philoblathici]: I vow you shall not, that's mine.

CLOT: Cannt you lend it me now and then brother? I'le have I swear then, and come as nigh swearing as I can.

NICK: I swear but you must not, that's mine you know.

CLOT: I protest then, I'le have I protest, that's a City-word, and best to cozen with.

CAPT: Come boyes, fall to some practice. Let me see about at the new French balls, sprung out of the old English vapours.

CLOT: I protest come on. I'le make a third man.

ANT: Whose man are you?

NICK: Whose man is not to be asked, nor scarce whose subject, now he is of our Brotherhood.

CLOT: Yes, by your favour he may ask.

ANT: I ask no favour, sir.

NICK: That may be granted.

CLOT: You can grant nothing in this kinde.

NICK: I swear, I neither can, nor will grant that.

CLOT: That, I protest, may bear exception indeed.

ANT: Exceptions amongst us? nay, then I vow.—

NICK: I swear.

CLOT: And I protest— [*Up with their Battoons* (cudgels)]

CAPT: Part faire, my boyes; 'tis very, well perform'd; now drink a round to qualifie this bout.

III, i

Their exercises completed, the roaring boys were ready to take on all comers and to spawn such gallants of the Restoration as Rochester, Sedley, and their cronies.

The professor of Greek during Byron's days at Cambridge, the great scholar Richard Porson, on whose handwritten script the Cambridge University Press still models its Greek type, was a three-bottle man in an age of two-bottle men; he was not profane, but his favorite oath was *Damn the nature of things*. He had good cause to damn them, for he was a much misunderstood and maltreated man of genius and one of England's genuinely great "characters." In argument he was a formidable opponent, as the following incident will show. "Mr. Porson," someone, after a heated argument, said to him, "my opinion of you is contemptible." "I know of no opinion of yours that is not contemptible," answered Porson.[8] *Damn the nature of things* is a generous oath that does not err on the side of exclusiveness; in fact, it can be said not only to be all-embracing, but to constitute a critique of the very organization of matter—and that is not only a theological heresy but also a secular one. It is possible that the structure of the atom could have been otherwise and "better" organized than it is, and that things might then have turned out better than they have, but one may suspect that however things are organized the manner in which they will "turn out" will largely depend upon the alembic through which they are made to pass—the creature man.

God created man in his own image, and man, as Voltaire remarked, has returned the compliment. God also created the world, but man, alas, has re-created it—in *his* image. It was a far better world before man began tampering with it. It is not the nature of things that is damnable, but man's, we hope temporary, aberration from the realization of his better self and purposes. And "self" as well as "purposes" are made, made by man, who makes himself.

> Nature never did betray
> The heart that loved her.

It is only man who betrays—that same man who is capable, if he would but avail himself of the opportunity to cultivate them, of the highest loyalties. The fault lies not in the nature of things, but in ourselves, and a man is the substance of the things he either loves or hates. In that luminous book *The Human Situation*, W. Macneile Dixon puts it well:

How simple then is our duty—loyalty to life, to the ship's company and to ourselves, that it may not be through our surrender that the great experiment of existence, whose issue remains in doubt, come to an end in nothingness. "We must not obey," said Aristotle, "those who urge us, because we are human and mortal, to think human and mortal thoughts; in so far as we may we should practise immortality, and omit no effort to live in accordance with the best that is in us."

What a handful of dust is man to think such thoughts! Or is he, perchance, a prince in misfortune, whose speech at times betrays his birth? I like to think that, if men are machines, they are machines of a celestial pattern, which can rise above themselves, and, to the amazement of the watching gods, acquit themselves as men. I like to think that this singular race of indomitable, philosophizing, poetical beings, resolute to carry the banner of Becoming to unimaginable heights, may be as interesting to the gods as they to us, and that they will stoop to admit these creatures of promise into their divine society.[9]

The nature of the human situation is what man makes of it. It is, therefore, not irremediable. What man has made he can unmake and remake as he ought. In this manner, instead of cursing the nature of things, he can remake them by remaking his own nature. But, as Byron reminds me:

> 't is no time to chat
> On general topics: "books" must confine
> Themselves to unity, like this of mine.

Barnaby Brook, in his recollections, *Mock Turtle*, nicely illustrates the intensive qualities of our fiery particle:

Although topics of conversation were carefully guarded, there was a
very free use of harmless oaths. My father, like Melbourne, Wellington
and Palmerston, plentifully belarded his talk with "damns" and "Goddams." To his friends and him no affirmative or negative was complete
without its expletive. "No, by God," and "Yes, by God," were common
form. There was some show of moderation among the ladies, but it was
half-hearted, and I had at least one old aunt, born in 1787, who out-
rivalled the men in the frequency of her appeals to the Deity.[10]

A quietus has, for some obscure reason, been put upon the proficiency of women in swearing. This conspiracy of silence was, no
doubt, a well-meant attempt to preserve what might be called the
"pedestalian" view of womankind, so popular during the Victorian
period. No lady, of course, would ever swear. Indeed, she would
rather swoon than swear. The farmer, in Mr. Johnson's shop in
Mrs. Gaskell's *Cranford* (1853), on learning that his note on the
Town and County Bank is worthless, exclaims, "Dang it!"—a nice
combination of *damn* and *hang*, but the only oath that Mrs. Gaskell
would permit to sully her charming book. Of course, it is not
sworn by a member of the gentler sex. In the Tudor period ladies
swore quite proficiently if not as varicoloredly as men. Queen
Elizabeth, for example, swore *By God, God's death*, and *God's
wounds*, and the ladies of her court did likewise. But in the seventeenth and eighteenth centuries ladies no longer swore, and in the
nineteenth century they never even thought of doing so, though
they might resort to such euphemisms as *Fiddlesticks, Fudge*, and
the like. Women, however, as distinct from ladies, of the lower
classes never ceased to swear as colorfully as their men. Indeed,
"to swear like a Billingsgate fishwife" still is as much as to say
that the performer has reached the apogee in the art of swearing.
Fishwives, for some obscure reason, seem to excel at swearing.
As early as classical Greek times "to swear like a fishwife" was
a common expression.

In 1778 Captain Cook discovered that Pacific paradise he named
the Sandwich Islands, later to become known as Hawaii. Cook's
men, and those who followed, sedulously swore their way through
the islands so effectively that when Captain Basil Hall visited the
Sandwich Islands in the 1820s an islander officiously greeted the
group with a full sense of the distinction of his exalted visitors:

"Very glad see you! Damn your eyes! Me like English very much. Devilish hot, sir! Goddam!"[11]

Beryl Lee Booker, in her book *Yesterday's Child* (1937), tells of her grandfather, an admiral, "who read the menu while he said grace with some such explosive result as: 'For what we are about to receive . . . God damn you, Adelaide, *cod* again!"

Captain Corcoran of Gilbert and Sullivan's *H.M.S. Pinafore* (1878), who never used "a big, big D———," would have been shocked. If only the admiral had been advised by the First Lord of the Admiralty, Sir Joseph Porter, K.C.B.:

> For I hold that on the seas
> The expression "if you please,"
> A particularly gentlemanly tone implants.

But in fairness to the admiral it is a matter of history that Captain Corcoran, unable to repress his rage did, on one occasion, cry, "Why, damme, it's too bad!"

Cousin Hebe and female relatives having overheard this, all exclaim, "Oh!" Captain Corcoran replies, "Yes, damme, it's too bad."

During this shameful exhibition, Sir Joseph has appeared on the poop deck. He is horrified at the bad language.

HEBE:	Did you hear him—did you hear him?
	Oh, the monster overbearing!
	Don't go near him—don't go near him—
	He is swearing—he is swearing!
SIR JOSEPH:	My pain and my distress,
	I find it is not easy to express;
	My amazement—my surprise—
	You may learn from the expression of my eyes!
CAPT:	My lord—one word—the facts are not before you
	The word was injudicious, I allow—
	But hear my explanation, I implore you,
	And you will be indignant too, I vow!
SIR JOSEPH:	I will hear of no defence,
	Attempt none if you're sensible.
	That word of evil sense
	Is wholly indefensible.
	Go, ribald, get you hence
	To your cabin with celerity.
	This is the consequence
	Of ill-advised asperity!

For I'll teach you all, ere long,
  To refrain from language strong
For I haven't any sympathy for ill-bred taunts!

II

In 1878, when *H.M.S. Pinafore* was produced at the Opéra
Comique in London, *damme* was, indeed, a "word of evil sense
. . . wholly indefensible," to a sizable number of squeamish souls,
but not those particularly likely to visit the Opéra Comique. Even
Swinburne, who was not incapable of an occasional expletive, when
it came to writing the word, couldn't muster the courage to do so.
He wrote from Mentone on January 19, 1861, to Paulina, Lady
Trevelyan: ". . . the aggravation of having people about one who
undertake to admire these big stone-heaps of hills, and hideous
split-jawed gorges! I must say (in Carlylese) that 'the (scenery)
is of the sort which must be called, *not* in the way of profane
swearing, but of grave, earnest and sorrowing indignation, the d——
sort.' (I wd. rather die than write it at length.)."[12]

Swinburne's diffidence was very real, especially in writing to a
lady, and not in the least pretended. His feeling about writing the
word serves to convey something of the dread in which it was held.

The horrid little sister in Booth Tarkington's novel *Seventeen*
(1916) is forbidden by her mother to mention the word *damn* in
recounting an adult conversation. So she substitutes *word* for *damn*
and *wordest* for *damndest* and at one stroke satisfies the requirements of morality, conscience, convention, and decency. But such
filtrates of "language," it could be argued, do not prevent the full
fragrance of the rose from making its presence felt even though
it is called by another name, but it is not so. John Macy, referring
to the exchange between mother and daughter in Tarkington's
novel, says, "It is a good bit of comedy, and part of the humor
of it lies in the mother's assumption that the interests of morality
have been served by the substitution. It burlesques the prudery
of good people who weaken the oral language and disfigure the
written for the sake of appearances, and, worse than that, are
themselves deceived by appearances, duped into believing that
an altered exterior acquits them of responsibility for the interior
meaning."[13]

But the refusal to use the "indefensible" word *does* acquit the
refuser of any responsibility for it or its meaning. *Word* is not
the same thing as *damn*, and a good thing, too, for if it were,
anarchy would prevail and speech would have no meaning. Macy

has simply failed to understand that the mana that attaches to a word ceases to operate as soon as some innocuous word is substituted for it. Every member of a nonliterate society understands this, but in literate societies in which the sophistication of thought has proceeded to rational extremes the magic omnipotence of some words as distinguished from others is sometimes forgotten. A man will not give you his real name in many nonliterate societies because he knows full well that it contains something of his essence, that you could endanger his very life were you in possession of it. One will even change names in order to deceive the ghosts of the departed. Certain words—for gods, kings, priests, animals, and the dead—may not be mentioned because of the magical or supernatural power that attaches to them. And so one uses substitutes for them, and the dangers inherent in the original words are in this way avoided. No one is deceived by the appearances, as Macy implies, indeed says, they are, and no one is duped, except the ghosts.

The expression *I don't care a damn*, rather more asseverative than its contemporary *I couldn't care less*, needs to be rescued from the clutches of the pseudohistorians who have obscured its origins by mythologizing it.

In a letter written March 6, 1849, Thomas Babington Macaulay wrote, "How they settle the matter I care not, as the Duke says, one twopenny damn." George Otto Trevelyan, Macaulay's biographer comments on this that the Duke of Wellington was the inventor of this oath.[14] Now the form in which the Duke is said to have employed the oath was *not* a twopenny *damn*, but a twopenny *dām*, a dām being an Indian coin of the minutest value. The victor of Assaye, it is said, coined the expression after the valuelessness of the Indian piece of money. The *Oxford English Dictionary* disagrees and says that in the sense of *not worth a damn*, "the conjecture that the word is the Hindi *dām, dawm*, an ancient copper coin, of which 1600 went to a rupee (see Yule), is ingenious, but has no basis in fact." Ernest Weekley, on the other hand, in *An Etymological Dictionary of Modern English*, states his belief:

at any rate the popularity of the expression is of this origin. In all langs. expressions of this kind are from (i) small coins and sums (*twopence, brass farthing*), or (ii) objects of no value (*button, straw*). Such expressions swarm esp. in OF [Old French]. I know no parallel to *damn* in this sense, for not to *care a curse* is really an argument in favour of the small coin suggestion. The popularizer in E. [English] of the *twopenny damn*, in which the coin association seems to survive, was a great Anglo-Indian, the Duke of Wellington.[15]

Weekley's points are all very plausible as to the origin of the expression, but the facts are with the *Oxford English Dictionary*. When I was a boy in London tinkers—notable swearers in their own right—were among the last "criers" of the town. For two-pence they would repair a hole in a pot or a pan, and they did this by building a dam of mud around the hole, to keep the molten metal in place until it cooled. They would then remove the dam by brushing it away. Not "to care a tinker's dam" expressed the feeling of little worth as graphically as possible. The *twopenny dam* chronicles the exact price of the tinker's service up to 1914. With respect to expressions based on small coins, there is Tristram Shandy's phrase *'Tis not twopence matter* (v, ch. 39), which reflects a much earlier usage. William Baxter in 1691 wrote: "All our righteousness is not worth two-pence"; and William Bramston in 1729, in *The Art of Politicks*, wrote: "He cares not two-pence for the land-tax bill," and so on. In fact, as a disparaging epithet *twopenny* goes well back into the sixteenth century, if not earlier. In *Citizen of the World* (1760), Oliver Goldsmith wrote: "Not that I care three damns what figure I cut"; and the Reverend Christopher Anstey, in *The New Bath Guide* (1766), wrote:

> Absurd as I am,
> I don't care a damn
> Either for you or your valet-de-sham.

Always remembering that novel expressions are given utterance, especially when they are considered of questionable propriety, long before they are permitted in print, we may be reasonably sure that *I don't care a damn* was in use in conversational English long before the middle of the eighteenth century. For a man of the cloth to have used such a phrase in print in the second third of the eighteenth century means that it must have been in use con-siderably before that. "Wisdom and wit is not now worth a curse" (x, 17) occurs in *Piers Plowman* (1377), so the style of the phrase is clearly of considerable antiquity. It is here, then, suggested that while the Iron Duke may have been the most prominent person to have used *I don't care a twopenny damn*, he was almost certainly not its inventor. The process of perseveration, which is a constant linguistic phenomenon whereby words having the same sound but somewhat different meanings are amalgamated and, by a sort of alloyed hybrid vigor, communicate meanings somewhat more puissant than the original words, has probably been at work in the genesis of *I don't care a twopenny damn*. The Hindi *dām* and the English *damn* combined with the appropriate element in *'Tis not twopence matter*—all attempting to convey the same thought—would produce as their progeny the expression in question. If this is so, then it is probable that the expression was already in use by the middle of the eighteenth century.

Euphemisms for *damn* are innumerable. For New England alone —not to mention Old England—*The Linguistic Atlas of New England* gives the following examples:

dem, dum, dim, deam, dan, dang, ding, dash, dast, dag, dad, drat, blame, blast, bust, burn, bother, bugger, butter, confound, condemn, consarn, condarn, curse, cuss, crump, gast, gum, hang, rat, ram, rabbit, shuck, torment, plague, dunder, tarn.

A large proportion of these euphemisms are of English origin. *Darn* is the general American euphemism for *damn*, and *durn* is perhaps not less frequent, and *proxime accessit* is undoubtedly *dern*. It is greatly to be doubted, in spite of some lexicographers to the contrary,[16] that *dern* is derived from the Old English *dern* or *derne*, meaning secret. Dr. Louise Pound has suggested that *darn* and its cognates *dern* and *durn* are more likely to have sprung from the American contraction for eternal, namely *tarnal*—an intensive widely used during the tumultuous days of the Revolution. The process is linguistically known as aphesis, in which a short unaccented syllable at the beginning of a word is dropped. From the expletive *eternal damnation, darn, tarnal*, and *darnation* or *tarnation* are easily developed, as is the participial adjective *darned*.[17] *Go darn your socks* is still a ladylike expletive in certain parts of New England. But whatever may be the case there, it is otherwise in New York, for no less a personage than a federal judge sitting in New York in July, 1941, threatened a lawyer with punishment for contempt of court for using the word *darn*.[18] Indeed, a lawyer so little mindful of the dignity of the court and so little aware of the power of words in their proper places has no business being a lawyer at all. The judge was quite right to bring the fact to his attention. The awful consequences of such a thoughtless act of self-indulgence on the part of a lawyer are something for their clients to reflect upon.

Tormented as a euphemism for *damned*, as in "I don't give a tormented cent," was not uncommon in nineteenth-century New England.

But to return to *damn*, a popular American expletive is *doggone*. One would have supposed that the origin of this expression was obvious, namely, that it was a euphemism for *goddamn*. But the authorities make no reference to such an origin. *The Dictionary of American English* traces its first usage to the middle of the nineteenth century, and it is suggested that its source is to be looked for in the Scottish *dagone*. I gravely doubt it. This is to miss the point that during the second half of the nineteenth century in England the expletive *dog on it* as a euphemism for *Goddamn it* enjoyed a certain popularity and was almost certainly carried to the New World by English immigrants during that period. *God* has for hundreds of years been converted to *dog* in profane oaths, and *dog on it* is a perfect substitute for *Goddamn it*. Since, according to Partridge, the oath flourished around 1860 to 1890 in England,[19] we do not have to look any further for the origins of *doggone* or *doggone it*. Terms such as *goldarn* and *goshdarn* are clearly euphemisms for *Goddamn* and linguistically originate in precisely the same manner as *doggone*.

During World War I the commander of the tank fleet issued an order echoing an earlier famous one before the Battle of Trafalgar: "England expects that every tank will do its damndest." That was November 20, 1917, and that day, it is recorded, every tank did.

Bob Acres was wrong. *Damns* will never cease to have their day.

CHAPTER FIFTEEN

The Four–Letter Words

‹‹ ‹ › ›››››››››››››››››››››››››››››››››››

Immodest words admit of no defence,
For want of decency is want of sense.

WENTWORTH DILLON, Earl of Roscommon,
Essay on Translated Verse, 1684

Oh perish the use of the four-letter words
Whose meanings are never obscure;
The Angles and Saxons, those bawdy old birds,
Were vulgar, obscene and impure.
But cherish the use of the weaseling phrase
That never says quite what you mean.
You had better be known for your hypocrite ways
Than vulgar, impure and obscene.
Let your morals be loose as an alderman's vest
If your language is always obscure.
Today, not the act, but the word is the test
Of vulgar, obscene and impure.

ANONYMOUS

E PPUR *si muove!* Indeed, the world does move, progress has been made, and four-letter words are now permitted in books, and even in magazines, but their employment in speech is still interdicted. However, as life becomes more secularized the demythologization of the elements of spiritual power, the pantheon of the gods and their minions, will serve to empty most of the swearer's traditional words of their proscribed potency. In this way the words' power to produce spiritual shock will be lost while their ability to fulfill their diverse functions in communication will be retained. A similar evolution may be foreseen for the four-letter words. These words largely draw their force from the dark and tumultuous arcanum of sex and the eliminative functions. The very word "sex" is one that could not be freely uttered, especially in mixed company, until after World War I. Nor could there be any direct reference to elimination. In many circles it is

to this day considered bad taste to refer to any of the functions
of sex or elimination.

A society characterized by such attitudes, especially toward sex,
and so wracked and confused by it provides an inexhaustibly rich
and highly ionized atmosphere from which the positively charged
libido can produce something more than sparks when it collides
with the terrestrially bound negative particles. Of the latter there
always seems to be a ready supply. The emotional charges attach-
ing to the taboo on virtually everything relating to sex renders the
words alluding to its intimate aspects uncommonly potent. So long
as Western societies cling to their chaotically unhealthy attitudes
toward sex, the swearer will never want for four-letter words.

It is observable that since the relaxation of Victorian attitudes
toward sex and their replacement by perhaps anarchically per-
missive ones in many quarters, four-letter words have appeared
in the vocabulary of many who can scarcely be said to be undisciplined in the choice of words. Indeed, their use gives some individuals a certain cachet, a quality of ultrasophistication. But for
the rest of the world such words are still generally considered
vulgar, obscene, and impure.

Four-letter words are deemed obscene because they refer to an
aspect of life that has long been considered *ob caenum*, that is,
filthy. Christianity and the church have, in their various forms,
been largely responsible for the uncleanness of sex.[1] Sin and sex,
as everyone knows, have somehow come to be inextricably inter-
related, so that the swearer who draws upon the forbidden sources
of sexuality adds to the force of his obscene words the power of
both a scatological and a sacrilegious act. "Love has placed its
palace/ In the place of excrement," wrote Yeats, and to the early
church fathers this constituted sure proof of the degradation and
sinfulness of those parts.

A distinction must be recognized between the swearing that
draws its power from the forbidden sources of religious authority,
deity, subdeity, saint, and the sacred, and the swearing that depends upon prohibited secular sources for its force, such as the
arcanum of sex. It is unnecessary to dwell here upon the Christian
view of sex as an evidence of man's innate depravity, his original
sinfulness, and the dangerous and powerful force for evil that sex
constitutes. This is fairly common knowledge, and innumerable
works have been devoted to the subject. The dark and evil powers
that inhabit man's body, and especially woman's, it is held, daily

and dreadfully put the temptations of the devil in his way. And so it is better to repress any thought of these concupisciently horrid and evil shapes and put them behind or beneath one. It is today well established that excessive restraint in the control of sexual expression is purchased at the cost of unremitting destructive inner turmoil. We recall Swift, driven mad by terrible unnatural repressions. It is this compelling and strenuous inner preoccupation with the forbidden sexual drives that provides the secular swearer with the main materials for his power to shock— achieving with the bolts he looses the jolting force of an electric convulsion.

This explanation will perhaps enable us to understand why four-letter swearwords possess so much more power to shock than those drawn from purely religious sources. The four-letter words are stronger because they deliver a fusillade from both barrels at once, the profane and the obscene. And it is presumably for this reason that there has been so much resistance to these words. The emotional charges carried by some words are so great that they can make the difference between life and death and all the states of being in between. They can raise men up and strike them down, elevate and depress them, infuriate and amuse them, shock and physically repel them. Such words are dangerous, and so they come to be forbidden, tabooed. Both the individual and society must be protected against the unconscious, irrational anxieties that such words are capable of evoking so anarchically.[2] The horror and fear of the un-understood, of the mysterious, of the forbidden, is capable of resulting in the most uncontrolled behavior —hence, the savage punishments that society, through its laws, has with such barbaric severity inflicted upon those who in any way tampered with the sluice gates that contained the reservoir of these anxieties.

It is not difficult, therefore, to understand in what manner the four-letter words achieve their peculiarly puissant charges. Those charges do not draw their power from the violation of the religious and secular prohibitions alone; what is perhaps an equally important source is the great cistern of anxieties that have bedeviled so many human beings in the Western world. Man's displacement activities, in the form of various customs, mores, rituals, and institutions, constitute a universal means through the agencies of which he is able to canalize and express his anxieties in more or less satisfying ways—to discharge his impulses over substitute social

pathways. The function of many religious, magical, ritual, ceremonial, and other social devices is to afford the opportunities for
such displacement activities and thereby to assuage and alleviate
anxiety. As cultures become more secularized and the supernaturals
become superannuated, the secular devices designed to afford relief from anxiety tend to increase. Swearing constitutes one such
device; psychotherapists who indulge the patient in conversation
ad libido, constitute another.

It is a curious fact that the words universally considered the most
foul and indecent in the English language are all four-letter one-
syllable words. It is, however, perfectly understandable that these
words should relate to parts of the body and their functions traditionally considered the most unclean. The organs of sex and their
functions, as well as those neighboring upon the sexual, the organs
of elimination, furnish most of the material for the inveterate
swearer's vocabulary, the material that "superior" people have
never deigned to acknowledge—at least, not until the second half
of the twentieth century had launched itself into space.

The principal four-letter words are *fuck, cunt, cock, arse, shit,
piss,* and *fart*. Each of these words has formed part of the swearer's
vocabulary for many centuries. In the hierarchy of forbidden and
dirty words *fuck*, in its various shapes and forms after its fall from
grace, has always been considered the most heinous. Hardly less
objectionable has been, and still is, the vulgar term for the female
genitalia, *cunt*. The other four-letter words do not really belong
in the same class as these two, for they carry much less powerful
charges and are considered not nearly as obscene.

In a certain sense Edward Sagarin, in his book *The Anatomy
of Dirty Words*,[3] is quite right when he says that there is only
one four-letter word in the English language. *Fuck* is, indeed, the
nonpareil of all the foulest and most inadmissible of all swearwords, four-lettered or otherwise. However, as everyone knows,
there are other four-letter words not of equal potency, to be sure,
but powerful enough to provide an inexhaustible reservoir of
energy for the swearer's uses.

Such is the power of the great four-letter word that it has
been completely banished ever since the eighteenth century
from all general dictionaries. Even Weekley in his *Etymological
Dictionary* (1921)[4] makes not the slightest reference to it, nor does
he acknowledge the word's existence or any of its derivatives in
any of his other lexical works. Nor, fourteen years later, does

H. L. Mencken in his great work *The American Language*[5] pay the slightest attention to it. The earliest dictionary to record the word in English was John Florio's Italian-English dictionary, *A Worlde of Wordes* (1598),[6] in which the word was entered as one of the five equivalents of the Italian *fottore*. The first English dictionary to enter the word in its proper alphabetic place was Stephen Skinner's *Etymologicon Linguae Anglicanae* (1671).[7]

Nathaniel Bailey in his *Universal Etymological Dictionary* (1721)[8] gives the word and defines it as "*subagitare foeminam* (to lie with a woman)." Nine years later, in his *Dictionarium Britannicum* (1730),[9] Bailey added to the definition: "a term used of a goat." In 1775 John Ash in his *A New and Complete Dictionary*,[10] describes the word as "low" and "vulgar," and gives various definitions. In 1785 Francis Grose included the word in his *Classical Dictionary of the Vulgar Tongue*,[11] but felt obliged to take refuge in asterisks for the two middle letters. Not so Dr. Edward Harwood, the editor of the twenty-fourth edition of Bailey's *Dictionary*, who, in 1782, completely banished the word from the book. Samuel Johnson had set the example by omitting the word from *A Dictionary of the English Language* (1755),[12] as Marchant and Gordon did in *A New Complete English Dictionary* (1760),[13] taking, as they wrote, "especial care to exclude all those Terms that carry any Indecency in their Meaning, or have the least Tendency to corrupt the Minds of Youth." In 1890 the word appeared in Farmer and Henley's *Slang and Its Analogues Past and Present*,[14] apparently on the simple ground that it could not possibly be omitted from such an unordinary dictionary. But no such considerations occurred to the editors of the abridged one-volume edition of Farmer and Henley that appeared in 1905. In this edition all references to the four-letter words are omitted.

The editors of the greatest of all English dictionaries, the *Oxford English Dictionary*, issued between the years 1884 and 1928, declined to have anything to do with the four-letter words.[15] When the Supplement was published in 1933, the taboo still held fast, as it does to the present day in all dictionaries published by the Oxford University Press.

Contemporary dictionary makers, yielding to established prejudice and obscurantism are still forced by the threat of economic disaster to ban the word from their pages. The third edition of *Webster's New International Dictionary*,[16] published in 1962, while including the principal four- and five-letter words, deliberately banned *the* four-letter word. The omission was defended not on lexical but on purely practical grounds. It was felt that the inclusion of the word would evoke denunciation and boycott. Since this would have imperiled the whole enterprise, it was reluctantly decided not to include the word in this latest edition. Indeed, apart from Partridge's *Slang* (1936)[17] and *Origins* (1958)[18] dictionaries, Wentworth and Flexner's *Dictionary of American Slang* (1960),[19] and Leitner and Lanen's *Dictionary of French and American Slang* (1965)[20]—the latter two having reference to American rather than to English usage—I know of no other dictionary in the English language of the twentieth century in which the word appears.

The Random House Dictionary of the English Language, published in October, 1966, omits all reference to four-letter words. In the Preface to the dictionary the editor in chief, Jess Stein, writes that it is "the function of a dictionary to provide the user with an exact record of the language he sees and hears." However, the dictionary stops short of providing "an exact record" of the four-letter words the seeker after knowledge sometimes sees in print and not infrequently hears. Before deciding to omit the offensive words from the dictionary, Stein made tests with a group of editorial workers and with a meeting of sales managers. He found that almost everyone in the editorial group contended that the "bad" words should be included, but he observed that no one actually used the words during the discussion of the subject.

According to a report in *The New York Times* for September 16, 1966, Stein said, "When I uttered the words, there was a shuffling of feet, and a wave of embarrassment went through the room. That convinced me the words did not belong in the dictionary, although I'm sure I'll be attacked as a prude for the decision."

The "residual prudishness" of which Mario Pei complained when reviewing the Merriam-Webster dictionary in 1961 will not be quickly dissipated, despite the frequency with which such "offensive words" now appear in contemporary literature and in the speech of educated people. The reader who seeks for enlightenment on the transitive verb for the most transitive of human actions will look in vain for it in the latest dictionaries of the English language. Mrs. Grundy is still, alas, with us, and with mittened hands folded over her "chest" and out of her bleary eye peers over the shoulders of our dictionary makers to make sure that they exclude from their pages any word that might be considered offensive, even though it may be among the most frequently used in the language.

It was not until 1936 that Eric Partridge took the plunge and put the word into his magnificent *Dictionary of Slang and Unconventional English*—not without the expected repercussions. There were protests to the police, school authorities, and libraries, with the result that to this day the book cannot be obtained in many libraries, and in some is kept under lock and key and may be looked at only after special application! But even in 1936 Partridge was not allowed to print either of the two words in full. Progress, however, had been made; three of the four letters were allowed, an asterisk being substituted for the vowel. This was much better than three asterisks preceded by the first letter. But trouble soon developed. Mrs. Grundy was not to be satisfied with so brief a miniskirt as a single asterisk. Hence, with the publication in 1958 of Partridge's *Origins: A Short Etymological Dictionary of Modern English*, the miniskirt had to be lengthened to two asterisks for each word. They are, as Partridge wrote in 1958, "the only two Standard English words that, outside official reports and learned papers, still cannot be printed in full anywhere within the British Commonwealth of Nations."

Even Partridge confesses, in his Preface to a *Dictionary of Slang* (1936), that in the matter of "unpleasant terms" his rule has been "to deal with them as briefly, as astringently, as aseptically as was consistent with clarity and adequacy; in a few instances, I had to force myself to overcome an instinctive repugnance." For these occasions Partridge begs the indulgence of his readers. Burges Johnson in his *Lost Art of Profanity* (1948) omits any discussion of the four-letter words on the ground of a natural squeamishness.[21] Most other evaders of the words have considered any explanation for doing so an act of abject supererogation and, in silent league with their readers, have offered none at all. But as Allen Walker Read has said, "These words are definitely a part of the English vocabulary, no matter how puritans may deplore them or dictionaries ignore them."[22]

Many of us have been so powerfully conditioned against four-letter words that upon encountering them we tend to react with something close to a feeling of physical revulsion. The forbidden words are so repugnant that it is not surprising that evasive tactics should be resorted to upon any threat of their imminence. For example, Burges Johnson in his book on profanity tells us that he is not really quite fair to himself when he attributes the failure to print the four-letter words to a lack of courage. He has not printed the words, he says, because suggestion is always more intriguing than complete revelation, and because he owes the reader who may object to such words a degree of courtesy! But, surely, a reader who purchases a book on profanity is hardly likely to be intimidated by the words he is expecting to find there. Johnson finally acknowledges the true reason for excluding the words from his engaging book. "I do not," he writes, "see myself as a crusader engaged upon breaking . . . down" the taboos against such words. "They will fade of themselves," he sagely concludes, "as civilization advances."[23]

How, one cannot help wondering, did Johnson believe "civilization advances"? By snuffing the candle and drawing the sheet? Whatever remains of the taboos that once made it impossible for scholars of an earlier day to discuss the four-letter words in print, they have crumbled to such an extent that it is today possible to consider such words as soberly and seriously as one would any ordinary word.

"So you have been looking for them, Madam?" was Dr. Johnson's splendid interrogatory rejoinder to the lady who congratulated him upon omitting all improper words from his dictionary. Word watchers, word chasers, and word lookers will find the "improper" words here.

⟮ Fuck

What is the etymological origin of this copulative word? No one knows. It should not, however, constitute an insoluble problem. No one seems to have been beguiled enough into undertaking the necessary research. The Latin verb *futuo, futuere* (to copulate) may well be the ancestors of the Standard English word, as may the German *ficken* (to strike, hence, to copulate). The combination of the German and Latin words, the vocalism of the one with the consonantism of the other, would yield *fuck*. The Greek φυτεύω and French *foutre*, both meaning to have sexual connection, almost certainly have contributed to the ancestry of the word. The verb and noun *fuck* and the adjective *fucking* first appear in print at the commencement of the sixteenth century in a poem published about 1503 by the Scottish poet and onetime

Franciscan friar William Dunbar, "Ane Brash of Wowing" ("A Bout of Wooing"). The last four lines of the poem read:

> He clappit fast, he kist, and chukkit,
> As with the glaikis* he wer ouirgane;*   *Feeling. *Overcome.
> Yit be his feirris* he wald have fukkit;   *Manner.
> Ye brek my hart, my bony ane!

About 1555 Sir David Lindsay, usher to King James V of Scotland, reproving the king's licentious mode of life, in a poem entitled "The Answer quhilk Schir Dauid Lindesay," wrote:

> For, lyke ane boisterous Bull, he rin* and ryde   *Run.
> Royatouslie lyke and rude Rubeatour,*   *Libertine.
> Ay fukkand lyke and furious Fornicatour.

In the same period Alexander Scott, in "Ane Ballat maid to the Derisioun and Scorne of wantoun Women," wrote:

> Fairweill with chestetie
> Fra* wenchis fall to chucking,*   *When. *Fondling.
> Their followis thingis three
> To gar* thame ga in gucking*   *Cause. *Fooling.
> Brasing,* graping,* and plucking;*   *Embracing. *Feeling. *Pulling about.
> Thir* foure the suth* to sane?*   *These. *Truth. *Say.
> Enforsis thame to fucking.

There are a good many other poems of the period in which the word is uninhibitedly used. The Scots seem to have been particularly free with this handy word, and as a people noted for their frugality they had clearly sought not to waste many words where one would do. The word occurs frequently in Scottish folk songs and was much in use by Burns.[24]

In the latter half of the seventeenth century the Earl of Rochester unashamedly made play with the word, but he, as in so many other ways, was the exception; for by the end of the third quarter of the sixteenth century the word had ceased to appear in print, except in the clandestine literature, not making its serious reappearance in that medium till the second quarter of the twentieth century.

The most redoubtable citadels of respectability were occasionally breached by a member of the glorious race of compositors. Readers of *The Times* (London) on January 13, 1882, could scarcely have believed their eyes when they came upon the fol-

lowing passage in the report of a speech delivered by the Attorney
General, Sir William Harcourt:

I saw in a Tory journal the other day a note of alarm, in which they
said, "Why, if a tenant-farmer is elected for the North Riding of Yorkshire the farmers will be a political power who will have to be reckoned
with." The speaker then said he felt inclined for a bit of fucking. I think
that is very likely. (*Laughter*).

The shock at Printing House Square was so great that it took
four whole days before the editors could bring themselves to
make reference to the regrettable incident, to print an apology,
and to add:

No pains have been spared by the management of this journal to discover the author of a gross outrage committed by the interpolation of
a line in the speech by Sir William Harcourt reported in our issue of
Monday last. This malicious fabrication was surreptitiously introduced
before the paper went to press. The matter is now under legal investigation, and it is to be hoped that the perpetrator of the outrage will be
brought to punishment.

Whether the villain was ever discovered is unknown. It is to
be hoped that he was not. Perhaps it was this selfsame sprite or
someone else inspired by his example who, in June of the same
year, struck again. This time it was in an advertisement for a
book, which read as follows:

Every-day Life in our Public Schools. Sketched by Head Scholars.
With a Glossary of Some Words used by Henry Irving in his disquisition
upon fucking, which is in Common Use in those Schools . . . *Church
Times.*—"A capital book for boys."—"The book will make an acceptable
present."

The Times seems never to have recovered from these two blows,
even though incidents of a similar kind have since been successfully avoided. When the law, in 1960, finally gave its sanction to
the word as Standard English, *The Times* alone demurred. The
Old Lady of Fleet Street and Mrs. Grundy stood fast together.

The heyday of the word in its various forms was the period
of World War I, a period during which to the British Tommy it
was the only term that permitted him to express his exacerbated
feelings. I well remember sometime during 1916 in London hearing one such soldier, in full battle dress, just back from the western

front, and still carrying the mud of the trenches on his boots and puttees, colorfully recounting the pleasures of his journey back to "Blighty." Until that moment I had no idea that one word could be so frequently used in a single sentence. But this heroic creature, short though he was of stature, managed to infuse his talk with so many *fuckings*, I had never heard the like before, nor have I since. It was a chronic condition among British soldiers of every description, though limited largely to the ranks. As Brophy and Partridge wrote in *Songs and Slang of the British Soldier, 1914–1918*, the word was

so common indeed in its adjectival form that after a short time the ear refused to acknowledge it and took in only the noun to which it is attached. Dean Inge recently remarked of *bloody* as used by working men that it means nothing, it is simply a warning that a noun is coming. So with the soldier's use of this sexual word. From being an intensive to express strong emotion it became a merely conventional excrescence. By adding -ing and -ing well, an adjective and an adverb were formed and thrown into every sentence. Thus if a sergeant said, "Get your ——ing rifles!" it was understood as a matter of routine. But if he said, "Get your rifles!" there was an immediate implication of urgency and danger.[25]

T. E. Lawrence, in *Revolt in the Desert* (1927),[26] tells a lovely story. Lawrence had been having difficulty with the water transport people in Cairo. "I got through again to the Inland Water Transport and talked like Chrysostom. It had no effect, so I became vivid, when friendly northern accents from the military exchange floated down the line, 'Its no bluidy good, sir, talking to the fookin water boogers.'" There could have been no balm more comforting than those sympathetic Yorkshire accents uttering the right words at exactly the right time.

It was, however, the rare exception for such words to appear in print so soon after World War I. Richard Aldington, in the prefatory note to his magnificent novel *Death of A Hero* (1929), tells how, at the request of his publishers, he removed what they considered to be objectionable words, inserting asterisks where the excisions had been made.[27]

During the late 1950s legal actions brought by the public prosecutor under the Obscenity Act made it quite evident that the basis of these actions had been the violent antagonism provoked by the four-letter words, and particularly *the* four-letter word. In 1959 Grove Press of New York published an unexpurgated edition of D. H. Lawrence's *Lady Chatterley's Lover.* On June 11, 1959, the Postmaster General, Arthur E. Summerfield, refused the book passage through the United States mails on the ground of obscenity. He also banned circulars advertising the book. The publisher brought action seeking to restrain the Post Office Department from enforcing this decision and asking for a decision that the book was not obscene within the meaning of the statute barring obscene matter from the mails, or if it were that the statute was unconstitutional as violating guarantees of the First and Fifth Amendments.

On July 21, 1959, federal Judge Frederick van Pelt Bryan handed down a decision in favor of the publishers and of the book. "Four-letter Anglo-Saxon words," wrote the judge in his decision, "are used with some frequency . . . this language understandably will shock the sensitive minded. Be that as it may . . . the language which shocks, except in a rare instance or two, is not inconsistent with character, situation or theme."[28] Upon appeal the decision of the lower court was unanimously upheld by the Second Circuit Court of Appeals in New York on March 25, 1960.

Encouraged by the American decision, in England Penguin Books, by prior arrangement with the Attorney General, "published" the unexpurgated version of *Lady Chatterley's Lover* by handing over a number of copies to the police. Some difficulty had been encountered in finding a printer willing to print the text, but this was finally overcome. Publication was announced for August 25, 1960. On August 19, 1960, the Public Prosecutor then applied for a summons against the publishers. The publishers elected to be tried at the Central Criminal Court, the Old Bailey. The trial began on October 21, 1960, and after a trial lasting five days, on November 2, 1960, the jury returned with a verdict of "not guilty." *Lady Chatterley's Lover* at long last was published in England exactly as Lawrence had written it. The press received the verdict with general approval—always, of course, excepting *The Times. The Guardian* (November 4) and *The Observer* (November 6) went so far as to print the no longer guilty word in all its four letters and without a single asterisk or eliminative dash. This greatly upset Sir Charles Taylor, who, in an article in that most proper newspaper *The News of the World* (November 13, 1960), expressed himself entirely in favor of the morals of *The News of the World* as contrasted with those represented by Lawrence's book. Later, the Press Council, a body supposed to exercise some influence upon the conduct of the press, felt obliged to rebuke the *Spectator, The Guardian,* and *The Observer* for their objectionable and unnecessary printing of the offending words (*The Observer,* February 19, 1961).

But the four-letter word was free, no longer condemned to pursue a fugitive existence. In the 1960s it began to be freely printed in books in the full panoplied glory of all its letters four.

However, the printed word is one thing and the spoken word quite another. The reader who is able to accept the word *fuck* in a novel or in some other work in print may react quite differently when he hears the word. And what we are here concerned with is not so much the printed as the spoken word. Since what is printed often affects what later comes to be uttered, and since attitudes toward forbidden words are often best understood from what is recorded of them, being careful to avoid confusing matters of obscenity with those of swearing, it is very necessary to refer to the printed word.

While the prohibition has been significantly relaxed for the printed word, it has not been equally relaxed for the spoken word. Anyone choosing to utter *the* word in polite society is, however, not quite as likely to find himself as permanently consigned to Coventry, as he would have been in earlier years. In 1965 Kenneth Tynan, Director of the National Theatre, in a television interview on the BBC used the forbidden word quite casually. It was a brave thing to do. The expected barking of the dogs of St. Ernulphus was widely heard throughout the land, but gratifyingly Tynan remained unmoved—and triumphant. As becomes a great pioneer, his stock has considerably risen in the world.

⟨ *The Forms of* Fuck

With the exception of the mid-eighteenth century *fuck-beggar,* an impotent man whom only a beggar woman would allow near her; *fuck-finger* or *finger-fucker,* a female masturbator; and *fuck-fist,* a male masturbator, the forms of *fuck* are mostly nineteenth–twentieth century inventions.

Fuck (it), a low expletive, correctly described by Partridge as "Very gen. among those for whom delicacy and aesthetics mean little—or rather nothing."[29]

Fuck off, get out, go, depart, make off. *Fuck you Jack, I'm all right*, a catchphrase directed at callousness or indifference, said to be of nautical origin, popular among military personnel in World War I and later abbreviated to "I'm all right Jack." *Fuckable*, sexually desirable, nubile. *Fucked-up and far from home*, in the depths of misery, a British military catchphrase, *circa* 1898. *Fucker*, chap, fellow, man, lover. *Fucking*, an intensive as adjective; the sexual act, as a noun. *Fuckish*, ready for copulation. *Fucksome*, sexually desirable. *Fuck-pig*, an unpleasant man. *Fuck up*, to make a mess of, as in *Snafu*, Situation normal, all fucked-up. *Fuckster, fuckstress*, a notable performer or an addict to the sexual act. To *get fucked* or *to get a fucking*, to be cheated or betrayed. *To fuck around* or *to fuck the dog*, to waste time, loaf or idle. *To fuck one's way out*, to cheat or defraud.

The word *motherfucker* first appears in print in the 1960s. In speech it is not much older. It would seem to be an American Negro invention, and in the mid-1960s it had just reached other parts of the English-speaking world. In a society in which the image of the mother is idealized and incest is a strong prohibition, the word is capable of producing a variety of pyrotechnical effects. Among American Negroes, to whom the word's usage is still largely limited, the word is constantly employed as an intensive, as "This motherfucking thing won't fucking work." It is also employed as a noun. It may be used as a pejorative or as an honorific. A flattering appellation is that a man is a "mean motherfucker" or a "tough motherfucker," but, as Abrahams tells us, "to call him just a 'motherfucker' is to invite reprisal."[30] As Abrahams points out in his fascinating book, *Deep Down in the Jungle* (1964), the success of this most frequently used obscenity among Negroes is inherent in the ambivalently satisfying capacities of the word itself, which makes it at once usable as curse, expletive, epithet, and intensive. The mother is the most powerful figure among the families in which such powerful words flourish, so that if one desires to play the role of a mother defier, a rebel, an antifeminist, in such a context *motherfucker* becomes an honorific conferring an accolade upon the speaker and upon whomever he is addressing. The emotional and biological bonds one bears to one's mother makes the accusation insulting, activating the taboo against incest and equally strong oedipal wishes. Hence, when used in the personal sense strongly antagonistic and conflicting emotions are activated, often provoking equally violent reactions. As Abrahams writes, "it is especially significant . . . that in this matrifocallyreared group with their violent attraction-rejection of mother-woman's world that the most frequent obscenity should be so obviously and overtly directed at mother."

Renatus Hartogs, a psychiatrist who has had much experience with juvenile delinquents in New York, tells us that the emotional dread surrounding the term *motherfucker* is so strong that "it is usually pronounced in its entirety only by persons relatively exempt from its effects. Men in whom Oedipal fears predominate usually say only 'your mother' (pronounced 'ya mudder') when invoking the spell (or, in Spanish, *'su madre'*). The meaning, however, is clearly understood."

Hartogs also tells us that the term is beginning to find its way into the middle classes, where the procession of temporary fathers, in the legalized form of serial monogamy, gives rise to much the same conflicts as occur in the males of the Negro family.[31]

It may be predicted that this Negro invention will spread quite rapidly to a great part of the English-speaking world.

As an adjectival modifier *fucking*, or in its other forms, *fuckin* or *fucken*, was the most often employed of the small arms of the servicemen of World Wars I and II. And if we are to judge from such books as Norman Mailer's novel *The Naked and the Dead*, the American GI outdid his English counterpart prodigiously in the use of this word. For the soldier, far from home and "all fouled up," it was an incomparable benison to have such an expletive at his command, all the more so since he had so very little else at his command.[32]

As an adjective, the word, among its customary users, is scarcely a swearword. It represents a statement of quality and color about the noun that is to follow. Its adjectival use is so much the normal thing that the word is employed much more frequently for other purposes than to refer to the act for which it is the name. So far has it departed from its original meaning and use that it will be employed in every other way than to describe the sexual act. For this, words like *screw, knock, lay, sleep,* and the 1,200 other English synonyms that have been recorded will be engaged.[33] Wayland Young (Lord Kennet) in his book *Eros Denied* (1965)[34] makes the same point, and by way of illustration quotes the following "rigmarole," which he thinks is possibly of Australian origin: "I was walking along on this fucking fine morning, fucking sun fucking shining away, little country fucking lane, and I meets up with this fucking girl. Fucking lovely she was, so we gets into fuckingconversation and I takes her over a fucking gate into a fucking field and we has sexual intercourse."

Another young man, when he could not make the engine of his car work, explained that "the fucking fuck won't fuck," which certainly put all that needed to be said into a minimum number of words.

In *fuckingconversation* we observe once more the process of infixing. Other examples are *irrefuckinsponsible*, *infuckinpossible*, *unfuckinconscious*, and *unfuckinsociable*. And as Sagarin points out, in each instance it is possible that the *e* rather than the *i* following the *k* more closely approximates the actual pronunciation of the word.[35]

Of all the euphemisms or circumlocutions used for the verb *to copulate* the commonest and most respectable is "to sleep with," or "to make love," usages that have not infrequently given rise to considerable confusion. But here we are clearly in the realm of the obscene and not of that of swearing at all. We need pause here only to remark that Wayland Young has most effectively dealt with the nonsense of such euphemisms and has cogently made the point that there really is no substitute for the word *fuck*, which clearly and unequivocally says what it means, and therefore Young employs it throughout his book. It is the first serious work published in the modern period to do so.

❮［ *Cunt*

As a swearword *cunt* does not appear to have an origin more ancient than the nineteenth century, although as a Standard English word for the female pudenda it is of considerable antiquity, dating from Middle English times. Chaucer, in 1387, spelled the word *queynte* or *queinte*, as in *The Miller's Tale*. Nicholas wooed Alison

> And prively he caughte hire by the queynte.[36]

Our interest here is not in the permissible but in the nonpermissible use of the word. From the fifteenth century to the present day the word was avoided in written and polite spoken English. From the beginning of the eighteenth century to 1960, except in the reprinting of old classics, the word was held to be obscene when printed in full.

As a pejorative description of a fool, a stupid person, the word was widely used during the first decade of the twentieth century and enjoyed considerable popularity among the fighting forces during World War I. While retaining this sense it also shifted in meaning to be applied pejoratively to material objects, and in yet a third sense came to be applied in a spirit of amiability to old friends, as in "How are you, you old cunt?"

Does a term that continues to be used as a swearword cease to be a swearword when it is used as an honorific? It does not. The swearword's intensity, its energy charge, is borrowed for the occasion to convey to the other the depth as well as the kind of feeling one has for him. The other usually gets the message without the slightest misunderstanding.

⟪ Cock

Cock, referring to the penis, has not been used as a swearword itself, but in a combined form such as cocksucker, meaning a toady, is of late nineteenth-century vintage. Sagarin, writing in 1962, says that within the course of an hour he heard a group of men employ the term 161 times. The term is often used as a pejorative of disapproval.

The synonym of cock, namely prick, is first recorded in 1598 in R.D.'s Hypnerotomachia, but is of undoubtedly much earlier spoken currency. Prick as a pejorative swearword has done service for cock and also as a term of contempt for a male.

⟪ Arse

Until about 1660 arse was Standard English for buttocks; thereafter it became a vulgarism. When, in 1930, Frederic Manning insisted on having the word printed in full in his war novel Her Privates We, he was considered very daring.

A silly or a foolish or a stupid man is an arse, however qualified. In America the word is misspelled ass; and even though one doesn't own one, one may be threatened with a kick in the "ass." The confusion is widespread, as is noted in an exegetical limerick:

There was a young woman named Glass
Who had a most beautiful ass,
Not round and pink
As you might think,
But gray, and had ears, and ate grass.

On February 24, 1905, a reviewer in *The Times Literary Supplement*, commenting on Oscar Wilde's *De Profundis* wrote: "It is impossible, except very occasionally, to look upon his testament as more than a literary feat. Not so, we find ourselves saying, are souls laid bare."

Arse is the mildest of the four-letter words and has enjoyed a certain permissiveness in polite conversation for many years.

❡ *Shit*

Shit as feces or excrement was Standard English from the sixteenth to the early nineteenth century. During the latter period the word in both its forms, *shit* and *shite*, became a vulgarism. The word was used as a term of contempt for a man, rarely for a woman. As an expletive the term is of nineteenth-century origin, possibly a little earlier.

The variant forms are all nineteenth century in origin, as *shit-arse*, a contemptible person; *shitbag*, one full of wind, an unpleasant person; *shitpot*, a worthless humbug or sneak. As an expletive in response to frustration, disgust, or dismay, *shit* grew to increasing popularity among both sexes in the 1960s.

❡ *Piss*

As urine or to urinate *piss* from the middle of the thirteenth to the middle of the eighteenth century was Standard English. The word became a vulgarism from about 1760, although it occurs as a vulgar expletive in Etherege's *The Man of Mode* (1676). The exclamation was, in fact, quite popular during the Restoration.

Piss-off, as an imperative injunction to its object to remove himself immediately, is of nineteenth-century vintage and is popular during the twentieth century. To be *pissed-off*, that is, to be disabused, disenchanted, let down, annoyed, is of mid-twentieth-century origin. *Shit, piss and corruption!* is an early twentieth-century exclamation that with unhurried deliberation expresses a feeling of utter dismay. It bears a close relation to its kindred *Hell, fire, rape and sodomy!* a nineteenth-century contribution.

((*Fart*

Glossed as to break wind, *fart* was from the thirteenth to the middle of the eighteenth century a Standard English word. By the middle of the seventeenth century it had been brought into service as a term of contempt for a worthless person, as *A silly fart*. A *fartsucker*, now obsolete, was in use in the late nineteenth and early twentieth century for a parasite.

What has been described as the finest bit of scatological pornography in the language, Mark Twain's *1601—A Conversation At the Social Fireside as it Was in the Time of the Tudors*, written in the 1870s, has never been permitted open publication because its theme is a fart at the court of Queen Bess, "the fellow to which the Queen had admiringly not heard the like before." The work seems to have been written for Twain's friend, the Reverend Dr. Joseph H. Twichell, whom we have already encountered in an earlier chapter. *1601*, pursuing its clandestine existence, has been published throughout the English-speaking world and even in translation, in innumerable editions—but never legitimately. Thus do little minds drive away the work of their betters.

Four-letter-word swearing was largely limited to the lower classes until after World War II, when it was gradually and selectively adopted by some of the more sophisticated of both sexes. It is no longer true to say that contemporary men and women swear because of any limitation in vocabulary—"He knew not what to say, and so he swore." On the other hand, it is in order to enlarge and render more colorful their vocabulary that many persons of education resort to the formerly forbidden words. The truth is that with the breakdown of class barriers, the growth of the principle of equality, and the relaxation of inhibitions, the educated classes have discovered a new wealth of language in the forbidden words, and especially in the four-letter words. These words have been endowed with a new elegance, and in the star-studded language of a gentlewoman are worn like a diadem upon her brow. They blossom like flowers in the verbal spring of a man of character.

Prudery has lost all the skirmishes and most of the battles in the struggle toward the liberation of the human spirit, and in speech this is reflected in a freer and more disciplined use of words formerly considered obscene. The old standards of propriety and good taste have, with the rust of time, yielded to those of a newer generation. Their view of the human condition is rather more liberating than that of the Victorian relicts who have presided as arbiters over these matters for more than a century.

As Allen Walker Read wrote in 1935:

That anyone should pass up well-established words of the language and have recourse to the Latin *defecate, urinate,* and *have sexual intercourse,* is indicative of grave mental unhealth.

The stigma on the obscene words was caused in the first place by unhealthy attitudes towards the bodily functions; but at the present time the stigma is a principal instrument for the perpetuating of the attitudes. If the stigma can be removed, a source of infection will thus be eradicated.[37]

Similar sentiments were expressed by J. Donald Adams, who wrote:

There are things to be said in favor of even the coarsest of the four-letter words. They are forthright and vigorous, and for that reason preferable to the more ponderous and somehow less direct Latinities which, in polite usage, supplanted them. What more than a sort of aseptic merit can be urged in support of *copulate, urinate, defecate, vagina,* and even though Anglo-Saxon, break wind?[38]

Who would disagree?

In November, 1965, Pertinax, the regular columnist of the *British Medical Journal,* commenting on Adams' statement pointed out that even in a journal like the *British Medical Journal* the "aseptic" words can be as safely employed as they are in the lay press, but not the short and expressive four-letter equivalents of the Anglo-Saxons. Making all allowances for propriety and good taste Pertinax concluded that "If I had to cast my vote for the short word or the long one, for the Anglo-Saxon (or Old Frisian) against the Latin, I would vote for the former."[39] Editorializing on this in the *Journal of the American Medical Association* in March, 1966, the writer opines that few would take kindly to a verbal revolution in which four-letter words were substituted for the conventional ones on laboratory requisitions or in the dialogue between physician and patient.[40]

One wonders. The fact seems to be that where, as among the classes in which such terms are regarded as Standard English, physicians use such words, they manage to communicate with their patients rather more effectively than those who do not.[41] The manner in which laboratory technicians might react upon seeing such terms on a requisition cannot be predicted with certainty. It may, however, be suspected that it would be with a great deal less trauma than the writer in the *Journal of the American Medical Association* supposes. The fact that such matters can be discussed at all in such organs of respectability as the British and American medical journals testifies to the distance that has been traveled toward the rehabilitation of the four-letter words.

The significance of the trend for the future of four-letter words is unpromising. It has been the usual experience that with the relaxation of the taboos and the appearance of forbidden words in print, it is not long before they lose their power to frighten and annoy and are employed more openly in speech. It is probable that this will happen with the four-letter words, for as soon as these words again become acceptable Standard English, the power that they enjoyed during their pariah period will gradually become attenuated, and, thus weakened, the four-letter words may disappear entirely from the swearer's vocabulary and vanish into husks and the formless ruin of oblivion.

CHAPTER SIXTEEN

Olla–Podrida

Nay, let me alone for swearing.
WILLIAM SHAKESPEARE, *Twelfth Night*, III, iv, 1601

WISE men, and not infrequently wise women, have recognized that swearing is the art of achieving eloquence with an economy of words. This or something like it is probably what Dr. Johnson had in mind when he remarked, "I like a good swearer." He has enjoyed much company in his inclination for the accomplished swearer, though Dr. Johnson was not himself given to the use of crimson words. Purple language, whether edged with brimstone or not, is no longer a mark of Cain distinguishing the lower orders of men at the nethermost fringes of society, from their betters. The abstract inconsideration of good intentions leads only too often to hypocrisy, and the silliness of which the pejoratively good are capable, have often acted like so many bunions designed to impede the pilgrim's progress toward the enrichment of the language and their own ability to explain themselves. Theirs has been the loss, for their recurrent and persistent attempts to interfere, no less, with the growth and development of the common tongue has served only to reinforce the power of the forbidden expressions and to perpetuate many that would otherwise have fallen by the way. The obsessive inadvertence of so many would-be reformers is but a token of their compulsive enslavement to unrealistic ideals and destructive certainties. These demonologists who have sought to exorcise the spirit of the language and cleanse it of what they deemed unclean have often behaved like fiends. In the name of the law they have hung, drawn, quartered and otherwise abused their victims. In fifteenth-century France, for example, swearers and blasphemers had a lip slit, and if they persisted they might have their tongues removed.

At the very least, well into the twentieth century, civilized Europe imposed graduated series of fines upon swearers and otherwise intimidated them—ignoring that fundamental right of civilized life, that every man should enjoy the freedom to speak as he chooses and that others shall enjoy the equal right to think what they will of his speech. Freedom does not embrace the right to abuse the freedom of others or to be deliberately offensive, and this holds for the swearer as well as for the nonswearer. A gentleman, as Dr. Johnson said, refrains.

To the inarticulateness of nature man has added a new dimension, speech. It is speech that makes man human, that makes the unintelligibility of the universe intelligible and serves to put man into contact with his fellow man. As Edward Hyams, in a charming essay, "Demotic English," put it, "As my own speech is naturally 'foul,' I have to remember self-consciously, not to speak in a certain mess-deck, machine-shop, plough-tail way when I am among persons of both sexes in the lower-middle to upper classes."[1] The civilized man will no more think of using improper language in the presence of others who may find it objectionable than he will engage in any other kind of unfitting conduct. Yet indecorous behavior, in various forms, is still received with greater tolerance than the inappropriate word, so much greater is the power of the word than the act.

Swearing is itself a displacement activity, but it is one that is negatively sanctioned in Western societies and for this reason achieves an additional ascendancy and power it would otherwise lack. In this manner words develop an omnipotence that often serves the dual function of achieving the discharge and relief of sexual pressures and the expression of contempt for conventional taboos. In this way they act both as a catharsis and as an expression of resentment or protest against the constraints of society. Swearing of this kind, therefore, performs a most useful function: it disposes of a great deal of aggressive energy that might otherwise have been devoted to more damaging purposes. But we have already dealt with this aspect of the subject in an earlier chapter. Malinowski, in discussing swearing among the Trobriand Islanders, confirms our views by both his examples and the conclusion he draws from them, namely, that "one of the main forces of abuse lies in the relation between the reality and plausibility of a desire or action and its conventional repressions."[2] Malinowski points out that that the incestuous type of swearing, in which the individual addressed is told to have sex with a forbidden relative, usually the mother, was in Europe the specialty of Slavic peoples, among whom the Russians easily took the lead, with their many combinations of *Yob twayu mat* (Have sex with thy mother). In the Trobriand Islands similar forms of swearing occurred. The Trobrianders' three incestuous expressions were: *Kwoy inam* (Cohabit with thy mother), *Kwoy lumata* (Cohabit with thy sister), and *Kwoy um' kwava* (Cohabit with thy wife).

As Malinowski remarks, the combination of these three expressions is curious, for the most lawful and at once the most illicit types of sex are used for the same purpose of being offensive and inflicting pain. But even more curious is the gradation in intensity of the three expressions. Being invited to indulge in maternal incest is considered rather a mild piece of chaffing or a joke, as one might say, "Oh, go to Jericho." But to be enjoined to commit incest with a sister is most serious and is used only when one is really angry. The most serious insult of all, however, was the command to have sex with one's wife. Malinowski heard this expression used only twice, and he learned of its existence only after he had been long in the Trobriands. Indeed, no native would pronounce it other than in a whisper or consent to make any jokes about it.

What is the psychology of this gradation? It is evident that from our own standpoint there is no distinct relation to the enormity or unpleasantness of the act enjoined upon the swearer's object. What then, is the explanation? It lies in the differences in the attitudes of the Trobrianders toward their relatives. The development of attitudes toward mother and sister are such, as well as to sexual life generally, as to make maternal incestuous desires almost absent, while the taboo against the sister is rigid, and the inclination to break it is much more real. But in the case of a man's wife reference is made to the plausibility and reality of the act, together with the feeling of shame, anger, and social humiliation experienced when the barriers of etiquette are broken down and the naked reality brought to light.

For the sexual intimacy between husband and wife is masked by a most rigid etiquette, not so strict of course as that between brother and sister, but directly aiming at the elimination of any suggestive modes of behaviour. Sexual jokes and indecencies must not be pronounced in the company of the two consorts. And to drag out the personal, direct sexuality of the relation in coarse language is a mortal offense to the sensitiveness of Trobrianders."[3]

It is not so much the power of the negative sanction as the force of the Trobriander's fierce anxiety to keep his conjugal sexual life a matter of the utmost privacy that renders the imperative to have sex with his wife a mortal insult. Malinowski quotes a case of fratricide that was in part due to the use of this expression. In Western societies a similar admonition to have sex with his wife might affront a Don Juan as a reflection upon his virility, but it would scarcely produce a laugh in others. On the other hand, incest, especially with one's mother, is considered so heinous an offense and the thought of it is so anxiety-producing in most men that anyone sworn at in such terms is likely to regard the epithet as a fighting matter. The epithet used derives its strength not so much from the respect in which men in Western societies hold their mothers, but from the anxieties that are associated with maternal incest and constellate about the Oedipus motif.

Imputations reflecting upon the chastity of one's sister are peculiarly offensive to men of the Western world, although not limited to that world, but swearing, drawing upon this resource is rather scanty. I cannot agree with Robert Graves that the chastity of a sister or daughter has become a far more serious consideration than the faithfulness of a wife; and although Graves made the statement in 1927, I believe it was as unsound then, and earlier, as it is today. This may perhaps be confirmed by the story about the orator in the Albert Hall in London in 1915, attempting to persuade Englishmen of their duty to join the army. "And what," he asked rhetorically, "would you do if a Hun broke into your home and attempted to rape your sister?" He paused for effect. Whereupon a cockney voice shot down from the "gods," "I'd ask me bloomin sister!"

Graves recounts the story of the master of a Thames tug who, having fouled a pleasure boat and broken one of the oarsman's oars, was remonstrated with by the aggrieved party for having thus disabled him. "Oh, I did, did I, Charley? And talking of oars, 'ows your sister?" Now the point to this story is that the oarsman was undoubtedly a young man; there would have been no point to making any reference to his wife, for he almost certainly had none, but almost as certainly he would have a sister, and hence the reference to that relative.

Graves notes that there is a great opportunity for ethnological research in swearing of this sort. He is quite right, but unfortunately ethnologists have neglected to follow his lead, for hardly a reference to the subject is to be found in any of their works.

In India, in Urdu, Swahili, and Arabic the common expletive *brother-in-law* is an unforgivable insult carrying the implication that the swearer has had intercourse with the victim's sister. Such an expletive would not be as mortally wounding to a Westerner.

Reference to the sexual deviations of a man's parents is, in Western societies, a grave insult. Terming a man a *bastard* succinctly makes the point. To be born out of wedlock was until recently considered a disgrace so enormous that nothing but the letters patent of nobility conferred upon the bastard could remove the stigma from him. Such a one could thus be transformed into a "natural son." In this manner were created many of the founders of the noble families of England, to the splendors of which land they have contributed not a little. Years ago—in fact, not so long ago, and for all I know it may still exist—an office of the English Civil Service was devoted to "The Escheated Estates of Intestate Bastards." Among the governing classes of England bastards were of quite another race from that of other classes of men, and tolerance for bastards was far greater among the governing classes than in the middle and lower classes. This reflected more relaxed and unanxious attitudes toward sex than those that prevailed among the subordinate classes. Hence, among the upper classes one would no more refer to a bastard in the pejorative than one would to a mistress of the king. It would be much more discreditable to the object of such a barb to refer to him euphemistically as the uncertificated son of an unlicensed mother. *That* would put the creature exactly where he belonged—outside the pale.

Our concern here is not with the uses of the word *bastard*, interesting as they may be, as with the word as an example of a potent swearword that depends upon its force because it refers to the sexual irregularities of the target's progenitors and his own displaced and equivocal status. For these reasons it is by many people considered one of the worst swearwords in the English language, for it reflects not only upon the object of it but upon his mother and father—and that is very offensive, indeed. But by that peculiar evolution that such intensives follow, the word has come to be employed in all sorts of situations, even as a term of affection or admiration. A cockney will greet an old friend with the words "Well, 'ow've ya been, ya old bastard?" or describe a highly competent performer as "A bastard with the girls—just slays 'em" or "We don't 'ave to worry about 'im, 'es a proper bastard 'e is." And finally, in an expression of sympathy, he may say, "The poor bastard, 'e never 'ad a chance." A bad idea may be referred to as "a bastard idea," and the forms "I'll bastardwell show 'im" and "'E's up to some bastardry," meaning some deviltry or unpleasantness, are not uncommon.

The equivalent of *bastard* for the female is *bitch*. In its original fifteenth-century meaning, the word referred to a lewd woman, and this meaning is strongly retained today, though it has more generally come to mean an excessively unpleasant female. Here, too, the original power of the word derives from its sexual connotation, with the addition of the modern meaning as unpleasant, spiteful. The full double meaning of the word is retained in the expression *Son of a bitch* and its euphemism in contracted form, "S.O.B." Recent Presidents of the United States have on occasion been known to apply the term to newspapermen (and others) whom they failed to appreciate. So widely was this expression used by the United States army in France during World War I that, so the story goes, when an American visitor shortly after the conclusion of hostilities gave his name as Beach to a French concierge, she exclaimed, "Ah, Beach! You are the son of the great American mother! Not so?" Well, perhaps not quite so, but as the Italians would say, *Se non é vero, é ben trovato.*

Son of a gun may represent a transmogrification of *son of a bitch* and, like the latter term, according to Partridge, dates back to the early eighteenth century. Jon Bee, in his *Dictionary* (1823), gives the meaning as "A soldier's bastard," but Admiral W. H. Smyth, in *The Sailor's Word-Book* (1867), states that the term is a nautical one and that it was "originally applied to boys born afloat, when women were permitted to accompany their husbands to sea." "One admiral," he added, "declared that he literally was thus cradled, under the breast of a gun-carriage." It may well be that in the cramped conditions existing in early men-of-war the cabins were usually situated under the gun emplacements and, hence, any children born aboard . . . but this is mere speculation.

It has been suggested to me (by Peter Putnam) that the term may have originated—and he was always under the impression that it had—from the Yiddish for "thief," (*gunnif*). *Son of a gun* would therefore mean *son of a thief*. It is a plausible suggestion, but

Yiddish does not appear to have had the least influence upon English until the twentieth century.

In the eleventh canto of *Don Juan* Byron makes the very nicest application of the term.

> Besides the ministers and underlings,
> 　Who must be courteous to the accredited
> Diplomatists of rather wavering kings,
> 　Until their royal riddle's fully read,
> The very clerks,—those somewhat dirty springs
> 　Of office, or the house of office, fed
> By foul corruption into streams,—even they
> Were hardly rude enough to earn their pay!

> And insolence no doubt is what they are
> 　Employ'd for, since it is their daily labour,
> In the dear offices of peace and war;
> 　And should you doubt, pray ask of your neighbour,
> When for a passport, or some other bar
> 　To freedom, he applied (a grief and a bore),
> If he found not in this spawn of taxborn riches,
> Like lap-dogs, the least civil sons of b——s.

That was in 1824. The manners of the European flunkeys have not much changed since. One can only express regret that Byron never enjoyed the opportunity of applying for a passport or a visa in the United States. Courtesy and expedition appear to be the principles by which the issuing offices work—unlike the customs service of the United States, one of the most improvable in the world.

If anxiety is the voice of fear and often shows itself in the repressive measures taken against swearers, the proscriptions and prohibitions represent the rationalizations of anxiety.[4] Similarly, under certain conditions swearing itself may constitute a rationalization of anxiety, as, for example, among soldiers in the front lines faced with the constant threat of death or injury. It was not for want of anything better to do that soldiers, whether in the front line or not, swear prodigiously. Most soldiers are frustrated civilians —and the term "soldiers" is used here to embrace all fighting men— and in addition to their anxieties there are the accumulated frustrations incident to being a member of the armed forces, a conscript, torn away from hearth and home. This makes for the powerful accumulation of a reservoir of aggressiveness that finds easy relief in swearing.

Under the pressures and tensions of warfare swearing is not unstrangely allied to prayer. The swearer and the prayer both appeal to the gods, both in their own ways hoping with their magical words to add to their firepower and their survival. Kingsley Amis tells of an ex-World War I infantryman who once told him "that when his platoon went over the top everybody was shouting as loud as he could, about half of them praying, the rest swearing."[5]

As everyone knows there is an army way of doing things and a human way. The explanation is simple; all one need do is look up any encyclopedia on the subject and one will find intelligence listed and defined in descending order of merit as human intelligence, animal intelligence, and military intelligence. So uncomprehending are the military authorities of the value of swearing as a safety valve, an equilibrator of morale, an invaluable auxiliary arm, that every so often some brass-headed general or admiral proclaims that no member of the armed forces under his command shall henceforth swear. Thus, in May, 1933, the commander in chief of the United States navy, Admiral R. H. Leigh, under a Norfolk dateline, issued a dispatch directing all commanding officers to "take immediate steps to eradicate the undesirable habit of using profane and obscene language, and to take suitable disciplinary action in the case of each infraction reported."

This *Pinafore* propriety was, I am happy to report, greeted by most landsmen, as well as seamen, with the derision it deserved —with an outcry as great as that when Secretary of the Navy Josephus Daniels docked the sailors' grog. "With these two features of deep-water existence supprest by executive fiat, it is possible," editorialized the New York *Herald Tribune*, "that in the near future tattooing may be proscribed and the hornpipe be one with the cat-o'-nine-tails. The holystone has vanished, and so must now (presumably) the emphatic damning, blasting, infernal-consigning, and genealogical exchanges which once relieved the spirits of seafaring fellows in moments of pique." The editorialist found it difficult to believe "that the essential vocabularies of sailors can be amended in this fashion, and it is still doubtful," he wrote, "if sailors' parrots will make suitable gifts for maiden aunts. We will have to be shown before we will believe that Sailor Bill can satisfy his outraged emotions with 'oh, fudge,' or 'bother it,' or 'gracious goodness me.'"[6]

What a pity Admiral Leigh had not had the advantage of reading Mr. Chucks' animadversions on swearing in Captain Marryat's *Peter Simple*.

Mr. Chucks, the boatswain on H. M. ship *Diomede*, is not aware that Captain Kirkwall, in command, had in his very first advice to young Simple urged him never to swear or drink spirits, because the one is immoral and the other not gentlemanlike. Mr. Chucks assures Simple, "I never lose my temper, even when I use my rattan."

"Why, then, Mr. Chucks," says Simple, "do you swear so much at the men? Surely that is not gentlemanly?"

"Most certainly not, sir. But I must defend myself by observing the very artificial state in which we live on board of a man-of-war. Necessity, my dear Mr. Simple, has no law. You must observe how gently I always commence when I have to find fault. I do that to prove my gentility; but sir, my zeal for the service obliges me to alter my language, to prove in the end that I am in earnest. Nothing would afford me more pleasure than to be able to carry on the duty as a gentleman, but that's impossible."

"I really cannot see why."

"Perhaps, then, Mr. Simple, you will explain to me why the captain and the first lieutenant swear."

"That I do not pretend to answer, but they only do so upon an emergency."

"Exactly so; but, sir, their 'mergency is my daily and hourly duty. In the continual working of the ship I am answerable for all that goes amiss. The life of a boatswain is a life of 'mergency, and therefore I swear."

"I still cannot allow it to be requisite, and certainly it is sinful."

"Excuse me, my dear sir; it is absolutely requisite, and not at all sinful. There is one language for the pulpit, and another for on board ship, and, in either situation, a man must make use of those terms most likely to produce the necessary effect upon his listeners. Whether it is from long custom of the service, or from the indifference of a sailor to all common things and language (I can't exactly explain myself, Mr. Simple, but I know what I mean), perhaps constant excitement may do, and therefore he requires more 'stimilis,' as they call it, to make him move. Certain it is, that common parlancy won't do with a common seaman. It is not here as in the scriptures, 'Do this, and he doeth it' (by the bye, that chap must have had his soldiers in tight order); but it is, 'Do this, d——n your eyes,' and then it is done directly. The order to *do* just carries the weight of a cannon-shot, but it wants the perpelling power— the d——n is the gunpowder which sets it flying in the execution of its duty. Do you comprehend me, Mr. Simple?"[7]

Mr. Simple, who is the son of a country parson and aged fifteen years, replies, "I perfectly understand you, Mr. Chucks." And if the reader does, too, as I expect he does, he will surely regret with me that Admiral Leigh was not as well informed on the psychology of swearing as the humble boatswain Mr. Chucks.

Admiral Leigh's prototype in *H.M.S. Pinafore*, Captain Corcoran, was not quite of the same opinion as Mr. Chucks on the efficacy of swearing in emergencies:

> Bad language or abuse,
> I never, never use,
> Whatever the emergency;
> Though "Bother it" I may
> Occasionally say,
> I never use a big, big D——

The more spiritually minded among the pirates of the main forbade swearing on board. And the Duke of Cambridge deprecated it to his men as "a damned ungentlemanly habit." Izaak Walton, better acquainted with rivers than with the high seas, advised anglers to "be patient, and forbear swearing, lest they be heard and catch no Fish."

Among army men the silly season never seems to come to an end. In October, 1948, General Jacob L. Devers, chief of the army ground forces announced that in the new peacetime army no one was to use profanity. Such orders do not seem to work. In July, 1776, General George Washington issued a General Order in New York in which he stated:

The General is sorry to be informed that the foolish and wicked practice of profane cursing and swearing, a vice heretofore little known in an American army, is growing into fashion. He hopes the officers will, by example as well as influence, endeavor to check it, and that both they and the men will reflect, that we can have little hope of the blessing of Heaven on our arms, if we insult it by our impiety and folly. Added to this, it is a vice so mean and low, without any temptation, that every man of sense and character detests and despises it.[8]

The revolutionary army continued to swear, and Heaven, judging the cause to be just, blessed its endeavors with ultimate victory. Washington was himself, upon occasion, a not unaccomplished swearer. W. C. Ford, in his biography of the hero, *The True George Washington*, records that the Secretary of War, having inquired whether he had seen Randolph's pamphlet, replied, "I have, and by the eternal God, he is the damndest liar on the face of the earth"; and as he spoke he brought his fist down upon the table with all his strength. On another occasion, Paul van Dyke states, in his *George Washington*, "General Scott, noted for his great skill in copious and artistic swearing, was asked, 'Did Washington swear?' He replied, 'Yes, Sir, he did once at Monmouth and on a day that would make any man swear. Yes, he swore that day until the leaves shook on the trees. Charming, delightful! Never have I enjoyed such swearing before or since. Sir, on that day he swore like an angel from heaven."[9] There is also a surviving legend in Washington, Pennsylvania, that Washington was fined by the judge for swearing at a man in the courtroom, and Burges Johnson states that the record seems to bear this out.[10]

Late in 1775, John Adams, serving on the so-called naval committee was directed by the Continental Congress to enjoin navy commanders to punish profane and blasphemous sailors "by causing them to wear a wooden collar or some shameful badge"; but the order does not seem to have been enforced in the newly formed American navy.[11]

In 1942 there appeared an article by J. E. Harris, in *The Sunday School Times*, entitled "Does Profanity Matter?" This was reprinted by the Moody Press of Chicago in a pamphlet headed "Questions for the Man in Uniform." I am informed that many thousands of copies were distributed among the armed services. Washington's General Order of 1776 enjoining officers and men of the American army to desist from the impiety and folly of swearing, appears as the epigraph on the first page of the pamphlet, without any reference to the general's own volleys that way. An "old writer" is quoted as having said, "Some sins are productive of temporary profit or pleasure, but profaneness is productive of nothing . . . it is the most gratuitous of all kinds of wickedness. . . . Profanity never did any man the least good. No man is the richer, or happier, or wiser for it."

As Darwin once remarked, a man who does not in the least understand what he is talking about is absolutely invulnerable. It would, indeed, be foolish to take the errors enshrined in these remarks seriously, for, surely, everyone is aware of the fact that profanity is productive of a great deal more than "nothing." Even the religious bigot knows better, else he would not be so much concerned with it. But bigots are forever constellating ahead of experience, and like the pupil of the human eye, the more light they are exposed to, the narrower they grow. What experience tells us is that profanity is productive in many ways, not only in its ability to produce change, but as a cathartic conferring great physiological and psychological benefits upon the individual—not to mention upon society. Indeed, a professor of psychology at the University of Manchester, John Cohen, suggests that swearing could be put to good use in international affairs as a substitute for war. Cohen proposes the imitation, by the members of the UN Security Council, of the Eskimos' traditional manner of settling disputes by "assaulting" each other with reproachful songs. In this way, Cohen thinks, political talent might finally discover its appropriate medium of expression.[12] It is an idea, borrowed by Cohen, from an earlier work of mine,[13] and it is an idea vastly more to the point and rather more contributory to the welfare of man than the Moody Press pamphlet. How much more to the point and revelatory of a humane understanding, which so many so-called Christians would do well to imitate, is Julian Sharman's sympathetic comment, written some sixty years before J. E. Harris' pusillanimous piece. Writes Sharman:

In numberless courts and alleys, in the sinks and hiding-places of a great city, we may be sure there are innumerable spots where oaths and imprecations never for a moment are laid aside. They are as punctual and as regular as the ticking of a clock. No word is uttered that has not its accompaniment of an oath; no bread broken that is not devoured with cursing. For why? Human nature is at all times bent upon possessing, and upon increasing what it has acquired. The very act of producing is sufficient to uphold the equilibrium of the mental frame. But this same nature, when pinched and starved, becomes a perfect storehouse of enmity and ill-feeling. Among the denizens of these holes and crannies humanity has been driven very hard. It has been crushed and bruised to a point beyond endurance. The possibility of possessing is very faint, that of enjoying still more remote. No graceful thing—no pleasant thing, can readily come to its hand. Yet there is one chattel they *can* possess when every stick and stone is denied them. They can be tenacious of their swearing. See how manifestly useful a thing it is! It can give a man an eloquence where none would otherwise belong to him. It can set him up with a semblance of bodily strength, when otherwise he would be puny and fragile. He can assail authorities, and they dare not answer. He can drown the voice of missionaries, and they are halting in reproval. There are beings so dejected—so penurious —that this swearing constitutes their whole store of worldly opulence.

They know it too, in a fashion, although it has never been told them and they themselves are incapable of the telling.[14]

Sharman had the heart to perceive what swearing meant to the poor as a worldly possession that the penurious in spirit seem never to have understood. At the same time Sharman points to the reason why it is among the lowest classes that swearing has flourished in such grim earnest: those who have been most frustrated in life can, by the magic omnipotence of words, achieve something of the power that in all other respects has been denied them. And it is for this selfsame reason that those who have consciously or unconsciously recognized the dangers to themselves inherent in the possession of such power have done everything they could to suppress it. Profanity is, by definition, a revolt against authority, the expression of contempt or disregard of things sacred; it is irreverent. Swearers, therefore, are subversive of existing institutions. Such men are dangerous, for they bring into contempt not alone the gods and the regions over which they preside, but also the very sanctions that hold the institutions of men together. Subverting these they would be capable of subverting anything. Such men cannot be tolerated. Hence the sorry history of punishments and repression that have so barbarously and ineffectually been instituted against them.

But it still goes on. In San Salvador, *The New York Times* reported on September 23, 1935, the police started a campaign against the use of "bad language" in public. The authorities claimed this as necessary because the language frequently used in public "would make walls blush." The campaign was, predictably, a dismal failure.

In Czarist Russia swearing of the most pulverizing kinds was a widespread habit. In that kingdom the people had a lot to swear about. It is, however, doubtful whether swearing has declined since 1917. That the habit is still a problem in Soviet Russia is evident from a 1965 United Press report:

Moscow (UPI)—Using vile language is a crime that should be punished, Russian newspaper readers are quoted as saying in a recent survey.

The Government newspaper *Izvestia* published an article attacking swear words and asking its readers what they thought.

"Cursing is verbal hooliganism—a crime to be punished," one of them wrote.

"It is categorically condemned, not only by public opinion, but also by law," said another.

"I heard there was a fine for swearing in pre-war years," wrote a third. "If so, I would like this measure to be revived."

"The Russians, like the Greeks, have a word for almost everything, and their language is especially rich in obscenities, but nobody in authority tries to keep them in bounds," one of *Izvestia*'s readers said.

"Cursing is flourishing in our society only because of the indifference of public organizations of factories and administrations," he wrote.

"Some of those who love swearing have the title of member of 'Advanced Socialist Labor Team,'" another noted. "This is incompatible."

Izvestia agreed. "Those who break the norms of Socialist conduct should be responsible for their deeds," it said.[15]

Legislators would do well to reflect carefully upon the possible consequences of so ill-considered an act as the proscription or punishment of swearing. Seeds of unrest thus thoughtlessly planted could produce dangerous amounts of frustration and, hence, of aggressiveness.

In September, 1949, it was widely reported in the press that a young woman employed in a glove factory in the Middle West expressed herself unfavorably on the ancestry of her glove machine. Whether she said of it that like the mule it had neither pride of ancestry nor hope of posterity or whether she uttered words of a more colorful complexion is not recorded. In any event, she was discharged by her employers. The young woman and her union appealed to Louis Plost, trial examiner of the National Labor Relations Board. After due reflection, Examiner Plost handed down the following sensible decision:

The day when a curse was designed and intended to call down the wrath of heaven upon any object, animate or inanimate, has happily passed. Today, the words of imprecation, cursing and blasphemy survive in our speech shorn of their real meaning.

Time was when even the use of such "swear words" devoid of blasphemous intent or meaning had a proper and respected place in our language. Their use was a great art, reaching its noblest . . . among men whose lives were bound to beasts of burden . . . the cavalry man, the artillery man, but most of all the mule skinner . . .

But, alas, the coming of the gasoline engine has removed the living spur to expressive, non-blasphemous profanity until now only a pale substitute survives—the words are remembered but the music has been lost.

Plost ruled that the young woman's "vulgar expressions . . . were not in any sense real blasphemy" and she should get her job back.[16]

The Very Reverend W. R. Inge, late Dean of St. Paul's, agreed with Plost. Writing in 1930, he said, "most people if they swear do it to relieve their feelings, without evil intent." Words, of course, as Bilioso says in Marston's *The Malcontent*, are terms of disport —which naturally brings us to swearing as sport and play.

One of the amenities of civilized communication consists in the application of words, and especially adjectives, to original and unusual uses. This requires a feeling for words that is the very essence of literary skill, of style. Good swearers, therefore, have everywhere evoked the admiration that the skillful performer on any instrument elicits. Sportive swearing resembles the light shafts of Apollo or the fine and philosophical flashes of Uncle Toby, not the crab stick of Hercules or the Samsonian mandible of a donkey. For example, when in a London club a rather young member was put down by another, whose effrontery and arrogance stood in inverse relation to his erudition, for not knowing what he meant by calling him "a Philistine," the young member appealed to Lord Salisbury, who was sitting in a nearby chair. "Sir, can you tell me, who were the Philistines?" "Why, yes," replied the noble lord, implying by his inflection that the parallel was immediate, "the Philistines were a people who were slain by the jawbone of an ass."

There is also the story of the club bore who announced that his grandfather had fought in the Zulu war. "Which side?" queried the club wit. Or the other club bore who boasted that his father was a baron, eliciting the response, *sotto voce*, "It's a pity your mother wasn't."

If swearing is chastisement with words, then these are genuine examples of refined swearing. Invective is but another name for polite swearing. Swinburne, who was very delicate upon such matters, made this abundantly clear when, referring to Emerson as "a gap-toothed and hoary-headed ape," he declared that he had confined himself to "language of the strictest reserve."

William IV said to a Captain Towers, "I hear, Towers, that you're the greatest blackguard in Portsmouth." Whereupon Captain Towers answered, "I hope your Majesty hasn't come down here to take away my character."

Louis XI, noticing that a man about the court resembled the royal family asked, "Was your mother about the court?" "No, sir," was the reply, "but my father was."

Early in the nineteenth century someone offered to bet that no one could successfully chaff Miss Skittles. The man who took the bet accosted her as she entered the room: "Why, Skittles, what a fine arse you have!" She, affecting modesty, replied, "Oh, you shouldn't kiss and tell!"

Tennyson considered these the three best things of their kind, and, indeed, their rank is very high (a comment that is not to be taken as a pun). About the same quality is the response of the Reverend Sydney Smith, "The Smith of Smiths," to a young man who had rudely said to him, "If I had a son who was an idiot, I would make him a parson." "Your father was of a different opinion."

John Curran, on being asked by a Member of Parliament if he had heard his last speech, replied, "I hope I have." Samuel Rogers, on entering a drawing room during a sudden silence, remarked, "I see that Hallam has just been telling a joke." This recalls the sage observation that "A German joke is no laughing matter." Disraeli described the difference between a misfortune and a calamity: "If Gladstone fell into the Thames it would be a misfortune. But if someone dragged him out again, it would be a calamity." And Henry James said of Carlyle, "The same old sausage, fizzing and spattering in its own grease." Carlyle remarked on Darwinism, "I have no patience whatever with these gorilla damnifications of humanity." And then there is the ringing reply of Thomas Henry Huxley to "Soapy Sam" Bishop Wilberforce at the 1860 Oxford meeting of the British Association for the Advancement of Science. Wilberforce was out to do the Darwinists in. He spoke for half an hour, with what one of his more sympathetic auditors described as "inimitable spirit, emptiness and unfairness." Finally, he turned to Huxley and with smiling insolence begged to know "Was it through his grandfather or his grandmother that he claimed descent from a monkey?"

Huxley, turning to Sir Benjamin Brodie, who was seated near him, and with a slap upon his knee, quietly remarked, "The Lord hath delivered him into mine hands." When the applause for the Bishop subsided, Huxley was called upon by the chairman to speak. Huxley was at that time thirty-five years old, a tall slight figure, stern and pale, very quiet and very grave. He rose slowly and said:

I have listened with great attention to the Lord Bishop's speech but I have been unable to discover either a new fact or a new argument in it—except indeed the question as to my personal predelictions in the matter of ancestry—It would not have occurred to me to bring forward such a topic as that for discussion myself, but I am quite ready to meet the Right Rev. prelate even on that ground. If, then, the question is put to me would I rather have a miserable ape for a grandfather or a man highly endowed by nature and possessing great means and influence and yet who employs those faculties and that influence for the mere purpose of introducing ridicule into a grave scientific discussion—I unhesitatingly affirm my preference for the ape.[17]

The effect, as one present wrote, recalling the event thirty-eight years later, "was tremendous."

Never was a bishop more gracefully sworn at, or a monkey more effectively made out of a bishop. It is said that when another bishop communicated to his wife the intelligence that the horrid Professor Huxley had claimed, at the Oxford meeting, that man was descended from an ape, she exclaimed, "Descended from an ape! My dear, let us hope that it is not true, but if it is, let us pray that it will not become generally known." The dear lady's prayers had no effect. It *has* become generally known—man is *descended* from an ape, and continues to descend, or so it would sometimes seem. What a pity the bishop's lady was unable to respond with something akin to Congreve's remark in 1695: "I confess freely to you, I could never look upon a monkey, without very mortifying reflections." Or have said to herself, "There but for the grace of Time, go I."

These references to apes and monkeys recalls the rejoinder of Alexandre Dumas, who, when asked the question by an impertinent upstart, "Who was your father?" replied, "My father was a Creole, his father was a Negro, and his father a monkey. My family, it seems, begins where yours left off."

Burges Johnson rightly laments the decline in the art of swearing:

What a pity that vituperation—the communication of feeling by word symbols hot from the furnace—should no longer be an art or even a common skill! Music and painting have their own symbols representing scorn, anger, derision, contempt. But might not words themselves flicker and sparkle and flare up into flames of emotion if one had imagination and artistry in their use? Invective is indeed a lost art, a forgotten skill! Its harp strings are loosened; its pigments have hardened on the palate.[18]

Johnson wrote those words in 1948, when perhaps the last of the great exponents of political invective was alive and flourishing: Winston Churchill, the man who said, "I do not resent criticism, even when, for the sake of emphasis, it parts for the time with reality." Who said of Mussolini, in April, 1941, "This whipped jackal, who to save his own skin, has made of Italy a vassal State of Hitler's Empire, is frisking up by the side of the German tiger with yelps not only of appetite—that could be understood—but even of triumph." And on another occasion referred to *Il Duce* as "A mere utensil of his master's will." He referred to Hitler as "this bloodthirsty guttersnipe," and on another occasion as that "squalid caucus boss and butcher." In a speech delivered at Margate October 10, 1953, Churchill described socialists as "Collective ideologists—those professional intellectuals who revel in decimals and polysyllables." Socialism Churchill described as "Government of the duds, by the duds, for the duds," a kind of government that would vanish "unwept, unhonoured, unsung and unhung." On Sir Stafford Cripps he remarked, "There but for the grace of God goes God."

Possibly apocryphal is Churchill's reply to an invitation by Bernard Shaw, who sent him two tickets to the opening night of his new play, suggesting that he bring a friend, if he had one. Churchill regretted that he had a previous engagement but asked Shaw to send him two seats to the second performance, "if there is one."

"Small curses, Dr. Slop, upon great occasions are but so much waste of our strength," said Mr. Shandy. And it is equally true that great oaths (as Mr. Shandy was fully aware) on small occasions are quite as unfitting, the merest folly. Shakespeare, a profound student of the hidden springs of swearing, was quite alive to the risibilities that might be educed from the incongruity of the major oath attached to the minor object, as when Rosalind says, "Where learnt you that oath, fool?" And Touchstone replies, "Of a certain knight who swore by his honour they were good pancakes."

Stephen Leacock, in one of his essays, suggested that the thoughtful asterisk that replaced the naughty word in some printed works be transferred to ordinary speech. "Asterisk," shouted the pirate. "I'll make it two asterisks," snarled the other, "and throw in a dash!" The suggestion has not found much favor; swearers seem to prefer the genuine article to the counterfeit—no sterilized ejaculations for them.

Negative swearing, in which innocuous words are substituted for the most sulfurous oaths, possesses a power all of its own. The temperature and the pressure on such occasions almost reaches the bursting point, but instead of the appropriate thermodynamic explosion the gentlest of sounds is produced or the most inaudible. Here are a few examples.

The dean of a cathedral, the guest of the officers of the regiment stationed nearby, at golf brought up a sizable quantity of turf. "Tut, tut," he exclaimed—an expression that for months afterward replaced every other oath uttered on the station. The spiritual relief this afforded the men is said to have been considerable.

Another clerical golfer, asked how he managed to exhibit such self-control after so many bad shots, replied, "Perhaps you have noticed that after each bungling effort I pause and spit. You will find that where that spit falls, the grass will not grow for a year."

And yet another clergyman playing against Chief Justice Harlan Stone, after the latter had made a 200-yard drive, stepped up to the tee, swung furiously, and missed. He stared at the ball for a full minute, then stepped up to the tee again. Whereupon the Chief Justice said to him, "That was the most profane silence I ever heard in my life."

Such men were never whipped for false quantities at school but have lathered themselves into ineffectual fury over the swearing of others. Bishop Weldon, the Dean of Durham, in a letter to *The Times*, in 1923, censured the "vulgar profanity" of the language used by some Labour Members of the House of Commons and inquired whether there was "no adequate means of preventing or punishing it," which elicited from E. M. Forster, the following, among other, lines:

> My brethren, nothing on earth is finer
> Than a truly refined inarticulate miner
> (Or may we say "under the earth," for there
> Is a miner's place, not up in the air?);
> But he must be refined, he must be meek,
> Expert at his job, yet unable to speak,
> He must not complain or use swear words or spit;
> Much is expected of men in the pit.

There was a time when clerics swore, and some, like Jonathan Trelawny, had it both ways. Reproved for swearing by a brother cleric, he made reply, "When I swear I do not swear as a Bishop. I swear as Sir Jonathan Trelawny, a country gentleman and a baronet." It is a fine distinction. Rabelais' Friar John, whose illustrious performances have been recorded in an earlier chapter, was no mere figment of the author's imagination, for he was modeled on the churchmen of his day, against whose immorality and vileness Luther so strongly protested. The luxuriant and fanciful swearing of Friar John has not, so far as is recorded, been equaled by any man, though Luther himself was no mean performer (see his *Tischrede*), but nothing like the Free Preachers of Rabelais' day, whose sermons in many respects may be regarded as his literary forebears. Rabelais had been both novice and monk in Franciscan and Benedictine monasteries and spoke from intimate knowledge of their supplicants. Undoubtedly Friar John had his models and represents a composite of them all.

It would be both sacrilegious and blasphemous in the proximity of one who, like Friar John, lived by a morality so touched with emotion, even so much as to refer to those modern clergymen who consider it necessary, from time to time, to intone their puling pulpit puerilities against the use of profanity. Friar John entertained a more charitable posture toward his fellow clerics, when in the Fifth Book, in Dionysian ecstasy, he utters the following prayer:

> O God, thou holy sire divine,
> Who out of water made the wine,
> Make of my rump a lantern bright
> To guide my neighbour through the night.

One of the most telling examples of refined swearing in the language is Robert Browning's scorching comment on "Omar Khayyam" Edward FitzGerald's remarks on Elizabeth Barrett Browning, published in 1889 in Aldis Wright's *The Life and Letters of Edward FitzGerald.* In that work the editor printed a letter by FitzGerald in which he delivered himself of the following offensive observations:

Mrs. Browning's death is rather a relief to me, I must say. No more Aurora Leigh's, thank God! A woman of real genius, I know; but what is the upshot of it all? She and her sex had better mind the kitchen and the children; and perhaps the poor. Except in such things as little novels, they only devote themselves to what men do much better, leaving that which men do worse or not at all.

This passage was quoted by a reviewer of the book in *The Athenaeum*, where Browning saw it, upon which he immediately dashed off the following sonnet and sent it to the same journal, where it appeared on July 13, 1889:

To Edward FitzGerald

I chanced upon a new book yesterday:
I opened it, and, where my finger lay
'Twixt page and uncut page, these words I read
—Some six or seven at most—and learned thereby
That you, FitzGerald, whom by ear and eye
She never knew, "thanked God my wife was dead."

Ay, dead! and were yourself alive, good Fitz,
How to return you thanks would task my wits:
Kicking you seems the lot of common curs—
While more appropriate greeting lends you grace:
Surely to spit there glorifies your face—
Spitting from lips once sanctified by Hers.

FitzGerald was, in fact, a man of the gentlest temper, but his staggeringly unpleasant remarks about Mrs. Browning could not be allowed to pass by her husband, to whose heart and head his sonnet is itself a tribute.

The exchanges between James McNeill Whistler and Oscar Wilde in *The World* in 1889–1890 are famous. We need quote only one example. Wilde replies: "With our James vulgarity begins at home, and should be allowed to stay there." To which Whistler rejoins, "A poor thing, Oscar!—but, for once, I suppose, your own."

Wit unredeemed by vulgarity is too often characteristic of invective, but it need not be so.

Labour leader J. H. Thomas approached Lord Birkenhead at a Buckingham Palace garden party and asked, "Birken'ead, what do you recommend for a 'eadache?" "I'd suggest a couple of aspirates," the recently elevated F. E. Smith replied. Samuel Johnson observed to Boswell of a man walking ahead of them, "I don't like to say anything unkind behind a man's back, but I believe that man's an attorney." And on another occasion he remarked of a man, "I believe it is not quite accurate to say that his mother was the keeper of a bawdy house. I believe she was a receiver of stolen goods." Lord Balfour remarked of an acquaintance, "He pursues me with a malignant fidelity." Jowett, Master of Balliol, said to a student with whom he was very annoyed, "What you have done is gravely offensive to me, and most displeasing to God."

The Earl of Rochester's epigram on his friend Charles II belongs in a class of its own:

Here lies our sovereign lord the king,
Whose word no man relies on:
Who never said a foolish thing,
Nor ever did a wise one.

To which Charles replied, "My sayings are my own, my actions are my ministers." When F. E. Smith, Lord Birkenhead, was a rising young barrister he was engaged in a case in which a boy had been run over by a tram and his parents were suing the tram company. F. E. was defending the company. The case for the boy was that the accident had led to blindness. The following exchange took place between the judge, a kindly though somewhat garrulous soul, who allowed his sympathies to outrun his discretion.

"Poor boy, poor boy!" he exclaimed. "Blind! Put him on a chair so that the jury can see him."

This was weighting the scales of justice rather heavily in favor of the plaintiffs, and F. E. was moved to protest.

"Perhaps your Honour would like to have the boy passed round the jury-box," he suggested.

"That is a most improper remark," observed the judge with some acerbity.

"It was provoked by a most improper suggestion," came the astonishing reply. There was some hesitation on the part of the discomfited judge while he was ordering in his own mind the decisive retort. In a few moments more he had it.

"Mr. Smith," he said, "have you ever heard of a saying by Bacon —the great Bacon—that youth and discretion are ill-wedded companions?"

Without a moment's hesitation F. E. replied, "Yes, I have. And have you ever heard of a saying by Bacon—the great Bacon— that a much-talking judge is like an ill-tuned cymbal?"

"You are an extremely offensive young man," opined the judge.

"As a matter of fact," said Smith, "we both are; but I am trying to be, and you cannot help it."

"What," in exasperation the judge demanded to know, "do you suppose I am on the bench for, Mr. Smith?"

"It is not for me, your Honour," came the instant reply, "to fathom the inscrutable workings of Providence."

Thus did the incipient incumbent of the Woolsack make his way to glory.

A predecessor of Birkenhead's, Lord Ellenborough, to a young counsel who paused after saying, "The unfortunate client, on whose behalf I appear—" remarked, "You may go on, sir. So far, the court is with you."

In official circles attitudes toward profanity are much relaxed, but while mild profanity is permitted in parliamentary debate, the official record of what is said, *Hansard*, either euphemizes or ignores it. However, the Lord Chamberlain, the censor of plays, still feels compelled to earn his keep as guardian of the public morals. As recently as August 15, 1966, he suggested to the students of the University of Keele that they should not stage a modern translation of Chaucer's "The Miller's Tale" at the Edinburgh Festival.[19] O' Holy Willie, where art thou?

> O Lord, Thou kens what zeal I bear,
> When drinkers drink, and swearers swear,
> An' singing here, an' dancing there,
> > Wi' great and sma';
> For I am keepit by Thy fear
> > Free frae them a'.[20]

Harry Whewell in an article, "The Crisis in Swearing," published in *The Guardian* (February 18, 1967), referring to the case of a South Yorkshire miner who was fined for using obscene language, and who protested that he had heard worse on television, asks the question, since "Formal religion counts for little or nothing in most people's lives, and if nothing is sacred how can anything be profane?" The answer surely is that, while it is true that most Christians can scarcely be described as pillars of the church, more closely resembling flying buttresses, and while they may no longer believe in gods, ghosts, and goblins, like Madame de Staël, they continue to be afraid of them. And even when they are not, the strength and power of the words remain because they are still largely forbidden —forbidden by those who consider them to be profane.

Whewell is worried about the future of British swearing. He need not be. The traditional deities and their minions may, like old soldiers, fade away, but they will not be forgotten. Furthermore, secular deities will arise to take their place, and as the peoples of the world draw more closely together, they will cross-fertilize each other to produce hybrids of even greater vigor than most of the ancient oaths.

Whewell quite rightly remarks that "one of the least attractive features of British profanity and obscenity is their drear repetitiveness. Most practitioners" he adds, "have a vocabulary of no more than a dozen or so words which are employed over and over again, usually without regard to context, euphony, or even alliteration." This is fair enough. British swearing, unlike that of many other peoples, has never been very imaginative. Whewell wants to see it reformed on a broader and more secure foundation, and toward this end he suggests some kind of bad language commission. It is a splendid idea.

The time is now ripe for such a body in England to invent and inject into the language a whole series of new swear words, curses, and oaths which are completely irreligious and asexual—some round rolling phrases like George Bernard Shaw's "Thirty thousand thunders!"

Once devised, getting them into circulation should be easy enough. Television playwrights could be given subsidies for writing them into their scripts. Newspapers could have a "Curse of the Week" corner, and most useful of all, perhaps the GPO could introduce a "Dial a Swear" service.

Clearly, while guardians and critics of Whewell's quality remain, there need be no anxiety for the future of British swearing.

A much-neglected form of swearing is gestural swearing. This is entirely nonverbal, although on suitable occasions the gestures may be accompanied by the appropriate words. Shaking a clenched fist at the object of one's wrath is perhaps the most familiar of the nonverbal expressions of animosity. Holding up a middle finger means "Go fornicate with yourself." Holding up the middle and index fingers, means "Stick it up your arse." Thumbing one's nose is a general expression of contempt.

These are fairly well known gestures. There is, in addition, a whole class of private gestures that may be peculiar to a particular individual or a group. These are probably numerous, and need not be considered here.

A good example of gesticulatory swearing is offered by Tobias Smollett in *Humphry Clinker*, where, in describing the battle of the Amazons at the party in Bath, he writes, "Some swore, and the tropes and figures of Billingsgate were used without reserve in all their native zest and flavour; nor were those flowers of rhetoric unattended with significant gesticulation. Some snapped their fingers, some forked them out, some clapped their hands, and some their backsides."

Notes

Chapter One

1. H. Jackson, "The Pathos of Profanity," *Occasions* (London, 1922), pp. 45–66.

Chapter Two

1. Ashley Montagu, *The Human Revolution* (Cleveland, Ohio, 1965).
2. W. D. Whitney, *The Life and Growth of Language* (New York, 1898), p. 288.
3. C. H. Grandgent, *Imitation And Other Essays* (Cambridge, Mass., 1933), p. 16.
4. For a discussion of these theories see Otto Jesperson, *Language* (London, 1928), pp. 413–446.
5. Ashley Montagu, *op. cit.*
6. B. Malinowski, "The Problem of Meaning in Primitive Languages," in C. K. Ogden and I. A. Richards, *The Meaning of Meaning* (London, 1923), pp. 451–510.
7. D. F. Thomson, "The Joking Relationship and Organized Obscenity in North Queensland," *American Anthropologist*, 37 (1935), 468.
8. H. Basedow, *The Australian Aboriginal* (Adelaide, 1925), p. 167.
9. Thomson, *op. cit.*, p. 465.
10. *Ibid.*, p. 466.
11. *Ibid.*, p. 467.
12. *Ibid.*
13. *Ibid.*, p. 469.
14. *Ibid.*
15. *Ibid.*, p. 478.
16. See W. La Barre, "The Psychopathology of Drinking Songs," *Psychiatry* 2 (1939), 203–212.
17. Thomson, *op. cit.*, p. 465.
18. *Ibid.*, p. 472.
19. See M. F. Ashley Montagu, *Coming Into Being Among the Australian Aborigines* (London, 1937).
20. W. Pleyte-Rossi, *Papyrus de Turin* (plates XLII ff.), quoted in G. Elliot Smith and W. Dawson, *Egyptian Mummies* (London, 1924), p. 176.
21. T. Carlyle, *Sartor Resartus* (Boston, 1836).
22. J. Sharman, *A Cursory History of Swearing* (London, 1884), p. 68.

23. Lucian, *The Works of Lucian* (London, 1921), III, 329.
24. *Ibid.*, p. 363.
25. Plutarch. Quoted by Sharman, *op. cit.*
26. F. Porché, *Charles Baudelaire* (London, 1928), p. 172.
27. Aristophanes, *The Clouds.*
28. Demosthenes, *De corona,* 208.
29. From the *Demis* of the comedian Eupolis, a contemporary of Aristophanes.
30. Longinus, *On the Sublime* (XVI, 3-4), translated by W. Hamilton Fyfe (London, 1927), pp. 179-183.
31. Athenaeus, *The Deipnosophists* (IX) (London, 1939), IV, 175-177.
32. *Journal des Savants* (Paris, 1839), p. 37.
33. Arnaius. Quoted by Sharman, *op. cit.*
34. F. T. Welcker, *Hipponactis et Ananii lamborgraphorum fragmenta* (Gottingen, 1817).
35. Plato, *The Laws* (London, 1926), II, 461-462.
36. *See also* Plautus' *Audria,* II, 2, 338, 347; III, 2, 495; *Captivi,* III, 1, 461; 4, 562. Terentius, *Hecyra,* V, 4, 860.
37. Juvenal, *The Eighth Satire*; George Stepney's translation edited by John Dryden, *The Satires of Decimus Junius Juvenalis* (London, 1693).
38. Ovid, *Heroical Epistles.*

Chapter Three

1. H. Basedow, *The Australian Aboriginal* (Adelaide, 1925), p. 175.
2. *Ibid.*
3. W. B. Cannon, " 'Voodoo' Death," *American Anthropologist,* 44 (1954), 169-181.
4. E. and P. Beaglehole, *Some Modern Maoris* (Christchurch, New Zealand, 1946), pp. 80-81.
5. R. Wünsch, *Defixionum tabellae atticae,* 1897; A. Andollent, *Defixionum tabellae,* 1904; F. B. Jevons "Defixionum tabellae," *Transactions of the Third International Congress for the History of Religions* (Oxford, 1908), II, 131-139.
6. J. C. Lawson, *Modern Greek Folklore and Ancient Greek Religion* (Cambridge, Eng., 1910).
7. Aeschylus, *Eumenides,* 417.
8. M. P. Nilsson, *Greek Popular Religion* (New York, 1940), pp. 114-115.
9. Plato, *The Laws* (XI) (London, 1926), II, 449.
10. W. Sherwood Fox, "Cursing as a Fine Art," *The Sewanee Review Quarterly,* 27 (1919), 460-477.
11. G. L. Hendrickson, "Archilochus and the Victims of His Iambics," *American Journal of Philology,* 44 (1925), 103.
12. *The Greek Anthology,* Book 7, 69, translated by W. R. Paton (London, 1917), II, 43. Lycambes was to have been Archilochus' father-in-law, but the latter at the last moment refused to sanction the marriage of his daughter to Archilochus, whereupon Archilochus rimed them both to death.

13. R. C. Elliott, *The Power of Satire* (Princeton, 1960), p. 9.
14. F. B. Jevons, "Graeco-Italian Magic," in R. R. Marett ed., *Anthropology and the Classics* (Oxford, 1908), pp. 118–119.
15. Demosthenes, "De falsa legatione," translated by C. A. Vince and J. H. Vince (London, 1926), pp. 291–293.
16. A. B. Cook, *Zeus: A Study in Ancient Religion* (Cambridge, Eng., 1940), III, 606, Pt. I.
17. Fox, *op. cit.*
18. *Ibid.*, p. 467.
19. A. D. Fraser, "The Ancient Curse—Some Analogies," *Classical Journal*, 17 (1921–1922), 454–460.
20. Fox, *loc. cit.*
21. *Ibid.*
22. Plato, *The Laws.*
23. E. R. Dodds, *The Greeks and the Irrational* (Berkeley, Calif., 1957), p. 194.
24. F. Bock, *Studien zum Politischen Inquisitions prozess Johanns XXII* (Berlin, 1937), p. 33. See also G. G. Coulton, *Inquisition and Liberty* (London, 1938), p. 188.
25. G. H. Kinahan, "Cursing Stones in Counties Fermanagh, Cavan, . . ." *Folk-Lore*, 34 (1894), p. 5.
26. Ovid, *Metamorphoses*, 8, 4.
27. J. H. Hardiman, *Irish Minstrelsy*, quoting Owen Connellan, *Transactions of the Ossianic Society*, 5 (1860), xxx.
28. Cited by J. H. Todd, *Proceedings of the Royal Irish Academy*, 5 (1850–1853), 355 ff.
29. See "Simon Forman," *Dictionary of National Biography* (London, 1899), XIX, 479.
30. W. Henderson, *Notes on the Folk Lore of the Northern Counties of England and the Borders*, with an Appendix by S. Baring-Gould (London, 1866), p. 192.
31. B. Thorpe, *Northern Mythology, Comprising the Principal Popular Traditions of Scandinavia, North Germany and the Netherlands*, 3 vols. (London, 1851), III, 94.
32. Anonymous, *The Man of the World's Dictionary* (London, 1822).
33. S. T. Coleridge, "Fire, Famine, and Slaughter" (1798).
34. R. Graves, *Lars Porsena, or the Future of Swearing* (London, 1927), p. 40.
35. *Ibid.*, p. 38.

Chapter Four

1. For accounts of the oath among primitive peoples see R. Lasch, *Der Eid, Seine Entstehung und Beziehung zu Glaube und Brauch der Naturvolker, eine ethnologische Studie* (Stuttgart, 1908); J. Hastings, (editor), *Encyclopaedia of Religion and Ethics* (Edinburgh, 1917), IX, 430–438.
2. For accounts of the oath in antiquity see S. A. B. Mercer, *The Oath in Babylonian and Assyrian Literature* (Munich, 1911); H. I. Bell, "An

Oath Formula of the Arab Period in Egypt," *Byzantinische Zeitschrift* (Leipzig, 1913), Bd. 22, pp. 392–405; R. Hirzil, *Der Eid: ein Beitrag zu seiner Geschichte* (Leipzig, 1902). J. M. Sullivan, "Judicial Oaths in Ancient Ireland," *Green Bag*, 14, (1902), 85–86; P. Stengel, "Zu den Griechenischen Schwuropfern," *Hermes, Zeitschrift fur classische Philologie* (Berlin, 1914), Bd. 49, pp. 90–101; J. W. Taylor, "The Athenian Ephebic Oath," *Classical Journal*, 13 (1918), 495–501; F. W. Wright, "Oaths in the Greek Epistolographers," *American Journal of Philology*, 39 (1918), 65–74; J. J. Modi, "Oaths among the Ancient Iranians and the Persian Saogaud-nameh," *Anthropological Society Journal*, 12 (1922), 204–244; F. J. Coffin, *The Third Commandment* (Norwood, 1898); R. de La Grasserie, "Phenomenes sociaux de survivance, Du Serment," *Revue Internationale de Sociologie*, 7 (1899), 796–814, 874–893.

3. R. Aubert, Abbé de Vertot, "A Dissertation on the Ancient Form of Oaths us'd among the French," *Vertot's Miscellanies* (London, 1723), pp. 110–143; O. Towles, *Prepositional Phrases of Asseveration and Adjuration in Old and Middle French* (Paris, 1920); L. K. Goetz, "Verwundchung und Fluch im serbokroatischen Volkslied," in *Westmark* (Köln, 1922); J. Sharman, *A Cursory History of Swearing* (London, 1884), pp. 22 ff.

4. R. G. Ingersoll, *The Oath Question: Falsehood Put in Partnership with Theology* (New York, 1895); M. D. Conway, *The Oath and its Ethics* (London, 1881); E. Lewis, *Observations on Legal and Judicial Oaths; Including a Brief Notice of the Measures of the British Government for the Abolition of Unnecessary Oaths* (Philadelphia, 1846); C. Bradlaugh, *Mr. Bradlaugh and the Oath Question: Being a Letter Which Was Written by the Author on the Occasion of the Rejection of the Government Affirmation Bill, 3 May, 1883, and Which Was Refused Publication by Some So-Called Liberal Papers* (London, 1883); Quaker Boy (pseudonym), *A Religious Test, and Trial for Blasphemy* (Philadelphia, 1897). United States Judiciary Committee (House 70:1), *To Provide for Dispensing with Oath or Affirmation as a Method of Verifying Certain Written Instruments. Hearing before the Committee on the Juridicary, House of Representatives, 70th Congress, 1st session, on H. R. 9343 February 28, 1928* (Washington, U.S. Government Printing Office, 1928); T. R. White, "Oaths in Judicial Proceedings and Their Effect Upon the Competency of Witnesses," *American Law Register*, 51 (N.S. vol. 42) (1903), 373–446; Great Britain Standing Committee B, *Report . . . on the Oaths Bill with the Proceedings of the Committee* (London, 1909, 1899), pp. 69–82; B. P. Moore, "The Passing of the Oath," *American Law Review*, 37, (1903), 554–568; H. Formby, *The Oath of Religion in Public Life: The Real Malice and Impiety of the Call for Its Removal* (London, 1883).

5. Sharman, *op. cit.*, p. 26.

Chapter Five

1. F. Rabelais, *Pantagruel*, 2 (London, 1927), 314.
2. *Ibid.*, pp. 124–125.

3. *Ibid.*, p. 125.
4. L. Sterne, *The Life & Opinions of Tristram Shandy, Gentleman* (London, 1760–1767).
5. S. T. Coleridge, *Fire, Famine, and Slaughter* (London, 1798).
6. J. Sharman, *A Cursory History of Swearing* (London, 1884), p. 39.
7. R. Graves, *Lars Porsena, or the Future of Swearing* (London, 1929), p. 32.
8. W. N. P. Barbellion, *The Journal of a Disappointed Man* (London, 1919), entry for November 14, 1914.
9. H. W. Hulbert, "Profanity," *Biblical World*, 54 (1920), 69–75.
10. B. G. Steinhoff, "Of Swearing," *East and West*, 12 (1913), 992–998.
11. J. Dollard, *et al.*, *Frustration and Aggression* (New Haven, 1939).
12. M. F. Ashley Montagu, "Problems and Methods Relating to the Study of Race," *Psychiatry*, 3 (1940), 493–506. M. F. Ashley Montagu, *Man's Most Dangerous Myth: The Fallacy of Race*, 4th ed. (Cleveland, 1964).
13. G. W. T. Patrick, "The Psychology of Profanity," *The Psychological Review*, 8 (1901), 113–127.
14. E. Linklater, *Magnus Merriman* (London, 1934), pp. 295–296.
15. G. Schaller, *The Year of the Gorilla* (Chicago, 1964). J. Goodall, "New Discoveries Among Africa's Chimpanzees," *National Geographic*, 128, (1965), 802–831. B. Harrisson, *Orang-Utan* (New York, 1962).
16. L. L. Bernard, *Instinct* (New York, 1924). O. Klineberg, *Social Psychology* (New York, 1954). M. F. Ashley Montagu, "The Nature of War and the Myth of Nature," *Scientific Monthly*, 54 (1942), 342–353. M. F. Ashley Montagu, "Is Man Naturally Aggressive?" *Think*, 26 (1960), 24–27. M. F. Ashley Montagu, *The Human Revolution* (Cleveland, 1965).
17. R. M. and A. W. Yerkes, *The Great Apes* (New Haven, 1929). I. DeVore, ed., *Primate Behavior* (New York, 1965).
18. Patrick, *loc. cit.*
19. L. W. Simmons, ed., *Sun Chief: The Autobiography of a Hopi Indian* (New Haven, 1942), p. 117.
20. For a discussion of the theories and nature of laughter see J. C. Gregory, *The Nature of Laughter* (London, 1924); D. H. Monro, *Argument of Laughter* (Melbourne, 1951); M. F. Ashley Montagu, "Why Man Laughs." *Think*, 26 (1960), 30–32.
21. H. Campbell, "The Therapeutical Aspects of Talking, Shouting, Singing, Laughing, Crying, and Yawning," *The Lancet*, II (1897), 140–142.
22. Steinhoff, *loc. cit.*
23. J. Forthergill, *An Innkeeper's Diary* (London, 1932), p. 125.
24. Ephes. 4:26.
25. M. F. Reiser, *et al.*, "Effects of Variation in Laboratory Procedure and Experimenter on Cardiac Data in Subjects," *Psychosomatic Medicine*, 17 (1955), 185–189.
26. S. H. King and A. F. Henry, "Aggression and Cardiovascular Reactions Related to Parental Control Over Behaviour" *Journal of Abnormal and Social Psychology*, 50 (1955), 206–210.
27. D. W. MacKinnon, "Violation of Prohibition," in H. A. Murray, (editor), *Explorations in Personality* (New York, 1938), pp. 491–501.
28. S. Freud, *Civilization and Its Discontents* (New York, 1930), p. 114.

29. S. Freud, *Wit and the Unconscious* (New York, 1930). "On Obscene Words," in S. Ferenczi, *Sex in Psychoanalysis* (New York, 1950), pp. 132–153. Otto Fenichel, *The Psychoanalytic Theory of Neurosis* (New York, 1945).

30. HAMLET: O, Vengeance!
            Why, what an ass am I! This is most brave
            That I, the son of a dear father murder'd
            Prompted to my revenge by heaven and hell,
            Must, like a whore, unpack my heart with words,
            And fall a-cursing, like a very drab,
            A scullion!

Hamlet, II, iii

31. Philadelphia *Evening Bulletin*, September 16, 1942.

32. H. E. Ross, "Patterns of Swearing," *Discovery* (November, 1960), pp. 479–481.

33. R. G. B. Brown, "Patterns of Swearing," *Discovery* (January, 1961), p. 40.

Chapter Six

1. R. Graves, *Lars Porsena, or the Future of Swearing* (London, 1929), p. 45.

2. T. Smollett, *Roderick Random* (London, 1748), III, 109.

3. E. Thompson, *A Farewell To India* (London, 1931), p. 26.

4. G. O. Trevelyan, *The Life and Letters of Lord Macauley* (London, 1877), II, 257. See also J. Sharman, *A Cursory History of Swearing* (London, 1884), p. 58.

5. E. Partridge, *A Dictionary of Slang* (London, 1938), p. 205.

6. C. Marriott, *Modern Movements in Painting* (London, 1920), p. 49.

7. B. Harte, *In the Carquine Woods* (New York, 1884), p. 78.

8. M. Cole, *Growing Up in a Revolution* (New York, 1949), pp. 111–112.

9. A. Strindberg, *The Confession of a Fool* (New York, 1925), and *The Father* (New York, 1912).

10. Graves, *op. cit.*, pp. 26–27.

11. A version resembling this is given in B. G. Steinhoff, "Of Swearing," *East and West*, 12 (1913), 992–998. The latest version is in Graves, *op. cit.*, pp. 24–26.

12. A. C. Swinburne, Letter to Ralph Waldo Emerson. January 30, 1874. In H. Kingsmill (editor), *An Anthology of Invective and Abuse* (London, 1929), pp. 174–75.

13. A. C. Swinburne, "A Study of Shakespeare," in E. Gosse and T. J. Wise, eds., *The Complete Works of Algernon Charles Swinburne* (London, 1926), XI, 3–222.

14. Mark Twain, *Pudd'nhead Wilson's Calendar* (Hartford, 1894).

15. *Ibid.*

16. Ardery *v.* the State, 56 Ind. 329 A.D. 1877. Quoted by Theodore Schroeder, "Legal Obscenity and Sexual Psychology," *The Alienist and Neurologist*, Vol. 29 (1908).

Chapter Seven

1. Ethelbert. Quoted in J. Sharman, *A Cursory History of Swearing* (London, 1884).
2. A. Howell, *A Sword Against Swearers* (London, 1611).
3. E. Weekley, *Etymological Dictionary of Modern English* (London, 1921), p. 439.
4. A. W. Pollard, *Miracle Plays, Moralities and Interludes* (Oxford, 1890), I, 92.
5. W. S. Skeat, ed., *The Lay of Havelock the Dane* (London, 1868), l. 1,930.
6. Quoted by G. G. Coulton, *Inquisition and Liberty* (London, 1938), p. 186.
7. G. R. Owst, *Literature and Pulpit in Medieval England* (Cambridge, Eng., 1933).
8. *Ibid.*
9. Coulton, *op. cit.*, 275n.
10. J. Sharman, *A Cursory History of Swearing* (London, 1884), pp. 79–80.
11. W. Sparrow Simpson, "Five Wounds," *Journal of the British Archaelogical Association* (December, 1874).
12. The sources of all these oaths will be found in A. E. H. Swaen, "Figures of Imprecation," *Englische Studien*, Bd. 24 (1898), pp. 16–71.
13. For further examples see *ibid.*
14. *St. James's Gazette*, June 20, 1884.
15. For the sources of these oaths and the others listed above see Swaen, *op. cit.*
16. F. J. Furnivall, ed., *Robert of Brunne's "Handlyng Synne,"* A.D. 1303 (London, 1901), pp. 25–29.
17. R. Morris, ed., *Dan Michel's Ayenbite of Inwyt*, A.D. 1340 (London, 1866), pp. 63–65.
18. D. B. Wyndham Lewis, *François Villon* (New York, 1928), p. 33.
19. Ms. Bibliothéque Nationale, *Collection Complet des Mémoires* (Paris), Vol. 8.
20. W. Butler-Bowdon, ed., *The Book of Margery Kempe, 1436* (London, 1936), pp. 64–65.
21. J. Myrk, *Instructions for Parish Priests* (London, 1450).
22. A. Barclay, *The Ship of Fooles, 1509*, edited by T. H. Jamieson, (London, 1874), II, 132.
23. T. Elyot, *The Boke Named the Gouernour*, Edited by H. H. S. Croft (London, 1531), II, 252. See also I, 275 (London, 1880).
24. Sharman, *op. cit.*, p. 195.
25. T. Becon, *An Invective Against Swearing* (London, 1543).
26. *The Acts of the Parliament of Scotland, 1424–1567* (London, 1814), II, 485.
27. *Ibid.*
28. J. G. Nicholls, *Literary Remains of Edward VI* (London, 1857).
29. N. Drake, *Shakespeare and his Times* (London, 1817), II, 160.
30. R. Hutchinson, *The Image of God* (London, 1560), pp. 20–21.

Chapter Eight

1. R. Holcomb, "The Antiquity of Congenital Syphilis," *Bulletin of the History of Medicine*, X (1941), 148–177.
2. *The Oxford English Dictionary*. Oxford, vol. 7, p. 1216.
3. J. Sharman, *A Cursory History of Swearing* (London, 1884), p. 35.
4. British Museum, Sloane ms. No. 2530, XXVI. D.

Chapter Nine

1. J. Palmer, *Ben Jonson* (New York, 1934). M. Chute, *Ben Jonson of Westminster* (New York, 1953). N. Zwager, *Glimpses of Ben Jonson's London* (Amsterdam, 1926).
2. *Collection of State Papers, Domestic, 1635–1636* (London).
3. R. H. Whitelock, *Memorials: Biographical and Historical* (London, 1860).
4. A. H. A. Hamilton, *Quarter Sessions from Queen Elizabeth to Queen Anne* (London, 1877).
5. W. Powell, *A Summons for Swearers* (London, 1645), p. vii.
6. *Ibid.*, p. 76.
7. R. Boyle, *A Free Discourse Against Customary Swearing and a Dissuasive from Cursing* (London, 1695).
8. W. Bridges-Adams, *The Irresistible Theatre* (London, 1957).
9. J. P. Collier, *History of Dramatic Poetry* (London, 1831).
10. Anon., *The Swearing-Master: Or, A Conference Between Two Country Fellows Concerning the Times* (London, 1681).
11. *The Character of the Beaux*. Written by a Young Gentleman (London, 1696), reprinted in G. Murphy, *A Cabinet of Characters* (London, 1925), pp. 335–339.
12. J. Collier, *A Short View of the Immorality and Profaneness of the English Stage* (London, 1698), pp. 56–57.
13. J. Dryden, *Epilogue* to Fletcher's *The Pilgrim*, 1621.
14. J. Vanbrugh, *A Short Vindication of the Relapse and the Provok'd Wife* (London, 1698).
15. J. Collier, *A Defense of the Short View of the Profaneness and Immorality of the English Stage, &c.* (London, 1699).
16. D. Defoe, "Of Academies," in *An Essay Upon Projects* (London, 1697).

Chapter Ten

1. F. Rabelais, *Gargantua—Les Grandes et Inestimables Cronicques du Grand et Enorme Geant Gargantua*. Lyons, 1532.
2. F. Rabelais, *Pantagruel* (Lyons, 1532).
3. F. Rabelais, *The Complete Works of Doctor François Rabelais*, translated by T. Urquhart and P. Motteux (London, 1708).
4. E. Dering, *The Fower Cardinall-Vertues of a Carmelite-Fryar, Fraud, Folly, Foul-Language, Blasphemy* (London, 1641).

Chapter Eleven

1. F. Grant, *A Discourse Concerning the Execution of the Laws Made Against Swearing* (Edinburgh, 1700).

2. [J. Woodward?], *A Letter From a Minister to His Parishoners. Shewing the Indispensable Duty Incumbent on All Persons to Give Information to the Magistrate as Well Against Prophane Swearing and Cursing, as Against Other Crimes and Misdemeanours* (London, 1701?).

3. [J. Woodward?], *A Disswasive From Prophane Swearing and Cursing, Offered to Such Unhappy Persons as Are Guilty of Those Horrid Sins, and Are Not Past Counsel* (London, 1702?).

4. [J. Woodward?] *The Oath of a Constable, so Far as It Relates to His Apprehending Night-Walkers, and Idle Persons, and His Presenting Offences Contrary to the Statutes Made Against Unlawful Gaming, Tipling, and Drunkenness, and for the Suppressing of Them* (London, 1702).

5. [J. Woodward?], *The Obligations of a Justice of the Peace, to Be Diligent in the Execution of the Penal-Laws Against Prophaneness and Debauchery, for the Effecting of a National Reformation. In a Letter to a Friend* (London, 1705).

6. [J. Woodward?], *A Kind Caution to Prophane Swearers. By a Minister of the Church of England* (London, 1705).

7. J. Swift, *The Swearers' Bank* (London, 1720).

8. *State Papers. Domestic, 1592* (London, 18??) p. 12.

9. J. Swift, *Polite Conversation* (London, 1738).

10. W. Blackstone, *Commentaries on the Laws of England* (London, 1765–1769), Book IV, p. 59.

Chapter Twelve

1. P. Fryer, *Mrs. Grundy: Studies in English Prudery* (London, 1963).

2. A. Myerson, *Speaking of Man* (New York, 1950), p. 98.

3. F. Boas, *The Mind of Primitive Man*, 2nd ed. (New York, 1938), p. 231.

4. H. C. Wyld, *A History of Modern Colloquial English* (London, 1920), p. 386.

5. C. Gessler, *The Reasonable Life* (New York, 1950), p. 59.

6. [Dean Mansel] *Phrontisterion, Or Oxford in the 19th Century* (Oxford, 1852).

7. R. Southey, *The Doctor* (London [1847], reprinted 1930), p. 339.

8. H. James, *William Wetmore Story* (Boston, 1903), II, 25.

9. W. S. Landor, *Dry Sticks Fagoted* (London, 1858), 10.

10. James, *loc. cit.*

11. B. Perry, *And Gladly Teach* (Boston, 1935), p. 13.

12. P. Noyes, *My Father's House: An Oneida Boyhood* (London, 1937), p. 262.

13. C. Darwin, *Autobiography in Letters* (London, 1867).
14. H. Spencer, *An Autobiography* (London, 1903), I, 486.
15. Mark Twain, *The Autobiography of Mark Twain*, edited by Charles Neider (New York, 1959), p. 276.
16. *Ibid.*, p. 278.
17. *Ibid.*, pp. 214–217.
18. W. D. Orcutt, *In Quest of the Perfect Book* (Boston, 1926), p. 172.
19. C. Torr, *Small Talk at Wrayland* (Cambridge, Eng., 1932), p. 106.
20. R. Barham, *The Ingoldsby Legends* (London, 1840–1847).
21. J. Plumptre, *The English Drama Purified* (London, 1812).
22. S. Marcus, *The Other Victorians* (New York, 1966).
23. B. Russell, *Sceptical Essays* (New York, 1928), p. 113.
24. E. Weekley, *Words: Ancient and Modern* (London, 1926), p. 16.
25. W. J. Tobey, letter in *Natural History*, 41 (April, 1938), p. 304.
26. T. H. Huxley, "Letter I," in Nora Barlow, ed., *The Autobiography of Charles Darwin* (London, 1958), p. 211.
27. J. B. Greenough and G. L. Kittredge, *Words and Their Ways in English Speech* (New York, 1901).

Chapter Thirteen

1. J. Sharman, *A Cursory History of Swearing* (London, 1884), p. 180.
2. C. Mackay, "English Slang and French Argot: Fashionable and Unfashionable," *Blackwood's Edinburgh Magazine*, vol. 143, (May, 1888), pp. 690–704.
3. Sharman, *op. cit.*, p. 182.
4. *Ibid.*
5. E. Weekley, *Words: Ancient and Modern* (London, 1926).
6. *Ibid.*, p. 18.
7. "Swearing," *Chamber's Encyclopaedia* (London, 1930), IX, 800.
8. W. Duranty, *Search For a Key* (New York, 1943), p. 18.
9. H. L. Mencken, *The American Language*, Supplement 1 (New York, 1948), p. 681.
10. E. Partridge, "The Word Bloody," *Words, Words, Words* (London, 1933), p. 88.
11. Ernest Weekley, *Words Ancient and Modern* (London, 1962), p. 17.
12. Voltaire, *Commentaire sur Corneille* (Paris, 1764).
13. Partridge, *op. cit.*, p. 89.
14. Sharman, *op. cit.*, p. 178.
15. *Ibid.*, p. 190.
16. R. H. Dana, *Two Years Before the Mast* (New York, 1840).
17. E. B. Browning, *Letters of Elizabeth Barrett Browning Addressed to Richard Hengist Horne* (London, 1877), I.
18. H. L. Mencken, *The American Language* (New York, 1936).
19. J. B. Matthews, "The Function of Slang," *Parts of Speech* (New York, 1901), pp. 187–213.
20. I. J. Semper, "The King's English," *English Journal*, 18 (1929), 308–312.

21. "William Schwenck Gilbert, 1836–1911," *Princeton University Chronicle*, 21 (1960), 229.

22. S. Dark and R. Grey, *W. S. Gilbert. His Life and Letters* (London, 1924), p. 103.

23. S. J. Ervine, *Bernard Shaw: His Life, Work and Friends* (London, 1956), pp. 459–460.

24. W. V. Tilsey, *Other Ranks* (London, 1931).

25. Partridge, *op. cit.*, p. 86.

26. J. Brophy, *Songs and Slang of the British Soldiers—1914–1918*, 3rd ed. (London, 1931).

27. E. Thompson, *These Men Thy Friends* (London, 1927), p. 164.

28. The original Australian Poem, by W. T. Goodge, was published in the *Sydney Bulletin* 1899, as follows:

"_____"

The sunburnt —— stockman stood,
And, in a dismal —— mood,
Apostrophised his —— duddy;
"The —— nag's no —— good,
He couldn't earn his —— food ——
A regular —— brumby [wild horse]
                              ——!"

He rode up hill, down —— dale,
The wind it blew a —— gale.
The creek was high and —— floody.
Said he: "The —— horse must swim,
The same for —— me and him,
Is something —— sickenin',
                              ——!"

He jumped across the —— horse
And cantered off, of —— course!
The roads were bad and —— muddy;
Said he: "Well, spare em —— days
The —— Government's —— ways
Are screamin' —— funny,
                              ——!"

He plunged into the —— creek,
The —— horse was —— weak,
The stockman's face a —— study!
And though the —— horse was drowned
The —— rider reached the ground
Ejaculating: "——?" "——!"

29. C. E. Montague, *Rough Justice* (London, 1926), p. 100.

30. H. C. Wyld, *A History of Colloquial English* (London, 1920), p. 387.

31. R. Withington, "A Note on 'Bloody,' " *American Speech*, 6, (1930), 29–35.

32. W. R. Inge, "We Swear To-Day—And Mean No Harm," *The Evening Standard*, March 12, 1930.

33. See the English press of May 31, 1936.

34. Wyld, *op. cit.*, p. 387.

35. Partridge, *op. cit.*, p. 80.

36. A. Marjoribanks, *Travels in New South Wales* (London, 1847), pp. 57–58.

37. S. J. Baker, *The Australian Language* (Sydney, Australia, 1945), p. 251.

38. T. Wood, *Cobbers* (London, 1934), p. 175.

39. F. Ratcliffe, *Flying Fox and Drifting Sand* (London, 1938), p. 56.

40. G. H. Wilkins, *Undiscovered Australia* (London, 1928), p. 56.

41. S. Boal, *New York Post*, June 11, 1947.

42. J. Masters, *Bhowani Junction* (New York, 1954), p. 276.

43. J. Wortis, *Fragments of an Analysis with Freud* (New York, 1954), p. 128.

44. R. Hart-Davis, *Hugh Walpole: A Biography* (New York, 1952).

45. J. W. Robertson Scott, *The Story of the Pall Mall Gazette* (London, 1950).

46. A. S. Neill, *A Dominie Dismissed* (London, 1917), p. 76.

47. J. Franklyn, *The Cockney* (London, 1953).

48. S. Baker, *The Australian Language* (Sydney, 1945), p. 106, n. 22.

49. *Ibid.*, pp. 153–154.

50. F. Majdalany, *The Monastery* (London, 1945), p. 53.
51. Partridge, *op. cit.*, p. 86.
52. G. Orwell, *Down and Out in London and Paris* (London, 1933), pp. 176–178.
53. Fryer, *op. cit.*

Chapter Fourteen

1. W. Maginn, "Bob Burke's Duel," *Blackwood's Edinburgh Magazine*, vol. 35, 1834, pp. 734–55.
2. *Ms. Bibliothèque Nationale, Paris. Collection Complèt des Memoires*, Vol. 8.
3. W. Hone, p. 456.
4. J. Howell, *Epistolae Ho-Elianiae. Familiar Letters Domestic and Forren* (London, 1645), I, 237.
5. J. Sharman, *A Cursory History of Swearing* (London, 1884), pp. 54–55.
6. G. Mynshull, *Certaine Characters and Essayes of Prison and Prisoners* (London, 1618), p. 45.
7. T. Peyton, *Catastrophe* (London, 1652), p. 28.
8. M. L. Clarke, *Richard Porson* (Cambridge, Eng., 1937), p. 57.
9. W. M. Dixon, *The Human Situation* (London, 1938).
10. B. Brook, *Mock Turtle* (London, 1931).
11. B. Hall, *Fragments of Voyages and Travels* (Edinburgh, 1831), p. 89.
12. E. Gosse and T. J. Wise, eds., *The Complete Works of Algernon Charles Swinburne* (London, 1927), XVIII, 8–9.
13. J. Macy, "A Cursory View of Swearing," *The Bookman*, 57 (1923), 593–600.
14. G. O. Trevelyan, *Life of Lord Macaulay* (London, 1877), II, 257.
15. E. Weekley, *An Etymological Dictionary of Modern English* (London, 1921), p. 409.
16. T. Pyles, *Words and Ways of American English* (New York, 1952), pp. 140–141.
17. L. Pound, "The Etymology of an English Expletive," *Language* (June, 1927).
18. *The New York Times*, July 15, 1941.
19. E. Partridge, *A Dictionary of Slang and Unconventional English*, 5th ed. (London, 1966), p. 231.

Chapter Fifteen

1. R. Briffault, *Sin and Sex* (New York, 1931). G. Rattray-Taylor, *Sex in History* (London, 1954).
2. M. F. Ashley Montagu, "Failure of Compensatory Mechanisms in Anxiety," *Journal of Neuropsychiatry*, 5 (1964), 415–417.
3. E. Sagarin, *The Anatomy of Dirty Words* (New York, 1962).

4. E. Weekley, *An Etymological Dictionary of Modern English* (London, 1921).

5. H. L. Mencken, *The American Language*, 4th ed. (New York, 1936); Supplement One (New York, 1945); Supplement Two (New York, 1948).

6. J. Florio, *A Worlde of Wordes* (London, 1598).

7. S. Skinner, *Etymologicon Linguae Anglicanae* (London, 1671).

8. N. Bailey, *Universal Etymological Dictionary* (London, 1721).

9. N. Bailey, *Dictionarium Britannicum* (London, 1730).

10. J. Ash, *A New and Complete Dictionary* (London, 1775).

11. F. Grose, *A Classical Dictionary of the Vulgar Tongue* (London, 1785).

12. S. Johnson, *A Dictionary of the English Language* (London, 1775).

13. [J. Marchant and Gordon], *A New Complete English Dictionary* (London, 1760).

14. J. S. Farmer and W. E. Henley, eds., *Slang and Its Analogues Past and Present*, 7 vols. (London, 1890–1904).

15. The *Oxford English Dictionary*. 13 vols. (Oxford, 1884–1928).

16. *Webster's New International Dictionary*, 3rd ed. (Springfield, Mass., 1962).

17. E. Partridge, *A Dictionary of Slang and Unconventional English*, 2nd ed. (London, 1936), 1938; 3rd ed., 1949; 4th ed., 1951; 5th ed., 1961.

18. E. Partridge, *Origins: A Short Etymological Dictionary of Modern English* (London, 1958).

19. H. Wentworth and S. B. Flexner, *A Dictionary of American Slang* (New York, 1960).

20. M. J. Leitner and J. R. Lanen, *A Dictionary of French and American Slang* (New York, 1965).

21. B. Johnson, *The Lost Art of Profanity* (Indianapolis, 1948), pp. 74, 75.

22. A. W. Read, *Lexical Evidence From Folk Epigraphy in Western North America: A Glossarial Study of the Low Element in the English Vocabulary* (Paris, 1935).

23. *Ibid.*, p. 76.

24. R. Burns, *The Merry Muses of Caledonia*, edited by J. Barke and S. G. Smith (New York, 1964).

25. J. Brophy and E. Partridge, *Songs and Slang of the British Soldier, 1914–1918*, 3rd ed. (London, 1931).

26. T. E. Lawrence, *Revolt in the Desert* (London, 1927).

27. R. Aldington, *Death of a Hero* (London, 1929).

28. For the complete text of Judge van Pelt Bryan's decision see A. Craig, *Suppressed Books* (London, 1963), pp. 231–248.

29. Partridge, *Slang*, *op. cit.*, p. 305.

30. R. D. Abrahams, *Deep Down in the Jungle* (Hatboro, Penna., 1964).

31. R. Hartogs, *Four-Letter Word Games* (New York, 1967), p. 61.

32. N. Mailer, *The Naked and the Dead* (New York, 1948).

33. See Farmer and Henley, *op. cit.*

34. W. Young, *Eros Denied* (London, 1965).

35. Sagarin, *op. cit.*, p. 148.

36. F. N. Robinson, ed., *The Works of Chaucer* (London, 1957), p. 49, line 3,276.

37. Read, *op. cit.*, pp. 13–14.
38. J. D. Adams, *The Magic and Mystery of Words* (New York, 1963).
39. Pertinax, "Without Prejudice," *British Medical Journal*, 27 (1965), 124.
40. "With Prejudice," *Journal of the American Medical Association*, 195 (1966), 173.
41. A. Myerson, *Speaking of Man* (New York, 1950), pp. 98 ff.

Chapter Sixteen

1. E. Hyams, "Demotic English," *New Statesman* (April 19, 1958), p. 498.
2. B. Malinowski, *Sex and Repression* (London, 1927), p. 107.
3. Malinowski, *op. cit.*, pp. 106–107.
4. M. F. Ashley Montagu, "Failure of Compensatory Mechanisms in Anxiety," *Journal of Neuropsychiatry*, 5 (1964), 415–417.
5. K. Amis, "Aha!" *New Statesman*, 72 (1965), 917.
6. *The Literary Digest*, June 10, 1933, p. 16.
7. C. Marryat, *Peter Simple* (London, 1834).
8. W. C. Ford, *The True George Washington* (New York, 1910).
9. P. van Dyke, *George Washington, The Son of His Country* (New York, 1931).
10. B. Johnson, *The Lost Art of Profanity* (Indianapolis, 1948), p. 37.
11. P. Smith, *John Adams* (New York, 1962).
12. J. Cohen, "The Natural History of Swearing," *The New Scientist* (December, 1960).
13. M. F. Ashley Montagu, "On the Physiology and Psychology of Swearing," *Psychiatry*, 5 (1942), 189–201.
14. J. Sharman, *A Cursory History of Swearing* (London, 1884).
15. "Vile Language," *The New York Times*, July 27, 1965.
16. *Time*, September 19, 1949, p. 29.
17. L. Huxley, *Life and Letters of Thomas Henry Huxley*, 1 (New York, 1901), 196–200.
18. Johnson, *op. cit.*, p. 71.
19. *The New York Times*, August 16, 1966.
20. R. Burns, *Holy Willie's Prayer*.

Index

A

Abrahams, R. D., *Deep Down in the Jungle*, 313
Abusive swearing, 105
Acres, Bob, 299
Act of 1551, 158–59; of 1606, 157; of 1623 and 1627, 162–63, 164, 165
Act of Supremacy (1534), 128
Act for the More Effectual Suppressing Profane Cursing, and Swearing, An (1694), 178
Adams, J. Donald, 319
Adams, John, 331
Addison, Joseph, 227–28, 271–72; *The Tatler* and *The Spectator*, 207–208, 213
Adjurative swearing, 105
Aeschines, 28
Aggressiveness, 56, 57, 72–76, 77–78, 81, 85–86, 94, 96, 171, 327. *See also* Language, operative function of
Alcibiades, 40
Aldington, Richard, *Death of a Hero*, 261, 310
Althea's brand (Greek legend), 40; Irish version of, 50
Amis, Kingsley, 328
Ancestors and heroes, names of, used in swearing, 11, 16, 28–29, 103
Animals, and aggression, 77, 78; swearing by, 24, 26, 30, 33, 66, 104, 192, 193, 196
Anne, Queen, 178
Anstey, Reverend Christopher, *The New Bath Guide*, 297
Aphesis, 298
Arabs, 8
Archilochus, 41–42, 46
Ardery v. the State, 102

Argyle, Duke of, 203
Aristophanes, *The Clouds*, 27; *Ecclesiazusae (The Assemblywomen)*, 26
Aristotle, 40, 292
Arnaius, 30
Arnulf, *see* Ernulphus
Ash, John, *A New and Complete Dictionary*, 304
Asseverative swearing, 105
Athenaeum, The, 340
Attributes, oaths on valued personal, 104, 196
Augustine, Saint, 107
Australia, 259, 267–70
Australian aborigines, 8–18, 36–37, 55, 57, 80, 270

B

Bad language commission, proposed, 344
Bailey, Nathaniel, *Dictionarium Britannicum*, 304; *Universal Etymological Dictionary*, 304
Baker, Sidney J., *The Australian Language*, 268
Balfour, Lord, 341
Ballantyne, Robert Michael, *Coral Island*, 237
Barbellion, W.N.P., 67
Barclay, Alexander, *The Ship of Fooles*, 126–27
Barham, Richard, *The Ingoldsby Legends*, 234–35
Baring-Gould, Sabine, 51
Basedow, Dr. Herbert, 9, 10, 36
Bastards, Office of Intestate and Escheated, 96, 325
Baudelaire, Charles, 27
Baxter, William, 297
BBC, 312

Beaconsfield, Lord, *see* Disraeli, Benjamin

Beaglehole, Ernest and Pearl, 38

Beast, myth of the, 77

Beatty, Admiral David, 264

Beaumarchais (Pierre Augustin Caron), *Le Mariage de Figaro,* 283

Beaumont, Francis, and John Fletcher, *A King and No King,* 159

Becon, Thomas, *An Invective Against Swearing,* 129

Bee, Jon, *Dictionary,* 326

Beerbohm, Max, *Fifty Caricatures,* 257

Benes of Hamtoun, 111, 112

Bennett, Arnold, 262

Benson, E. F., *As We Are,* 271

Bernardino of Siena, Saint, 129

Besant, Walter, *All Sorts and Conditions of Men,* 253

Bible, 84, 114, 282; injunctions against swearing in, 19–23

Billy Liar, 263

Blackfriars (theater), 173

Blackstone, Sir William, *Commentaries on the Laws of England,* 213–14

Blake, William, 228

Blasphemy, 19–21, 87, 115, 123, 129–30, 132, 182, 214, 334; defined, 101–102, 105

Bloody, 104, Chapter 13

Bloody Instructions, 265

Blunden, Edmund, *Undertones of War,* 261

Boas, Franz, 226

Body, parts and functions of, as source of swear words, 13–14, 34, 109, 110, 193, 195, 198, 303. *See also* Obscenity *and* Sexual organs

Booker, Beryl Lee, *Yesterday's Child,* 294

Boorde, Andrew, *Dyetery of Health,* 132

Boswell, James, 341

Bouzýges, 43

Bowdler, Thomas, *The Family Shakespeare,* 235

Boyle, Honorable Robert, *A Free Discourse Against Customary Swearing and a Dissuasive from Cursing,* 169–70

Bradstreet, Dudley, 177

Bramston, William, *The Art of Politicks,* 297

Brant, Sebastian, *Das Narrenschiff (Ship of Fools),* 126–27

Bridgman, Percy W., 279

British Medical Journal, 319

British Museum, 147

Brodie, Sir Benjamin, 336

Brome, Richard, *The Covent-Garden Weeded,* 290

Bromyard, John, *Summa Predicantium,* 109–10, 111

Brook, Barnaby, *Mock Turtle,* 293

Brophy, John, and Eric Partridge, *Songs and Slang of the British Soldier, 1914–1918,* 310

Brown, R. G. B., 88

Browning, Elizabeth Barrett, 251, 340–41

Browning, Robert, 340–41; "Soliloquy of the Spanish Cloister," 281–82; "To Edward FitzGerald," 341

Bryan, Judge Frederick van Pelt, 311

Buchman, Dr. Frank, 51

Bunyan, John, *Pilgrim's Progress,* 172

Burghley, William Cecil, Lord, 211

Butler, Samuel (1612–1680), *Hudibras,* 55

Butler, Samuel (1835–1902), 95, 237

Byron, George Gordon, Lord, 254, 291, 292; *Don Juan,* 250, 284–85, 327

C

Cambridge University, 133; Press, 291

Campbell, H., 83

Campbell, Mrs. Patrick, 256

Canada, 276

Cape York Peninsula tribes, Australia, 10*ff.*

Carlyle, Thomas, 19, 98, 252, 336

Carson, Anthony, "Roman Scandals," 274

Catharsis, *see* Relief mechanism

Catholic Church, 61–64, 82, 107, 115, 126

Cavaliers, 289. *See also* Restoration

Cellini, Benvenuto, 13

Central Criminal Court (Old Bailey), 311

Chapman, George, *see* Jonson, Ben

Character of the Beaux, The, 178

Charles I, King of England, 163, 164, 165, 167, 171

Charles II, King of England, 95, 172–73, 177–78, 181, 341–42

Charles IV, King of France, 49

Chaucer, Geoffrey, *Canterbury Tales,*

112–13, 115, 116; "The Miller's Tale," 315, 343

Children and swearing, 10, 66, 70, 80–81, 270

Church, Christian, and swearing, 68–69, 301, 331–32. *See also* Catholic Church

Churchill, Winston, 337–38

Cibber, Colley, *The Careless Husband*, 203–204

Cicero, *Pro Sex Roscio*, 32

Clough, Arthur Hugh, *The Latest Decalogue*, 224

Cockneys, 59, 273, 324, 325–26

Cohen, John, 332

Cole, Margaret, *Growing Up Into Revolution*, 94

Coleridge, Samuel Taylor, Preface to "Fire, Famine and Slaughter," 53, 67; "Rime of the Ancient Mariner," 272

Collier, Jeremy, *A Defense of the Short View*, 182; *Maxims and Reflections Upon Plays*, 182; *A Second Defense*, 182; *A Short View of the Immorality and Profaneness of the English Stage*, 90, 180–82

Colman the Younger, George, 236

Colonial America, 102

Colum, Mary, 264

Commonwealth Ballads, 285

Congreve, William, 181, 337; *The Double Dealer*, 181; *Love For Love*, 181; *The Old Bachelor*, 181

Continental Congress, 230, 331

Cook, Captain James, 293

Coulton, G. G., 113

Cowley, Abraham, *The Puritan and the Papist*, 289–90

Crete, 30

Crimean War, 245

Cripps, Sir Stafford, 338

Cromwell, Oliver, 167, 171

Curran, John Philpot, 97, 330

Cursing defined, 105; stone, 50; and swearing compared, 35–36, 48, 52–54, 59; tablets, 39–40, 43–45

Cursor Mundi, 282

Curtain Theatre, 154

D

Daily Mirror (London), 273, 274

Dan Michel, *Ayenbite of Inwyt (The Again-Biting of the Inner Wit*, or *The*

Remorse of Conscience)*, 107, 112, 122–24, 128

Dana, Richard Henry, Jr., *Two Years Before the Mast*, 250, 253

Daniels, Josephus, 328

Dante Alighieri, 49

Darwin, Charles, 229, 237, 331

D'Avenant, Sir William, 172; *The Wits*, 173

Davies, Sir John, "Of a Gull," 266

Dead, names of, *see* Ancestors and heroes

Death curses, 26–27, 58

Decalogue, 19

Defixive cursing, 47–48

Defoe, Daniel, *An Essay Upon Projects*, 183–87

Deities, curses asked of, 43–44; names of, used in swearing, 18–21, 25, 27, 31–32, 34, 60–61, 100–101, 104, 109. *See also* Jesus Christ

Demophilus, 40

Demosthenes, 28–29, 40, 42

Denmark, 147

Dering, Sir Edward, *The Fower Cardinall-Vertues of a Carmelite-Fryar, Fraud, Folly, Foul-Language, Blasphemy*, 199

Devers, General Jacob L., 330

Devil, 118, 130, 220

Diagoras, 30

Dictionary of American English, The, 299

Dillon, Wentworth, Earl of Roscommon, *Essay on Translated Verse*, 300

Diodorus, 40

Dirty jokes, 13

Disraeli, Benjamin (Lord Beaconsfield), 97–98, 336

Dixon, W. Macneile, *The Human Situation*, 292

Dobbie, William, 265

Dollard, Dr. John, 72

Don Quixote, 181

Donald VI, King of the Scots, 108

Dryden, John, 181; *The Assignation*, 176; *The Tempest*, 175; *The Wild Gallant*, 175, 244–45

Duke's Theatre, 176

Dumas, Alexandre (père), 337

Dunbar, William, "Ane Brash of Wowing" ("A Bout of Wooing"), 308; "The Sweirers and the Devill," 130, 159

Duranty, Walter, 247
D'Urfrey, Thomas, 181

E

Earle, Bishop John, *Microcosmographie*, 163
Eddy, Mrs. Mary Baker, 51
Edinburgh Festival, 343
Edward VI, King of England, 132
Egoist Press, London, 264
Egyptians, ancient, 18–19
Ejaculatory swearing, 105
Elizabeth I, Queen of England, 49, 116, 127, 132, 139, 156, 162, 211, 212, 293
Ellenborough, Lord, 342–43
Elyot, Sir Thomas, *The Boke Named the Gouernour*, 128
Emerson, Ralph Waldo, 98, 99, 335
Emotional value of swear words, 90–93, 100, 230, 302, 313–14, 316
Ernulphus, Bishop, curse of, in *Textus Roffensis*, 62–63, 220–21, 312
Ervine, St. John, 256, 257
Eskimos, 13, 76, 332
Essex, Countess of, 51
Ethelbert of Kent, 107
Etherege, Sir George, *The Man of Mode*, 245, 247, 317
Euphemistic swearing, 105, 225–27, 254, 275, 298–99, 315, 326
Examiner of Plays, 236
Exclamatory swearing, 105
Excrement and other filth as source of swear words, 10, 11, 15, 57. *See also* Obscenity
Execratory swearing, 106
Expletive swearing, 104, 106

F

Farington, Joseph, 228
Farmer, J. S., and W. E. Henley, *Slang and Its Analogues Past and Present*, 304
Farquhar, George, *The Beaux' Stratagem*, 205; *Love and a Bottle*, 179–80, 245; *The Recruiting Officer*, 204, 245; *The Stage-Coach*, 204; *The Twin-Rivals*, 182–83
Field, Nathan, *Amends For Ladies*, 162, 287
Fines for swearing, *see* Penalties for swearing

FitzGerald, Edward, 340–41
Flaxman, John, 228
Fletcher, John, *see* Beaumont and Fletcher
Flexner, Stuart B., *see* Wentworth and Flexner
Florio, John, *A Worlde of Wordes*, 304
Foote, Samuel, *The Englishman in Paris*, 249–50
Ford, W. C., *The True George Washington*, 330
Fordyce, James, *Poems*, 222–23
Formon, Simon, 51
Forster, E. M., 257, 339
Forthergill, John, 84
Fox, Sherwood, 44, 45
France, 48–49, 109, 122, 124, 182, 321
Franklyn, Julian, *The Cockney*, 273
Freud, Sigmund, 271, 280
Frustration, as cause of swearing, 65, 70–75, 94, 238, 327
Function of swearing, 70–79, 83–86, 152, 237–38, 322. *See also* Relief mechanism
Fuseli, Henry, 228
Future life, words relating to, as swear words, 101

G

Gambier, Admiral James, 248
Gambling games as source of swear words, 33
Gaskell, Mrs. Elizabeth, *Cranford*, 293
George II, King of England, 213, 214
Genitalia as source of swear words, 11–12, 13, 14. *See also* Body, parts and functions of
Geraud, Hugh, Bishop of Cahors, 49
German High Seas Fleet, 263
Gessler, Clifford, 226
Gestural swearing, 344
Gibbon, Edward, 235
Gilbert, Sir William S., "Lorenzo de Lardy," 284; and Sir Arthur Sullivan, *H. M. S. Pinafore*, 294–95, 330; *Ruddygore*, 234, 254–55
Gladstone, William Ewart, 98, 236, 336
Globe Theatre, 288
Gods and goddesses, *see* Deities
Goldsmith, Oliver, *Citizen of the World*, 297
Goodge, W. T., "——— (The Great Australian Adjective)" ("The Australian Poem"), 259–60, 265, 267

Gordon, *see* Marchant and Gordon

Gordon, Leon, *White Cargo*, 262–63

Grandgent, C. H., 6

Grant, Sir Francis, Lord Cullen, *A Discourse Concerning the Execution of The Laws Made Against Prophaneness, &c.*, 200–202

Graphic (London), 254

Graves, Robert, 91, 96, 97, 324; *Goodbye to All That*, 262; *Lars Porsena, or the Future of Swearing*, 4, 53, 67, 264–65

Greeks, ancient, 23–31, 39–41, 47–48; modern, 48

Greenough, James Bradstreet, *see* Kittredge and Greenough

Greville, Fulke, *Maxims, Characters and Reflections*, 5

Griffin, Gwyn, *Shipmaster*, 274

Grose, Francis, *Classical Dictionary of the Vulgar Tongue*, 304

Grove Press, New York, 310

Guardian, The, 311, 312, 343

Gunpowder Plot of 1605, 157

H

Hall, Captain Basil, 293

Hannay, James, 271–72

Hansard, 343

Harcourt, Sir William, 309

Hardiman, J. H., 50

Harington, Sir John, *Epigrams*, 161–62, 287

Harris, J. E., "Does Profanity Matter?", 331–32

Harte, Bret, *In the Carquinez Woods*, 93–94

Hartogs, Renatus, 314

Harwood, Dr. Edward, 304

Havelok the Dane, 108–109, 111, 112, 126

Hawaii, 293

Hawes, Stephen, *The Conversyion of Swerers*, 128

Hendrickson, G. L., 41

Henley, W. E., *see* Farmer and Henley

Henry, A. F., 85

Henry I, King of England, 108

Henry VI, King of England, 124

Henry VIII, King of England, 115–16, 132, 138, 152, 212

Herbert, George, 165; "The Church Porch" in *The Temple*, 166

Herbert, Sir Henry, 165, 173

Herbert, Xavier, *Capricornia*, 269

Heywood, Thomas, *An Apology for Actors*, 160; *The Fair Maid of the West*, 160

Hipponax, 30, 42

His Majesty's Theatre, 256

Hitler, Adolf, 338

"Holy, Holy, Holy," 257–58

Homer, *Iliad*, 23

Hone, William, 285

Honor, oaths on inanimate symbols of, 104

Hook, Theodore, 228

Hopi Indians, 81–82

Horne, R. H., 251

Hortatory swearing, 106

House of Commons, 97, 157, 339

House of Lords, 157, 263

Howell, Alexander, *A Sword Against Swearers*, 159

Howell, James, *Epistolae Ho-Elianae, Familiar Letters Domestic and Forren*, 285

Huebsch, Ben, 264

Hulbert, Henry Woodward, *Biblical World*, 68, 69

Hull, University of, 87

Hundred Years' War, 282

Hungary, 25

Hunt, Leigh, *Autobiography*, 227, 229

Hutchinson, Roger, *Image of God*, 135

Huxley, Leonard, *Life and Letters of Thomas Henry Huxley*, 237

Huxley, Thomas Henry, 229, 237, 336–37

Hyams, Edward, "Demotic English," 322

Hypnerotomachia, 316

I

Illegitimacy, 95–96, 325

Incest, 17, 322–23

India, 325

Indians, North American, 12, 55, 80–82; languages of, 240. *See also* Eskimos

Infixing, 240, 257, 266, 269–70, 315

Inge, Very Reverend W. R., "We Swear To-day—and Mean No Harm," 262, 334–35

Instincts, 56, 77–78

Insults, 95. *See also* Invective

Interjectional swearing, 106
Invective, 76, 97–100, 255, 335–38
Iowa, University of, 72
Ireland, 48, 49–50, 208–211
Irving, Henry, 309
Italy, 25, 48
Izvestia, 333–34

J

Jackson, Holbrook, 2
Jackson, Hughlings, 83
James I, King of England, 156–57, 161, 164; *Daemonologie,* 49
James II, King of England, 178
James V, King of Scotland, 308
James VI, King of Scotland, *see* James I, King of England
James, Henry, 271, 336
Japanese, 55
Jeremiah, 38
Jesperson, Otto, 7
Jesus Christ, name, body and blood of, as source of swear words, 22, 110–17, 119–22, 128–35 *passim,* 225–26
Jevons, F. B., 42
Jews of antiquity, 19–23, 38–39, 208
Joan of Arc, 124, 282–83
John XXII, Pope, 48–49
Johns Hopkins University, Archaeological Museum at, 43
Johnson, Burges, *Lost Art of Profanity,* 306–307, 331, 337
Johnson, Samuel, 54, 307, 321, 322, 341; *A Dictionary of the English Language,* 304
Jones, Sir Lawrence, *Georgian Afternoon,* 263
Jonson, Ben, 244; *The Alchemist,* 160; *Bartholomew Fair,* 161; *Epicene, or The Silent Woman,* 158; *Every Man in His Humour,* 154, 155, 156, 158; *Every Man Out of His Humour,* 288; *The Magnetick Lady, or The Humours Reconciled,* 165; *Poetaster,* 41; and Chapman and Marston, *Eastward Ho,* 156
Jordan, Elijah, *Business Be Damned,* 279
Journal of the American Medical Association, 319, 320
Jowett, Benjamin, 341
Joyce, James, *Dubliners,* 264; *A Portrait of the Artist as a Young Man,* 264
Juvenal, *Satires,* 24, 34

K

Keele, University of, 343
Kempe, Margery, 125
Kenneth II, King of the Scots, 108
Khrushchev, Nikita, 274
Killigrew, Thomas, *The Parson's Wedding,* 174
King, Emma, *Questions in Church History,* 234
King, S. H., 85
Kipling, Rudyard, *Barrack-Room Ballads,* 254
Kittredge, George Lyman, and J. B. Greenough, *Words and Their Ways in English Speech,* 237

L

Laborers and swearing, 187, 214, 253, 262, 276
Lamb, Charles, "Christ's Hospital Five-and-Thirty Years Ago," 251
Landor, Walter Savage, 228; "The Modern Idyll" in *Dry Sticks Fagoted,* 228
Lanen, J. R., *see* Leitner and Lanen
Langland, William, *Piers Plowman,* 247, 297
Language, operative function of, 8–9, 16, 277; theories of origins of, 5–7. *See also* Aphesis, Function of Swearing *and* Infixing
Laughter, 78, 79–86
Lawrence, D. H., *Lady Chatterley's Lover,* 311
Lawrence, T. E., *Revolt in the Desert,* 310
Lawrence, Sir Thomas, 228
Law of the Words Used in Swearing, The, 100
Laws against swearing and cursing, 2, 25, 30–31, 47, 48, 107–108, 129–31, 153, 157, 158–59, 162–63, 167, 186, 200–202, 207, 208–10, 213–14, 302, 321; Biblical, 19–23. *See also* Taboos against swearing
Leacock, Stephen, 338
Leaf, Walter, 34
Lee, Nathaniel, *Constantine the Great,* 177
Leigh, Admiral R. H., 328, 330
Leitner, M. J., and J. R. Lanen, *Dictionary of French and American Slang,* 305

Lesley, Robert, 167
Lewis, D. B. Wyndham, 124, 265
Lichtenberg, G. C., 282
"Lillibullero," 219, 220
Limericks, 13, 316
Lincoln's Inn Fields (theater), 204
Lindsay, Sir David, "The Answer quhilk Schir David Lindesay," 308; *The Satyre of the Thrie Estaitis*, 131
Linguistic Atlas of New England, The, 298
Linklater, Eric, *Magnus Merriman*, 73
Lollards, 61, 113, 125
Longinus, *On the Sublime*, 28, 191
Lonsdale, Frederick, *Aren't We All?*, 263
López, Francisco, 250
Lorens, Frère, *Le Somme des vices et des vertues (Le Miroir du Monde)*
Louis IX (Saint), King of France, 111
Louis X, King of France, 49
Louis XI, King of France, 335
Lord Chamberlain's Office, 262–63, 343
Lucian, *The Lover of Lies*, 25, 26
Luther, Martin, 340
Lycurgus, 40
Lynceus of Rhodes, 30

M

Macaulay, Thomas Babington, 296
Mackay, Charles, 241
MacKinnon, D. W., 85
McLaren, Jack, 270
Macy, John, 295–96
Maginn, William, "Bob Burke's Duel," 281
Mailer, Norman, *The Naked and the Dead*, 314
Majdalany, Fred, *The Monastery*, 274
Malayans, 55
Malinowski, Bronislaw, 8, 322–24
Malory, Sir Thomas, *Le Morte d'Arthur*, 125–26
Manchester, University of, 332
Manning, Frederic, *Her Privates We*, 262, 316
Mansel, Dean, *Phrontisterion*, 226
Maoris, 37–38
Marchant and Gordon, *A New Complete English Dictionary*, 304
Marcus, Steven, 235
Marigui, Enguerrand de, 49
Marjoribanks, Alexander, *Travels in New South Wales*, 267–68

Marmion, Shackerley, *A Fine Companion*, 166
Marprelate, Martin, 51
Marriott, Charles, *Modern Movements in Painting*, 93
Marryat, Captain Frederick, *Peter Simple*, 329–30
Marston, John, 288; *Antonio and Mellida*, 155, 157; *The Dutch Courtezan*, 156, 235–36; *The Malcontent*, 155, 335; *The Parasitaster; or the Fawne*, 157, 243–44, 247; and Chapman and Jonson, *Eastward Ho*, 156
Mary Stuart, Queen of Scots, 129
Masefield, John, 93; *The Everlasting Mercy*, 242, 257; "The Yarn of The Loch Achray," 275
Massinger, Philip, *The City Madam*, 165; *The Parliament of Love*, 163, 288, 289
Masters, John, *Bhowani Junction*, 271
Matthews, J. Brander, 252
Melbourne, University of, 260
Mencken, H. L., 245, 251; *The American Language*, 304
Middleton, Thomas, *A Trick to Catch the Old One*, 175; and William Rowley, *A Faire Quarrell*, 162, 287
Miracle plays, medieval, 108, 116
Miroir du Monde, Le, 122, 128
Modes, of swearing, seven, 122–23
Montagu, Ashley, *Man: His First Million Years*, 279
Montague, C. E., *Disenchantment*, 262; *Rough Justice*, 261, 262
Moody Press, Chicago, 331, 332
Moralité des blasphemateurs, 199
Morality plays, 134
Morris, Edward E., *Austral English: A Dictionary of Australian Words, Phrases and Usages*, 260
Moser, Joseph, *Reflections on Profane and Judicial Swearing*, 223
Motteux, Peter, 188, 194
Mottram, R. H., *The Spanish Farm*, 261
Mule skinners, 334
Music, as an element of swearing, 68, 76, 187, 257–58, 332, 334
Mussolini, Benito, 25, 274, 337
Myerson, Dr. Albert, 225
My Fair Lady, 270
Mynshull, Geffray, *Certaine Characters and Essayes of Prison and Prisoners*, 288

Myrk, John, *Instructions for Parish Priests*, 126

N

National Library of Wales, 283
Negative swearing, 96–97, 100, 338–39
Negro, American, 313–14
Neill, A. S., *A Dominie Dismissed*, 272
New Custom, 134
New Monthly, 228
New Statesman, 274
News of the World, The, 311
Newtown Court, Sydney, Australia, 269
New York *Herald Tribune*, 328
New York Times, The, 257, 279, 305, 333
New Zealand, 37–38
Nicarcus, 33
Nilsson, M. P., 40
Norman conquest of Britain, 108, 109
Noyes, Pierrpont, 229

O

Oaths, 64, 103, 104, 125; judicial, 59–60, 109
Objects: names of sacred, used as swear words, 101; Resistentialism of, 70–71, 73, 74; swearing by, 23, 24, 26–27, 29–30, 192, 196, 197, 198
Objurgatory swearing, 106
Obligatory swearing, *see* Socialized swearing
Obscenity, 1, 11, 13, 87, 90, 93, 102, 103, 105, 172, 301, 310–12, 319, 334
Obscenity Act, 310
Observer, The, 311, 312
Ogden, C. K., 270
Opéra Comique (London), 295
Orcutt, William Dana, 234
Orwell, George, *Down and Out in Paris and London*, 275–76
Otway, Thomas, *The Atheist*, 174; *The Soldier's Fortune*, 173
Ovid, 34; *Ibis*, 45–46
Owen, Sir David, 128
Owst, G. R., 110
Oxford English Dictionary, The, 242, 248, 251, 282, 286, 296–97, 304
Oxford University Dramatic Society, 285–86
Oxford University Press, 304

P

Pall Mall, 271
Palmerston, Henry John Temple, Lord, 97
Pappe, 288
Paraguay, 250
Parliament, 162, 167, 213; Scottish, 170
Parny, Evariste, *Goddam! Poëm en quatre chants, par un french-dog*, 283
Partridge, Eric, 246–47, 249, 257, 275, 299, 326; *Dictionary of Slang and Unconventional English*, 305, 306, 313; *Origins: A Short Etymological Dictionary of Modern English*, 305, 306; "The Word Bloody" in *Words, Words, Words*, 265. *See also* Brophy and Partridge
Patrick, G. T. W., "The Psychology of Profanity," 72–73, 75, 80
Patt's Coffee-house, 211
Paul, Saint, 84, 114, 282
Peale, Reverend Dr. Norman Vincent, 279–80
Pei, Mario, 305
Penalties for swearing and cursing, 20–23, 30–31, 46, 49, 107–108, 109, 111, 131–32, 157, 159, 162, 167, 168, 171, 178, 186, 208–11, 213–14, 302, 321, 334
Penguin Books, 311
Pennant, Thomas, "Tour on the Continent," 283
Pericles, 40
Perrot, Sir John, 138, 212
Perry, Bliss, *And Gladly Teach*, 229
Persius, *Satires*, 33
Pertinax, 319
Peter of Blois, Archdeacon of Bath, *Epistolae*, 109–110
Petrus Cantor, Precentor of Notre Dame, 109, 114
Peyton, Thomas, 289
Philip II, King of France, 122
Philip IV, King of France, 49
Phocion, 40
Pigott, E. F. Smyth, 236
Pimps, 269
Pitcairn Island, 237
Places, names of sacred, used as swear words, 101
Plants, names of, used as swear words, 29–30, 104

Plato, 27, 30–31, 40, 47; *The Laws*, 30–31, 40; *The Republic*, 31
Plautus, *Aulularia*, 32; *Audria*, 32
Playhouse (London), The, 262
Plost, Louis, 334–35
Plumtre, James, 235
Plutarch, 26, 40
"Pointing," 36, 39
Polynesians, 55, 226
Pope, Alexander, 217
Pornography, 235
Porson, Richard, 291
Porter, Henry, *The Two Angrie Women of Abington*, 160
Portugal, 48
Pound, Ezra, 270
Pound, Dr. Louise, 298
Powell, Walter, 167; *A Summons for Swearers*, 168
Practical cursing, 36–52 *passim*, 58
Press Council, 311–12
Profanity, 109, 163, 214; defined, 101–102, 105
Prostitutes, 87, 210, 269
Provisional curse, 59–60
Prynne, William, *Histriomastix*, 166
Pudenda, *see* Genitalia as source of swear words
Punch, 70, 92, 240
Puritans, 61, 102, 153, 154, 157, 159, 162, 163, 165, 166, 171, 172, 181, 213, 236, 289
Purposes of swearing, 1–2, 12–13, 59, 70–79. *See also* Function of swearing
Putnam, Peter, 326
Pythagoras, 24

Q

Quakers, 23, 61, 81, 86, 172, 216, 222
Queen's Theatre, 205

R

Rabelais, François, 65–66, 339–40; *Gargantua and Pantagruel*, Chapter 10, 278
Ramses III, 18
Randolph, Thomas, *Hey For Honesty*, 118
Random House Dictionary of the English Language, The, 305
Ratcliffe, Francis, 269–70

Raven, Simon, 274
Read, Allen Walker, 306, 319
Reformation, English, 107, 115–16, 127, 134, 136
Reiser, D. M. F., 85
Relief mechanism, in animals, 78; laughter and weeping as, 79–86; swearing as a, 13, 18, 35–36, 52, 53, 59, 65–69, 72–73, 78, 83–86, 94, 238, 322, 327, 332, 335
Religion, as source of swear words, 56–57, 100–101; profanity as threat to, 163. *See also* Catholic Church *and* Church, Christian
Resistentialism, 70–71, 73, 74
Restoration, 154, 172–77, 213, 244, 248, 291
Revolution, American, 298
Rhadamanthus, 30
Richards, Grant, 264
Richardson, Samuel, *Pamela*, 245, 248
Roaring boys, 290–91
Robert of Brunne, *Handlyng Synne* (*Against Swearing Oaths* and *The Tale of the Bloody Child*), 118–22, 128
Robinson, Lennox, 256
Rochester, Earl of, 291, 308, 341–42
Rodenberg, M., 211
Rogers, Mr. Justice Halse, 269
Rogers, Samuel, 336
Romans, ancient, 31–34, 43–48; in Britain, 107
Rondelet, William, 192
Ross, Dr. Helen E., 87–88
Rowley, William, *see* Middleton and Rowley
Ruark, Robert, *Something of Value*, 273–74
Rufus, William, 108
Ruler or symbol of authority, names of, used as swear words, 103
Russell, Bertrand, 236
Russians, 323, 333–34

S

Sagarin, Edward, *The Anatomy of Dirty Words*, 303, 315, 316
Sailors and swearing, 213, 216–17, 223, 225, 238, 248, 253, 275, 313, 326, 328
St. Paul's Cathedral, 187

Saints' names used in swearing, 16–17, 101, 117, 189, 191, 194

Salt, 269

Sandwich, Earl of, 76

Sandwich Islands, see Hawaii

San Salvador, 333

Sassoon, Siegfried, The Memoirs of an Infantry Officer, 262

Savoy Theatre, 254–55

Scanderbeg (George Castriota), 155

Scheer, Admiral Reinhard, 263

Scotland, 108, 129–32, 156–57

Scott, Alexander, "Ane Ballat maid to the Derisioun and Scorne of wantoun Women," 308

Scott, J. W. Robertson, 271

Second Circuit Court of Appeals, New York, 311

Sedley, Sir Charles, 172, 176, 291

Semper, I. J., 253

Sermon on the Mount, 22, 140

Sex, attitudes toward, contemporary, 301; primitive, 11

Sexual organs and functions as source of swear words, 303, 315–16

Shadwell, Thomas, The Virtuoso, 176

Shakespeare, William, 83–84, 99, 126, 127, Chapter 8, 154, 173, 235, 244, 247, 338; All's Well That Ends Well, 143; Antony and Cleopatra, 150; Comedy of Errors, 124, 137–38, 286; Coriolanus, 84, 151; Cymbeline, 65, 86, 150–51; Hamlet, 117, 142–43, 286; Henry IV, Pt. 1, 143; Henry IV, Pt. 2, 139, 144–45; Henry V, 145, 244; Henry VI, Pt. 2, 141–42, 273; Henry VI, Pt. 3, 241; Julius Caesar, 147, 241; King John, 75, 137, 285; Henry VIII, 152; King Lear, 148–49; Love's Labour's Lost, 67, 140; Macbeth, 149, 242; Measure for Measure, 148; Merry Wives of Windsor, 118, 142, 278; A Midsummer Night's Dream, 134, 137; Much Ado About Nothing, 146–47; Othello, 152, 246, 286; Pericles, 150; Richard II, 143; Richard III, 143, 241; Romeo and Juliet, 146, 241, 289; Taming of the Shrew, 141; The Tempest, 35, 150; Timon of Athens, 151; Titus Andronicus, 91, 138–40, 241; Troilus and Cressida, 147–48; Twelfth Night, 160, 321

Sharman, Julian, A Cursory History of Swearing, 24, 64, 67, 114, 131, 146, 239, 242, 248, 249, 286, 332

Shaw, G. B., 253, 338, 344; Pygmalion, 234, 256, 257

Sheridan, Richard Brinsley, 97; The Rivals, 90, 278

Shirley, James, The Young Admiral, 166

Shute, Nevil, Marazan, 264

Sicily, kingdom of, 111

Sillitoe, Alan, Saturday Night and Sunday Morning, 270

Sir Gyles Goosecappe, 289

Skinner, Stephen, Etymologicon Linguae Anglicanae, 304

Smith, Adam, 285

Smith, F. E., Lord Birkenhead, 341, 342

Smith, Logan Pearsall, 239

Smith, Reverend Sydney, 336

Smollett, Tobias, The Adventures of Count Fathom, 217; The Adventures of Sir Launcelot Greaves, 217; The Expedition of Humphrey Clinker, 217–18, 344; Peregrine Pickle, 216; Roderick Random, 92, 214–18

Smyth, Admiral W. H., The Sailor's Word-Book, 326

Social swearing, 87–89

Socialized swearing, 11, 12–13

Societies for Reformation of Manners &c. in England and Ireland, 202

Socrates, 24, 26, 27, 29

Soldiers and swearing, 23, 85, 107, 124, 167, 171, 177, 178, 179, 204, 213, 223, 224, 225, 238, 253, 254, 257, 260–61, 309–10, 313, 314, 326, 327, 334

Solomon, 22

Somerset, Earl of, 51

Sources of swear words, 100–101, 103–104

South Sea Bubble, 208, 209

Southey, Robert, The Doctor, 227

Spain, 48

Spectator, The, 274, 312

Spencer, Herbert, Autobiography, 229

Spenser, Edmund, The Faerie Queene, 150, 256

Staël, Madame de, 343

State Papers (Domestic) 1595, 211

Steele, Richard, 227; The Tatler, 200, 205–207, 208, 213

Stefansson, Vilhjalmur, 272

Stein, Jess, 305

Steinhoff, B. G., 83

Sterne, Laurence, *A Sentimental Journey Through France and England,* 222; *Tristram Shandy,* 46, 62, 63, 66, 219–22, 297, 338

Stevenson, William, *Gammer Gurton's Needle,* 133, 134

Still, John, 133

Stone, Chief Justice Harlan, 339

Story, William Wetmore, 228

Strawshoes, 24

Stress and annoyance swearing, 87–89

Strindberg, August, *The Confession of a Fool,* 95; *The Father,* 95

Sullivan, Sir Arthur, *see* Gilbert and Sullivan

Summerfield, Arthur E., 311

Summerhill, 272

Sunday School Times, The, 331

Supplycacion to Kynge Henry the Eyght, 132

Swearing defined, 3, 105

Swearing-Master: Or, A Conference Between Two Country-Fellows Concerning the Times, The, 176–77

Swift, Jonathan, 245, 248; *Polite Conversation,* 211–12; *The Swearer's Bank,* 208–211

Swinburne, Algernon Charles, 98–99, 234, 295, 335

Sydney *Bulletin,* 259, 260, 268

Sydney (Australia) Divorce Court, 269

Sympathetic magic, cursing by, 36–37, 39

T

Taboos against swearing, among Australian aborigines, 11–12, 13, 17; among ancient Egyptians, 19; among Jews of antiquity, 19–20; contemporary, 1, 2, 31, 57–58, 134; Victorian, 224

Talayesva, Don, 81–82

Tarkington, Booth, *Seventeen,* 295

Tatler, The, 200, 205–207, 208

Tatler and Bystander, 265

Taylor, Charles, 311

Taylor, John, "A Dog of War," 164–65

Technology Review, 279

Tennyson, Alfred, Lord, 271, 336

Thackeray, William Makepeace, *The Newcomes,* 126

Theatre Royal, 175, 182, 203, 204, 244, 245

Thomas, Dylan, 271

Thomas, J. H., 341

Thompson, Edward, *A Farewell to India,* 92; *These Men Thy Friends,* 258–59, 261

Thomson, Dr. Donald F., 9, 10–12, 13

Tilsey, W. V., 257

Times, The (London), 265, 308–309, 311, 339

Times Literary Supplement, The, 317

Tobey, Mrs. W. J., 237

Tom Jones (Fielding), 227

Tooke, John Horne, 97

Torr, Cecil, *Small Talk at Wrayland,* 234

Tourneur, Cyril, *The Revenger's Tragedie,* 288

Towers, Captain, 335

Tree, Sir Herbert Beerbohm, 256

Trelawny, Sir Jonathan, 339

Trevelyan, George Otto, 296

Trevelyan, Paulina, Lady, 295

Trobriand Islanders, 8, 322–24

Tudor, Owen, 128

Twain, Mark, 68, 99, 187; *Autobiography,* 230–34; *1601—A Conversation as It Was by the Social Fireside in the Time of the Tudors,* 318; *Tom Sawyer,* 230

Twichell, Reverend Joseph, 230–34, 318

Tyndall, John, 229

Tynan, Kenneth, 312

U

Udall, Nicholas, *Ralph Roister Doister,* 132–33, 134

UN Security Council, 332

United States, 2, 102, 276, 327

Urquhart, Sir Thomas, 188, 190, 193

V

Vanbrugh, Sir John, 181–82; *The Provok'd Wife,* 179, 181; *The Relapse,* 179, 181, 204

van Dyke, Paul, *George Washington,* 331

Victoria, Queen, 229, 263

Victorianism, 95–96, 206, Chapter 12 *passim*, 240, 251, 293, 301

Voltaire, 246, 283, 292; *Letters Concerning the English Nation*, 222

Vulgarity, 105. *See also* Obscenity

W

WAACs, 261

Wain, John, *Living in the Present*, 270

Wakeman, Captain Ned, 230

Waldeby, Friar John, 110

Walpole, Hugh, 271

Walton, Izaak, 330

Washington, George, 330–31

Webb, Sidney (Lord Passfield), 97

Webster's New International Dictionary (3rd Ed.), 304–305

Wedmore, Frederick, 99

Weekley, Ernest, 236–37, 243, 244, 254; *An Etymological Dictionary of Modern English*, 296–97, 303

Weeping, 78, 79–86

Weldon, Bishop, Dean of Durham, 339

Wellington, Duke of, 92, 296–97

Wentworth, H. and S. B. Flexner, *Dictionary of American Slang*, 305

Werner, Bruno, *The Slave Ship*, 273

Whewell, Harry, "The Crisis in Swearing," 343–44

Whistler, James McNeill, 99, 341

Whitney, William Dwight, 5, 6

Wik Monkan tribe, 13–14

Wilberforce, Samuel, Bishop, 336

Wilde, Oscar, 341; *De Profundis*, 317

Wilkes, John, 76

Wilkins, Sir Hubert, 270

William the Conqueror, 108

William III and Mary II, King and Queen of England, 178

William IV, King of England, 335; as Prince Regent, 236

William of Waddington, *Manuel des Pechiez*, 119

Willis, Ted, 263

Wise, Thomas James, 98

Witch hunting, 48–49

Women and swearing, 86–87

Wood, Dr. Thomas, 268–69

Woodward, John, *A Disswasive From Prophane Swearing and Cursing . . .* , 202–203; *A Kind Caution to Prophane Swearers . . .* , 203; *A Letter from a Minister . . .* , 202; *The Oath of a Constable . . .* , 203; *The Obligations of a Justice of the Peace . . .* , 203

Worde, Wynkyn de, *Hickscorner*, 117, 127, 138

Wordsworth, William, 227; "It is not to be thought of," 136

World, The, 99, 341

World War I, 252, 257–58, 260–61, 263, 266, 299, 300, 301–10, 313, 314, 316, 326, 328

World War II, 87, 252, 260, 265, 274, 279, 314, 318

Wortis, Dr. Joseph, 271

Wren, Sir Christopher, 187

Wright, Aldis, *The Life and Letters of Edward FitzGerald*, 340

Wycherley, William, 176

Wyld, Henry Cecil, 226, 262, 267

Y

Yale University, 72

Yeats, William Butler, 301

Yintjingga tribe, 10

YMCA, 81–82

Young, Wayland (Lord Kennet), *Eros Denied*, 314–15

Z

Zeno, 24